RED CLOUD'S REVENGE

Showdown on the Northern Plains, 1867

TERRY C. JOHNSTON

ST. MARTIN'S PAPERBACKS

RED CLOUD'S REVENGE

ISBN: 0-312-92281-7

Printed in the United States of America

St. Martin's Paperbacks edition/August 1990

10 9 8 7 6 5 4 3 2 1

Author's Foreword

I believe it important to give a moment to a few thoughts before the reader dives into this novel with both feet. Not so much to explain anything of the story itself, but to give you a sense of what it is you are about to read.

This, above all, is the story of a time and characters largely forgotten, what with the pace of our comfortable, relatively untroubled lives. What strikes me as a shame is that most of those who have a speaking acquaintance with the opening of the West know little or nothing of that summer Red Cloud sought to purge his hunting ground of the white man forever. After the Fetterman Massacre the previous December of 1866, the confederated Sioux, Cheyenne, and Arapaho bands vowed to drive the soldiers and white travelers on the Montana Road from the Big Horn country.

In two long and pitched battles, each fight only ninety miles from the other in distance and but some twenty-four hours apart in time, the Indians failed to wipe out small bands of determined men. It is, therefore, ultimately ironic that while Red Cloud's bloody plan of exacting his terrible revenge on the white men at forts Phil Kearny and C.F. Smith failed miserably, the Oglalla chieftain did succeed with his summer of warfare in convincing the army to abandon not only its forts along the Bozeman Trail, but the Bozeman Trail itself.

To date, the Wagon-Box Fight at Fort Phil Kearny on the second of August, 1867, has been more thoroughly explored by historians. Never before in novel form.

The Hayfield Fight at Fort C.F. Smith on the day before has never received the historical attention due it. Perhaps because in the army's shortsighted view of things, it was not a military encounter, but instead one of hostile Indian forces pitted against civilian teamsters performing contract labor. Its story as well has never been told in a novel.

The drama of one battle cannot be torn from the story of the other. Both fights were planned as parts of the whole. They were far from being isolated skirmishes.

In a study of the era of the Indian Wars, again and again one runs across instances of small groups of determined defenders holding out against overwhelming odds of screeching, equally determined horsemen. And time and again I run across references in each and every one of those battles which clearly and unequivocally state that the white men thus surrounded and fighting for their very lives were nonetheless most ready to commit suicide at a moment's notice should the fight be lost and the red onslaught breech the walls.

Even more than merely being ready to commit suicide, I have read repeatedly of these frontiersmen and soldiers alike making concerted and careful *preparations* to take their own lives should the fight be lost.

Time and again in the writing of the Old West, one runs across the well-considered, oft-repeated, and most-popular notion that in the end a white man must take his own life before he is captured alive by a band of hostile warriors. To be taken prisoner simply meant unspeakable agony and torture. A slow death.

No death for a hero.

Instead, it is perhaps a paradox for those of us viewing that era from this distance and with our twentieth-century minds to attempt understanding the superstition, ignorance, and outright fear with which most white men approached a coming battle with what they viewed as naked, savage, pagan, and bloodthirsty minions of the Great Plains. Far too many of us today cannot accept that *brave* men would take their own lives rather than forfeiting those lives to an agonizing, tortured, and slow death.

But one must stop and consider the nineteenth-century mind of those who ventured beyond the confines of just wh.e scant civilization the West offered at the time. We are asked to consider that it was the last *brave* act of desperate, overwhelmed, and very courageous men *to take their own lives rather than submit to what they knew without a doubt would be unspeakable torture.*

So then, I tell these stories of the brave and the cowardly. Tales of those ready to die and those pleading to live, pinned down and without hope. Human conflict, pathos and passion —white men and red alike colliding on that farflung prairie during a summer like no other on the high plains. The time has come for the stories of those two obscure battles to be told. Both were waged beneath the same burning sun that still scorches the prairie in late summer, were fought between a small group of men determined to hold out against overwhelming odds and those mounted bands of thousands—what could possibly be richer backdrop for our cavalryman turned plainsman turned cavalryman once more: Seamus Donegan (pronounced "Shamus").

The writer of historical fiction assumes a perilous task: while he must remain true to history, there are the demands of fiction pressing the novelist to pace, dramatize, capsulize, omit. So with both battles studied and restudied, the sites visited and walked over, a sense of place and time finally in my grasp—the story of that summer of 1867 all but lay before me. I had only to let the characters of that day tell it.

As a work of history, I relied on many sources, a few of which I'll make mention. The first four I called upon most heavily—drawing much of the human element of the story, as those were four firsthand, primary accounts given by battle participants. Two from the Hayfield Fight. Two from the Wagon-Box. What remained was for the novelist in me to flesh their story out.

Finn Burnett, Frontiersman: the Life and Adventures of an Indian Fighter, edited by Robert B. David, was perhaps drawn upon more than any other source, as it proved one of the firsthand primary accounts by not only an eyewitness, but written by one who had a commanding presence in the Hayfield Fight, civilian Finn Burnett himself.

Every bit as useful was the second primary source, the story of Pvt. Sam Gibson, as told in E. A. Brininstool's historic work, *Fighting Red Cloud's Warriors.*

Cyrus Townsend Brady's *Indian Fights and Fighters* continues the tradition by recounting the story of another civilian teamster, R. J. Smyth, in his recollections of the Wagon-Box Fight.

In his book *Life and Adventures of a Drummer Boy; or, Seven Years a Soldier,* James D. Lockwood gives us a stirring account of his participation in the Hayfield Fight.

Roy E. Appleman's work on both battles appeared in *Great Western Indian Fights.* Both readable stories were well-researched, and thoughtful opinions rendered.

As I have stated before, the Wagon-Box Fight has received the greatest print. J. W. Vaughn in his monumental work, *Indian Fights: New Facts on Seven Encounters,* goes far to balance the scales of history and historical journalism with his enlightening theories on the Hayfield encounter.

One cannot write a historical novel of the Montana Road without mentioning the superb and highly readable account of that era portrayed by Dorothy M. Johnson in *The Bloody Bozeman.*

With these sources at my fingertips, what remained was for the novelist in me to flesh out the story with musele and sinew, giving these ghosts from our past voice once more. And voice I gave them, speaking most of the mood and flavor of both that time and that place. To accomplish this, I relied on two more firsthand accounts, both written by women married to officers at Fort Phil Kearny during those dramatic months portrayed in the first novel in this series, *Sioux Dawn* —the story of the Fetterman Massacre. Frances C. Grummond (later Carrington) wrote her story in *My Army Life, and the Fort Phil. Kearny Massacre.* In addition, Margaret I. Carrington accompanied her husband to the foot of the Big Horns, where the colonel would build his fort and protect the Montana Road, leaving us her *Absaraka: Home of the Crows,* published in 1868. Both women left us a rich legacy coupled with a sense of that time on the high plains in the shadow of the Sioux and Cheyenne.

Yet, beyond the mere *retelling* of history, it is left for the historical novelist himself to add something that history alon can't convey to most readers—a warm, throbbing pulse that truly allows the reader to *relive* history.

The era of the Indian Wars of the Far West is really the story of the final conquest of western America. During that quarter century we witness the conclusion to what had begun when the Pilgrims set foot on Plymouth Rock or Sir Walter Raleigh founded his Virginia Colony. By the end of the Civil War, America eagerly lurched westward, ready once more to grow. Until that time, the westward-expanding tide had only stretched its fingers tentatively beyond the Missouri and Mississippi Rivers, not as yet seriously driving before the white migration the mighty bands of Sioux and their allies—both Cheyenne and Arapaho.

But with the declaration of peace following Appomattox, the government of this reunited Union could now marshal its resources and devote vast amounts of money, matériel, and manpower to the pacification of the West.

The story told in *Sioux Dawn* of a bitterly cold December day in 1866, as Capt. William Judd Fetterman led his men beyond Lodge Trail Ridge above Fort Phil Kearny and into history, would not end until another bloody, cold December day twenty-four years later in 1890, with another massacre along a little-known creek called Wounded Knee.

The fever of that quarter century made the Indian Wars a time unequaled in the annals of time, when a vast frontier was forcibly wrenched from its inhabitants, during a struggle as rich in drama and pathos as any in the history of man.

This is a story of those soldiers come to man the forts that would guard the Montana Road—to protect those civilians in whose breasts burned the dream of untold wealth to be found by scraping a pick along the ground or washing some gravel from the bottom of a stream. The same dream that for years had driven men west to Sutter's Mill in California, Cripple Creek in Colorado, and now Alder Gulch in Montana—the latest strike to land upon the ears of war-weary soldiers, Union and Confederate alike. But to reach those northern goldfields of Montana Territory, a man had to march north from Fort Laramie, north into the jaws of Red Cloud's land, using John Bozeman's road, which pierced the very heart of prime Sioux hunting ground.

Any man who laid eyes on that country had to come away understanding why the Indians guarded their land so jealously. The whole of the Big Horn country was laced with clear, cold streams born of winter snows, feeding the luxuriant valleys teeming with abundant wildlife of all description. At the edge of the eastern plains, in the shadow of the Big Horns, roamed the mighty *pte,* the Sioux's buffalo, a nomadic animal, followed season after season by a nomadic people, providing the Indian with everything he required for his survival century after century.

Into the heart of this redman's paradise, the postwar army dispatched a handful of companies assigned to protect the Road from a series of forts. From the moment of their establishment in the summer of 1866 until the time of their abandonment some two years later, Fort Phil Kearny and Fort C.F. Smith to the north were under a constant state of siege. Both posts so vigilantly watched by hostile war and scouting parties that those virtually trapped in the forts found little safety outside the stockades unless accompanied by a troop of soldiers. Even then, sheer numbers did not always guarantee that the Indians would not swoop down to harass, burn, or drive off stock.

The stories of the Hayfield and Wagon-Box Fights give proof of the fact that sheer numbers of soldiers could not by themselves guarantee immunity to attack.

It is no exaggeration to state that Red Cloud's hostiles surrounded the forts at all times. Not one log was cut for the stockades, nor was any hay mowed for the stock, nor any mail moved without a heavy guard.

There is no richer story than to peer like voyeurs into the lives of those men and women under this constant stress of life and death. Wondering, as only a reader in the safety and comfort of his easy chair can, if he too would have measured up with the gallant defenders who held off charge after charge of the hundreds.

Important too is that the reader realize he's *reliving* the story of real people. From Lt. Col. Henry W. Wessells and his commander at Fort Phil Kearny . . . to the soldiers like Capt. James W. Powell and Lt. John C. Jenness, those killed and wounded, in addition to the oft-faceless civilians who found themselves trapped in two bloody little fights under a nameless hot sun across two days in August in 1867 . . . you are reading a story peopled with flesh and blood that walked and fought, cried and cheered on that hallowed ground.

So it is that good historical fiction fuses the fortunes, adventures, and destinies of numerous characters. Gold hunters and con men, sutlers and cowards, enlisted men and those few officers' wives who followed, trusting to some man's dream. All were actual, living souls walking across that crude stage erected on the high plains below Big Horns . . . all, save one.

Into their midst I send my fictional character, Seamus Donegan, late of the Union Army of the Shenandoah, cavalry sergeant turned soldier-of-fortune, having sought a change of scenery in the West, and some relief if not escape for his lonely, aching heart. Over a series of books that will encompass this era of the Indian Wars, you will follow Seamus as he marches through some of history's bloodiest hours. Not always doing the right thing, but trying nonetheless, for Donegan was no "plaster saint" nor "larger-than-life" dime-novel icon.

History has itself plenty of heros—every one of them dead. Donegan represents the rest of us. Ordinary in every way, except that at some point we are each called upon by circumstances to do something *extra*-ordinary . . . what most might call heroic. Forget the pain, the thirst and hunger. Forget the blood. Each man does what he must in the end.

That's the saga of Seamus Donegan that began with *Sioux Dawn.* If you will listen, you'll hear wagonmasters cursing their balky mules struggling with the mowing machines and wood wagons . . . the screeching war cries of Indians mingled with the screams of frightened women and the prayers of untried soldiers. Sniff the air—you'll likely smell the stench of gunpowder and your own blood slowly cooking as it drops from your wounded head into the overheated breech of your rifle, while you wait for the next rattle of gunfire or the hair-raising thunder of Indian pony hoofbeats bearing down on you.

There is, after all, a sense of something inevitable afoot here in this history of the Indian Wars. Something of destiny's impelling course sweeping man up in its headlong rush into the future.

So remember above all else—what is written here happened. This story needs no false glamor, no shiny veneer of dash and daring. What has always been the story of man at war—of culture against culture, race against race—needs be told without special lighting.

There's drama enough in that summer of Red Cloud's revenge for any man.

The stories of the Hayfield and Wagon-Box fights are really very old tales indeed, my friends. Tales whose time have come at last. I've done my best telling the whole cloth of that story in these pages. None alive can say if I've succeeded or failed . . . save for those ghosts still haunting the grassy meadows, ghosts both red and white who alone lived and perhaps died during those brutal hours when Red Cloud's thousands flung themselves against less than a hundred scared yet determined men who held out against all odds.

Terry C. Johnston
Fort C.F. Smith National Historic Site
Montana Territory
August 1, 1989

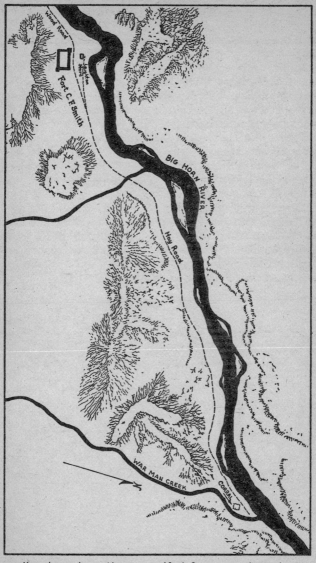

Map drawn by author, compiled from maps drawn by
Captain Edward L. Hartz (August, 1867),
and the National Park Service.

Map drawn by author, compiled from maps drawn by Colonel
Henry B. Carrington, Palacios, and the
Phil Kearny/Bozeman Trail Association, Inc.

Prologue

God, how he hated these primitive savages.

All their hocus-pocus and hoo-doo witchcraft, he brooded to himself.

What he needed most now was a good dose of fumaric in those bloody holes in his belly . . . and a jolt of whiskey down his gullet.

"Captain" Robert North adjusted himself on the bed of elk robes, easing a wool blanket from his shoulder to study his wound one more time. More to assure himself again that the soldier's bullet had passed on through his belly, out the small of his back. Sighing, he sank back on the buffalo robes, quietly whispering the words to the old Confederate song.

> "I'd rather be in some dark holler,
> Where the sun refuse to shine,
> Than to see you another man's darling
> And know you'll never be mine."

His nose filled with the smell of this winter place. The lodge reeked of smoked hides, sweetgrass and pungent roots a'boil.

That old harpy better not spit into my bullet hole no more, he thought, yanking the blanket over his bare skin and singing more.

> "I don't want your greenback dollars,
> I don't want your diamond ring,

All I want is your love, darling,
Won't you take me back again?"

All that remained of his left hand were stumps of fingers an exploding pistol had left behind many years ago. With them North scratched at a week's worth of whiskers. Wondering how long it had taken his Arapahos to drag him back to this winter camp on the upper Tongue River. Their village sat upstream from Red Cloud's Oglalla Bad Face band. Opposite Black Eagle's Miniconjous. Within hailing distance of Sitting Bull's Hunkpapas.

Where the hell's that stick?

His fingers felt through his war-bag at the side of his bed by the fire. Finally he found the peeled willow stick. He counted the notches he carved in it every sundown. The only calendar a white man like North had to keep track of the days and weeks and months with these savages. Down from the twelfth ring carved clear around the stick he counted twenty-nine notches.

December . . . gawddamn . . . thirtieth today.

He struggled, fire through his belly and pain in his head, trying to remember how long ago he had been shot.

Seventh . . . no—the sixth, gawddammit.

He and his Arapahos had joined Red Leaf's Miniconjous, Crazy Horse's Oglallas and the rest when they ambushed the soldiers on the sixth of December, 1866. If his count was right, he'd been lying here more than three weeks, mending. His belly full of puggle and his wounds oozing poison. Worst of it was he'd even missed the big fight. The Sioux and Cheyenne called it their "Battle of the Hundred in the Hand." With their leader wounded and unable to move, North's Arapahos had followed Red Leaf and got in a few licks too.

For three days after that big fight, the bands had danced over soldier scalps and feasted.

"Just as sure as the dew falls
Upon the green corn,
Last night she was with me,
Tonight she is gone."

He closed his eyes. They burned with gritty lodge-smoke, tearing like he'd bitten into a raw prairie onion.

Yesterday he heard talk of the tribes breaking up for the rest of the winter. Going their separate ways. They were due, North figured.

By gawd, they killed every last one of those sonsabitches!

Ambushed. Trapped at the foot of Lodge Trail Ridge. And butchered to the last man. Every last army horse killed. Not one thing left living on that bare-bone, snow-crusted ridge.

Shit! How I wished I'd been there to see that!

He twisted to the side, his arm cradling his gut. The fire had come back, in a bad way. He fumed, wondering when that handful of Arapahos would get back from Fort Peck with his whiskey. Two hundred miles. Almost due north—cross the Yellowstone, then ride for the Missouri. He'd sent them there with some hides to trade for the white man's whiskey.

Bob North had always needed whiskey more than anything else. With it, he'd kill the pain in his belly. And then he wouldn't care that those two holes in his gut still oozed. Then he wouldn't care how their festering stank up this winter-lodge. Whiskey . . . and a woman now and then. Bob North could be happy with the simple things.

His thirst for whiskey had led to his capture by Union forces back in 'sixty-three. A tall, muscular Confederate cavalry officer—knocked from his horse by the concussion of artillery exploding around him . . . knocked senseless and captured. Ending up in irons and shipped to one hellhole after another. Time and again they shoved a paper under his nose . . . telling him to sign it . . . swear allegiance to the Union and they'd make him a soldier . . . wearing Union blue this time . . . and stationed on the frontier to fight Injuns.

The iron locked on his wrists and ankles grew heavier, and one day Bob North signed—just so he could get something to eat. And maybe a little whiskey, if he was good.

Gawddamn 'em!

"Galvanized Yankees" is what they called those former Confederates, officers and soldiers both, who had sworn allegiance to the Union, sent west to fight Indians instead of wasting away in a federal prison. At least until this last sixth of

December, things had been working out a whole hell of a lot
better for Bob North.

He'd deserted, escaping from his detachment up on the
Powder River. Country the Union officers were calling hostile
territory at that time. But to Bob North, freedom itself beck-
oned, and he didn't much give a damn about where he tried to
run. Lady Luck was at his side two days later when he ran
onto a small hunting party of Arapaho. Had they been Sioux
. . . well, Bob North tried not to dwell on that.

A few days later in the Arapaho camp he was taken to,
North began carving on his willow sticks, making his calen-
dars. And riding out with the Arapaho on raids into Ab-
saroka to bring back Crow ponies. Scalp raids against the
Crow and Ute and Snake and Flathead. With each new success, Bob North grew more daring. Until he started leading
his own war-parties out. If he couldn't find an enemy village,
Bob North always knew where the soldier forts were. The
Arapahos liked that in their renegade leader.

They said he had big bull's eggs.

*Damn right, I've got balls! Who the hell else is gonna let
himself get seen time and again by them white sonsabitches?*

But after three summers of daring and killing and living
with the Arapaho, the army moved their posts farther north
. . . right to the foot of the Big Horns . . . into the heart of
Sioux, Cheyenne and Arapaho hunting grounds. To protect
their Bozeman Road which took settlers and miners to Bozeman, farther still to Virginia City—Alder Gulch and gold.

From July of this year, 'sixty-six, through the twenty-first
of December, when the tribes had wiped out eighty-one
soldiers in a spare forty minutes, Red Cloud's confederation
had harassed the forts, killing civilians along the trail and
civilians working in the hayfields or timber. Last summer Bob
North made sure Red Cloud and the other chiefs understood
what the word "siege" meant. Bob North made sure the tribes
never let up their pressure on those forts hunkered defensively
along the white man's Montana Road.

And then he took that bullet in the belly. Bob North had
missed the finest day of fighting any of the tribes had ever
seen. Forced that day to lay here on these robes, drinking the

last of his whiskey . . . waiting for someone to return to camp with news of the success of the ambush and battle.

Damn, did he hate white men.

Bob North chuckled. "You're getting half crazy, ol' coon," he whispered to himself. "You got white skin yourself, gawd-dammit."

He recalled that during the last full moon he had led this small band of his adopted Arapahos to the upper Tongue. To join in struggle against other white men. But those white men weren't his kind. Where Bob North wanted to be left alone, those soldiers down at the new fort wanted to stir shit up. Where soldiers went, he knew, the shit always got stirred.

Bob North had learned that much by following Stephen Watts Kearny in and out of Mexico back to 'forty-six.

Suspiciously, he eyed the old woman who hobbled through the door flap and scooted around the fire in his direction. She bent over the kettle simmering at the edge of the fire and nodded, smiling toothlessly at him.

Gawd-damn! My belly hurts. This bitch goes sticking roots and other shit in them holes . . . could do with more whiskey . . . these brutes ever come drag this old harpy away . . . they ever show up with more whiskey like I told 'em. How many days ago now . . . I got knocked outta the saddle?

Back on that murky dawn in the first week of a white man's December, renegade Bob North had led his Arapahos to join the Sioux attacking the soldiers stationed in that new fort on the plateau. Dawn—and time for North to prove himself to Red Cloud's boys.

The sky had never really snowed. It just oozed icy, lancing flakes once the gray of predawn streamed along the hills to the east. Everything made slick and wet. Their short bows not worth much in such damp weather, the Arapaho would have to rely on their numbers. Their speed. And the incompetence of the fort's officers.

North could always count on that. Incompetence. Few officers like Capt. Robert L. North in either army anymore—those not raving lunatics by now had become roaring drunks.

Wish they'd get here with that whiskey of mine! he fumed, watching the old woman guardedly and grinding his hip down into the elk robes. *Could use me some drink.* He remembered

the good red whiskey aged in those Tennessee kegs. Not at all
like this amber-colored, tobacco-laced grain the traders sold
to the Indians along the upper Missouri.

Just 'nother drink . . . help me sleep.

As directed, his warriors had raced down on some soldiers,
then turned and darted away while the soldiers followed obe-
diently behind them. After a ten-mile chase took North's
Arapahos into the badlands northeast of the fort, North had
suddenly turned his warriors as the Sioux closed the trap behind their hapless pursuers.

Rather than shooting at the white men, the Arapahos and
Sioux had tried to pull the soldiers from their horses. Two
soldiers died along that trail. But the rest escaped. Soldiers
retreating, their withdrawal covered by a lone civilian.

Bob North would never forget that solitary civilian standing behind his big horse while the soldiers scampered past
him, dashing over the hill to safety.

Now his side hurt more than ever thinking about that son
of a bitch. *Gawddamn brazen file-closer . . . what he was.
Covering the rest of them . . . coolly covering their retreat.*

Again and again North had exhorted his warriors into
charging the civilian. Each time he watched a warrior fall.
Each time he swore in English. The big civilian had carried a
brass-mounted repeater that day north of the Lodge Trail
Ridge, using it to hold North's warriors at bay until the
soldiers were on their way.

Until Bob North himself grew furious with defeat, growling
ugly curses about cowardly Injuns and charged the civilian on
his own.

He remembered getting hit, with the slap of a painful claw
around his belly. Tumbling to the ground like a sack of wet
oats. Seconds later he remembered being yanked across the
wet sage between two flying Arapaho ponies. Rescued.
Dragged from the field.

The angry warriors had watched the big white man leap
atop his horse and disappear. Then took Bob North to this
camp on the upper Tongue to lick his wounds.

And remember that big, gray horse.

He would not easily forget the soldiers and civilians he had
fought that snowy dawn. He would not forget the feel of white

man's lead burning an icy track through his belly. And Bob North vowed never to forget the tall, bearded one who stood beside his big gray horse, firing that brass-mounted repeating Henry rifle of his . . . again and again and—

Until Bob North suffered the sting of that big man's bullet.

The renegade had stayed with the Arapaho to be left alone. To lay with the women now and again when it moved him.

But now them Yankee soldiers come to protect their gawd-damned road. Bringing these civilian sonsabitches in their shadow . . . like camp dogs.

His head hurt. Hangover, he figured. He was due for a whopper of a hangover all right.

It's gonna be fine, he told himself. *You're not a white man any longer, Captain North. You play by Injun rules now. You get hurt . . . you hurt back.*

North closed his eyes, hungering for his whiskey, gritting his teeth as the old woman ground the root fibers into his mean, oozy wounds.

He grit his teeth . . . and brooded on the tall, bearded man sheltered beside his gray horse. Dreaming how good it would be to wear that tall bastard's scalp one day soon.

"I'd rather be in some dark holler," he growled out the song's words against the pain in his gut, a pain he was beginning to think would never be washed away with all the whiskey at Fort Peck. Or with all the time in the world.

"Where the sun refuse to shine," and he coughed again.

"Than to see you another man's darling,

"And know you'll never be mine."

He shoved the old woman's hand away as she tried to feed him some slick, scummy meat.

Lordy, I wanna wear that tall bastard's scalp one day real soon!

One day real soon, he promised himself.

Chapter 1

*T*he old scout gazed over his steaming cup of coffee at the big Irishman sitting across the table. Jim Bridger had to chuckle a bit inside with it. After better than forty-four winters in these Shining Mountains, Old Gabe had seen a few he-dogs come west. And this big strapping youngster had to be one of the few himself, Bridger figured.

But it seemed Seamus Donegan had himself a natural-born talent for attracting trouble.

No matter the package, Jim Bridger figured. Whether it was one of Red Cloud's warriors, or an army captain, or a pretty young widow-gal—Seamus Donegan attracted trouble like bees drawn to honey.

"You're punishing that whiskey, Seamus," young Jack Stead advised. He was Bridger's young partner, a former English seaman who had become a competent scout in his own right, marrying a Cheyenne woman and settling into a life of working for the army as it sought to pacify the Far West this second year following the end of the Civil War. Stead himself admired the big, taciturn Irishman. Something about his twinkling eyes attracted friends.

Perhaps Seamus Donegan had been born that rare breed of soul who is blessed with as many good friends as he was cursed with mighty enemies.

"I haven't a right to drink my whiskey, you're saying?" Donegan growled over the lip of his tin cup. "Winter's got this land locked down tighter'n a nun's kneecaps . . . and not a nit-prick of us venturing out the stockade if he don't have at least a company of sojurs behind him, for fear of getting butchered like Fetterman's boys—bless their souls. Jack, me boy, seems drinking the sutler's red whiskey is all that's left a man to do."

"Then drink yourself silly again today, damn you!" Jack roared in laughter. "Can't think of a reason why we shouldn't get sacked together."

Bridger watched them clang their cups together, sloshing some of the strong liquid onto one of the rough-hewn tables in the sutler's cabin. He grinned behind his beard, despite the ache in his bones and the icy pain the rheumatiz stabbed at his every joint. And he remembered another cold day barely one month past.

A day Fetterman and Brown and Grummond rode out at the head of seventy-eight men to chase themselves some Sioux scalps. Jim brooded darkly to himself with the memory. *Twenty-one December last, 1866—when Fetterman's entire force disappeared over that goddamned Lodge Trail Ridge, not a man among the lot of them seen alive again.*

Sighing, the old trapper become army scout gazed at the hard cut of Donegan's face. The finely chiseled nose set beneath the gray-green eyes. Those full, expressive lips buried within the dark beard. And Bridger recalled the look carved on the Irishman's face that sub-zero night when Donegan returned with the somber rescue party with word that not a soul among Fetterman's command had survived. Bridger had never asked any more about it, for the look in Donegan's eyes had told any half-smart man not to venture a question.

Still, the old scout knew the young Irishman had seen far too much of the killing in his few years, what with four of those years spent fighting atop a horse down south against Confederate cavalry, not to mention all that Donegan had seen since he arrived in Red Cloud's Sioux country some seven months ago.

Seven months to some. A lifetime to most.

No way Jim Bridger would ever forget the look in the Irishman's eyes that winter night. A haunted look that somehow, even with all the time that had since passed, remained a look every bit as haunted still.

"Sun's going down behind the peaks," Stead remarked absently, nodding toward the window where he watched the milk-pale orb settle on the Big Horns mantled in white.

"Matters little," Donegan replied, never looking up from his whiskey cup. "Night or day—still cold enough to freeze the bullocks off a Boston snowman."

"You spent time in Boston, did you?" Stead asked, eager to make conversation to ease some of the constant electrical tension forever present around the Irishman like a frightening aura.

Seamus nodded. "It's where I landed . . . come here from the land of me birth. An English ship, filled with dirt-poor Irish farmers . . . come to these foreign shores hoping for better. Too oft handed worse. And me but a young lad shipped off by me mither to this new land with her hopes and her tears."

"She hoped you'd fare better here?"

"Aye." He nodded again. "To look up her two brothers, I was. A lad of fifteen, carrying all I owned in her wee carpet satchel. Most everything I had then a hand-me-down at that."

"Those uncles of yours help you find work there in Boston by the sea?"

Donegan shook his head, staring into the red of his whiskey. "Not a trace of 'em, either one."

"You came to Boston on a cold trail?"

"Nawww," and Seamus lifted the cup to his lips. "Last letter my sainted mither got from her brothers came posted from Boston . . . saying they'd both landed work as city constables." He snorted without any humor. "That's a bit of a laugh. Them two brothers of hers—constables! And in Irish Boston to boot!"

"What became of 'em?" Stead inquired.

Donegan froze the young scout with those gray-green eyes of his, then he finally gazed out the frosted window while the last light slid from the sky. His brow knitted. "No telling, Jack."

"You checked with the constables' office?"

"Never worked as constables," he answered with a wolf slash of a grin. "But the constables did know the both of 'em. One was quite the brawler, it seems. My dear mither oft shook

her head and said I took after his blood. And me other uncle
. . . well, now—the constables said he had a smooth way
about him, talking folks out of their money."

"Sounds a bit like sutler Kinney there," Stead whispered,
nodding toward the counter.

Jefferson T. Kinney leaned one pudgy elbow on the rough-
hewn pine-plank bar, wiping a dirty towel across some spilled
whiskey and laughing with two civilian workers who had bellied their way through the crowd to nurse their whiskey. A
former U.S. judge out of Utah and an ardent pro-slaver, Kinney had lost his bench when President Lincoln had entered
the White House. Kinney had been one of the many who had
rejoiced when the Great Emancipator was cut down in Ford's
theater not two years ago come April.

Bridger's eyes joined the Irishman's in glaring at the sutler.
Kinney must have felt the heat, for he looked up from the bar,
gazing across the noisy, smoky room with those black beads
he had for eyes. They locked on Donegan.

"No love lost on that one," Bridger whispered around the
stub of his pipe which kept a constant wreath round his gray
head.

"Aye," Donegan agreed as he nodded and went back to
staring at his red whiskey. "That's one bastard wishes Seamus
Donegan's body had been hauled back from the Ridge with
Fetterman's dead."

"What makes a man like him hate a man like you,
Seamus?" Stead asked, gazing at the sutler's plump fingers
pouring drinks for civilian workers pressing the bar.

"Man like Seamus Donegan here," Bridger began, snagging
the attention of the other two, "always brings out the fear in
little men like the judge over there. And in such men, fear is
the worst thing you want. No telling what a fella like him
might do you get him scared enough."

"What's a man like Kinney got to be afeared of from me?"

"Seamus Donegan, down inside where that fat, little bastard lives, Kinney knows he don't belong out here in these
mountains like you do," Bridger explained. "Somewhere in
his gut he knows he's bought his way out here—but he can't
ever earn what it is you already have for free."

"What's that, Jim?" Stead asked.

"The respect of other men. Strong men. Honest men. The kind of man it will take to tame this land. The kind of man Judge Kinney will never be, but will always try to buy, and failing that . . . will try to squash like a sowbug."

"Pour me more whiskey, Jack," Seamus said as he slammed down his empty cup, "and I'll drink a toast to the sowbug squashers in the world. Appears me uncles have much in common with our friend Judge Kinney over there."

Stead poured from a thick glass bottle packed in straw all the way from Omaha. "What keeps Seamus Donegan from being a sowbug squasher himself?"

The Irishman stared at the red whiskey a moment before answering. "I suppose I'm not the kind content to die peacefully in bed with me eyes closed. Because some time back on a hot, bloody battlefield they called Gettysburg, Seamus Donegan realized he would never die an old man's death. Now some cold and bony finger's always tapping me shoulder, telling me every day's borrowed time."

"The reaper has us all, sometime," Bridger added.

"To the reaper, then!" Donegan cheered, lifting his cup. "To the reaper—the last friend a dying man will ever know."

"To the reaper," Stead joined in, sloshing his cup into the air.

"To the old bastard himself," Donegan added after swilling down some of the burning whiskey. "This God-blessed, hell-forsaken country gonna keep the reaper plenty busy before this war with Red Cloud's over."

Seamus stood shuddering with the cold blast knifing his groin. Quickly as he could, he finished wetting the snowy ground at the corner of the latrine slip-trench behind Kinney's cabin, and was buttoning the fly on his faded cavalry britches when the voice startled him.

"Should have known, Seamus Donegan. If I don't find you drinking whiskey in the bar, you're outside in the cold, pissing good whiskey away!"

Donegan smiled at his old friend, Samuel Marr, as he pulled on a buffalo-hide mitten and swiped at his drippy nose. "Hate the smell of these places. Remind me of sojurs, a latrine like this does."

Marr chuckled. "Where the hell you think you are, boy? You spit in any direction . . . you'll hit a soldier."

"Curses be to 'em!" Seamus growled. Then he grinned and slapped the gray-headed Marr on the back. "Man tries to forget ever being a sojur and fighting that war—there's always mitherless sons like you want to remind him of the bleeming army! C'mon in to Kinney's place—I'll buy you a drink if the bastard will take my treasury note."

Marr stopped, pulling away from the tall Irishman's arm. "You can't, Seamus."

"And why can't I?" he asked, both hands balled on his hips and a wide grin cutting his face. His teeth glimmered beneath the thumbnail moon tracing a path out of the east.

"The girl," Marr replied. "She wants to see you."

"The Wheatley woman?" He felt his pulse quicken.

Marr nodded without a word.

Donegan's eyes narrowed suspiciously, not wanting to hope. "What would the widow be wanting with me?"

"You told her to call when she needed anything."

"Aye." He nodded, staring at the crusty snow beneath his tall, muddy boots. "The day we buried her husband. Brave man, that one."

"A few who marched with Fetterman were every bit as brave as they had to be on that hellish day," Marr whispered, taking a step closer to the tall man.

"She say what it was?"

Sam shook his head. "Not a word. Just asked me to fetch you to her place . . . small cabin outside the east wall of the quartermaster's stockade."

"I know where it is."

"Oh?"

"I've kept me eye on her since."

"I see."

"It's not what you're thinking, Cap'n," Donegan growled.

"Didn't say it was. Just, I've got a fatherly feeling for the girl. Not yet out of her teens . . . and with two young boys to raise . . . her husband butchered with Fetterman's command but a month ago this day. She's alone in the world now."

"No she's not, Cap'n." Then Donegan slapped a big paw

on the older man's shoulder. "She's got you . . . and me both watching out for her and the boys."

Marr winked in the pale light. "Best you get now. I told her I'd send you straightaway."

"You'll be at Kinney's for the evening?"

Marr nodded. "Nowhere else to be, is there, Seamus? You'll find me here." He turned and scuffed off across the old snow, his boots squeaking over the icy crust as he stomped toward Kinney's door.

Donegan watched after him while the old man's form faded from the pale snow. He loved that old man, he did. Capt. Samuel Marr, Missouri Union Volunteers.

When Seamus had mustered himself out in those months following Appomattox, he had wandered west with the big gray stallion, his yellow-striped cavalry britches now patched and worn, and the .44-caliber army pistol that had carved out a comfortable place for itself at his hip. Wandering into Missouri, he had run onto Sam Marr busy buying horses for the newly organized frontier army. After the canny horse trader Marr discovered he couldn't buy Donegan's gray stallion, they had learned together of the wealth to be made in the Montana diggings along Alder Gulch. And from that moment had begun forming a fierce friendship frequently tested as they fought their way up the Bozeman Road through Sioux hunting ground.

Seamus Donegan would not do a thing to hurt Sam Marr. Nor would he ever do anything to harm the widow Wheatley.

Purposely he slid to the door as quietly as a winter-gaunt wolf and listened. Inside he made out the muffled voices of the two young boys. The oldest, Issac, named for his father's best friend. Issac Fisher who had stood and stared cold-eyed into Red Cloud's Sioux ambush at Wheatley's side. Then Donegan made out the smaller boy's voice. Little Peter. Taking after his mother. A beauty she was, that woman. With so much to bear at her young age. He heard her scolding the two, then listened as she laughed.

Never was one to get hard with those boys of hers, Seamus thought, bringing his big fist up to the rough-hewn door.

Two pairs of little feet hammered to the other side of the door, accompanied by excited voices. He listened as her feet scuffled up, her whisper shushing the boys as she drew back the huge iron bolt and cracked the door an inch.

Seamus gazed down at the single eye peering through the crack at him under the pale moonlight. He cleared his throat.

"Mrs. Wheatley. It's Seamus. Seamus Donegan."

Then he suddenly remembered his hat. Quickly he raked the big, stiff, quarter-crowned brown-felt hat from his long, curly hair and nodded.

"Pardon me, ma'am. A man out in this country doesn't get much of a chance to be a gentleman."

By this time the door had opened and the shy, liquid eyes were blinking their welcome as she waved him inside. "Please . . . Mr. Donegan. Come in."

He stooped through the doorframe and stopped two steps inside as the woman urged the heavy door back into its jamb and slid home the iron bolt. She came around him, shyly reaching for his hat.

"I'll take that, Mr. Donegan," she offered, taking the hat from his mittened hands. "Your coat. Please. Make yourself to home."

Beyond her the two boys stood huddled as one, staring at the tall man who had to hunch his shoulders beneath the exposed, peeled beams of the low-roofed cabin. Their eyes wide with wonder, Issac finally whispered to his young brother.

"We see'd him afore, Peter. Day we put Papa to rest."

"It was cold, Issac," the little one whispered. "I don't remember him."

"I do," Issac replied protectively of his mother, never taking his eyes off Donegan. "I remember *that* one."

Jennifer Wheatley slid an old cane-backed chair across the plank floor toward the Irishman. Donegan slipped the heavy mackinaw coat from his shoulders and shook it free of frost before handing it to the woman. He settled carefully on the chair many-times repaired with nails and wire.

Things have to last folks out in this country, he brooded as he watched her pull up the only other chair in the one-room cabin.

He saw a wooden box turned on its end that served as a third chair at the tiny table where the family took its meals.

"You'd like coffee, Mr. Donegan?" she asked, pointing to the fireplace of creek-bottom stone and mortar.

"If it's no trouble, ma'am."

"Have some made. But you must stop calling me ma'am, Mr. Donegan," she said as she knelt by the iron trivet where the blackened and battered coffeepot sat warming over the coals.

"You're a married woman, ma'am," he started, then ground his hands over his knees, growing angry with himself for his careless words. Words that caused her to stop pouring the coffee. "You've got two fine boys here," Seamus tried again, hoping it would ease the pain of his thoughtlessness.

Jennifer rose slowly, two cups in hand. She passed one to Donegan. "My name's Jennifer. Family and friends back in Ohio called me Jennie. I . . . I want you to be my friend." For a moment she glanced at the two boys. "We . . . we all need a friend. So, please—call me Jennie."

He sipped at the hot liquid. The coffee tasted as if it had been setting in the kettle, reheating for most of the afternoon. Seamus nodded. "Make you a deal . . . ma'am. I'll call you Jennie—if you and the boys here call me Seamus."

Jennie looked over her shoulder at the boys huddled by the fireplace with wooden horses in hand. They had stopped play to stare once more at the big man sprawled over the tiny chair.

"Boys, I want you come over here now," the woman directed. "Want you meet a kind man who knew your papa."

Issac nudged Peter across the floor until both stood at their mother's side. "You knowed my papa?" Issac demanded gruffly.

Donegan nodded and smiled. "As fine a man as any I've met, Mr. Wheatley was." He stuck out his hand to the boy. "My name's Seamus Donegan. Who do I have the pleasure of meeting?"

Issac wiped his hand across his patched denims and stuffed it into the Irishman's paw. "Issac Wheatley, sir. Pleased to meet a friend of my papa's."

Seamus gazed at the youngest when Issac stepped back. Peter glanced up at his mother. She nodded before he inched forward.

"Peter, sir. I'm pleased."

"Not as pleased as me, Peter." Seamus felt the small hand sweating in his grip. "Your papa would be proud to know how his boys help their mother."

Seamus tried to blink away the stinging tears, glancing round the little cabin split in half by wool blankets suspended from a rope lanyard. In the back there was barely enough room for the one small bed he supposed the boys shared. Here in the front half of the cabin another small prairie bed joined the table and chairs, along with a battered old hutch where Jennie kept what dishes had not been broken in her travels west.

When he looked back, he found her staring at her hands in her lap, wringing them silently as she bit her lower lip between her teeth.

"Jennie?" his deep-throated whisper filled the tiny room. "You have nothing to fear now, ma'am. You and the boys got a friend."

Chapter 2

"*Y*our orderly said you requested to see me, Colonel."

Henry Walton Wessells looked up as his office door dragged across the plank floor in closing. The lieutenant colonel shuddered at the blast of cold air accompanying Capt. Tenedore Ten Eyck into the room. Wessells shuddered more with what stared him in the face this cold winter morning.

"Please, Captain. Take a seat."

Ten Eyck pulled up the straight-backed chair near the desk and settled stiffly, yanking off his buffalo-hide mittens.

"Damn cold, Captain."

"Yessir."

Wessells moved around his desk to the sheet-iron stove in the corner of his small office. He remembered this office had once belonged to another, tortured commander of Fort Phil Kearny.

"There's no easy way to do this, Captain."

"Sir?" Ten Eyck turned to the side, straining to keep his one good eye on Wessells.

He cleared his throat and turned back to his desk. "When I arrived here to assume command from Colonel Carrington . . . I personally requested that you alone remain behind when his headquarters group left for Fort Caspar."

Ten Eyck waited a moment, expectant of more. "Sir?"

"Captain, I wanted you to remain behind to help me during the transition of commands."

"After Henry . . . Colonel Carrington had his command wrenched from him by General Crook?"

Wessells stiffened, bristling. "I had nothing to do with that."

"Didn't say you did, sir."

Wessells caught how Ten Eyck emphasized that last word. Studying the Dutchman's face, he saw how the good eye was even more bloodshot than usual. Then he recognized it—what he had caught a whiff of as Ten Eyck swept into the room on that gust of winter wind. The smell of old whiskey and urine-stained britches. Wessells had smelled enough of that potent mix during the war. A lot of good officers grown tired of the army and its tedium. And the whiskey became an easy way out.

"I didn't have a thing to do with Colonel Carrington's dismissal."

"I'm sorry, sir."

Something in Ten Eyck's eyes reminded Henry of a wounded puppy at that moment.

The captain stared at the floor now. "I know it was Crook and Crook alone who drove Henry out. In fact, the truth be known—Henry wanted out. He'd requested a transfer, sir."

"I wasn't aware of that."

"Most men aren't," Ten Eyck said as he smoothed his mittens self-consciously across his legs. "The approval of his transfer just came at a bad time . . . making it appear like Crook was drumming Carrington right out of the Mountain District."

Wessells watched Ten Eyck stare at the rough-boarded floor under his feet. *Damn, this isn't going to be easy at all, Henry.*

"Captain."

"Yessir."

"Surely you're aware of what most of the men are saying in regard to you and your actions on the day of . . . Fetterman's slaughter?"

He watched Ten Eyck gulp, then finally bob his head in admission of it.

"Yes . . . sir. I hear talk. Can't help it. Talk saying I was afraid. Others say I took too long to get to the . . . the place where we found them . . . the bodies." Suddenly Ten Eyck wheeled in the chair, his eyes imploring Wessells. "Do you believe them, Colonel?"

Wessells straightened and inched forward so that he stood closer to the captain. "I wouldn't have asked for you to remain behind to help me when Carrington left . . . had I believed in any of that trash, Captain."

Ten Eyck visibly sank back into the chair with some relief. "I . . . thank you, sir."

"While I don't believe you were a coward in going to Fetterman's rescue, nor do I believe you purposely took too long in reaching the site of the . . . the savagery—I am presented with a dilemma."

"A dilemma, sir?"

"Yes." Wessells waited until he strode around his desk and settled in the horsehair-stuffed chair. It struck him again that, as post commander, Carrington must have sat in this chair with Captain Ten Eyck across the desk from him many a time. Just like this. None of it made an obedient career soldier like Henry Walton Wessells enjoy what he was about to say.

"Captain . . . what I want to say to you is for the good of this command. But, if it matters to you—I want you to know that I reached this decision in large part due to my respect for you and your abilities as an officer."

"Thank you, Colonel. But—"

Wessells waved a hand to silence Ten Eyck. "Even more important, the decision is reached in large part for what you . . . endured during your imprisonment during the war in that Confederate hellhole."

Ten Eyck gulped, not sure where Wessells was leading him. "No man was ever the same coming out of Libby Prison, sir. Thousands like me."

"That's the shame of it. Dead men make heros." Wessells rose from the chair, nervous once again. He paced to the frosty pane of the single window that looked onto the parade. Gazing at the white monolith of Lodge Trail Ridge. "Dead men always make the best of heros, Captain. But those who the war ruined without killing them . . . men like you—are left to struggle on the best way you can."

"Ruined, sir?"

Wessells turned and was at Ten Eyck's side before the captain realized it. "Perhaps a poor choice of words. But, you can't tell me you don't drink because of the pain. The pain left you by that prison. The pain of your wounds. The pain of surrendering your command not once, but twice . . . for the sake of your men. That's a lot for any man to bear, Captain."

Ten Eyck's chin dropped. His one good eye blinked at the sting of tears. The other, droopy lid burned as well. "I . . . I do drink, sir."

Wessells put a hand on Ten Eyck's shoulder. "You must get a hold on yourself, Captain. For the sake of this command. For the sake of your own command. And for the record, as of today, thirty January, 1867—I am reassigning you."

"Reassigning me, sir?"

"Moving you from command of Company H—"

"My company . . . I fought with them during the—"

". . . to Company F."

"But why, sir?"

"There's far too much grumbling among your men."

"My men, sir?" Ten Eyck squeaked, rising from his chair as he twisted the buffalo-hide mittens ruthlessly.

Wessells nodded. "Yes, Captain. As cruel as it sounds, your men are your own worst critics on this post. Far too much grumbling. For the good of the command—"

"Yessir." Ten Eyck straightened and saluted. "As you command."

He was stunned a moment. "You . . . you are a good soldier, Captain."

Ten Eyck blinked, the sting back at his eyes. "I have a job to do, sir. When do you want me to report to my new assignment?"

"In the morning. The first of the month." Wessells wormed back behind the desk, pushing some papers aside. "I'm in hopes that not only will this new command better the morale on the post, but will work an improvement on you as well."

Ten Eyck studied Wessells's face. "On me as well?"

"I want you to tame your drinking, Captain. It's that simple."

"I don't abuse the bottle, sir. Just a little at times to dull the pain—"

"You and I both know that's a lie. But, I can sympathize with you wanting to dull the memories."

"And the pain of my own men calling me a coward . . . or worse behind my back."

"Well, yes." Wessells cleared his throat. "I've heard more than one soldier who rode with you that day say that a civilian advised you against following directly in Fetterman's tracks. Is that correct?"

Ten Eyck squinted the good eye a moment. "It's true, sir. What of it?"

"I've wanted to ask you that question many times in the past two weeks I've been here as post commander. Wanted to know myself just who that civilian was who advised you in taking a longer trail to the Fetterman site . . . and what business did a battlefield-experienced army officer have listening to a goddamned civilian?"

Ten Eyck coughed nervously, wiping the back of his hand across his lips. He had started to sweat in the small office, despite the fact that the stove had to struggle to put out any heat at all.

"His name . . . sir—Seamus Donegan."

"Donegan . . . Donegan," Wessells repeated, his hands pushing papers around atop his messy desk. "Seems I've seen that name written up in reports . . . yes—several reports, as a matter of fact." He stared at Ten Eyck. "What could this Seamus Donegan possibly know that would make a proven soldier like you want to listen to him while riding to the rescue of Fetterman's command?" Wessells pulled up the sheaf of papers with Henry Carrington's writing scrawled across them. Reports.

He gulped. "Donegan . . . sir. He was in the Second Cavalry during the war."

"That doesn't explain a thing, Captain."

Ten Eyck stiffened, his eyes locked on the dirty map behind Wessells's head. "Seamus Donegan is the best soldier—"

"He's no goddamned soldier!" Wessells roared.

Ten Eyck waited for Wessells to calm himself, his eyes still locked on the map. "Begging the colonel's pardon—Seamus Donegan is the best goddamned soldier this captain's ever had the privilege to run across."

"And just what the hell makes him the best damned soldier you've ever run across, Captain?"

"Two medals of honor, Colonel."

"Two?" Wessells choked. He knew only two men during the entire war had been awarded *two* medals of honor for heroism.

"Yessir. Both earned in the face of intense enemy fire as his unit assaulted Confederate artillery positions."

"I see." Wessells gazed into the distance through the window, shadows shifting beyond the glazed, frosty pane of glass.

"I don't think the colonel understands at all, begging the commander's pardon."

"I don't understand—"

"Seamus Donegan is the type of soldier we need more of out here, sir."

"What type of soldier is that, Captain?"

Ten Eyck turned on his heel and stomped to the door, where he pulled on his mittens thoughtfully. "The kind of soldier who cares more about his men than he does about his climb up the ladder."

Wessells stiffened noticeably. "You don't mean to—"

"No offense intended, Colonel," Ten Eyck interrupted. "You just might enjoy meeting Seamus Donegan one of these days, sir."

Wessells nodded. "I might at that, Captain. I just might at that. Two medals of honor, you say?"

Ten Eyck snugged the hat atop his greasy hair and swiped at his red nose. "He was awarded two, sir. Friend of his showed 'em to me. The friend said Donegan ain't the type that will show 'em off. But I saw 'em. And to hear Donegan's friend tell it, the way Donegan fought in the war—should've been more than two medals awarded him."

"Oh?"

"Time and again he did what no other man would."

"Meaning?"

"Seamus Donegan acted like he wanted to die at times, so his friend tells it."

"A bit crazy?"

"Perhaps, Colonel. But, Seamus Donegan always did the craziest things when he was looking out for his men."

"Tell me, Ten Eyck. Was this Donegan a captain . . . a major perhaps?"

"Lord, no, Colonel." Ten Eyck chuckled. "Seamus Donegan wore chevrons."

"A sergeant?"

He nodded. "Time and again turned down the chance to field-jump his rank."

"What do you suppose would have made a man like this Donegan want to turn down such promotions?"

"His men, sir."

"His men?"

"Yessir. And that's something I can learn from Donegan. Having your men care about you and respect you the way Donegan's men felt for him. Especially the way Seamus Donegan felt about the men who fought beside him."

Wessells felt the bite of cold as Ten Eyck pulled the plank door open, allowing the wind to force its way inside. "Something for us all to learn from, perhaps."

Ten Eyck smiled. "Difference between Donegan and the rest of us, Colonel Wessells—the rest of us order men into battle. Seamus Donegan, he leads his men into battle."

Wessells stared at the bare-plank door long after Ten Eyck had left. Wondering if having such a man as this Irishman Donegan on his post would be a blessing or a curse. In such a small command, there was little room for sharing command. Even sharing the command of the men's respect.

I haven't worked all these years and sweated in all those damned backwater commands to have my authority questioned by some dad-blamed ex-sergeant! He stared out the window as he fumed.

We'll have to see what this Donegan is made of, perhaps. To let him know who's in command here.

Make no mistake about it, Seamus Donegan.

Jack Stead leaped to the porch in front of Kinney's bar just as the door flew open. He was too late.

Through the doorframe struggled four soldiers, each one with a lock on Seamus Donegan. Jack had heard the ruckus begin clear across the parade ground, and raced across the starlit snow toward the sound of Donegan's roar. Too late to help.

"What the devil's going on here?" Jack demanded, planting his feet in front of the four troopers.

"Out of the way, Stead!" the voice growled. Major Benjamin Smith slipped past the four guards to confront the scout.

"I asked what's going on here—"

"No concern of yours . . . Stead—isn't it?"

"It is my concern." Stead held out an arm to slow the soldiers from dragging the semiconscious Donegan off the porch.

"It most certainly is not," Smith replied, waving the soldiers past the scout and into the night toward the guard-house across the parade.

Stead stood his ground on the porch, jostled by soldiers and civilians alike pouring back into the sutler's saloon like a retreating tide. A shadow forced its way against the crowd until it stood beside him.

"Captain Marr!" Stead whispered. "What happened to you?"

Sam Marr held a bandanna over one eye. "I'm afraid I'm not as young as I used to be, Jack. When Seamus gets to brawling, he'll have to brawl alone from now on. This ol' warhorse ain't as spry as he once was."

Stead laughed easily with the civilian. "What'd Seamus do this time to land in the guardhouse?"

Marr stopped laughing. He stared off across the parade toward the guardhouse. It would not be the first visit Seamus Donegan had made to Fort Phil Kearny's constabulary.

"A brainless wonder—Donegan is," Marr growled under his breath. "Like he wanted to pick that fight—"

"And he's forbidden to return to my establishment!"

Marr and Stead jerked around at the barking voice. In the doorway stood Judge Kinney, post sutler, wringing his hands on a soiled apron.

"You had a good deal to do with his going to the guard-house, Kinney!" Marr flung his words.

"I want him in my place no more, Captain. You behave yourself—you'll be welcome."

"You'll get no more of my business!" Marr snapped.

"Suit yourself, Marr. I've plenty enough as it is. You'll not hurt me nor my standing here at this post."

"Was I to have a chance at carving up your fat carcass—"

"You threatening me too?" Kinney barked. "Like your friend Donegan?" He shook an arm after the group that was nothing more than a shadow now on the old snow as they trudged on across the parade. "Look what he got for causing me trouble . . . threatening me. *Me!* I'm as good as government property, I am. And no one the likes of him will get my respect. Seamus Donegan. Colonel Wessells himself was asking 'round about him just yesterday, and I gave him a word or two on that black Irishman."

"I'll bet you did, Kinney," Stead growled.

"Best you watch yourself, young scout!" Kinney glared. "Told Wessells what I thought of a man who stirred up trouble with all the finest of soldiers this post has ever seen. Fetterman and Brown both. Not to mention that Sergeant Garrett himself."

"And I'll bet Wessells was all ears, wasn't he?" Stead demanded.

Kinney smiled broadly, his cherubic face grown ruddy in the cold. "He was damned interested in what I had to say about Seamus Donegan. Appears the colonel isn't one to allow the morale and condition of this post be affected by the likes of an unruly drunk civilian like your friend Donegan."

"Way I saw it, you baited him," a new voice added.

All three turned to watch a young soldier push from the shadows at the door.

Kinney sputtered. "Who the hell are you, soldier? And what business is it of yours anyway?"

"Private Gibson. Sam Gibson, Judge. And I know a setup when I see it. You baited that Irishman."

"Baited?" Marr asked.

"Set the Irishman up, most like," Gibson replied. "I can see it now. Why Major Benjamin and them four guards was at the bar when the judge started arguing with Donegan."

"He's the bastard started it!" Kinney sputtered.

"Arguing over what?" Stead asked.

"Who the real soldiers were on Massacre Ridge when Fetterman took his men to their deaths."

Marr and Stead glared at Kinney. A suddenly silent Kinney.

"The judge here said Fetterman and Brown, Grummond too—was the real soldiers that bloody day."

"And Seamus said what?" Stead asked.

"He laughed, is what!" Marr answered.

"That he did, and said Fetterman and Brown was cowards. Put pistols to their heads and killed themselves before the Injuns could have at 'em. Said Grummond was the bravest of the officers on that hillside that day—covering the retreat up the ridge until he was cut down."

"Aye," Marr nodded. "I saw the body myself. It was down in the bottom near where Wheatley and Fisher made their stand. He covered the retreat of the rest up the hill . . . to the rocks where they was finished off."

"That's when Donegan grabbed hold of the sutler here," Gibson continued.

"So that's why you pulled your club, eh, Judge?" Marr demanded.

"The mick threatened me!" Kinney squeaked.

"It's what he said to the judge that's most important," Gibson added. "Grabbed the judge and was lifting him over the bar with his one arm . . . his one goddamned arm, it was! Screaming that the bravest man on that bloody field was some bugler."

"Metzger," Marr whispered. "Adolph Metzger. Company C. Second U.S. Cavalry."

"Good lord!" Kinney choked. "No wonder—"

"Seamus told me how they found Metzger's body in the center of the rocks on Massacre Hill. His was the only body left untouched, while the rest were hacked piece from piece. And in his hand still—his dented, battered tin horn."

"The vision haunts Seamus. I know it does," Stead said as he turned on Kinney. "Donegan and Metzger fought through four years of war down South. And to know his friend was left with no other weapon but his tin horn in those final, terrible moments—you must understand why Donegan went to pieces in there."

Kinney shook himself. He wrung his hands on the apron once more. "None of my concern that a man blows his cork over a dead friend. Lots of those men in there . . . on this post . . . lost friends on that bloody ridge. Donegan has no monopoly on grief."

"It's not grief he's feeling when he thinks about Metzger alone on that hillside with all those screaming Injuns," Marr growled, stepping off the porch. "I figure it's rage."

"C'mon, Captain," Stead said as he joined Marr at the foot of the steps. "Mr. Gibson, I'd like you to join us. We're going to see Colonel Wessells about getting Seamus freed."

The trio turned as gusty laughter roared out of Judge Jefferson T. Kinney.

"Try your damndest, gentlemen," Kinney scoffed. "But your pleas will fall on deaf ears, let me assure you."

"Neither Wessells nor you gonna stop me getting Seamus Donegan out of that guardhouse." Marr leaped halfway up the steps, startling Kinney and forcing the sutler to scurry back to his door.

"Be my guest, Captain Marr."

"I will, Judge," the civilian whispered loudly. "I won't rest until I see Seamus Donegan safely away from this post—away from you and Colonel Wessells both."

Chapter 3

"Go away!" he mumbled through swollen, cracked lips.

"Seamus—you can leave now."

"I'm fine right here."

"C'mon, Seamus. Wessells gave the order to free you. Wants to see you right now." Marr clung to the cell bars.

Donegan rolled away from the wall, clutching the two thin blankets around himself, hoping still for some warmth as the first shaft of sunlight broke through the small window above him.

"Wessells, eh?"

"C'mon, Seamus Donegan."

The Irishman blinked, working to clear his bleary eyes so he could focus on the new voice. "By glory!" he whispered. "If it ain't Cap'n Ten Eyck. How's the Dutchman?"

"Glad to see you're among the living. C'mon—the colonel wants a word with you, you troublemaking blaggard."

Seamus stood, weaving and unsteady at first. Every inch of him hurt. What hadn't been beaten during last night's scuffle at Kinney's ached from the intense cold of the unheated guardhouse. "Gonna snow again, it 'tis."

Marr watched his friend stumble toward the cell door. "How you so blamed sure of that, Seamus?"

"Feel it to my bones, Cap'n Marr. The ones what aren't bruised or broke, you see." He tried to laugh, but it hurt his face.

"You're a mess, Seamus Donegan."

He saluted. "Present and accounted for, Cap'n. Sergeant Mess, reporting for conference with the post commander."

"Maybe you should wash up a bit," Marr said, looking for something he might use to wipe off the crusted blood.

"No time," Ten Eyck advised. "Wessells wants to see him first off . . . and that means now."

"You heard the man, Seamus." Marr grabbed Donegan's arm as he stumbled out of the cell. "You're off to see the brass."

"I always love seeing the brass." Donegan giggled. "It's the highlight of me day. Almost as much as I love getting the piles."

The three of them laughed together as they pushed into the sunlight just breaking over the east wall of the stockade.

"So you're Seamus Donegan," Wessells declared as he stood and cornered his desk toward the trio who entered his office. He held out his hand halfway there. "Been wanting to meet the man who single-handedly wrecked the sutler's place three times."

Donegan stared down at the offered hand. "I had help—each time."

Wessells glanced at his hand hanging in the air between them, then dropped it. He drew himself up expansively and stomped back to the desk, his collar a little warmer. Flinging an arm toward the young lieutenant standing close to the stove, Wessells announced, "You've not met the officer of the day? Lieutenant John C. Jenness. He'll be in charge of you until you leave the post, Donegan."

Seamus watched the post commander gaze down at his papers without seating himself at the desk. Dumbfounded, he took two steps closer to that desk. "Did I hear you right, Colonel? *Until I leave the post?*"

Wessells put both palms flat on the desk and leaned toward the Irishman. "You heard me correctly, mister."

"On what grounds are you throwing me off the post?"

This time Wessells settled into the horsehair chair before speaking. He seemed self-assured as he gazed up at Donegan. "I'm having you removed from this military reservation for the good of my command and the morale of the men assigned a task in this godforsaken wilderness."

"The good of your command?" Marr joined Donegan in glaring at the officer.

"Winter in this country is not a good time at all to have someone of your color here, Mr. Donegan. The lack of activity, the length of the nights . . . all of that goes a long way to making my men restive. Prone to excitement. You're just the sort of excitement I can do without."

Seamus shook his head, gazing from Ten Eyck to Marr. The captain found a place for his eyes on the far wall so he would not have to meet Donegan's glare. Marr wore a look of undisguised anger matched only by the Irishman's.

"What do you suppose he's to do, Colonel?" Marr demanded at the edge of Wessells's desk.

"If you're asking how Mr. Donegan's to survive in this wilderness, you have every right to know."

"You bet I wanna know!" Donegan barked, beside Marr now at the desk, his big hands clenching at his sides, seeking something to throttle. From the corner of his eye he watched Lieutenant Jenness free the mule-ear on his holster.

"You'll not need that pistol!" Seamus snapped without looking over at Jenness. He straightened. "Your post commander's in no danger . . . at least from the likes of me, Lieutenant."

Wessells's eyes darted between the two, coming to rest on the Irishman. "Well," he gulped. "I'm certainly not going to be guilty of driving you from this post without a means for you to survive in this godforsaken winter desert, Mr. Donegan."

"Oh?"

"I have need of someone of your . . . talents, shall I say."

"Talents?" Donegan asked, his eyes flicking momentarily to Marr.

"Most definitely. A man of your resolution. Your undoubted strength. Your determination in the face of great odds—as witnessed by your repeated attempts to take on the soldiers of this post—"

"After I've been drinking some."

"Be that as it may, Mr. Donegan," Wessells continued, "it's just that determination I need."

"To do what?"

"Make your way to Fort C.F. Smith."

"Fort Smith?" Donegan's voice rose an octave. "Hear tell that's ninety miles north of here on the Bighorn River. Through this snow and cold?"

"We've had no communication with that post since November last. For over three months the two posts have been shut off from one another."

"So you want me to ride up there and say how-do?"

Wessells grinned. "You, and two of my best men who will be going along."

"Three of us."

"That's right. Carrying mail and dispatches for the men and officers at our northernmost outpost on this road to the Montana gold camps."

"Why haven't you had any contact with Fort Smith before now?"

"Mr. Donegan, surely you're aware I took command of this post from Colonel Carrington little over two weeks ago. I can't explain why the former District Commander failed to open communication with Fort Smith. But I can tell you I will surely try."

"You haven't explained *why* you haven't had any contact."

"Until now, Mr. Donegan—we've had no volunteers."

"Vol—Volunteers?" Seamus snorted. "You bleeming idjit! I'm volunteering?"

"No," Wessells snapped. "Two of my sergeants have volunteered to break their way through to Fort Smith and return."

"And you want me to 'volunteer' to go with them?"

"You can volunteer . . . if volunteering would make you feel better."

"I don't have another choice, do I?"

"You're smarter than I gave you credit for, I suppose. Seems you've begun to see things in a better light, and quickly at that, Mr. Donegan."

"All right. Say I go with your two sergeants—"

"Grant and Graham."

"I go with them to your Fort Smith and back again—then what?"

"Ah . . . no. You've misunderstood. Grant and Graham will be returning here to Fort Phil Kearny."

Donegan waited a moment for Wessells to continue. "Ahhh," Seamus finally sighed, "I see. I'll be staying behind at Fort C.F. Smith."

"Correct."

"And while I'm there?"

"You'll support yourself as you have here. You will carry my notice to the post commander there, informing him of your need for employment."

"And telling him why you've thrown me out of Fort Phil Kearny."

Wessells nodded, swallowing. "Captain Nathaniel C. Kinney would naturally be curious as to why you couldn't work the winter here."

"He'll love you for sending him a troublemaker like me, won't he, Colonel?"

"I suppose he has little choice."

"About as little as I." Donegan sighed. He looked at Marr. "Say, Cap'n . . . no sense being so dog-faced 'bout this. I'll be that much closer to the gold camps when we're ready to make ourselves rich men!"

"Want me go along, Seamus?"

"Naww." Donegan glanced at the fire in Wessells's eyes. "You stay put. The Wheatley woman needs someone to watch over her and the boys."

Marr scratched his chin. "I'd clean forgot about the widow. You best go explain this to her yourself."

"I intend to. Soon's the brass monkey here's done with this stupid Irishman. When're your men fixing to leave on this little trip of yours, Colonel?"

"In the morning."

"Of course," Seamus replied, nodding. "Not much time for this mick to get himself in trouble, is it?"

Wessells nodded once.

"I'll be here before first light." Donegan saluted.

The gesture evidently surprised the post commander. Before he realized what he was doing, Wessells started to salute, catching his hand before it slapped against his forehead.

"We'll be expecting you, Mr. Donegan. Dismissed."

* * *

"Won't it be dangerous?" Jennie Wheatley asked, handing the steaming cup of coffee to Donegan.

"Not much a man does in this part of the world what isn't dangerous, Jennie."

She sighed, settling in the other chair with her own cup. After sipping at the scalding liquid, she tried a valiant smile. "At least I got you to calling me Jennie these few days we had together."

Donegan returned her smile. Already he ached. "I'll miss you . . . the boys." He spoke quietly, glancing across the room beyond the blanket partition where Jennie's boys lay on their straw tick, peeking over the covers at him.

"The boys will miss having you bounce them on your knee, Seamus."

An uneasy silence grew between them as Jennie stared into her cup and Seamus sipped at his, eyes smarting already.

Such a thing is never easy, he reminded himself. *Your time with Jennie is yet to come. Let things be. Just, let them be.*

"You've done well fattening me for the journey." He tried out a smile on her.

That did it. She smiled back, her eyes filling. "You look a little healthier than the day we buried . . . the day I met you."

He cleared his throat. "Not been fed so well since I left my mother's table years ago."

She giggled lightly in that way of hers that was like mountain water over a pebbled streambed, eyes shining with moistness. "Nor eaten so much, I'd imagine."

"I don't remember ever passing up a meal, Jennie."

"Surely not a free one, Seamus."

He laughed with her, then fell quiet, gazing at her dark, almond eyes, studying the moist, pink lips formed in a pouty bow and the high-boned cheeks rouged with heat from the fireplace. The ruddy ivory of it all surrounded by a cascade of auburn curls. "Never would I miss a meal with a lady as beautiful as you. If only to drink you in with my eyes."

The color in her cheeks darkened. Her eyes fell from his, staring once more at her coffee. "I remember once . . . once you drank in all of me, Seamus Donegan. Down at the creek when I was . . . bathing."

"I felt like such a beggar that day . . . peeking at you from the willows. Gazing at your . . . your beauty. I'd watched all day had you not spotted me." Suddenly Seamus was struck with the feeling he had done something wrong. "Did I say something . . . something I—"

She glanced up, eyes moistening, and shook her head. "No, no, Seamus. Nothing wrong. I'll miss you so." The sob caught in her throat. She swallowed it down like something bitter. "The boys will miss you so much."

"Cap'n Marr will be by to see how you three are doing." Seamus's voice sounded rough, hiding the thick knot that threatened to betray him. He set the cup on her table and stood, sweeping up his coat.

He watched her eyes as they implored his, their moist depths betraying some small fear in them at his leaving so abruptly. "I best be going, Jennie. An early start. No telling what the day will bring. No telling how hard—"

She dropped her cup to the table and struggled to help him into his heavy, double-breasted coat. Standing before him, Jennie Wheatley slowly shoved each of the eight huge buttons through their holes. He looked down at the top of her head as she worked her callused fingers at their task. The crown of her auburn curls almost reached his bearded chin.

So close. This smell of her. Never closer than this moment. His mind burned with the fragrance . . . the feel of her inches from him.

Seamus crumpled the brim on his big hat, yearning. A man who had had his way with women for years, first initiated into the wonders of pleasure as a boy who looked and performed as if he were much older. For such a man to feel this unsure, this nervous . . .

She's dangerous, Seamus Donegan. Making a man like you feel the way you do about her.

For the longest moment she stared up at him, bottom lip caught between her teeth. "Aren't you going to kiss me, Seamus Donegan?"

"Kiss you?"

"To say, good-bye?"

"Good-bye?" His cheeks burned.

"Until you return . . . to me?" The first drop slid free from her pooling eyes.

He swept her into his arms, holding her against him fiercely for long minutes. Over the top of Jennie's head he watched one set of dark eyes peeking over the covers at them by the door. At last Seamus held her away from him.

She raised her face, ruddy cheeks stained with glistening tracks. "Put your mouth on mine, Seamus."

He had never needed so much prompting. Not knowing at this difficult moment if he hesitated because she was barely more than a month a widow. Or, if he hesitated because of the boys. A man used to stealing kisses and feeling no remorse when he was slapped, Seamus Donegan felt his own cheeks warm again as he bent over her opening mouth that invited him to taste her.

Jennie pressed into him, her small, full breasts straining against the heavy wool shirt she wore, straining against him as he clutched her every bit as eagerly as he would driftwood in a raging torrent. When his mouth met hers, Jennie's lips opened more fully. Greedily he drank in the taste of her, sensing the tingle race across his loins. Seamus felt her shudder as well, just before Jennie took hold one of his hands, bringing it from the small of her back, slowly around the fullness of her hip. She placed his hand on her breast.

He trembled as he drew back, ready to curse himself for his stupidity, had she not spoken first.

"Seamus," she whispered huskily. She still imprisoned his hand against her breast straining beneath the oversized wool shirt. Her husband's wool shirt. "Please."

He shook his head, bewildered, wondering for a moment what made him refuse. "I've never had . . . such a delicious offer, Jennie. I . . . I can't."

"I need you."

"Not like this . . . not so soon."

"Please—"

He clutched her against him roughly, smoothing her curls with his rough, gnarled hand. "Ssshhh," he whispered. "I'll be back, girl."

"You'll . . . you'll *be* . . . with me when you return?"

With a finger he raised her chin so he could gaze down into her eyes. "Count on it."

"Hurry back to me." She whispered the words prayerfully, eyes closing. Her lips parted again.

Seamus dipped once more into the taste of her full-mouthed headiness, lingering there for the longest time before he turned and threw himself into the night.

Chapter 4

"*F*or a g-goddamned Irishman, you're all right," Noah Graham stammered with cold lips, smiling. He blew on his bare fingers, watching Seamus Donegan feed the struggling newborn flames of the tiny fire he was building beneath the overhanging bows of a pine out of the howling wind.

"We get this fire going, get some water a'boil," Seamus replied. "Got to get something hot into Grant here." He nodded to the soldier seated next to Graham, who stared dumbly at the fire near his feet.

"He's a good man, really he is, Donegan."

Seamus glanced up at Graham. "No question of it. Any man volunteer for this duty . . . got him bullocks as big as a herd bull."

"That, or he hasn't got the sense got gave a buffalo gnat!" Graham stammered, his teeth chattering.

"You know why I'm trudging off to Fort Smith." Seamus held his bare hands over the fire a moment, then went back to snapping twigs into the growing fire. He gazed steadily at Graham. "What leads a veteran like you to chance this cold walk?"

Graham swiped a hand beneath his red nose, taking with it a cold, drippy pendant the color of a pearl. "Chance to get out of that damned post. Simple as that."

Donegan snorted. "You gotta be joking, Graham."

"Bound to go crazy . . . snowed in the way we were. Both

of us, we knew Wessells been asking civilians for volunteers. No man would touch it for less'n a thousand in gold."

"And the three of us sit here on our asses," Seamus said, waving his arm in an arc, "in the middle of this goddamn winter—doing Wessells's work for free. We oughtta have us a drink to commemorate the occasion."

"If we had any, I'd join you." He hung his head, then glanced at Grant beside him. "Probably drink his too."

Seamus stuffed a hand inside his wool mackinaw. "He needs it worse'n us both together." And pulled out a battered tin flask. He worried the cork from it, to Graham's astonished expression. The fragrance of the raw whiskey escaped the flask.

"You're shitting me, ain't you, Donegan!"

"Give a taste," Seamus suggested, handing the flask to Graham. "Then see if you can get some down him."

As he dribbled some on Grant's half-frozen lips and tongue, Graham continued. "We get out of this, I'll damn sure remember this winter as the coldest I ever seen."

"That's why you need Irish blood pumping in your veins, Sergeant. Irish blood keep a man warmer'n most."

"A good woman would do me every bit as much good as Irish blood."

Seamus nodded, recalling the fragrance of her but a handful of hours ago. "No argument there, Sergeant. No argument there."

It had been a sleepless night for Seamus Donegan after leaving the widow Wheatley, tossing under his blankets in the civilian quarters, waiting for the first hint of dawn, remembering the double-barreled feel of her pressed against him, and cursing himself for ever leaving the excitement of her. Finally admitting it was the only thing he could have done.

In Wessells's office that morning before dawn, the stove had begun to warm and there was hot coffee poured into steaming cups and as quickly poured into empty bellies, joining old hardtack and some pasty, ancient jerky. The remainder of the trail food had been packed in some canvas satchels by the two sergeants and a private who had volunteered to come along, wanting to see a friend up at Fort C.F. Smith. The satchels and four sets of snowshoes had been lashed to their mules.

With another check of the big gray's hooves and shoes, Donegan crawled into the saddle, following the soldiers out the main gate and down the northern cut of the Sullivant Hills. They reached the valley of Peno Creek near the foot of Massacre Hill.

Funny, what difference a month will make, Donegan thought as he stood shivering in the wind on that gray slope at first light inking off the eastern plains. *The snow had come and covered everything. No man would know what happened on this ground—had he not seen it for his own eyes.*

By the time they were struggling out of the Peno drainage, it had grown clear to Donegan they were not going to make it on horseback. The animals were floundering too badly, swimming through the drifts. He had suggested a halt to Graham and the others, the four of them huddling within the corral of their animals, stomping their boots, stuffing mittened hands under their armpits, teeth chattering beneath the shrill keening of a wolfish wind slicing off the Big Horns themselves.

"Fellas," Donegan began, "no sense in trying to push these animals any farther. We'll move faster, and stay warmer to boot—we march north on foot."

"On f-foot?" Grant stammered.

He nodded. "We won't flounder in the deep stuff, where it's piled in the ravines and against the lee of every hillock," Seamus explained.

"All right," Graham agreed, nodding. "Suppose we do march on foot. What the hell we gonna do with our mules? You're not fixing to leave that big brute of yours behind, are you now?"

Donegan glanced back at the quivering sides of the gray, the ice glazed round its nostrils as steamy mist exploded with each breath exhaled. "He's going back too."

"How?"

Seamus regarded Graham, then Grant. And finally the young private. "Him." He nodded to the private. "He'll take the animals back."

"I'll what?" the young man squeaked.

Graham paid no attention to him. "I'm listening."

"We'll take everything from here on our backs. The lad here can make it back to Kearny well before dark."

"I ain't going back!"

"Shuddup!" Graham snapped, then stared at the tall civilian again. "You're crazy, figuring us to make it ninety miles on foot, Irishman!"

Seamus grinned, straining to hide his own chattering teeth. "If a Irishman can make that walk, boys—surely the two of you can as well."

Graham nodded to the private. "He ride your gray back?"

Seamus studied the youth. Then finally nodded once. "He'll do to ride him back. Lash the mules together. Tether 'em to the back of me saddle."

Then he turned to face the young private. "You get this horse to a man named Sam Marr. First thing you do when you get in that stockade. You find Sam Marr. Give him my horse."

"He'll know what to do?" Graham asked.

"Best horse man this side of Gettysburg," Donegan replied.

"He's gonna have to be," Grant moaned. "Stock there at Kearny running out of food. Can't get down to the Pinery for cottonwood the way we should to feed the animals."

"Marr'll see to the stallion."

"You won't see that animal till spring."

Something stung Seamus a bit, something like the reality of parting from the stallion. First he had pulled himself away from the girl, knowing it was right not to bed her. Not this way. And now, it was every bit as right for him to send the gray back. Back to Sam Marr at Fort Phil Kearny, where the animal stood a chance of surviving the winter.

Out here in this wilderness, the gray might not last out the struggle north to Fort C.F. Smith.

He stroked the stallion's neck. "C'mon over here, sojur." Seamus waved. "Best we get these stirrups adjusted for you."

"You're a damned sight taller'n me, mister." The young trooper's teeth chattered.

"Damned sight taller most men," Grant mumbled, his lips paling in color as he stammered.

"Just means I'm gonna make a bigger hole, Sergeant," Seamus said.

"A bigger hole?" Noah Graham asked.

"When I fall down dead-froze in the snow!"

He and Graham had laughed about it, then lashed the mules together and bid farewell to the young trooper. Graham stood watching Donegan. Seamus watching the stallion disappear beyond the ridge.

"Let's march, Mr. Donegan."

He nodded to Graham, bringing up the rear of the little procession turning its nose into the north wind, busting through the snow climbing from their calves to well past their hips by mid-afternoon. Time and again Seamus pulled Grant out of the snowdrifts and icy banks. As the sun began to sink onto the spires of the Big Horns, Donegan had begun lugging Grant along under his arm, struggling to stay in the trail Graham busted ahead of him, one step at a time.

When Noah Graham found it impossible to rise from his knees that last time, Donegan growled they had to cache for the night. Near the side of the trail the two of them spotted a likely place to camp, both struggling to drag the semiconscious Grant out of the wind and the snow. As many times as he had stumbled and fallen, breaking through the icy crust, Leonard Grant appeared in bad shape. Some time ago he had ceased mumbling incoherently. Now by the fire, Grant sat like a statue, staring into the leaping flames, dazed and half dead.

Forcing small sips of warmed whiskey diluted by Donegan with melted snow, Graham eventually got his fellow sergeant responding by the time the wind picked up and a coal-cotton darkness descended on their little campsite.

By the next morning, Leonard Grant had awakened to complain of his hunger and his frozen toes.

"By the by, Irishman," Grant gazed across the fire Donegan had spent a fitful night feeding with limbs, "you have any more of that whiskey you nursed me with?"

Seamus snorted, patting the side of his mackinaw. "Not much, Sergeant. I'll keep what I've got left for a real need. Not just your whiskey thirst."

He watched Graham wrap his shoes with wide strips of burlap sacking.

Graham glanced up. "Army still don't make a good pair of boots for a man."

Donegan nodded. "A shame they march a man out West to

fight Injins and the winter, and don't give him something fit and decent to march in. Boots falling apart, are they?"

"Stitching ain't worth a red piss," Leonard Grant said as he finished lashing the burlap around the split leather of his army shoes. That burlap was probably the only thing keeping the soldiers' feet from freezing fully.

"How come your boots ain't fallen apart?" Graham asked.

Donegan patted the calf-high Jefferson boots with their tall Cuban heel and squared toe. "These boots was the last pair give me before Appomattox. Drew 'em out hoping they'd make me through to the end of the war. They did that and better—all 'cause of a man named Sam Marr. Met him, and he showed me how to take care of leather—be it a boot or the saddle on that gray I sent back under that sojur of yours yesterday."

"Some secret?" Graham asked as he stood, shook his legs and hoisted a canvas satchel over both arms.

"Not now, t'ain't. Lampblack and grease. But you must start with good leather. Not the third-class cowhide the army buys from its suppliers because someone in the War Department's getting paid off."

"Ain't that the blessed truth," groaned Leonard Grant.

"Sam Marr had a fella he knew back in Independence, Missouri, rebuild my boots from the ground up, using prime leather. And, for more than a year now I've kept 'em oiled—not a crack to be seen for it."

Grant stood shouldering his load. Donegan stepped between the two soldiers. Graham stared off into the north, where dark clouds scudded along the ridges, forbidding and angry. The wind moaning off the Big Horns with the coming light sliced at the trio as surely as a saber swung at close quarters. Cutting. Brutal. Bloody as well.

"C'mon, Irishman." Graham tapped Seamus before he led off. "Let's hope these shoes of mine will outlast each miserable mile we've got to put behind us today."

The same insistent wind snaffled the single braid along the young war-chief's cheek. Crazy Horse pulled the hairy buffalo robe more tightly about his shoulders and stared into the south.

Whereas the Cheyenne stayed close to the Tongue River and the Arapahos under white renegade Bob North, who hunkered for the winter along the banks of the upper Bighorn, Red Cloud's Oglalla Sioux had wandered north to the lower reaches of the Powder River after the great defeat they had dealt the soldiers near the Pine Woods fort, the place the white man called Phil Kearny.

"My nephew is touched-by-the-moon?"

Crazy Horse turned, finding his uncle Little Hawk approaching with Man-Afraid. Both huddled against the predawn winter wind, beneath buffalo robes and wool leggings.

The young Oglalla chieftain smiled. "I am young. My blood runs hot. Tired old men like you both should not come to greet the morning."

The three laughed before all fell quiet once more as they listened to the pained keening of the wind slashing the ridges above the Powder.

"You come to seek a winter vision, nephew?"

Crazy Horse turned to Little Hawk. "No, uncle. I come to wish the winter away. So we may be at our war once more."

"The young are so anxious for blood," Little Hawk said to Man-Afraid.

"This one, I think he hasn't had his fill of white blood for the winter," Man-Afraid agreed.

"Red Cloud, High Backbone . . . even the Cheyenne war-chief Roman Nose himself—all were certain that in the *Moon of Deer Shedding Horns* we would deliver one terrible blow to the soldiers at the Pine Woods fort . . . and the rest would flee to the south, beyond our hunting grounds."

Man-Afraid clucked, "The soldiers did not run."

"Even though we had a hundred in the hand that day on the ridge where blood muddied the snow and my moccasins grew slick with the gore of soldiers who fought bravely until there was but one."

"You left your robe behind to cover his body," Little Hawk commented.

"Yes," Crazy Horse said, nodding. "He was the bravest among the rocks." He spat on his fingers. "Some of the soldiers threw themselves away."

"Killed themselves?" Little Hawk asked.

"Threw their spirits away rather than fight like men," the young Oglalla chief spat again.

Man-Afraid was quiet for a long time, feeling the moan of the wind in his soul as well as in his bones. Then he finally spoke. "We defeated those soldiers with bow and lance, my young friend. Now, after fighting these white men along the road since last summer's sundance, more than half our warriors have rifles."

"They are old rifles, Man-Afraid," Crazy Horse replied. "You will need much ammunition to feed those soldier rifles when we resume our attacks on the forts come the short-grass."

"Red Cloud already speaks of going to Laramie to trade for powder and lead. We will load these soldier rifles taken on that icy day . . . and kill more soldiers with them come the short-grass time."

Little Hawk gazed at Crazy Horse. "My nephew is not satisfied with talk of war come the time our ponies grow sleek on the new grass?"

"No uncle." He shook his head, staring into the south, beyond the ridges and hills, the canyons and badlands, to where the two soldier forts still stood like fists shoved down the throat of the Lakota. "I cannot wait to crush the forts themselves this time."

"Your heart follows Red Cloud in this?"

"Yes." Crazy Horse nodded to his uncle. "Enough of attacking the wagons and those who journey on the white road to Crow land. Enough of burning the grass the white man cuts to feed his horses. Enough of killing a soldier here, a soldier there as he chops down the trees to burn in his wood lodges at the forts. Yes, my heart rests with Red Cloud. We make war until the white soldiers are no more."

"There are many among the bands who say the diseases our people suffered last robe season and this are the magic of the white man," Man-Afraid barely whispered. "They say the white man will stay, because he knows this magic . . . and he knows he will prevail. All *Wakan Tanka's* red children will be as the dust that blows from the face of the earth. Gone away before the white man's magic sickness."

"I do not believe this." Crazy Horse whirled on his mentor,

the man who taught him not only war, but courage as well. And he wondered why the fight had gone out of Man-Afraid, like the juices dried from the prairie grasses come the cold winds of autumn. Grasses gone brittle before the onslaught of winter, like Man-Afraid's hope gone brittle before the coming of the white man.

"You tell me, Crazy Horse. I will listen."

"We grow sick when we touch the white man. If only he will stay away, our children will not cry in pain. Our women will not carry the oozing sickness between their legs. There is no magic to that. We drive the white man from our lands, there will be no more sickness. Our children will not cry from pinched, hungry bellies. Our women will not shame themselves. Nor will our young men hunger for the crazy water these white men bring to dull the fighting spirit of our warriors."

Man-Afraid brooded on it for a moment. His young protégé must surely be right. "There is no magic."

"*Aiyee*," Crazy Horse whispered, his arm bare as it crept from his robe, pointing off to the south. "There is no magic . . . none strong enough to save the white men who huddle in their pitiful forts. Come the short-grass time, and after the strength that grows in our people from the sundance, we will follow Red Cloud."

"To the forts, nephew?"

"Yes, Little Hawk," he answered. "We will crush every last man, woman and child in those forts. That is the only way. Then the white man will send no more into our country. When we wipe the breast of our earth-mother clean of all traces of the white man at last."

Chapter 5

"*I* already told you this morning, Leonard," Sgt. Noah Graham growled wearily to the man plodding behind him. He stared once more at the back of the tall Irishman busting through the snow ahead of the two who followed, and shook his head. Leonard Grant was in bad shape and getting worse.

"I don't remember, Noah," the soldier whined. "Tell me again. I promise I won't ask no more."

"You've asked me twenty times this morning already!" Graham snapped. "I'm not going to tell you again, goddamn—"

"Tell him!"

Graham slid to a halt behind Seamus Donegan, who stood waist deep in the snow, his Henry rifle cradled across his chest, glowering like a monolithic beast with sunken, red-rimmed eyes.

"The sonuvabitch keeps asking what day—"

"Tell him, goddammit," Donegan ordered. "You tell him, or come up here to break trail."

"Who're you to order me, you goddamned mule-headed mick!"

Donegan sighed. It was too cold to fight. Graham wanted to fight, but it would take too much out of the both of them. And poor Leonard Grant just needed to keep moving. Seamus decided he'd keep them moving, if he had to knock them unconscious and drag them along by himself.

"It's the seventh, Sergeant." Donegan flung his voice over Graham's shoulder to the weary soldier bringing up the tail of their sad procession.

"The seventh." Grant chewed on that as he chewed on his chapped lips, seemingly trying to make sense of it. "How many—"

"This is our fourth day, goddammit!" Graham shouted, snatching his fellow sergeant by the collar and shaking him.

"Four days?"

"Let's march," Donegan said, turning. "You foot sloggers know how to do that, don't you?"

"Your goddamned idea to leave the mules and that gray brute of yours behind," Graham snarled. "We'd be riding now you hadn't—"

"Your turn to bust trail, Graham." Seamus said it softly as he turned.

The sergeant ground to a halt, his legs buried in Donegan's tracks, snow up to his crotch and more swirling like white buckshot that stung his cheeks. "I . . . I don't figure I've got the strength left—"

"Then you best find the strength to shut up and keep marching behind me. You won't break trail for me . . . you bloody well shut your bleeming mouth. Leonard?"

"Yeah, Seamus?" the other sergeant answered.

"Sing me some more."

"Anything in particular."

"Just sing. I figure I gotta walk like a goddamned foot-sloggin' infantry sojur . . . I best have me some marching songs to go 'long with this little walk. Sing, Leonard."

"Come unto me, ye heroes—"

"Louder, Leonard! Louder!" Donegan ordered. "This wind carries your voice away."

"Come unto me, ye heroes,
Whose hearts are true and bold,
Who value more your honor,
Than others do their gold."

"Than others do their gold!" Donegan repeated lustily, his deep voice rocking the branches of the trees, all the time reminding himself to keep putting one boot before the other. Just sing and walk. Sing and walk.

"Give ear unto my story," Sergeant Grant continued, feeling some warmth in the singing, the march, the swinging of his arms beneath the heavy Springfield rifle he clutched like a lover.

> "Give ear unto my story,
> And the truth to you I'll tell,
> Concerning many a soldier,
> Who for his country fell."

Through the shank of that icy morning and into midday Seamus Donegan kept Leonard Grant singing. And Noah Graham grumbling angrily between them both. *A man does what a man must,* Seamus reminded himself. And thought on other things.

The shriek of shells and the whistle of minié balls. The jets of earth erupting and the showers of shrapnel from the throat of the artillery he rode hellbent to capture. And always stray bullets hissing, tearing at his jacket sleeves as he hacked and carved his way in red through the Confederate positions at Gettysburg.

His beloved 2nd Cavalry. With the war over, his own Company C dispatched to return to Fort Laramie under Capt. James Peale, on orders of Lieutenant Colonel Wessells to save the horses at Fort Phil Kearny from starvation that late January of 1867. It would be weeks before word came up from Laramie that Peale and every man along had arrived safely. But not until spring would Wessells learn that Peale's command had reached Laramie without a single horse. One hundred fifty carcasses strewn south along that stretch of the Montana Road, bones bleaching to mark every mile for years to come.

"One small loaf of bread is all issued to us each day."

Seamus recalled what Graham had talked about last night, huddled at their little fire after the last of the jerky and hardtack had been swallowed.

"Nary a strip of fresh meat, nor vegetables!" Graham had

laughed. "We ain't seen a potato in better'n four months at Kearny."

"Time was when we finished our bread each day," Leonard Grant had continued explaining, filling his mouth with words when no food was left between them, "a man had to fall back on the wormy hardtack left the army after the war. That, and the frowzy bacon or salt-pork. A'times all we had for days was white-bean soup and coffee."

"You've lived," Donegan had reminded them this morning as they all awoke to growling bellies and short dispositions. "We'll find something to eat today."

"What you figure we'll run into—"

"Something," Seamus had snapped, then quickly turned his nose into the wind slashing out of the north.

"Least we was warm last night, Noah," Grant tried cheering his fellow soldier. "Not like back at Phil Kearny where we had to stay up bucking wood past nine o'clock, just to keep the stoves fired till break o'day."

Later, as the sun had risen like a dull pewter plate behind the thick clouds, looking more like a glob of buttermilk gone to clabber, Grant had sniffed noisily, his runny nose raw and aching. "You stink, Noah."

"You don't smell no better, Grant," the sergeant growled.

"Maybeso we can take a bath we get to Smith."

Graham laughed mirthlessly. "You crazy loon. What with all the creeks froze up solid 'tween now and spring, no soldier's bound to waste water on washing. You best get used to smelling your friends, Leonard Grant."

Through the morning Seamus listened to them arguing, bickering like bitchy women. He minded not at all, as it kept the soldiers' minds off the march. Off the cold. And off the coming storm boiling up in the west and headed their way over the hills.

There'd been times this last few months, Seamus had to admit, times when he had wondered privately of putting his name to a recruiting form once more. Then, he would hear the soldiers at Phil Kearny grumbling of their diet. For lack of vegetables, the post hospital had grown crowded by men down on their backs with scurvy. With no relief outside of Surgeon Horton's medicines, the entire garrison was threatened. A pitiable sight to see so many young soldiers grown emaciated and weak, flat on their backs and afflicted to the extent that their teeth were ready to drop from their mouths.

Food. Army troubles always came back to food.

That's when Donegan spotted it, off to the side of the trail he was breaking through the wind-carved snow.

The animal's tracks crossed the trail Seamus was cutting. He stopped, studying the country ahead. To his left—the snow pounded and trampled by many footprints. And in the center lay the carcass of an old buffalo bull.

"That what I think it is?" Graham pushed past Donegan.

Seamus flung his left arm out, trying to stop the sergeant lunging ahead into the tracks beaten by moccasined feet.

"Sergeant!" he whispered hoarsely. "Get your ass back in the trees." Donegan whirled, stumbling back to keep from falling as Grant barreled by him.

As fast as they could stumble through the trampled snow-drifts, both sergeants lumbered up the bare slope to what was left of the buffalo carcass. His Henry held at ready, ears pricked for any foreign sound and eyes scouring the skyline, Donegan trudged behind them warily.

He joined the soldiers at the carcass as they both freed knives and hacked slices of raw, cold meat from the ribs, stuffing the bloody flesh into their gaping mouths. "Don't you realize what this carcass means?"

"A blessing, that's what it is!" Grant exclaimed.

"The Injins killed it," Donegan replied, placing a bare hand against the cooling flesh. "Not here long, either. We best be moving quick." He rose, nudged Graham with the muzzle of his Henry.

The sergeant shoved the rifle barrel aside. "Lemme alone, Irishman. Gonna eat my fill and cut some for supper. No telling when we'll eat again."

"You're more worried 'bout your belly than your scalp, is it?"

"Lookee here," Graham retorted. "Red bastards butchered what they wanted and hot-footed it back to their camp. They long gone by—"

"Just how far you think they are from here?" Seamus snapped, his muzzle trying to nudge Grant from the carcass.

"They wander out on foot to hunt, they don't wander far from camp at all." He backed off a few steps, sensing something on the change of wind as it shifted to a norther. His eyes crawled to the ridgeline.

"I ain't gonna be long, I told you," Graham snapped, slicing meat.

"You ain't at that," Donegan barked, his voice loud now. "You ain't got time for nothing but running now, boys."

Grant was the first to look up, see where Donegan pointed his rifle. Off the top of the ridge poured a dozen or more warriors wrapped in wool capotes and brandishing rifles over their heads as they screeched their way down the slope.

"It'll be a merry chase, sojurs . . ." Donegan said as he turned back to the carcass, finding the sergeants gone, seeing and hearing them beating a path into the timber along the north brow of the ridge. "Why you bleeming fools! Leave me to close the file for you, eh? Cover your backsides, worthless as they are."

Donegan was running full tilt by now, the warriors closer to him than he was to either Grant or Graham. He doubted he could make the stand of timber more than a quarter mile off, where his companions had disappeared in shadow, but he had to try.

Halfway there his boots scoured too deep through the soft snow. He realized he had run off the crust of icy snow onto the exposed underbelly of a deep drift burying a hidden ravine. The snow gave way beneath him like a yawning, spongy bed of moss. After five feet of slow descent, Donegan broke through, sliding uncontrollably through the icy shelf—plummeting down the side of a ravine. Staring wide-eyed at a two-hundred-foot drop below his boots.

Frantically digging with his heels and the butt of his Henry, Donegan slowed his precipitous fall, bounced off a small boulder with his left shoulder, catapulting him better than ten feet into the air. As he hit the icy slope on the exposed southern slope, Seamus careened out of control again. No way to prepare for the rocks he was hurled against. His stomach shoved up around his tonsils as he slammed onto a narrow ledge. Light shot across his eyes, meteors of pure, red heat. The black velvet of blessed darkness threatened, like slow-moving molasses creeping over his mind.

Donegan shook his head, sensing the cold at his cheek. He opened his eyes when the wild shrieks echoed overhead, up the slope.

Holy mither of Mary!

His side ached. *Must be a goddamned rib.*

The shouts drew closer, directly overhead. Seamus jerked up as the snow fell on him.

One of the bastirds is coming down!

Pulling his rifle up, he cocked the Henry, checking the load. Then quickly patted the pistol belt around his waist. The mule-ear on the regulation holster had held the pistol during his headlong descent down the slope. In his pockets he had another hundred rounds of ammo. Heavy, but damned comforting right about now.

They followed my tracks to the hole, he thought, looking around quickly. Then he scooted back against the inside of the rock ledge with the southern exposure. More snow tumbled down from the underside of the snow ledge. He tightened the latigo strap holding his hat beneath his chin.

More yelling. Taunts. Savage cries of anger. Finally the thump and crash of rocks the warriors tossed down, trying to dislodge the white man.

By Jesus—they can't see me!

At least, Donegan knew he couldn't see them when he looked up. Looked up and got himself a face full of snow. Hearing what sounded like a body sliding down the hole in the snow ledge.

'Bout time to dance, Seamus, me boy. One of them red h'athens coming down to dance.

Seamus worked to make himself small, pushing himself into the ledge wall as he spotted the buffalo-hide moccasins inching toward him. The moccasins dangled, then plopped on the rock ledge four feet away.

"Arrggghhh!" Donegan growled, shoving the muzzle of his Henry toward the wide-eyed Sioux.

Unprepared for the surprise of finding the white man so close, the warrior misstepped going back. His arms flew up, reaching for a handhold on the ledge, a root, grasping for the

white man himself. Donegan put his hand out, but only to
snatch the rifle from the lip of the ledge as the warrior tumbled off backward, screeching louder than ever.

Donegan flung himself back into the shadows of the snow
ledge, listening to the warrior's body bounce on the jagged
rocks two hundred feet below his tiny sanctuary. He glanced
down at the rifle as more snow showered from above.

Henry! Some poor bastard gave up more'n this rifle to—
Another warrior was on his way down.

Seamus pulled the Indian's Henry up, levered a shell into
the chamber and inched out of the shadows.

The warrior hung against the snow ledge a moment before
dropping onto the rock ledge three feet below him. There was
a moment there as he dropped that seemed suspended in time.
Two men staring at one another above the yawning chasm.
One painted and hungry for blood. A hand filled with a
bloody skinning knife and the other holding a tomahawk.

The second man had him a red cheek where a jagged chunk
of granite had scoured a bloody gash along it. This one pulled
the trigger before the warrior ever touched the rock outcrop
where he stood.

In a way, it looked damned pretty to Donegan, if he'd really had time to consider it. How the Sioux hunter had never
touched foot on the rock ledge but continued his descent to
the rocks below without a sound over the echo of the Henry.
His dark mouth opened and moved frantically as he fell out of
sight into the shadows below. No sound but the keening wind.

Donegan pushed himself back into the lee of the snow
ledge. Waiting. Watching for more snow. More moccasins.
Another to try to dislodge him. Like a snowshoe hare or al-
pine marmot nested in the snow and waiting for the wolves to
leave the entrance to its den.

He huddled there and waited. Thinking on all sorts of
things. About her.

And just when he realized his feet were starting to freeze,
Seamus ventured a look. The sun had fallen from overhead
and was in the last quarter of the western sky behind him. He
figured it had been over an hour since the last screech he had
heard come from the ridge overhead.

With less than two hours left him before the sun fell from

the sky. What with him alone and on foot. No telling how far left to go until he reached Fort C.F. Smith. No choice but to crawl back atop the ridge the way he'd come down. Up through the snow ledge, a handhold at a time.

On the top Seamus lay exhausted on the cold crust of trampled snow where a dozen warriors had stomped around the hole angrily, trying to flush their white quarry unsuccessfully. Finally his heart slowed. His breathing grew more regular.

He rose shakily, squinting into the gray distance of the horizon that blended like a smooth pond of dirty rainwater into the lowering sky of dusk. Then he looked down at the Henry rifle he had taken from the warrior as spoils of his victory.

Sour bile snagged his tonsils. He swallowed hard, forcing it back down. Remembering the sight of that narrow ring of rocks clustered at the base of Massacre Hill after the hostiles had retreated and Ten Eyck led his men down to the bodies. Remembering the sight of what was left of that tiny group of brave defenders who had held their lonely position while the rest retreated up the hill to die with Fetterman and Brown.

Donegan breathed deep of the coming night-gloom and lengthening shadows, staring mesmerized at the name scratched crudely on the Henry's stock.

Remembering the two civilians who had ridden over Lodge Trail Ridge with Capt. William J. Fetterman's doomed command. Issac Fisher and

JAMES WHEATLEY
Troy, Ohio

Chapter 6

$\mathcal{F}$or the better part of two hours Seamus Donegan waded through old snow and new, beginning to shudder as badly as Leonard Grant had their first night out from Fort Phil Kearny. Trouble was, Seamus realized he had no one to start a fire for him come nightfall.

Keep walking, he told himself, fiercely clenching his chattering teeth. *Just keep walking.*

The snow slapped against the wide brim of his hat with tiny, moist sighs as the sky lowered, nudging the sun down upon the peaks of the Big Horns. And with every step, he dreamed of the warmth come of a woman's desire for him. That, and whiskey—whiskey potent and red as a bay horse raised on Kentucky bluegrass. Women and whiskey, the only things in life worth living for. Worth dying for.

Women and whiskey kept Seamus Donegan climbing those hills toward the mouth of the Big Horn canyon.

Off to his left the winter sun had just settled behind the peaks. A cruel wind tumbled more insistently off those same granite spires. He'd have to find himself a place to roost for the night. No food to speak of. Damned little whiskey. But he figured a belly full of gumption was enough to see him through a sleepless night. That, and the sulfur-head matches he had packed in every pocket, coated with lard so they wouldn't be soaked.

Up top of that rise, you'll see the next stretch of country, Seamus, me boy, he confided to himself. *See what your next*

*move is . . . where you can find a place to spend the lonely
hours. Come nightfall.*

Leaning against a stunted cedar near the skyline, Donegan
blew the way the big gray would after the climb. An afternoon
filled with many long ascents. About done in, he squinted into
the lengthening gray of distance before him, glad for once
there hadn't been any sun to speak of all day. Otherwise, he'd
have snow-blindness to contend with as well. A burning agony that felt like hot grains of sand rolling beneath his lids.

*That's all you'd need, boy. Talk about being useless as a
priest in a St. Louis whorehouse—*

He blinked again, doubting what he saw . . . blinked to be
sure it wasn't the changing light, nor the beginnings of snow-
blindness that made his eyes swim at the enormous distance
stretching from his feet.

No, the objects were there, shimmering dark like liquid
shadows against the graying snow. Creeping from his right to
left a good three hundred yards from him. And headed into
valley there before him as well.

His empty belly lurched, complaining as he slid back into
the cedars, making himself small, no small task for a man
pushing better than 230 pounds along the skyline. Seamus
settled in a clump of cedar, checked the loads on both Henrys.
After adding nine shells to Wheatley's rifle, he looked up to
find the party of two had been joined by another pair of riders. Yet something about the way they sat their horses in the
dimming light began to work on him.

At a hundred yards, Donegan was certain. Certain enough
to gamble stepping out of his cedar sanctuary and waving an
arm to the four horsemen. One of the riders stopped, pointing
in Donegan's direction. The remaining three stopped, turning
their horses along the edge of the slope. Then kicked their
animals into a snowy fury as they yelped.

Of a sudden he wasn't all that sure anymore. The frantic
way they drove their animals toward him, their mouths oooed
and hollered as they splashed through the snow. Four of them
—he could make a good show of it anyway, make up for the
mistake of showing himself. He slid back into the cedars.
Cocked both Henrys and knelt. A man ready to make a stand.

"Ho! Donegan!"

That surprised him. One of the riders stood in the stirrups and shouted his name amid the cheers of the rest. *Besides,* he told himself, *h'athen Injins don't use stirrups, you cuddle-headed fool!*

Seamus Donegan rose stiffly, shuddering and shaky from the cold knifing at the marrow of him. He stepped to the edge of the cedars.

"Donegan!"

The Irishman stepped out of the cedars, smiling at last. "Who is it wants to know?"

The riders splashed up the lip of the ridge. Fifty feet away. One held his hand aloft, slowing the rest. "You Donegan . . . then I'm Thompson. Private James W. Thompson."

"I'm Donegan," Seamus sighed. "Cheeroo! Where the bleeming saints you come from?"

Thompson brought his laboring mount to a halt feet away from Seamus. It snorted frosty sprays of white gauze around the Irishman. "Why, Fort C.F. Smith, of course. Where would you be heading?"

He chuckled at first, having almost forgotten where the devil he had been going. Then he burst out laughing long and loud as all four soldiers stared at him like they were watching a lunatic. "Heading straight to hell in the end, sojurs! Same as you. But, Fort C.F. Smith would do just fine for now. By glory, I'm glad I spotted you!"

Thompson nudged his horse closer, ripping off a mitten and presenting a hand down to the Irishman. "Mr. Donegan, another few minutes and we'd've spotted you. One of us would've cut your trail. It been them goddamned Sioux cut your trail first, we'd not be standing here talking to you . . . ready to ride you in to Fort Smith where you're expected."

"Expected?"

Thompson nodded. "That's right. 'Bout three hours ago them two sergeants from Phil Kearny stumbled in, half froze from cold, and fright too. After getting a couple cups of coffee down 'em, they told us there was one more of you left out here—civilian named Donegan."

"Bless those spineless beggars," Donegan growled. "Left me to worry about a band of red h'athens by meself. Many was the time I cursed 'em both straight to the pits of hell. Bless their little souls for telling you I was still out here."

"Simmons," Private Thompson turned, "you're the smallest. Climb over behind Purdy there." He looked to Seamus. "Pull yourself on Simmons's horse. You're a big load, mister —but that animal will get you to Fort C.F. Smith . . . since I ain't found the way to hell myself."

"Soon enough for us all, Private," Seamus said as he clambered aboard the army horse.

Thompson led off, riding beside Donegan. "Them two from Phil Kearny claimed there was at least a dozen screaming Sioux on your tail when last they saw you. That true, Mr. Donegan?"

"Could be, Private," and he grinned, teeth chattering still. "But I wasn't one to stop and count, you see."

"So tell me how you pulled your tail outta that scrape."

"Sometime I will," he replied. "For now, it's enough to say that Seamus Donegan knows well enough that life ain't in holding a good hand, but in playing a poor one well."

It wasn't long before Seamus was at the fort, explaining how he had pulled himself out of the scrape to Private Thompson and a growing crowd of listeners, officers and enlisted both. His coffee mug never drained itself before some hand refilled it while Donegan regaled the soldiers of Fort C.F. Smith with his hair-raising tale, basking in the attention. Enjoying the eager faces to talk to.

A cold, silvery winter moon hung over the Big Horns by the time Seamus Donegan stumbled along beside Thompson toward the low log-and-dirt shack that served as a barrack where he would be assigned a bunk in the midst of rows of snoring soldiers. Seamus sighed contentedly beneath the smelly, scratchy wool of familiar blankets, listening to the varied chorus of sleep-starved troopers.

After what seemed but a moment of relief, the Irishman squinted into pale, gray light streaking the oily window to his left with a foretaste of dawn. Around him scuffed thick-soled brogans and growling soldiers, roused from their slumber for another day of labor. And a cold day at that. Seamus pulled the blanket against his cheek, watching his breath turn to steamy vapor before his face.

The figure hunched over before the open door of the sheet-iron stove turned, his face familiar to the half-groggy Donegan. Thompson stopped beside the Irishman's cot.

"Sleep in if you can, Mr. Donegan," the private said. "You and me got dinner plans this night."

His eyes grew from slits. "Dinner plans, eh?"

"Ever eat in a Indian lodge?"

He pulled the blanket down from his chin. "Can't say as I have, Private."

"Crow," Thompson replied. "Warrior by the name of Iron Bull. Him and some others camped for the winter not far from the stockade. I wrangled an invite for you from him . . . seems Iron Bull wants to meet the big soldier who escaped the Sioux war party that's been raising hell in the neighborhood."

"Iron Bull, is it?"

"See you here to sundown, Mr. Donegan."

"Wouldn't miss it for the world, Private."

Iron Bull was the sort who made much of this white-man habit of shaking hands. He performed the ritual with zest, and kept pumping Donegan's arm until Seamus had to pull his hand free. The older Crow warrior had about him the scents of stale tobacco and tanned hides, pleasant smells if not pungent. Iron Bull's woman squatted at the fire near their feet in the buffalo-hide lodge. Behind her sat two other swarthy guests, who measured Donegan closely before Iron Bull motioned for them to stand. They presented their hands to the Irishman as well.

"John Reshaw," the first one said.

Seamus shook his hand. Thompson took Reshaw's grip in turn.

"Mitch Bouyer," the second, darker one introduced himself.

"Bouyer, you say?" Seamus asked.

The dark man slowly pulled his hand from the Irishman's grip. "That's right."

"Jim Bridger spoke of you."

"You know Bridger?"

"I do, Mr. Bouyer."

"Call me Mitch. My friends call me Mitch. And any friend of Jim Bridger's is a friend of mine."

"Says he taught you everything you know about tracking."

Bouyer laughed. "Ol' Big Throat always telling folks that. He just forgets to tell 'em I grew up in Sioux camps." Mitch watched the Irishman's eyes narrow, studying his face. "That's right, Seamus Donegan. I'm half-breed. Reshaw too. We both had Sioux mothers."

Seamus smiled, easing himself down on a pallet of buffalo and wool blankets. "As you said, fellas—any friend of Bridger's is a friend of mine as well. What brings Sioux blood to camp with the Crow this winter?"

Bouyer glanced at Reshaw for the flicker of a moment. "You are a direct man, Mr. Donegan."

"Don't mean to offend, Mitch." He accepted a steaming tin of coffee handed him by James Thompson. "Just can't figure you being here . . ."

"Unless we mean to spy on the fort? That it, Seamus Donegan? You figure we're spies for Red Cloud?"

He gazed over the steamy lip of his cup. "I seen with my own eyes what the Sioux did to those soldiers at Kearny." Seamus saw interest brighten Bouyer's dark eyes. "Seems reasonable now that winter covers the land, Red Cloud's got half-breeds like you out scouting things over . . . waiting for spring."

"Come the short-grass time, Mr. Donegan, both John and I plan on being far from here. It's not healthy for either of us in Sioux country. Sitting Bull, even Red Cloud himself, have both put prices on our heads."

Seamus almost choked. "That don't figure."

Bouyer grinned, his teeth luminescent in the firelight as sparks popped up toward the indigo smokehole above them. "We no longer live with the Sioux. We have Crow wives. My wife is Iron Bull's niece."

"With the whole country choosing up sides," John Reshaw said, joining the conversation for the first time, "Mitch and me stay with the Crow. Our scalps worth a lot to Red Cloud for it."

"Turning your back on your people? Sioux can't like that."

Reshaw smiled. "They don't. Hate it about as much as your

soldiers plopping forts down in the middle of their prime hunting grounds. And they'll do anything they can to drive you soldiers away."

Seamus glanced over at Private Thompson, an eager listener. "I'm no sojur, fellas." He said it quietly, as if he had thought it over first.

"You were at Kearny in the *Moon of Deer Shedding Horns*?"

"Meaning December?"

"When the hundred in the hand were killed."

"Weren't a hundred," Donegan protested a little too strongly. "Eighty of 'em is all."

"The Sioux call it their 'Battle of the Hundred in the Hand.' "

Donegan stared at the fire for a long moment, sipping at his coffee, the dancing flames giving way to remembrance of the butchered bodies. "They had those soldiers in their hands, all right. Crushed 'em, like a man crushes a handful of dried stalks of grass."

He watched Reshaw glance at the other half-breed a moment across the fire. Bouyer eventually nodded.

Reshaw looked back at Donegan before he spoke. "The Sioux, Cheyenne, and their Arapaho cousins did not kill all the soldiers in that fight."

Donegan scratched his beard, grinning. "I know. I saw the two who shot themselves with my own eyes."

This time Reshaw glanced at Thompson and Iron Bull, finding their attention riveted on him. "No, Seamus Donegan. More than two threw themselves away."

Seamus sputtered some coffee down his shirt. "More'n two? You saying more'n two killed themselves on that hill?"

Reshaw nodded. "It is the word of those who watched it happen."

Seamus gazed at Bouyer. "This true? More of them soldiers shot themselves?"

Bouyer nodded. "Except for those at the foot of the ridge, where a handful did much damage in a small circle of horses and rocks . . . the rest near the top of the ridge fell too easy."

"Fell too easy?" Thompson squeaked this time.

Seamus nodded. "Near the boulders."

Bouyer nodded as well. "Near the boulders. Yes. We have heard from those who were there. Some gave up. Throwing their guns away. Many more turned their guns on themselves."

Seamus gazed at Thompson. "Always wondered how that fight was over so damned fast. Now it all makes sense."

Thompson gazed through the Irishman. "Shot themselves?"

Bouyer nodded again. "A few kept up the fight as long as they could, so I'm told. While around them one after another of the soldiers shot himself."

"Those bastards," Seamus growled.

"Who?"

"Fetterman and his friend Brown," Seamus answered. "They likely started it—killing themselves. With their officers committing suicide . . . the rest of those poor boys saw all hope disappear on the wind like a puff of old smoke. Damn their souls to hell!"

After a moment Bouyer sipped at his coffee, then spoke again. "Not all killed themselves."

"I know. You said the group at the bottom of the hill fought. I had . . . friends die there."

"They were brave. But not the only brave ones," Reshaw added.

"Yes," Bouyer replied. "At the rocks, the Sioux covered the bravest with a buffalo robe, and did not mutilate his body as they did the others."

The Irishman's gray eyes snapped onto Bouyer's face. "I knew him too. An old friend." He swallowed hard. "Adolph Metzger. Good soldier. A brave man."

"At the end, he had only his brass horn for a weapon," Bouyer explained.

"I found it beside him."

"We are told he fought like a warrior to the end," Bouyer added.

Seamus sighed, sipping at the stinging coffee to keep from sobbing. "Not enough goddamned warriors wearing army blue that cold day on Lodge Trail Ridge. Too damned many sojurs led to the slaughter by their officers. Not enough war-riors to give the Sioux a fight of it."

"You figure to give the Sioux some taste of their own, Mr. Donegan?"

He studied Bouyer's face a moment. "No, Mitch. I figure to stay as far away from trouble as I can."

But as he said it, Seamus Donegan knew the lie of his words. Try as he might, Seamus knew he was the sort who just naturally attracted trouble the way a frontier post's slit-trench attracted flies.

Chapter 7

"Sure you don't wanna come along now, Seamus Donegan?" Sgt. Noah Graham asked with a smile on his face, lips trembling and teeth chattering as he stuffed hands into his wool-lined buffalo-fur mittens.

Donegan slapped a big hand on the man's shoulder. "Believe I'll stay put, Sergeant. You and Grant tried your damnedest to kill me on the trip here. I'll stay put and watch your backsides disappear over the hills."

"No you're not," Sergeant Leonard Grant growled. "Too goddamned dark for any man to watch us after we slip out the stockade."

Donegan glanced at the starless sky, dark as the inside of a tin-lined army coffin. "You got two, maybe three hours till moonrise, boys. You'll make good time this night. Just keep your mouths shut and follow Bouyer. Do as he says, and you'll make out."

"I just wanna make it back to Kearny wearing my hair," Grant grumbled, sour as usual.

"Do as the scout says, we'll both keep our hair," Graham suggested.

"'Fore you slip out, Mitch," Donegan began, pulling the half-breed off to the side where fewer ears might overhear, "I got a letter I'll trust you to take back to Phil Kearny with you. Got reason not to trust them two sojurs to do it."

Bouyer chuckled. "You got every right for suspicion there, Seamus Donegan. I'll take your letter."

The Irishman handed it over, watching Bouyer pull up the flap of the rawhide packet in which the army's mail would be carried back to Fort Phil Kearny some ninety miles away. Seamus stopped the half-breed's hand.

"No, Mitch," he whispered with a hiss. "This ain't official mail. I want you should deliver it for me . . . personal."

"Personal, eh?" He smiled again. "Who would you want to get this personal letter?"

Seamus glanced over his shoulder at the small crowd clustered around the two sergeants preparing to leave, shaking hands, slapping backs, everyone shivering in the moonless cold of the tiny stockade built in the shadow of the Big Horn Mountains.

"You'll find her place right outside the quartermaster's stockade, Mitch. Small place. Cabin made of logs. Give her my letter."

"Her?"

"Wheatley. Mrs. Wheatley."

"Missus, huh? I see why you want it delivered personal."

"You got it figured all wrong. She's . . . she's a widow. Her man was one of the handful in the rocks at the bottom of the ridge, that black day back to December."

Bouyer fell quiet a moment, but Donegan thought he had heard a gasp from the half-breed. "They put up the fight, those few," Mitch replied. Inside his coat, he stuffed Donegan's envelope down in his shirt. "I'll see this letter gets to Mrs. Wheatley."

"You can't find her—see it gets to Sam Marr."

"Marr?"

"You'll find him there. A friend. Civilian camp. Thanks, Mitch. I owe you one."

Bouyer grinned in the pale starlight. "Seamus Donegan, I'll be back to collect."

The Irishman slapped the half-breed on the shoulder again. "I'll count on it. Whiskey?"

"Never made a habit of turning down an offer of whiskey."

"Knew I was going to like you, Bouyer," Donegan replied. "We'll drain the pond water off the lily when you get back."

"Don't know when that'll be."

"Don't matter, does it?"

"I suppose not."

"I figure you'll bring back a thirst, whenever you come."

Bouyer grinned wider, sticking out his bare hand. "I'll miss you, Seamus Donegan."

"Likewise, you Sioux runt!" He pumped Bouyer's arm for all it was worth. "Give that old man Bridger an Irish kick in the arse for me, would you?"

"Be a pleasure!"

Seamus watched Bouyer signal the sergeants. The trio creaked across the frozen snow to the small water gate where some guards waited. They opened the gate. All three crawled out on their knees. The gate closed. And the night fell silent once more. For a moment, the snow outside the compound was disturbed by footsteps. Then all sound faded like water into thirsty earth.

In small groups, the soldiers turned away, headed for their barracks and warm bunks.

Donegan stopped near the center of the small parade. Watching the smears of dark shadows disappear from the white background. He stood alone. Sensing the winter night. In his own way praying to that three-in-one God of his mother's church that Mitch Bouyer would find Jennie Wheatley. Praying that his words would convince the woman to wait. It was the ninth of February. She should hold his letter in her hands before the middle of the month.

More than anything he had ever wanted in his young life, Seamus Donegan wanted Jennie Wheatley to wait for an Irishman to return to Fort Phil Kearny.

The fifteenth of February dawned cold and clear as rinsed crystal.

Seamus joined Thompson's company in mess for the hardtack and moldy salt-pork every man grumbled over, but ate nonetheless. The pasty combination softened by several cups of strong coffee, Donegan strolled onto the muddy parade as the sun rose full above the stockade wall. Seeing in that fiery red ball the glint of red in Jennie Wheatley's hair beneath a summer sun reflecting off the water of the Little Piney, where she went daily to bathe.

Seamus Donegan hoped by now the widow held his letter in

her hands. Hoped she kept his promise to return for her in her heart.

Named in honor of General Charles Ferguson Smith, who had served with distinction during the Mexican War, this northernmost fort along the Montana Road was raised on a high plateau some hundred fifty yards east of the Bighorn River. A scant two miles west of the post the river itself issued from the mountains. The Bighorn turned to flow eastward past the post, but soon twisted slightly toward the northeast, not far from the stockade. The plateau gave a commanding view of most of the surrounding countryside, running as it did along the river for better than a mile before a spur extended northward for a quarter mile. There the valley of the Big Horn opened into wide hayfields that come spring would guarantee the stock of Fort C.F. Smith all the pasturage and lush fodder they could want.

The former commander of this Mountain District, Col. Henry B. Carrington, had dispatched Capt. Nathaniel C. Kinney here the previous August to establish a post where the Bozeman Trail crossed the Bighorn. Two walls of the stockade were constructed of logs buried in trenches. The other two walls were of baked adobe. One of those mud walls, the north, contained the only gate to the compound.

At the south and west sides of the parade squatted the barracks, mud hovels that had a tendency to leak mud on days such as this, when the sun made an appearance and the temperature climbed above zero. On the east side of the stockade stood the quartermaster stores and a ramshackle stable affair. On the north at either side of the main gate stood the post offices along with the one-roomed, low-roofed structure that served as Smith's jail.

In coming to this place, Captain Kinney's soldiers had struggled to lower their burdened wagons down the face of the rugged bluffs into the valley of the Bighorn River at the end of ropes. Through that summer and into the fall, some three hundred soldiers slept in tents until completing the stockade and its buildings.

Far from the magnificence of Fort Phil Kearny, Fort C.F. Smith nonetheless had a homier feel to it. Small, and nowhere near as pretentious as Kearny, this farflung post made Seamus

Donegan a bit more comfortable than had Col. Henry B. Carrington's spectacular post at the junction of the Pineys. What Fort C.F. Smith lacked in grand appointments, it made up for in plenty of whiskey, red as a bay horse and with twice the kick.

Seamus Donegan felt right at home here.

Most of these soldiers hungered for talk with a new face. There came a constant string of questions for the Irishman, asking for news of the outside world. Having no word from Kearny since last November, old newspapers had been tacked onto the bulletin board adorning one end of the small parade. The newsprint weathered and yellowed, read again and again by those starved for word of the world outside the Big Horn valley.

Again and again Seamus was asked to repeat the story of Fetterman's disappearance over Lodge Trail Ridge contrary to Colonel Carrington's orders. Asked to tell the gruesome details of Captain Ten Eyck's relief party discovering the mutilated bodies of eighty-one men. Still, Donegan only confirmed what had been rumors from the friendly Crows like Iron Bull, camped in the valley for the winter. From those Indians the garrison at Fort C.F. Smith had learned of a big fight ninety miles away at Kearny. The Crow told of a detail of soldiers ambushed, wiped out to the last man.

Most had refused to believe the gruesome news brought to the stockade walls by the moccasin telegraph of the Crow, Sioux and Cheyenne. Who could consider such a massacre possible?

Until Seamus Donegan described how the carcasses of the horses lay frozen on the slope of Lodge Trail Ridge, their noses pointed back to Fort Phil Kearny in retreat. He told the soldiers how three groups fought alone and out of sight of one another against the overwhelming numbers of warriors who had waited in ambush. How those warriors had torn the soldier bodies apart, limb from limb, in a fury. All but one. The little German bugler with streaks of gray in his hair.

Seamus Donegan did not tell these soldiers that many of their friends had died at their own hand. He did not have to. It was a rare soldier who did not lose a friend on Lodge Trail Ridge.

* * *

"Tomorrow is the first of March, Captain." Henry Wessells's eyes locked on the papers strewn across his desktop.

"Yessir," Ten Eyck answered, uncomfortable, and thirsty for more of the whiskey that helped dull the pain.

Wessells finally settled in his chair and looked up at Ten Eyck sadly.

"I've got more problems than having to cut the rations for March, Ten Eyck."

"There's enough grumbling as it is."

"And scurvy to go around," Wessells replied, waving a hand for the captain's silence. "I know. I know. Few men not beginning to suffer. Roll call every morning finds more cases at the hospital. But," he sighed before continuing, "I take heart that our two sergeants made it to Smith and back again."

"That cheered the garrison, sir—to learn that Smith is faring as well as they are."

Wessells nodded. "We're cut off even more than they, Ten Eyck."

"Yes, sir." And for the first time, Ten Eyck sensed a cloud cross Wessells's face. It had been there all along, from the moment he had marched into this post commander's office and watched the others scurry out, leaving him alone with Wessells as if on some unspoken cue. But, Tenedore Ten Eyck had been too concerned with his own physical pain to notice until now. Wallowing too much in his own emotional prison to recognize what was coming.

Wessells wiped a hand across his mouth, swallowing hard. As if this were some bitter medicine he himself were forced to take.

"Captain, I'm relieving you of command of Company F."

Ten Eyck sensed his throat constrict. Too long dry now. His tongue longed for the familiar sting of Kinney's whiskey. "Sir?" he struggled with the one word.

Wessells swept past him, unable to look Ten Eyck in the eye. "More grumbling from the men."

"My . . . my men, sir?"

"Yes, dammit," he answered quietly. "And other officers as well."

"I see."

"You'll have another chance with A company."

"Another . . . another chance, Colonel."

"Your last here, Ten Eyck," Wessells said dryly, turning from the oily window that looked out onto the snowy, gloomy parade.

It was just the way Ten Eyck felt, even though his eyes were locked straight ahead on a knothole in the rough-hewn plank of Colonel Wessells's office wall.

"I had hopes when I moved you from H Company to F . . . that the grumbling would eventually quiet itself."

"My cowardice?" Ten Eyck's hands balled into fists involuntarily.

Wessells nodded, though the captain could not see. "That, and the drinking. For your sake, Captain, I hope you make this assignment stick."

Tenedore hungered for the red whiskey more than ever. His throat gone dry, words hard as clods to dredge up. And, more than ever, he wanted to drink himself to forgetfulness with the Irishman. But, Donegan was far gone from this place of bitter memories, memories daily reminding Tenedore Ten Eyck of that bloody day in December as he watched the warriors reluctantly pull back from the mutilated bodies down the ridge. Taunting the soldiers to come on, luring and profane like some red-mouthed camp whore following his regiment from battleground to battleground during the war. Seductive, and deadly as well.

Donegan alone knew the loneliness and despair Tenedore felt.

Ten Eyck swallowed. Admitting he was alone here now. As alone as was Donegan at Fort C.F. Smith.

"I'll make this command stick, Colonel," Tenedore finally answered. He saluted the wall, turned and strode toward the door.

The cold slapped him like a brutal hand as the door slammed behind him. The gray of the parade reminded him of how his insides felt. Hollow, ringing with pain. And loneliness.

Chapter 8

"*Y*ou're Cap'n Sam Marr?"

The gray-headed civilian turned at the sound of the young soldier's voice.

"I am." Marr's eyes narrowed in the bright reflection off the snow. "What is it, son?"

"I was told by Colonel Wessells to find you."

"What he want with me?" Marr asked, turning back to soaping the harness in his lap. "I'm busy enough these days, keeping harness repaired for the woodcutters, Private. Wessells can see me when I'm not so—"

"Wanted me to give you this, sir."

"Sir, is it?" Sam looked over his shoulder again, regarding the young soldier. He stared at the envelope the young man held between them. "For me?"

"Colonel said you could see it got delivered, Cap'n Marr."

Sam studied the much-handled, wrinkled envelope, a tight scrawl neatly centered on its face. "He did, did he?"

"Yessir," the soldier answered. "I'll be going now, sir."

Marr looked up suddenly. "Son?" The soldier stopped in his tracks. "Didn't catch your name."

"Ketcham, sir. Private Henry."

"Good making your acquaintance, Private," Sam said with a smile. "Where you hail from?"

"Southern Illinois, Cap'n."

"Thought I heard that flavor in your voice. I'm Missouri, through and through."

The young soldier grinned. "Yessir."

"Tell you what, Private Ketcham—you a drinking man?"

"At times, sir."

"Good, son. I'll buy you a drink this evening . . . up to Kinney's place. Much as I hate the man, he's the only one with whiskey in these parts."

"Tonight it is, Cap'n."

"See you there, Private," Marr replied as Ketcham turned away. Sam bent over the envelope again.

No mistake about it, the address read:

> Seamus Donegan
> Fort Laramy
> U.S. Army Fort
> America

He looked up, finding Ketcham moving off at a brisk clip. "Private!"

Ketcham turned. "Cap'n?"

"How'd this come in?" Marr hollered.

"Supply train come in this morning, Cap'n. Had a slew of mail on it."

"Supply train?"

"From Laramie, sir. And long overdue."

"Food come in the wagons?"

"Yessir."

" 'Bout damned time, Private. Nearly every man down with scurvy. I ain't seen it this bad since the war. What day is it, son."

"The seventeenth, as I remember."

"February?"

"No!" Ketcham laughed. "March, Cap'n."

"Thankee, son." Marr waved Ketcham off once more and gazed down at the wrinkled envelope, for the first time noticing the soiled and greasy smear that formed the long-ago postmark inked across the top of the folded parchment.

Beware the Ides of March, Sam Marr, he thought to himself. *And what the Ides of March bring on their heels.*

Sam turned the envelope into the light so he could read the inking better.

Town Callan
County Kilkenny
Ireland

"Lord, if that don't beat all." He slapped the envelope across his thigh. "Coming all the way across the ocean, to rest now in the hand of Sam Marr. If that don't beat all."

"What don't beat all?"

Marr turned, finding Finn Burnett, another civilian teamster striding up, his shoulders encased with harness.

"Letter for Seamus."

"Donegan, eh?"

Marr nodded. "All the way from Ireland."

"Where my mother and father both come from," Burnett replied. "What's it say?"

"I ain't read Seamus's mail, Finn."

Burnett grinned, then winked. "Not yet anyway. He's been run off, all the way up to Fort Smith. Won't hurt none you reading that letter come all the way from the green isle, will it?"

Marr shook his head. "Wouldn't think of it, Burnett." For the first time he noticed the harness weighing down Finn's shoulder. "Where you heading with all that?"

"Leighton's heading south with a train of wagons in two days," Burnett began, explaining about their civilian employer who had contracted with the army for freighting supplies, expecting to cut hay for Fort C.F. Smith come cutting season. "At Laramie he'll turn east to North Platte, Nebraska. Bring back supplies for Smith up north . . . once we can get through come spring, and start cutting grass."

"You going along?"

"Better'n hanging 'round here, staring at ugly mugs like yours, Cap'n Marr."

Marr chuckled, staring back at the letter. "I suppose it is."

"Besides, I'll get to look at a prettier face than yours on that long ride."

"Oh?" Marr's interest was piqued.

"The widow," Burnett replied. "Leighton tells me she's heading back east to her husband's people in Nebraska."

Marr jerked, startled. "The widow Wheatley?"

Burnett nodded. "That's right."

Sam's eyes narrowed. "I suppose it gets hard on a woman out here . . . left alone. What with two boys and no man to help her. Young as she is."

"And quite the looker too," Burnett said, grinning. He dropped the harness in a pile near the sawbucks where the men soaped the leather to keep it supple. "I'll be plenty pleased to ride east with that one."

Marr slapped the envelope across the palm of his hand. "I'll be back in a bit, Finn."

"Be back?" Burnett called out as the old man trotted up the snowy slope toward the quartermaster's stockade.

"Leave me my share, Burnett!" Marr shouted over his shoulder, waving the envelope in the air.

"Damn right I will, Cap'n!" Burnett hollered back. "Damn right you'll find your share waiting for you."

"Best you wait for your own people, Mrs. Wheatley."

Jennie looked into the old man's eyes once more, seeing them plead with her as much as did his voice. She wrung her hands in her soiled apron, glancing once at the boys playing on the bed. "But . . . what if my brother doesn't come?"

"You yourself told me you wrote your folks back in Ohio to come fetch you."

Jennie nodded. "If only my letter gets there." She watched Marr chuckle merrily.

"Get there, Jennie? Why, lookee here!" Marr pulled a greasy envelope from inside his shirt. "This got here all the way from Ireland."

"Ireland?" she asked, eyes widening. "Someone write you from Ireland?"

"Goodness no, child. It's for Seamus."

"Seamus?" she whispered, as if once more sensing the fragrance of him. His presence pungent with the strong smell of working animals and whiskey, wood smoke, and gun-oil. And sensed a tightening across her loins for him. Aching for his return.

"From the town his folks call home."

"His . . . his folks?" she asked, taking the envelope into

her slim hands, creased with grease and dirt, callused with hard work.

Marr nodded. "If you won't stay to wait on your own family come from Ohio . . . stay for Seamus."

"He's not here," she whispered, her eyes never straying from the envelope, holding it like she would a piece of him.

"He will be soon as he can, Jennie. You told me he promised you."

Jennie caressed the stiff, wrinkled paper. "He promised."

"You'll stay till Seamus comes back?"

She looked up at the merry wrinkles creasing his eyes. There was a softness there wrought by the decades of Sam Marr's life. "That . . . or my kin comes from Ohio to fetch me. Whichever happens first."

"Pray it be Seamus Donegan, Jennie Wheatley."

It seemed the old man hung suspended, waiting for an answer from her. "Yes, Sam. Pray Seamus Donegan comes for me first." She gazed down at the envelope once more. Something chill ran through her. Certain it was the letter enclosed within her fingers. "What news is this?"

"I ain't read Seamus's mail."

"Read it."

"I can't, Jennie."

"You must."

Sam Marr shook his head stubbornly. "It's private. Come from the town where he was born. His soil, Jennie. Family matters—"

"Read it to me, Sam," Jennie interrupted, pleading, suddenly afraid. No longer curious. More so scared of the letter. She stared hard into his eyes until something behind them weakened, and smiled softly. "All right, Jennie. I'll read it . . . we'll read it, together."

She began to tear at the envelope.

"Carefully, child. Carefully."

"Here, Sam. You open it for me."

One old, gnarled finger slipped beneath the flaps, sealed with wax and long-ago dried glue. Inside lay a single folded page. Gently spreading the sheet, they could see the ink on the paper was brighter than that on the envelope. Not smudged and dulled with many hands and countless miles.

"It's from Seamus's mother," Jennie whispered, her hand flying to her mouth. She turned away, sinking to a crude stool beside the washtub where the water grew tepid. Knowing as only a mother could what tidings a letter from the woman in Ireland could foreshadow. "Tell me the news, Sam. Tell me."

Marr gulped. His old eyes quickly scanning Katie Donegan's tight scrawl. When he had reached the bottom of the page, his eyes found Jennie Wheatley's eyes anxiously searching his for some explanation.

"Just tell me, Sam."

"Jesus H. Christ, Jennie!" Marr whispered low, like a rush of hard water bouncing off the rocks of the Big Piney. "Seamus ain't gonna believe this!"

His big hand shook as he read the few words Sam Marr had scrawled in explanation of the letter from Ireland being opened. It didn't matter now. Not that much. More important the old man's explanation of reading it to Jennie Wheatley. Why she had wanted Marr to read it to her.

Seamus stuffed Marr's letter in his pocket, only then turning from Capt. Nathaniel C. Kinney's door, where the captain's adjutant passed out mail just arrived from Fort Phil Kearny this twenty-sixth day of March. He would find a place in the sun to read his mother's letter. More than three years now since last he had written her. During the war. That summer of Gettysburg.

The smells of that battlefield as fresh in his nostrils now as they were that steamy July. Hot gun oil and fresh blood. The stench of men's bowels and their gore baking beneath a relentless sun. Before the rain came that third day, cleansing the rocks and grass and hillsides of the bloody epitaph.

Seamus Donegan settled nervously to his haunches against the north wall, licked his lips, wishing he had a drink before him right now. And read his mother's tight hand.

My dearest Seamus,

It has been so long since I have heard from you. Years now. I can only trust to God himself that my words will find you. He alone knows my anguish of sending you on that fool's errand.

I ask your forgiveness. Your mother thought it best to send you to America. A new land. Better to find your uncles there than die with the rest here in the land of your birth. Sweet Eire.

Do not think harsh of me that I wait until now to reply to your last letter. It caused me so much hurt to read your words, explaining to me my brothers were not what they had told me they were. Not finding them in Boston. Learning only they had joined the army as you were forced to do. Fighting in a foreign war, against a foreign enemy. Taking the lives of other men—against the commandments of God himself.

I trusted my brothers when I sent you to that foreign soil, Seamus. You must believe that I would not release you from my bosom if I had known they would prove unfaithful. They promised such riches. A bright future for you in America. Where there is none here in the land of your birth. The young ones grow old so quickly here. And the old ones die, haunted.

Do not harbor harsh thoughts of your mother, Seamus Donegan. She meant well. Always meant well for you. Even above your brothers and sisters. She wanted the best for you, Seamus. It pains me to write this, but you must know beside this page lies a letter from your uncle Liam. No word at all from Ian. But Liam has written. From California, in America.

He explains that he went west. Never was in the Union army at all. Says Ian talked of nothing else. But Liam headed west to the goldfields of California. He stayed there as long as he could. Wasn't anywhere near Boston when his nephew came to America.

Now, this old letter, wrote back in 1861, says he's headed for a place called Colorado. To find gold in some place called Cripple Creek.

Always hoping, that one. Liam. Not like Ian, my dark brother. Liam would chase a leprechaun to the ends of the earth to find his pot of gold, he would.

Liam said his letter would come to me in a packet ship, round the horn of South America, by way of New York City. It came last week, Seamus. He said he would send word next when he was a rich man in Cripple Creek. Lord knows when that will be, the way Liam is.

Seamus, your mother weeps for her brothers. She weeps for her son adrift in a new land. Find them both, Seamus Donegan. Find Liam and Ian both.

If you do nothing else for your mother's soul, so I can rest in peace when the Lord calls—find your uncles and bring them home where you all belong. Bring them home to the land of your birth, Seamus Donegan.

I am ill and dying, Seamus. Bring them home.

> May the saints watch over and preserve your soul among the wicked and the heathen,

> Your Mother

Chapter 9

$\mathscr{M}$arr had no time to get out of the man's way.

Ten Eyck rammed into him, spilling both of them onto the steps in front of Colonel Wessells's office.

Sam Marr sat sprawled in a puddle of icy water at the foot of the plank steps, staring at the captain. A grin appeared, then grew into a smile. "By damn, you are a sight, Ten Eyck."

Tenedore's face finally cracked a reluctant smile. He wiped mud and slush from the front of his coat, smearing it all the more. "You're no better yourself, Cap'n Marr."

"Why the billy-hell you come roaring outta that door for?" Marr asked, crabbing to his feet, his legs soaked with slush. "That's Wessells's office, ain't it?"

"It is," Ten Eyck answered, rising as well. The smile was gone. "A man can only take so much." His eyes glared at the door.

Marr recognized well enough the fires of hatred behind Ten Eyck's eyes. "C'mon, Tenedore. Lemme buy you a drink of Kinney's whiskey."

"Rye would do nicely, Cap'n Marr."

"Rye it is."

By the time Marr had purchased two rounds and the third sat before them on the small table, Ten Eyck was past his anger, well past the tears, and finally where Sam wanted him to be. Laughing at last. If at nothing more than himself.

"Sonuvabitch transferred you again?"

Ten Eyck nodded. "This time to C Company. Says my next move is out the gate."

"He serious?"

"If he's not, I sure as hell am," Ten Eyck grumbled, staring into the amber liquid before him on the table. "I've had it with him . . . and Fort Phil Kearny. 'Bout goddamned time I moved on anyway."

"Tomorrow's first of April. A whole new chance for you, Cap'n." Marr fell silent for long moments after Ten Eyck didn't reply. Instead the soldier sipped at his rye without a word. Like a man relishing the numbing forgetfulness that would soon arrive to rescue him.

"Man like Wessells—he needs someone like you to blame for his troubles." Marr thought he recognized a hint of thanks in Tenedore's eyes.

Ten Eyck hoisted his cup, then tossed back the rest of the rye in one swallow. "Blames me for everything now. Because he can't keep on blaming Carrington now. He's gotta find someone to blame for the rations . . . and the scurvy . . . and the low morale."

"Morale?"

"Worst it's been since we arrived here last summer. At times a man's got no choice but to drink until he forgets."

Marr threw back the rest of his whiskey and pushed the cup aside. "That's your whiskey talking, Cap'n. Sure, you got pain. It's the God's-honest truth you pulled through something during the war that any of the rest of these fellas would've died from. That Libby Prison killed many a lesser man—"

"It don't matter, Cap'n Marr."

"It matters, Ten Eyck. Matters that a soldier like you is drinking to forget Libby Prison . . . to forget your pain."

"More'n that," Ten Eyck replied quietly, the pink tip of his tongue darting across his bottom lip. "Trying to forget those bodies over Lodge Trail Ridge."

"You . . . and Seamus Donegan both."

"I wake up in the middle of the night, sweating like it was August at Libby Prison in that swamp. Shaking—in a sweat, Cap'n. And everywhere 'round me lays those bodies . . . arms, legs . . . their cocks shoved in their—"

"Hush now, Cap'n Ten Eyck."

He swallowed hard, raking the back of his hand across his mouth. "Problem ain't what the others say about me . . . that I was a coward—"

"You wasn't no coward. You and Seamus both figured it best to ride the ridge north of the Lodge Trail. And it made sense."

"Sense?"

"Yeah, Ten Eyck. You didn't do that—there'd been another pile of mutilized bodies left behind by them red bastards."

Tenedore wagged his head, glancing over at the bar. "You suppose?"

"You've had enough for now, Ten Eyck."

He nodded once, staring dumbly at his hands. "The real problem, Cap'n Marr . . . ain't what the others say about me being a coward. Real problem is that *I* figure I am. And a little bit of rye always helps to kill the pain of that when it gets too much to bear."

"You ain't no coward—"

"You're wrong," he whispered with a hiss, his head hunching into his shoulders protectively. "And there's come times when I wonder if it'll be the rye whiskey . . . or the bullet I'll put into my own brain that kills me first."

Marr watched in disbelief as Captain Ten Eyck clambered to his feet, swaying a moment before he lurched out the door of Judge Jefferson Kinney's stinking watering hole. Sam wondered a moment if he should have himself one more bracer before braving another night alone himself. Glancing over the soldiers who had watched the captain leave, Marr thought better of it.

Enough liquid painkiller in his gut for one night.

He moved carefully into the cold, sensing his own light-headedness. Wondering when Seamus Donegan would be riding back to Fort Phil Kearny to claim the widow Wheatley as his own. That, or passing on through to find his two uncles and answer his mother's prayer.

Seamus breathed deep, the air electric with the sun's rising. In a moment the orb would show itself red as a mare's afterbirth in the east. But for this singular moment, the earth hung in the balance.

Here, to this hillside overlooking the plateau, he had wandered more than an hour ago, in the cold of this mid-April dawn. To think on things he doubted a simple man should have to trouble himself with. Matters of the heart. And of family. Enough to trouble any three men, the weight of it like a railroad tie cutting into Seamus Donegan's wide shoulders this cold morning as the breath vapor before his face turned pink, then a bright rose with the sun's rising.

Below him the garrison of Fort C.F. Smith slowly stirred. While Fort Phil Kearny had quivered in the death throes of low morale, scurvy, and continued reports of Indian attacks through the winter, the Big Horn post had been left to its isolation, cut off from the outside world since the twenty-eighth of November. It was not until the twenty-sixth of March, when mail arrived from Fort Phil Kearny, up from Laramie, that the isolation was broken. News of the East. Word from beyond the shores of America.

From time to time across his two months here, Seamus had heard Mitch Bouyer and John Reshaw say the Cheyenne and Arapaho were gathering nearby. The warnings of the half-breeds had fallen on Kinney's and Burrowes's deaf ears. The captains had only laughed at such assertions of danger. After all, Fort C.F. Smith had already missed the serious harassment of Red Cloud's Bad Face Sioux, sitting so close as it did to Crow lands.

If anyone knew Red Cloud and the others who gathered around the Bad Face camps, Seamus figured Bouyer and Reshaw did. As surely as officers like Kinney and Burrowes had no business laughing at anyone, much less half-breed scouts every bit as savvy as army brass was stupid.

He stood. Taking in the full glory of the red globe's rising off the far lip of the earth like a healing wound tearing open, turning the April frost on the ground pink like pale blood. Off to his left the Bighorn River burst from its mountain prison, shimmering like a silver-red cleft through the awakening valley below his feet.

Seamus turned back to the fort, curious with the clamor. Three riders. Five horses approaching. A pair of pack animals. One burdened with a winters' worth of furry treasure. The other dragging travois as well. Most likely Indians coming in with hopes of trading. He could see these didn't ride like white men. Legs loose and feet flopping outside their stirrups.

Indians for sure.

By the time Donegan lumbered down the slippery, icy slope warming beneath the April sun, two of the newcomers were dropping from their ponies. The third stayed in the saddle, huddled against the morning chill in a furry buffalo robe.

"By God, it's Bouyer!" Donegan shouted as he recognized the half-breed. Mitch turned. His companion as well. "Reshaw! You've fared well, you old half-breed pissant!"

Both lunged to greet the huge Irishman. He swung his arms wide to enclose the two small half-breeds in his embrace, like small terriers attacking the herd bull.

"You ain't froze yet?" Bouyer asked.

"Me?" Donegan roared. "Not a chance. Till we run low on whiskey, me friend. Where you been since last you left?"

"Wessells hired me on to scout for him at Kearny," Mitch began, waiting for Seamus to nod. "And you know Reshaw come down to sign on too."

"But that's been better'n six . . . seven weeks now. You been out trapping in the meanwhile?" Donegan flung an arm at one of the pack animals burdened with a full load.

Reshaw flicked his ebony eyes at Bouyer, then toed the frozen mud at his feet.

"Not trapping, Seamus Donegan," Bouyer admitted quietly as more soldiers drew around them. He shouldered his way over to the pony burdened with the full load slung over its back. Pulling at the canvas tarp covering the load.

"What the devil you hauling, if it ain't—"

The words froze in Donegan's mouth as surely as water in a kettle these early spring mornings. The half-breed scout yanked the tarp off the pony.

"Who the hell is that poor fella?" Donegan moved beside the body. Head fully scalped, eyes gouged out. The muscles in the face relaxed and sagging, what with the scalp gone. His throat had been deeply slashed, looking like so much cleaved pork.

Old wounds.

"John Bozeman," Bouyer whispered.

"B-Bozeman?" Captain Kinney squeaked as he shoved his way through the crowd, still buttoning his shirt against the morning chill.

Reshaw nodded. "Found him . . . and what was left of his goods the Sioux didn't take—about ten mile from here." He pointed.

"Bound from Missouri City," Kinney clucked, wagging his head. He waved two young soldiers over. "Get the body over to the hospital. And wake that damned surgeon. Sleeping off another drunk, that one is. Played cards till damned near sunrise with the bastard myself. Easy there, fellas. That's John Bozeman himself."

"Man who cut this road?" Donegan asked.

"None other," Kinney said, turning to the Irishman. "Been supplying us since last fall. When he could get through. Usually he brings at least two wagons of goods down from the settlements. Hadn't been for John Bozeman bringing in what he could last fall before the road became impassable with snowdrifts . . . Fort C.F. Smith would likely be a ghost town now." Kinney looked at Bouyer. "He bring only the one wagon?"

Bouyer shook his head. "Not so. Found tracks of two more wagons."

"Damn!" Kinney muttered, shivering slightly.

"More bodies?" Seamus asked.

"No sign," Reshaw answered. "Likely dragged off with the other wagons. For what fun Red Cloud's warriors can dream up."

"They'll turn Bozeman's men over to the squaws, most likely," Bouyer growled.

Donegan sensed the hair on the back of his neck stand. "Squaws?"

Bouyer gazed up at the bearded Irishman, nodding sourly. "The women are really good—it comes to carving a man up. Better'n the warriors . . . making a fella suffer before they outright kill him. Women got a natural talent for causing a man misery, Seamus Donegan."

"I want to see you both in my office—in five minutes,"

Kinney pointed toward the north wall, where his small office huddled itself against the adobe brick darkened by morning frost. "Goddamned paperwork . . . reports." He walked away, wagging his head and muttering. "Sonuvabitch. John Bozeman himself . . ."

For the first time Donegan paid real attention to the third Indian, still seated atop a pony, bundled in the furry robe, a few streamers of black hair gleaming in the new sun on the breeze.

"A friend?"

Bouyer looked at Reshaw and winked. "No, Seamus Donegan. A relative of mine."

"Crow, eh?" Seamus asked, stepping over to the pony with every intention of introducing himself, as the most polite of the Irish were wont to do.

"Yes," Bouyer answered again, a grin growing. "Crow."

"By the saints . . . he's—a woman!" Seamus stammered. "It's . . . she's a woman!"

Bouyer and Reshaw chuckled along with the soldiers who had hung back to gaze at the oriental beauty encircled in the buffalo robe.

"My wife's youngest sister, Seamus Donegan," Bouyer explained as he stepped beside the Irishman. *"Eyes Talking."*

Seamus was at a loss for words. What with all the warriors he had laid eyes upon, this was his first up-close, arm's-length look at an Indian woman. And this one proved a feast for any man's hungry eyes.

"Why, she can't be more'n a girl . . . young as she—"

"Seventeen summers, Seamus Donegan," Bouyer interrupted. "The last of my wife's family. They're hoping she will marry."

"Marrying age among your people?"

Reshaw and Bouyer laughed. Mitch explained, "As ol' Bridger would say, she is prime doin's!"

Despite himself, Seamus found himself blushing. Staring unashamedly at the girl's beauty. "Why she not interested in a Crow husband?"

"Like many Crow squaws, she believes a white man will treat her better. And if not a white man . . . then a half-breed like John or me."

"So," Seamus said, smiling, as he clapped a big hand on Mitch Bouyer's shoulder, "you brought her over to marry her off to one of these soldier boys, eh?"

Bouyer winked at Reshaw. "No such, Seamus Donegan. Soldiers go off where the officers tell them. They cannot marry and keep a wife."

"Not all the officers here took up with wives, Mitch."

Bouyer wagged his head. "Eyes Talking would not make good wife for army officer. This one has spirit . . . like young pony needing to be broke."

"You figuring to take her down to Kearny, then?"

Bouyer finally laughed, loud and lusty. "Seamus Donegan —you fooled me. I thought you were smart man! Eyes Talking would not be wife for a soldier. She could only be wife to a free man. A man like Seamus Donegan!"

It took a moment to sink in through that thick, battered skull of his. Then he reluctantly tore his eyes from the face of Eyes Talking. Staring at Mitch Bouyer. Registering disbelief. The half-breed nodded again, his round face cut with a wide grin.

"You gotta be pulling me leg here, Bouyer!" he roared. "I ain't about to take your wife's sister here to marry!"

"Why not, Seamus Donegan?"

"I—I—I—" he stammered, hands flying. "I never . . . such a thing . . . your wife's sister—"

It was Bouyer's turn to grab hold of Donegan and turn him round so the Irishman would look at the woman. "Tell you what, Seamus Donegan. Eyes Talking brought all her plunder, even dragged along her own lodge. She's heard us talk all about you, so she was dead set on raising her lodge down with Iron Bull and the other Crow nearby."

"I don't understand at all," Seamus stammered, staring at the young woman's smiling face, fully exposed now as she slid the buffalo robe from her head. "Don't see what this—"

"Don't be late, Seamus Donegan. She expects you for dinner," Bouyer went on. "Tonight."

"Tonight?" he squeaked, feeling helpless.

Bouyer nodded, slapping the big Irishman on the back while the soldiers about them hooted and whistled in merriment. "Tonight you pay court to Eyes Talking!"

Chapter 10

She was beautiful.

Of little consequence that she had white skin. And beneath her breasts beat a white heart.

To Crazy Horse, the woman was beautiful.

There was a sad, haunting look to her dark eyes, like sunken pockets in the creamy skin. Reminding him of dark pools of cold water captured in the low places on the endless prairie after a spring thunderstorm.

And her mouth, so brightly rouged. He had seen a few mouths like hers around the forts. Soldier women.

This one had belonged to a soldier as well.

He held her tiny picture in his palm. A portrait encased in a small, gold cameo locket the soldier had worn about his neck.

At his waist hung that soldier's scalp.

Lieutenant Grummond had fought bravely. More courageously than most that day beyond Lodge Trail Ridge. He had sold his life dearly, slashing out with saber and taking five lives with the six shots in his pistol. He died as bravely as he had fought, wielding his long-knife against the young Oglalla warrior who claimed his scalp. Crazy Horse, who had plunged a lance already bloodied with frozen gore into the breast of George Grummond.

The scalp was his to take. As was the locket bearing the tintype photograph of Francis Grummond, already pregnant with George's child that day they had the daguerreotype made. Two days before moving west, orders in hand, to join

Col. Henry B. Carrington's men defending Fort Phil Kearny, Dakota Territory.

Crazy Horse closed the locket, hearing footsteps in the soft, wet snow outside the small lodge he alone used. Quickly he stuffed the amulet down the neck of his war shirt once more, where it hung suspended on a thin leather thong. Exactly as he had found it hung round the soldier's neck that cold day in the *Moon of Deer Shedding Horns,* a day when blood froze on the snow.

"Crazy Horse! You are there?"

He recognized the voice. "I am, Man-Afraid. Join me."

Man-Afraid-of-His-Horses stooped through the lodge entrance. He stood just inside the buffalo-hide circle of poles, shaking wet snow from his blanket. "Every year we see one last snowfall like this," he said, grinning as the blanket slipped off his shoulders. "Here in the *Moon of New Grass* before Winter Man is through with us until next robe season."

"Sit, my friend," Crazy Horse said, indicating a seat at his left hand. "What brings you out so late on this cold night?"

Man-Afraid sat, staring at the fire for long moments, left to his thoughts by The Horse before he finally spoke. "Already they are calling me *Old*-Man-Afraid-of-His-Horses. And not only behind my back."

"I have heard such talk," Crazy Horse admitted, nodding once. "Don't let it bother you."

Man-Afraid stared back into the low flames that radiated a warmth to the small lodge. "I have grown old perhaps . . . sensing this war of Red Cloud does not go well."

Crazy Horse nodded. "After our fight of the Hundred in the Hand, some soldiers left the fort near the Piney Woods. But not until other soldiers had come to take their places."

"It is so. We all believed the soldiers would scamper away from our land, with their tails between their legs like so many whipped dogs. I believed it as strongly as any."

"When they did not," Crazy Horse replied, his voice rising with enthusiasm, "I realized we were in for a long, long fight of it. Come soon the short-grass time, our ponies will be strong once more. And again we can ride—"

"My young friend," Man-Afraid interrupted, "perhaps the fight is now for others to take up."

"You are finished fighting the soldiers?" He stared at his mentor, disbelieving.

"Perhaps. The magic of the fight is gone from my heart. Red Cloud sends us here to the fort the white man calls La-Ramee, to trade our hides for powder and bullets."

"The soldier traders will not sell us powder or bullets," Crazy Horse agreed sourly. "They do not talk of trading with us. Their mouths are full only with the story of the soldiers who died near Piney Woods."

"Some died bravely, taking many Sioux spirits with them."

"Yes," The Horse said and nodded, his eyes seeing once more the snowy, bare ridge. "Others took their own lives. Like cowards."

Man-Afraid regarded his young warrior friend and protégé. "You would not call me a coward . . . were I to stay here in the south this season? Hunting the buffalo along the Shell River."

"The waters of this river the white man calls the Platte grow warm in this place closer to the sun . . . this far south, Man-Afraid."

He nodded in agreement, eyes fixed on the red coals near his feet. "Already Little Wound has taken his band of Oglalla from this place, and travels east toward the rising of the sun."

"I have heard he left two suns ago. Pawnee Killer and his warriors go with them. They are angry with Red Cloud's war on the white soldiers in the north. So now Pawnee Killer goes south to fight the soldiers who guard the iron tracks of the white man's great horse that belches smoke as it travels farther and farther west across our hunting grounds."

"Pawnee Killer will bring himself trouble," Man-Afraid mused. "I am glad he is gone. And Little Wound with him."

He fell quiet for a long time. Allowed his gathering of thoughts by Crazy Horse.

At long last Man-Afraid sighed. "I do not like all this quarreling among our peoples. The medicine is gone for now. The fight is not good."

"I think Red Cloud is afraid the medicine has gone bad for him as well."

He stared at Crazy Horse a moment. "Is that why Red Cloud speaks so loud, speaks so long—haranguing us all that we must wipe the country clean of the white man once the short-grass grows in the shadows of the Big Horn Mountains?"

Crazy Horse nodded sadly. "Red Cloud is worried. His power is as stake now. Among all the Lakota, his medicine becomes a question."

"You will stay, Horse?"

Crazy Horse stared at the fire a long time too. And when his eyes rose to meet Man-Afraid's shining across the lodge, he nodded once.

"I will stay with Red Cloud. He may grow desperate. He may flail wildly at the white soldiers come here to our last, best hunting grounds taken from the Sparrowhawks many winters ago. Red Cloud may thrash about loudly, reminding one of a war-eagle with a broken wing—but I believe in him still. More important, my old friend—I believe in the fight."

"It will be hard to drive these white men from their forts, where they bury their heads like ticks in an old bull's stinking summer hide."

"Yes. These white men are like those ticks. But, like Red Cloud—I still believe we can rub our hides like the old bull rubs his . . . to scrape the land clean of the white man who sucks the blood from our bodies. The soldiers who draw our very life from our land."

He wasn't sure he had ever heard such silence before. Silence so all-encompassing that he could hear the slap of wet, fat flakes against the damp hides of the lodge.

He sighed, eventually opening his eyes. The glow of the coals in the small firepit brushed a crimson light up the poles as they gathered in a graceful spiral near the smokehole.

She snuggled more tightly against him, her black hair tangled across his chest, her copper skin burnished with the red glow like a sheet of rusted iron, still moist to his touch. His nostrils drank of the damp muskiness that was her secret perfume.

That had done it, he thought, remembering. *The smell of her.*

Seamus had gone, unwilling and not a little unsure, with Mitch Bouyer to this lodge of Eyes Talking.

As the sun sank off the peaks of the Big Horns. As the sky lowered like the muddy sole of a boot on the land. As the wind shifted out of the north, snarling with a bite like that of a ravenous wolf.

And with it came the wet spring snow.

"I'll be back for you come morning, Seamus Donegan!" Bouyer had flung his voice over his shoulder, disappearing into the wild flurry as the Irishman stood dumbfounded at the doorway.

"Come morning?" Donegan had shrieked into the white buckshot snow.

When the only answer for him was the soft sprat of fat flakes against the brim of his hat, Donegan reluctantly turned back to the lodge, finding Eyes Talking there, pulling back the elkhide doorflap for him.

For the longest time Seamus had been sure his nervousness showed. So many times he wanted to leap up and bolt from the lodge. But what kept him there was Eyes Talking, and the fact that she seemed more anxious than he. They spilled the blood soup on one another and eventually laughed together over it. After that, Donegan relaxed enough to swallow the elk stew she had simmered most of the day in a battered iron kettle steaming by the edge of the coals.

Dinner over, Eyes Talking pulled a blackened coffeepot from the fire. Into two small white china cups she poured her thick brew, then added heaping teaspoons of sugar Bouyer had supplied her. Donegan was beginning to realize how the Indian loved the white man's sugar. Coffee and tobacco, powder and lead, were all one thing. But when it came down to it, Sioux squaw or Crow, the women wanted sugar most of all in trade for those hides they had toiled over all season long, scraping . . . chewing . . . and softening.

It wasn't until after the third cup that Donegan pulled off his muddy boots. Or, more truthfully, Eyes Talking pulled them off for him. Then his damp stockings. Only looking at the white man from behind her long eyelashes, the Crow woman smiled shyly, keeping her distance. Once his feet had dried and warmed there, cozied up to the fire, Eyes Talking took one foot into her lap and began working her magic.

By the time she had talked him out of his undershirt so she

could knead the muscles of his back, Seamus Donegan would gladly have traded twenty fine ponies for the girl. The lodge grew warmer as the fire fell to worming red coals. The Irishman hadn't felt like this since . . . well, he hadn't felt like this in too long.

Feeling the insistent pressure of her hip against him as she worked all those secret places along knotted ribbons on his shoulders, Seamus slowly rolled over, luxuriating in the furry warmth of the buffalo-robe bed. For a moment he stared into her black-cherry eyes, liquid with rust-flecks in the red light.

Not knowing if it were right, he pulled her close, brushing his lips against her full, moist mouth. And then realized he did not care if it were right or wrong.

After their kiss, Seamus cradled her against his bare chest, excited by the fragrant tickle of her long, perfumed hair spread across his flesh. Only then did he sense her tremble in his embrace. And realized he too shook with anticipation.

When at last she stood above him, slowly pulling the fringed leggings from each long, brown limb, then raised the hem of the long deerskin dress over her head, Donegan gasped at the supple, firm beauty of her young body. Almost more than he could take, the fragrance of her heated body as she sank beside him on the buffalo robe drove him near mad.

Too long he had been without a woman. Too long wanting others he could not have. Now at last given this girl, this night. Here in this wilderness.

For some reason, dear God—you have blessed me tonight . . . with this warm island in a cold, snowy land haunted with ghosts.

Seamus Donegan realized he had done nothing to deserve what Eyes Talking offered him. But he had never been one to turn down red whiskey. Nor would any Irishman admit to turning down the warmth of loving flesh.

Her fingers found all those places too long untouched. Surprising him with her softness, she had pulled him to her. For a moment Seamus felt like a great bear lowering himself over her glistening, copper body. So small was she compared to his great size, yet Eyes Talking urged him down, down upon her.

When Donegan pressed himself inside her moist warmth, Eyes Talking gasped at first. Then sighed when he began to move atop her, the sound in her throat like a raw, growing hunger that frightened him.

Of a sudden she was gasping again, raking her fingers along the great muscles of his back, clawing again and again at the long, white snake of a scar left there by Confederate cavalry steel.

Himself like a saber, slashing back at her fury with that of his own . . . until both lay spent upon the damp robes, their moist bodies glistening forms of shadow and diamond.

After his heart had slowed and his breathing softened, Seamus felt the young woman stir. Eyes Talking raised her face above his, raking her hot lips across his. Then, with another sigh caught deep in her throat, she sank her head into the crook of the Irishman's shoulder.

He listened while her breathing became rhythmic. Knowing she slept against him. Watching the glowing, wriggling, writhing worms of red coals in the firepit, shadows dancing against the lodgepoles spiraling with sparks to the smokehole above them.

Only then did Seamus realize he was crying himself to sleep.

"Just thinking 'bout what Red Cloud done to Fetterman's men is enough to pucker any man's asshole," the settler grumbled at Mitch Bouyer and John Reshaw that first night's camp out from John Bozeman's Missouri City.

"I ain't so all-fired sure this is such a good idea anymore," moaned another civilian recruited from the Montana settlements.

It was early May. Just four days after Bouyer and Reshaw rode into Missouri City with the body of John Bozeman. And from the sign they had crossed along the way, the two half-breeds figured what Sioux had been in the area were now gone east. If only temporarily.

"It's safe," Bouyer answered over the lip of his tin cup. "Me and Reshaw the closest thing you'll see to an Indian."

"I ain't so sure this ain't a trap," grumbled the first settler again. "You two lead us out here . . . what, with all these goods—we'd be sitting pretty for Red Cloud to jump us."

Reshaw eyed those in the group gathered around his fire.

There were other fires nearby, but to this fire more of the forty-two settlers were drawn by the shrill tone of the less-than-courageous settlers among them.

"Mr. Martin," Reshaw began politely, a sense of danger pricking him, feeling his place as a half-breed among these men new to Montana Territory, "you never did like me none. Mitch either, did you? Even though we was with your train when Jim Bridger himself brought you up here. Don't trust us, do you?"

"I'm for heading back to town come morning," another shouted as he stood, rallying support.

There was a smattering of cheers and huzzahs. Then silence as a tall, thin, pockmarked man stepped into the firelight behind Bouyer and Reshaw.

"I'm staying," he said quietly, then sipped his coffee.

More of the white settlers drew close to the flames. When Harrison McNeal talked, most of them had learned to listen. Not given to loud brag the way of other men, McNeal had come to this country years before with John Bozeman himself. Enough said.

"I smell something that stinks 'bout all this, Harrison," a gray-headed sutler from Missouri City declared.

McNeal emptied his coffee cup. "Nothing but foul air from the beans we et for dinner, boys." He waited for some of the nervous laughter to quiet itself. "I'm going on. And the wagons stay with me and those who'll push on. Rest of you fixing to go back, you make your own way, best you know how."

"We can't walk all the way!"

"Maybe you'd like to ride on to Fort Smith with us then," McNeal replied calmly. "Them soldiers done the best they know how to protect the road. They deserve the help we got in those wagons to bring 'em."

He flung an arm behind him at half a dozen long freight wagons, filled to the sidewalls with foodstuffs for the beleaguered army post so long cut off from the outside world. Four days ago Bouyer and Reshaw had brought the body to Missouri City, it and word that Fort C.F. Smith was in a bad way, with no supplies coming up from the south. Something had to be done, so the half-breeds had marched off to see John Bozeman's best friend. Harrison McNeal.

McNeal enlisted forty-one other settlers and sutlers to donate what they could, load it into borrowed wagons and point themselves east to the Yellowstone, from there to the mouth of the Bighorn canyon where the squat, adobe-walled fort stood, waiting in desperation for some word from Wessells at Fort Phil Kearny.

"Besides," McNeal continued, "any man been out in this country more'n one winter knows the Sioux are moving east . . . just like Bouyer says."

"Why you so sure it's east?"

"Now, Asa—you oughtta know better'n most the Sioux move east this time of year. Sundance time. By next month all the bands be gathered up on the Powder or the Rosebud somewhere. Red Cloud will hold his big sundance and his warriors will hang themselves from that tall pole . . . working themselves up for another summer of bloody work along the road."

"By God," Asa replied with a wag of his head, "I'm glad mother and me already here in the Montana settlements. Red Cloud gets his boys all het up with another sundance, there's no telling what hell will be paid along the road this summer."

"And those soldiers at Smith the only ones stand between you and Red Cloud's thievin' bastards marching into Missouri City to lift your hair," McNeal stated.

Bouyer waited a moment more, studying the faces of the white men, lit copper by the red firelight. He stood and stretched, glancing quickly at McNeal.

"Best I turn in for the night, Mr. McNeal. Reshaw's gonna pick a handful for the first guard. No sense in me losing any more sleep. We've got a big day ahead of us tomorrow—get these wagons a little closer to Fort Smith and them soldiers."

Chapter 11

A dewy, May moon had stolen out over the Big Horns, giving a silver luster to the spring night. Shadows of four-legged animals slithered along the unlit fringes of this place at the foot of the Big Horns where man gathered. Shadows drawn here by the fragrance of the offal left in the army's slaughter yard down by the Little Piney.

All winter long wolves had visited this place where Capt. Obadiah Dandy's quartermasters butchered game and what few beef remained in the herd for the post mess. Concealed in the shadows, the wolves snarled and fought over their bloody feast after a long and hard winter, a winter spent as near to starvation as had any of the two-legged animals who inhabited this place.

When the wolves made their first appearance, boldly slinking into the twilight shadows near the fort walls, post sentries repeatedly shot at the unwelcome visitors throughout the cold spring nights to drive the wolves away. Wasn't long before enough soldiers complained about the gun fire that Commander Wessells changed procedure. His troops were jumpy enough already, waiting for Red Cloud's renewed attacks on Fort Phil Kearny. No need for the pickets to needlessly interrupt the sleep of the rest just to frighten four-legged beggars away.

Quickly learning there would be no threat from the soldiers now, the wolves ventured to the foot of the stockade itself. As a solution, Captain Dandy himself offered the idea of sprinkling poison on the meat.

"If enough of their kind die," Dandy had explained to Wessells and staff a week before, "the rest will get the message. They'll avoid the slaughter-yard like death. And you know—that's just what I want to do with Red Cloud's scheming bastards. Kill enough of them to start with . . . the rest'll get the message and steer clear of Kearny and the road. Hell, they might even abandon the country!"

A marvelous plan, Dandy reminded himself now as he strolled back to his quarters from the slaughter-yard. The damned Sioux were no better than uncivilized predators themselves. Animals.

Without a doubt, Dandy most enjoyed this part of his evenings. His work complete for the day. The evening mess behind him. Time now his own to enjoy, what with a little help from his bottle of spirits. And a new friend.

"Got to tell you, Lieutenant," Dandy poured more of the amber liquid into John Jenness's cup, "how greatly I admire your war record!"

They clinked cups and sipped at the burning liquid.

"I figure we both did our share of damage, sir."

"No, no," Dandy replied quickly. Then in a whisper, "You are among friends when you're with me. Please, let's not be so formal, John. Call me Obadiah. I feel we have much in common."

Lt. John C. Jenness, recently transferred to Fort Phil Kearny from the East, studied the strong jaw of the officer seated opposite him on the only other camp stool in Dandy's small quarters.

Careful with this one, Jenness told himself. "What sort of things do we have in common . . . Obadiah?"

Dandy rose, cup in hand. It went to his lips as he reflected. "Matters most important to men like us. Having to do with honor and duty to our regiment. A sacred way of life that must not be polluted with those who would give in to the Quaker apologists and weak-kneed peacemakers who want to be friends to the Indian. It's up to strong, resolute men like us to preserve what the army always has been: an iron glove in pursuit of our grand Republic's destiny!"

Jenness had to admit, the captain did have a way about
him. Dandy caused something to stir within the young lieutenant. "Yes. I think I know just how you feel about the army
. . . and our assignment here to oversee the settlement of the
West."

"Exactly!" Dandy grinned, pouring Jenness more of the
whiskey. "I was certain we two would find ourselves kindred
souls. Tell me, John—don't you feel at times a surge of deep
anger at some of the priggish dolts who run this army? Some
of those mindless pricks making their foolish decisions? Or,
perhaps the other spineless cowards making no move at all
until circumstances or Congress force them to play a hand?"

As the evening wore on, the young lieutenant grew increasingly amazed at what whiskey Dandy could swill and not be
stretched out on the floor. Jenness had been called to the
captain's doorstep immediately following supper. What with a
long evening of guzzling and talk behind them—Dandy was
still standing.

"I have only my personal experience to go on, sir . . .
Obadiah. Mind you, that doesn't include any fights with the
Sioux—"

"Yet, Lieutenant! You'll have a crack, as will I, at the red
niggers soon enough. But, little matter! Brave men like you
and me . . . and like Major Benjamin Smith himself—we
know what needs to be done, without ever fighting those naked, painted bastards." His face swept close to the lieutenant's, whiskey sour on his breath. "So, tell me what you
think."

"I agree." Jenness gathered his wits, choosing his words
carefully. "Yes, these Indians need a sound whipping. They
understand nothing else but war."

"How perfect!" Dandy slapped a knee.

"Yes, Obadiah! We must show them a strong hand now—or
we're asking for more trouble. More bodies. More fine officers
dead—sacrificed like Fetterman. Other good soldiers as well."

Dandy rose. Paced a moment. Then flew back to hover over
Jenness like a huge bird in need of a nest, his breath thick and
sour in the lieutenant's face again.

"Bless you, John. You've helped put things in the most
perfect light. Red Cloud and his cronies can't possibly under-

stand the peacemakers and those misguided soldiers like Carrington who handed out blankets and kettles to our enemies! Even poor Wessells himself sits on his hands now. Why is the army losing this fight? Because the red sonsabitches only understand *war!*"

He straightened, weaving slightly as he snapped his fingers, "Of course!" With a dramatic sweep he snatched up the bottle, refilling his cup. "We must show these stone-age savages that this post is under new leadership—no longer will Fort Phil Kearny be a haven for those who wish to pacify the warriors harassing the Montana Road. Instead, John, we'll show Red Cloud and his other banditti that our post alone is, at last, that mighty iron fist of our great Republic. An iron fist shoved down their red throats! If they cannot learn to live with that fist here—by God, then let the ignorant bastards choke on it!"

Jenness shuddered. Ashamed as quickly as the feeling washed over him. John recognized that fire in Dandy's eyes. Passion. The same look he remembered seeing on the grim faces of the Confederates he spent four years fighting, from Virginia to Georgia. Yet Jenness was certain that Capt. Obadiah Dandy shared something more than mere passion with those rebel soldiers.

It troubled Jenness to his core that he couldn't put his finger on just what that something was.

"Thank you, John." Dandy suddenly seemed more relaxed. Calmer now, sipping his whiskey rather than throwing it back in hungry draughts. "You've helped me sort out just how I'm going to squeeze my brevet out of that goddamned service review board. Right here—at Fort Phil Kearny, Dakota Territory—I'll earn my brevet. Earn it—if I have to kill ever last one of the red bastards who murdered Fetterman with my own two hands!"

Now Jenness knew what it was that had troubled him so deeply. Capt. Obadiah Dandy was every bit as obsessed in getting his promotion, and killing Indians while doing it, as Red Cloud's warriors were driven to earn their coups and drive the white soldiers from their hunting grounds. Though he shared much in common with the energetic Captain

Dandy, Lieutenant Jenness suddenly grew unsure who he actually feared more. The warriors of Red Cloud, or—

"Captain Dandy!"

Obadiah wheeled, flinging open the door. "What the devil is it?"

Over Dandy's shoulder Jenness saw the whole parade in an uproar. The light from more than half a hundred lamps spilled across the ground in greasy yellow splotches along officers row. Shadows of half-dressed soldiers spilled through those splotches, flitting like frightened starlings against the raw-boarded buildings.

"What's going on, soldier?" Dandy demanded again before the breathless sentry began.

"Thought you'd want to know, sir," the private heaved, catching his wind. "One of the pickets . . . up on the walk—murdered. A Sioux, sir. Got him with an arrow. Right through the heart!"

"A sentry?" Dandy's voice rose.

The private nodded, then raced off to spread the word as Dandy turned into his room and the white-faced Jenness. "John, it appears I won't have to wait that long for Red Cloud and his band of cutthroat, murdering fiends to make my promotion come true."

He splashed more whiskey into his cup, then held it out before him in self-congratulation.

"Here's to my brevet—and the Sioux scalps Obadiah Dandy will joyfully take in getting that promotion!"

Drops of whiskey glistened on his lips from swilling down the liquid. Dandy began to giggle, until the sound grew into shrill laughter that slashed across the bustling compound like the squeal of a huge cog set in motion.

"Their guns are poor," said the young warrior as he drew his pony to a halt beside the war-party leader, reporting his findings while the other Cheyenne tore through the overturned wagons.

"Powder?" asked the leader.

"Some."

"We will take it all with us," he said, waving a hand with

impatience. "Be about it, quickly. I do not want to stay here long."

Roman Nose watched the young warrior nod and turn away to join the others who clawed through the wagons or searched the pockets of the white teamsters they had killed. It was good to be back to raiding once more after a long and very hard winter. These white men who came to scare the game away from this sacred Cheyenne hunting ground must be driven away. If they persisted in using this road to the land of the Sparrowhawks, then those white men deserved to die.

Moon of Ducks Coming Back. The short-grass time before the summer gatherings for the celebration of the sundance. Red Cloud's Sioux had migrated slowly eastward for their celebration. For the time, that left the job here along the road to the Cheyenne. At least those who would not be traveling far to the east, to Bear Butte on the northern fringe of the Black Hills, where gathered the Northern Cheyenne every summer for their celebration of renewal and life.

The young warrior swept back to his side in a spray of dust to report. "We are finished, Roman Nose."

"Burn the wagons."

The young warrior smiled. "I will use these!" He held up the sulfur-headed matches, his face gleaming with anticipation.

Roman Nose smiled as well. "Do not use them all. We will find more work for them in the moons to come. There is much to be done before we drive the white man from our lands forever."

He watched his young firebrands gleefully set the wagons to the torch, carrying flaming shreds of burlap and canvas from place to place to ignite the entire circle.

"We are ready," the young warrior announced as he loped back to the side of his war leader.

"No," Roman Nose said, shaking his head. "The white men."

"We stripped them. We scalped them too. We cut their arms so everyone knows Cheyenne were victorious. We even put their manhood in their mouths, Roman Nose. We have done every—"

"Burn them."

"Burn?"

"Throw their bodies in the fire."

"Why?"

"This land must be purified of the white man's stain upon it. Only fire will purify our land."

When the last body had been hurled into the leaping yellow and orange flames in the midst of the wagons, the two dozen leaped atop their ponies and loped up the slope to the crest of the low ridge where their leader awaited them.

Roman Nose watched the oily smoke billow into the spring sky of robin's-egg blue. As the wind shifted, he could smell the burning of flesh, the cooking of blood. Time now to leave this place. He stared at the flames a moment more, listening to the heaving of his warriors' chests as their breathing slowed after the long rush of adrenaline. And as it grew quiet, he heard the crackle of those flames purifying what they had done here.

"Our land will be cleansed of the white man's stain." The tall, muscular Cheyenne leader pulled his pony away, the others following him over the ridge.

"This time," Roman Nose swore, "we will burn them out."

Chapter 12

"Why don't we just quit beating round the brush here, Judge," Jim Bridger growled, spitting into one of Judge Jefferson T. Kinney's shiny brass spittoons. "No sense fooling ourselves either. You don't like me. That's plain to see. And I sure as hell don't like you."

"Why, Mr. Bridger—"

"Don't go mistering me now. We'll get this goddamned testifying over and done with . . . so I can be gone from your place and you don't have to look at my face no more."

Kinney drew his squat, pudgy frame up in his high-backed chair at the opposite end of the table, his watery eyes slewing over the spectators gathered in the chairs behind Bridger. The old trapper figured the Utah judge turned post sutler was filled with his own self-importance. If not full of something a bit more fragrant.

Kinney pursed his lips, glaring beadlike eyes at the army scout. "All right, Mr. Bridger. You have laid the ground rules well enough. I don't like being around you any more than you like being here with me. But I didn't make that trip to Laramie to meet with the other members of the commission . . . preparing to take depositions—"

"Just who the hell's on this goddamned commission looking into Fetterman's massacre?"

Kinney smiled. Bridger had just handed him a chance to drop some important names upon the captive, curious audience in his sutler's cabin here at Fort Phil Kearny.

"General J. B. Sanborn. General Alfred Sully. General N. B. Buford and Colonel E. S. Parker representing the army—"

"Sounds to me," Bridger interrupted, turning half around to fling his voice back to the civilian and soldier spectators in the room, "like the commission's got its deck stacked against Henry Carrington from the get-go."

Kinney cleared his throat, attempting to silence some of the guffaws and sniggers from the onlookers. "You did not give me a chance to mention that besides myself as a civilian member of the esteemed commission looking into the unfortunate slaughter of Colonel Fetterman's command, there is also serving one G. P. Beauvais, a civilian trader from St. Louis who lived among the Sioux for many years during the height of the fur trade."

"Bull."

"What was that, Mr. Bridger?" Kinney asked, his pen poised over the paper in a threatening gesture.

"Spell it right, Kinney. I said *bull* . . . as in *bull*shit. I been better'n forty and four winters out here in these mountains, trapping and trading both. And I ain't never heard of no Beauvais living with the Sioux. Likely he's another one of the army brass lick-ups what already made up their minds about Carrington and Fetterman both. Just like you."

Kinney tugged at his collar, watching some of the spectators behind Bridger rock forward on their chairs. "I have yet to reach a conclusion—"

"More bullshit, Kinney," Bridger replied, spitting again. "You been looking for a way to hurt Carrington, as far back as last summer when he lined up on the opposite side of things from you, Brown, Fetterman, and the rest of you boys full of brag but damned short on the gumption."

"Carrington and I never hit it off, that much is true—"

"Let's get this over with so I can go get my supper," Bridger interrupted. "You got better things to do than talk to me. Never did listen to nothing I said before. Why you going to listen to what I gotta tell you now?" He looked out the window, waiting for Kinney's next move.

The former federal judge cleared his throat and shifted in his chair. "One James Bridger—"

"That's *Jim* Bridger, Judge."

"One *Jim* Bridger, being duly sworn before an official member of this commission, on this thirty-first day of May, in the year of our Lord, 1867, does hereby offer and make the following declaration in the form of affidavit, of his own free will and without prompting." He waited a moment, staring at Bridger, who continued to stare out the window at twilight descending on the snowy Big Horns. "You may go ahead now, Mr. Bridger."

Jim looked back at Kinney and sighed. "As you wanna know about this Philip Kearny massacre, it's been said that the Injuns didn't approach the fort with hostile intent, but that the commanding officer—that's Carrington hisself—mistook their intentions, fired on the Injuns and brought on the fight."

He watched Kinney scribbling furiously at his papers, transcribing Jim's spoken words.

"All of that's nothing but so much bullshit."

Kinney gazed up, his eyes glaring at Bridger once more. "May I have your permission to alter your wording . . . so that your statement will read, and I quote: " 'All of that's preposterous'?"

"Go right ahead, Judge. But, don't change nothing else."

"I wouldn't dare, Mr. Bridger," he growled, and bent over his papers once again.

"Up to the time of the massacre, the Injuns been hanging 'round the fort every day, stealing stock every chance they had, attacking trains going to the woods. Why, they even stole up at night and was shooting at Carrington's sentries . . . down in the valley at the civilians with the trains while they was sitting 'round their campfires at night. No more'n a hundred yards from the post."

Bridger waited while Kinney caught up, sipping at his black coffee from a steaming mug, tonguing his chew to the side of his cheek.

"But, a few days afore the massacre, a train going to the Piney Wood was attacked. In defending the train, Lieutenant Bingham of the Second Cavalry and a sergeant under him— both of 'em lost their lives. Killing white men is the funniest goddamned sign of friendship I seen from Injuns in all my winters out here."

Bridger grinned as he listened to more laughter from the spectators.

"Judge, you best get it outta your mind—and the commission's too—that the Injuns camped 'round Fort Philip Kearny was friendly. *Friendly?* I got better chance of being asked to dinner by Red Cloud hisself!"

"May we proceed, Mr. Bridger?" Kinney snarled, hurling his high voice over the laughter.

"O' course, Judge. Every person that truly knows the affairs of this country knows very well that the massacre at Fort Philip Kearny was planned weeks before. Any right-thinking man who comes up for sunshine once't a while knows that the Sioux, Cheyennes and Arapahos had been gathering up, preparing to make their attack from their camp on Tongue River. Where they had better'n some 2200 lodges.

"They intended to hit Fort Philip Kearny first, and if they was successful in driving the soldiers off, they was going to head north for Fort C.F. Smith.

"But at the present time, the entire tribe of the Northern Sioux are collecting on Powder River, below the mouth of Little Powder River, and they've vowed in blood to attack all three of the army's posts on the Bozeman Road—and kill every man, woman, and child what tries to use the road as well.

"Friendly Crow tell us Red Cloud's bands of Bad Faces are being supplied with ammunition by half-breed traders working for the Englishers' Hudson's Bay Company."

"I've sent word to the hostiles that I want to talk with them, Mr. Bridger. I'll get their testimony as well before the commission issues its findings."

Bridger snorted, causing Kinney to fidget a moment more. "It ain't no use sending out for any of them with Red Cloud, Judge. If they talk sweet to the army or traders, it's only to have time to trade for powder and lead to carry on the war against the army here on the Montana Road. Once they have more powder and lead, the next time you see their painted faces will be when they're lifting your scalp, Judge Kinney. Or what's left of hair on your bald head."

Kinney immediately ran a hand across his half-naked head, glaring at the hooting spectators.

"No, Judge—and you get this down, every word of it. The only way to settle the trouble with Red Cloud and these forts plopped down on their prime hunting ground is to send out enough troops to completely whip all Red Cloud's Sioux and Cheyenne . . . the whole shitteree at once. Make the bastards beg for peace."

"And if the army chooses not to devote the manpower and the expense to such a punitive expedition?"

Bridger chewed on that a moment, the way he would bite into a fresh cud of Virginia burley. "If the army ain't ready to fight a war out here to take this land from the Injuns, Judge Kinney—then by damned, the army better get ready to have itself drove right out of the country and turn it back over to Red Cloud."

Kinney looked up from his papers. "What you're saying is—"

"What I'm saying is, it's the Injuns or the army, Judge. Ain't the both of you gonna stay. It damned well may take a few winters . . . but army blue and redskins don't mix. Injuns ain't gonna give up without the biggest fight of it. And from what I seen, with Cooke and his bosses not ready to give Carrington what he needed to fight the war out here last year . . . the army just ain't got the gumption or the nerve to win the fight out here."

When Kinney finished writing, he cocked his head and stared at Bridger. "Anything else?"

He nodded. "I been in this country, among these very Injuns, for forty and four years. I'm familiar with 'em—like I know my own mule. I know their history. What I got to tell your commission is more important than any other testimony you might take. Red Cloud and his bunch won't respect any treaty until they've been whipped into it. And since it appears the army ain't willing to give a man like Carrington what he needs to do his job, then the army best haul its goddamned tail outta this country, and hole up in Fort Laramie until it works up the courage to back its officers."

"You're done now, Mr. Bridger?"

Jim stood before he answered, both palms flat on the table,

his empty cup between them. "I'm done all right, Judge Kinney. But you mark my words. Red Cloud ain't done. Not by a long chalk."

He pointed a bony, gnarled finger at Kinney. "You can put my money on that. Red Cloud ain't done with you yet."

"By damned you are one unlucky sonuvabitch," the soldier said with a smile as he raked in the pot that included a good deal of Seamus Donegan's money.

The Irishman wagged his head, smiling within his dark beard. He blew a kiss at the paper script as it was swept away from the center of the table by the soldier. "Farewell, my beloved lucre. How true it is what they say. Unlucky at cards, lucky at love."

"You been spending a lot of your time down in that Crow camp, ain't you, Seamus?" another soldier asked as the cards were shuffled and dealt.

"Man sleeps where it's warmest, I suppose," Donegan admitted with a grin. "Don't figger I got to be back up here to the fort till the new trader comes in and gets his mowing operation going. Then I'll have to go to work for a living again. Instead of living off army wages."

"Living off us poor soldiers, you mean!" A third player laughed.

"Man does what a man must to live, I say," Seamus added. "Hmmm. Not a bad hand you gave me, Wilcox. Not bad a'tall."

" 'Nother of your bluffs, Seamus?"

He gave a look of mock wounding. "Not me, Humphrey. Looks like I'll take two cards . . . and make 'em sweet ones this time. My poke's getting awfully light after those last two hands Riley swept away."

Donegan watched Humphrey staring at him over the top of his cards. "You worried 'bout me hand, soldier? You been staring at me hard most of the night."

Humphrey smiled. "Wasn't thinking about cards, Donegan."

"You figure to read my face—get an idea of my hand?"

This time Humphrey shook his head, laying his hand facedown on the table. "I been trying to place you, Donegan."

"Place me?"

"I run on to someone looks almost the spittin' image of you."

Donegan's eyes narrowed. The table around him grew quiet. He laid his cards on the table. "Looks like me, eh? Where?"

"Back in Kansas. Can't remember if was Fort Harker. Maybe Wallace."

"Kansas, you say. And he looked like me?"

"Close enough to be your brother."

Donegan eventually nodded, the beginnings of a smile creeping into his beard. A smile that eased some of the tension at the lamplit table. "Close enough to be my . . . uncle?"

Humphrey nodded. "Yeah. Sure—"

"You remember his name, sojur?"

Humphrey's eyes batted nervously. He licked his lips a moment, thinking on it the way he would heft a heavy object. "O'Connell . . . no." He swallowed hard. "I think it was O'Roarke."

Wilcox turned to Donegan. "Ain't that the name your uncles carry? Ones you said you was looking for?"

Donegan slowly picked up his hand, plus his two new cards. He smiled before he turned to Wilcox. "You betting?"

Wilcox regarded his new hand. "No," and he slapped the table with the cards. "Ain't it them, Donegan?"

Seamus ignored the question as his eyes sought out the other three soldiers around the lamplit table in this muddy, adobe hut the soldiers of Fort C.F. Smith called home. After two raises and a call, Seamus laid down his full house.

"Kings . . . and jacks, me boys!"

As he dragged the paper script toward his side of the table, Seamus looked again at Wilcox. "Best deal me out for now."

"Going to the Crow camp again, Seamus?"

"Not right away, Hastings," he answered the soldier across the table, stuffing the bills in his pocket. "Got me some thinking to do."

He stood and stared at Humphrey. "My mother's name was O'Roarke. And you knowing a soldier in Kansas named O'Roarke means I got better things to figure on than playing pasteboards with you fellas."

Humphrey stared at his hands, then cleared his throat loudly. "He ain't there anymore, Seamus."

"What?"

"O'Roarke ain't in Kansas no more."

"Where'd he go?" Seamus demanded, his fist banging the rough-hewn, wobbly table.

"Don't know."

"He was transferred to another outfit?"

"Never was in the army, least as I knew."

"Not in the army? How'd you know him? What's he doing on a post?"

"Wait . . . wait a minute. He was civilian," Humphrey began to explain. "He was hunting for the army . . . supplying meat—buffalo mostly, for the post."

"What post?"

"Can't remember."

"Remember, gawddammit!"

Humphrey swallowed hard. His Adam's apple bobbing in his neck like a turkey gobbler. "Wasn't Wallace. No, wasn't Fort Wallace. Was either Harker or . . ."

"Or what?"

"Or Fort Hays."

"Hays?" Wilcox asked.

Humphrey's head bobbed up and down. "Yeah."

Wilcox looked up at Donegan. "That's where your old friend is in command, Seamus."

"My old friend?" Donegan asked.

"Lieutenant Colonel . . . United States Seventh Cavalry," Wilcox announced it slowly. "George Armstrong—"

"Custer," Donegan finished the name. "By the saints! If I don't run across that bastard's tail again. The hanging general who first cost me my stripes. *George Armstrong Custer."*

Chapter 13

"*T*hey just waltzed right out?" Col. Henry W. Wessells shrieked.

For a moment it was all Lt. John C. Jenness, officer-of-the-day, could do to bob his head. "Y-Yessir. Bold as brass."

"Dressed like Crows?"

"From what the sentries can tell me—"

"How do we know the two weren't Crow to begin with?"

Jenness took a deep breath. He rattled the pages of the report before him. As Wessells snatched the papers from him, the young lieutenant answered, "The count of Crow warriors allowed in the gate this morning, sir. You'll read on page three—the notation by the second watch—their count of Crow warriors leaving the post this afternoon. Two more than arrived this—"

"I can damn well read, Lieutenant!" Wessells shrieked again, his face red from the collar up. He felt his stomach go cold.

So, this is the kind of thing that brought Henry Carrington to his ruin, Wessells brooded, not really looking at the report any longer as his eyes bored a hole in the floor. *More damned desertions . . . on top of all the rest of my problems, with the Sioux stepping up their forays at the herds again—I've got problems with desertions. And there's always Ten Eyck's drinking. The only thing saving him right now is that . . . he's not the only one . . .*

"Can you figure it, sir?"

"What's that, Lieutenant?" Wessells asked his officer-of-the-day, suddenly yanked back to the present.

"How'd they work it . . . looking like Crow? No wigs on the post, I know of."

The colonel shook his head. "Does it matter, Jenness? They pulled an old flea-infested blanket over their heads . . . put on some moccasins they traded off the warriors . . . walked out in the middle of that bunch from Fort C.F. Smith. Problem is, they did it. And I don't have the manpower to go traipsing off to find where the bastards ran off to."

"Any change in sentry policy, sir?"

He glanced at Jenness, then stared out the window at a shaft of sunshine just then pouring through the clouds to splatter its golden light across the muddy parade. Everything a soggy mess at Fort Phil Kearny. Spring come to the Northern Rockies.

"No, Jenness. Stand down your detail you were about to take after them."

"Sir?"

"If those two soldiers want to go to the trouble to dress up like the Crow and live with the goddamned flea-bitten beggars —then the best I can do is wish them well."

"But, sir—"

"Enough, Jenness! Good riddance to the bastards. Let them go north with Iron Bull and live by the walls of Fort C.F. Smith . . . like that Irishman."

"Donegan, sir?"

"Yes. I washed my hands of him too."

"Word has it—"

"I know all about Mr. Donegan, Lieutenant," Wessells cut him off. "He's . . . sharing the lodge of a Crow woman in her teens up there at Smith . . . and still Kinney allows him on the post—playing cards . . . regularly carousing with the contractors and enlisted."

"Nothing you can do, sir?"

He looked at Jenness hard for a moment. "Nothing I will do . . . for now. Come a time, I'll rid this department of scum like Donegan. Soon enough, Lieutenant. I'll not have his kind worrying me. Fomenting discontent. Drinking. Lallygagging 'round the posts—it's his kind creates these deserters,

Mr. Jenness. I've got enough to worry about right now," he growled, finding the dispatch on his desk. He waved it before him.

"Bad news, sir?" Jenness inquired. The eyes studied his commander's face.

Wessells nodded. "This informs me they've chosen a replacement for Carrington."

"I take it, then, they've selected someone else, Colonel?"

"Bloody well right, they have, Jenness!" he barked, flinging the dispatch down on the desk. "What with all I've tried to accomplish here since that incompetent clerk Carrington retreated with his tail between his legs. And this is the thanks I get from Department Command."

Jenness cleared his throat, waiting until Wessells looked up from the dispatch. "Who . . . who is it, sir?"

"Name's Smith. Colonel . . . John E. Smith."

"A new District Commander."

"That's right," he replied, softly this time. And marched to the window where he studied the shaft of sunlight breaking through the clouds. "A new commander for the Mountain District. I wish him luck."

"Luck, sir?"

Wessells wheeled suddenly. "Luck, Jenness. Luck accomplishing what Carrington couldn't do. Nor I in the short time allowed me here. Time to shape this district into something the army would be proud of."

Jenness swallowed hard. "The desertions, sir. They're not your fault."

Wessells smiled broadly. He saw the look of surprise that sudden smile brought to the young lieutenant's face. "Damn well right they're not my fault, Jenness. I know just who's fault they are, you see. So . . . come a time and soon—Mr. Seamus Donegan will get what's coming to him for causing all this trouble hereabouts. He'll get what's coming to him."

He had to admit he liked the softening thud of the warclub he smashed against the side of the soldier's head. The sensation of blood warm and sticky on his hands as he slashed the scalp from the white man's head.

War up close. Not fought at long distance the way the white

soldiers preferred to practice it. Roman Nose liked it up close. Where he could see the fear in another man's eyes as the knife or tomahawk or warclub was already singing through the air.

Close enough to smell the fear exuding from the enemy's pores.

The Cheyenne war-chief rose to his feet, shaking the scalp and screeching his victory song. All round him echoed the shouts of Sioux and Cheyenne warriors alike. Roman Nose stood over the body of the first soldier killed this fine morning, late in the *Moon of Ducks Coming Back,* exhorting the others on to feats of bravery of their own.

It seemed he always led the charges himself, as did his Oglalla friend, Crazy Horse. Unafraid of soldier bullets. Certain of his own medicine. Knowing lead from soldier guns would fall away before it reached his glistening, naked body atop the fleet, grass-fed pony.

As soon as it grew light enough to see the outline of the tents and horses picketed outside the walls of Fort Reno, Crazy Horse and Roman Nose led their combined forces down on the Powder River post. The drumming of their pony hoofs and their wild screams answered immediately by the fearful shrieks of the soldier guards. More of the white men, soldier and civilian alike, rolled from their tents into the chill dawn air, pulling up their britches with one hand while the other held their unpredictable muzzle-loading Springfields.

On the outskirts of the confusion the warriors circled their wide-eyed ponies, aiming their rifles at the dark forms darting against the backdrop of white canvas and purple dawn light. The Sioux and Cheyenne fired rifles captured long ago in the *Moon of Deer Shedding Horns* when the soldiers had given themselves up at the foot of Lodge Trail Ridge. Many rifles. Much ammunition found on the bodies bloodying the trampled snow.

Now the warriors would use soldier weapons and soldier bullets on soldiers at the dirt fort beside the Powder.

Roman Nose laughed as bullets sang around him. He felt them sting the air near his face, or whistle by his arms as he waved the scalp in one hand, a Winchester eleven-shot repeater in the other. No soldier lead would touch him. His medicine decreed it so.

A glorious day to fight! his mind sang out as he gathered up the long, looping rawhide rein and leaped onto his pony's back.

Less than a moon now until the time when all the bands would Dance for the Sun. Praying for the Sun's blessings. Praying for the gift of Life for the People. Enough time before the Sun Dance that Roman Nose had talked Crazy Horse into joining him in this raid on the dirt fort south of the Crazy Woman Fork.

Not the dirt fort the soldiers had built where the Bighorn River flowed from the mountains farther north.

Time enough to destroy that fort, Roman Nose brooded. *Time enough to butcher the soldiers there by the Bighorn River.*

At his side a young warrior careened off the back of his pony. Roman Nose recognized the familiar smack of lead colliding with a naked body.

He wheeled, waving the rifle in the air, signaling. On cue two young horsemen pulled away from their charge on the soldier camp, sweeping down on the fallen one. Leaning off their ponies, they yanked his limp body from the dusty sage, dragging him over the hillside.

The Cheyenne chief let his big pony prance a moment as he watched the battle rage before him. Inside the fort itself the white men were scrambling like beetles from an overturned buffalo chip. With no order. Only a mindless fear, a mindless obsession with self-preservation ruling them.

That was the thing about striking at the white man, Roman Nose thought as he hammered his heels against his pony's ribs, leaping back into the dusty fray. *The white man was slow to gather his wits about him when surprised. And that slowness is enough to spell his doom.*

On the far side of the camp where Crazy Horse had deployed his warriors, the soldiers dragged two more bouncing bodies across the sage toward the tiny ring of dirty tents where everything was a beehive of frantic activity. Puffs of gunsmoke blossoming above the dark-shirted troopers like white flower petals.

Already the air in his nostrils reeked of burnt powder. Roman Nose liked that smell. A strong, pungent odor always meant victory for him. Good that the sting of burnt gunpowder mingled with blood, sweat, pony droppings, and the acrid dust staining the coming of day in this place.

Off to his right another young warrior toppled from his frightened pony. Just beyond, among the sage and an over-turned wagon-box, Roman Nose watched a puff of dirty gray smoke rise to betray the soldier's position. Whoever fired from behind that wagon was good enough to kill one of his Cheyenne warriors. Good enough that the soldier must be stopped.

"Aiyee-yi-yi-yi!" the war-chief shouted, his voice high and shrill as he hammered his pony's ribs once again.

Beneath the barrel-chested Cheyenne the animal burst into a full gallop. Jamming the rifle barrel under his left arm, Roman Nose cocked the Winchester as the wind of day-coming whipped his face. Closer and closer still. He would wait until he was close enough to fire. Another soldier scalp this day—

He heard the bullet slam into the pony's chest. Felt the first quiver between his legs, and with it the change in the animal's stride. One of the war-chief's legs grew damp with the pony's blood. The animal slowed even more.

He goes down, Roman Nose thought.

To his left a puff of smoke betrayed where the soldier hid among the tents. Determined, Roman Nose reined his dying pony toward the soldier who had killed two warriors already. Vowing that the white man would kill no more this day.

The pony stumbled as it neared the wagon-box, pitching sideways.

Roman Nose was off the animal in a smooth leap, hitting the ground at full stride when the pony toppled over. Done for as it carried its master into the jaws of the white soldiers.

Running, yelling, waving his rifle wildly between shots, Roman Nose hurtled over the sage. Glancing at the first thumbnail of red-orange sun creeping atop the edge of the world beyond. Daybreak.

A good day for soldiers to die!

The soldier marksman stood, turning this way. Turning that. Ramming a new charge home. He stumbled backward two steps as the Cheyenne's bullet smashed into his chest.

Roman Nose always liked the look on a man's face when he

was hit with a fatal shot, but stood, his heart still pumping, not yet giving out.

Roman Nose slammed the soldier backward another two steps with a second bullet in the chest. Then a third to the belly as he drew close and eased his race. The soldier doubled over, sinking to his knees slowly, his face gone white as the alkali dust on the ground. He stared up at the Cheyenne, his mouth moving but no sound coming forth.

Swinging the Winchester's butt, Roman Nose was on the white man in two more long strides. The wooden stock smashing the soldier's jaw, his head flopping sideways like a sawdust doll's.

He dropped onto the soldier, one knee on the man's chest, sensing beneath him the rapid, frightened breathing. Roman Nose peered down into the glassy, blinking eyes. Then ripped his knife from its scabbard at his waist.

With a swift, practiced movement, Roman Nose slashed the blade across the soldier's throat like light in a mirror. So quickly no blood dirtied the gleaming blade. Instead, the hot crimson spurted onto the Cheyenne's legging.

The soldier jerked convulsively, his arms and legs flailing like an animal about to be butchered. From his throat bubbled thick, gurgling noises. With his left hand the Cheyenne rammed the greasy blond head against the ground, holding it steady as the soldier struggled against the weight over him, against the blood choking him, blood soaking into the thirsty soil as well.

Below Roman Nose the frightened, glassy eyes blinked clear, staring frozen up at his while the Cheyenne slowly dragged the knife blade across the soldier's forehead. Agonizingly slow, hearing the gurgle in the man's throat turn to a high-pitched bubbling wheeze. Down the side of the soldier's face, across the top of the ear and on to the nape of the neck.

Only when he had begun to pull the full scalp from the soldier's head did the white man quit moving. Roman Nose smelled the stench of voiding bowels. And knew his enemy died at last. He cursed the luck of it. The man had not lasted beneath the knife. Denying Roman Nose the joy of showing his victim his own scalp, shaking it in his face. The white man died too quickly.

He jerked up, recognizing the tone of the shouts and a quieting of the wingbone whistles. On the knoll to the north Crazy Horse waved his red blanket. The Sioux were breaking off the attack, dragging off their wounded. Their ponies splashed water and sandy grit into the sparkling red-orange sunshine of a new day. Across the Powder, up the sharp-lipped bank and into the sage.

Roman Nose cursed under his breath, flinging the limp body down into the yellow dust as more lead bullets kicked up spurts of dirt, whining into the ground around him like harmless buffalo gnats.

Come a day, he would no longer have to follow in the shadow of Crazy Horse. Come that day, Roman Nose promised himself as he sprinted off on foot, he would stand alone, his own prowess in war overshadowed by no man, Sioux or Cheyenne.

Out of the dust and powdersmoke, two young Cheyenne warriors swept up on either side of him protectively. Both grinned and shouted their greetings. One held out his bare leg and an arm. Roman Nose pulled himself behind the youth without breaking his stride. The ribby pony pranced around wildly in a circle as the heavy load settled on its back. Then its master kicked heels into its flanks and burst off, down the slope into the cool waters of the Powder, up the far side to join the rest of the Sioux and Cheyenne leaving this soldier fort.

Leaving the fight.

Come a day, Roman Nose promised himself, *I will not leave a fight until all soldiers lay dead. That, or my spirit will be freed. It can be no other way.*

He turned quarter-round to look over his shoulder at the small, squalid tent town beside the dirt walls of the soldier fort, raising his rifle and shrieking his oath.

A promise.

Come a day, I will give the last drop of blood in my body—to watch the last soldier die by my hand!

Chapter 14

"**B**y God, young man—Providence indeed holds us in the palm of its hand once more!" freighting boss A. C. Leighton roared, slapping his young employee on the back.

"Yessir, A.C.," the employee replied. "One of us was born under a good star, sir."

A good star or not, twenty-three years before that day the Missouri homestead home of Sheriff Reed Burnett had listened to the hungry wails of their first-born son, Fincelius Gustavus. A mouthful of a name for anyone, much less poor, grub-hoe Ozark folk like the Burnetts. The parents called their firstborn Finn.

For eighteen years Finn grew whipcord lean and wise in the ways of the woods, tracking barefoot through the hardwood forests after gray squirrel, rabbit and an assortment of birds, targets all for his practiced marksmanship. Cardinals and jays haunted the shaded hollers of his youth for those eighteen years spent growing up among the slave-owning people of Missouri and knowing of no other world beyond Taney County. There was little cause to wonder on anything beyond the shady hills of his youth.

Until the day news of war came home to Taney County.

For the next three years young Finn Burnett continued to work the family ground, repairing rail fence every fall and turning the dark soil each spring while his father sheriffed the county. Never was much said about the war between them, except that it stayed far enough away. Even with that battle down at Pea Ridge and all. The Yankees were still far enough away, Sheriff Burnett told his growing son. The day come soon enough to learn of the world outside. To learn of blood and death in the twinkling of a Yankee's eye.

But by late summer of 1864 the Union forces pressured the undermanned and underarmed Confederate home units something fierce. And what with Sherman turning Georgia to ruin and Sheridan burning his way up the Shenandoah, those of both political persuasions in Missouri saw it would be only a matter of time until the Union blue mopped up the eastern battlefields with the Rebel gray. Only a matter of time and who could throw enough manpower into the fray before the inevitable end for the once-hopeful and always-honorable Confederate States of America.

Both the Union blue and the Rebel butternut sent conscription units scouring the hill country of southern Missouri and northern Arkansas, searching out the half-grown sons of the men they had collected back in 'sixty-one. Surely by now, went the reasoning, some of the young lads would be old enough to carry a gun.

Sheriff Reed Burnett was not the sort to take any such chance. Better that his son should live among the enemy, than wear the blue uniform of that enemy's army.

Came time to go that misty, October morning in 'sixty-four, with the leaves turned pumpkin orange and sunset red, igniting his boyhood forest with a blaze of color. Finn turned once from the middle of the dusty road, his feet already pinched by the new brogans his daddy had bought him the day before.

Finn waved one last time. Then pointed his nose north. Not sure what the Nebraska frontier would bring. Only that his father had assured him the faraway place was far enough away for a twenty-year-old to disappear among settlers and sutlers, teamsters and buffalo hunters, faceless in the crowds of frontier army and railroad crews. To Finn Burnett it was not a cowardly thing to do, this running from conscription. Not cowardly to turn your back, to shuck it and leave it behind so that you didn't have to end up fighting against everything you had ever known. Everything you had ever loved as well.

Many were the times those first few weeks that young Finn Burnett's eyes stung with hot tears of remembrance and loneliness. Only those who have left home before they are ready to leave know just what memories do to a young man adrift in a foreign sea of strange faces and smells and fears.

At Omaha he stripped hide wagons of their rank buffalo furs brought in from the prairie beyond the tall-grass country of eastern Nebraska. When the hide men left, Finn nailed together board fence that would hold the growing hog population of the town's stockyards. And each night he ate his biscuit and bowl of stew, thinking on home. Thinking on someplace where the snow never fell so deep. Someplace like the shady hollers where the wind never cut through his clothes as it did here on the Great Plains of the buffalo and the mighty Sioux.

By the middle of March in 'sixty-five, twenty-one-year-old Finn Burnett had himself a job that guaranteed a little warmth to it. If he stayed close enough to the forge where he assisted the blacksmith in all his labors. If he stayed busy enough moving horse and mule, wagon and dray in and out of the livery on the outskirts of a burgeoning Omaha.

It was there in that smoky, stinking, sweat-smelly, dung-reeking livery that a freighter from Ottumwa, Iowa, watched the energetic Burnett working over three days of readying the wagons that would carry A. C. Leighton's goods west to Fort Laramie along with the contract to haul army supplies for General Patrick Conner's Powder River expedition against Red Cloud's haughty Sioux.

By God, Finn Burnett realized he had never seen a *real* Indian. Only the squash-eaters living along the Missouri River who wandered into Omaha, begging for coins and a drink or two of the white man's whiskey. Never a real, by God, Indian like Sioux or Cheyenne.

"Why not come see some for yourself, son?" Leighton had asked him that third afternoon, convinced that the swelling arms and the good common sense of the youth would prove worthwhile on this contract to the army.

"You saying . . . go with you to *Injun* country?"

"By damned, Burnett—that's what he's asking you!" The blacksmith slung the hammer down with a resounding clang against the anvil, red sparks spraying like fireflies. And he smiled. "You're a bigger ass than that cantankerous Jack back there in stall two if you don't go with this man."

"By God," Finn said, drawing himself up, "by God, Mr. Leighton. I will go with you!"

"Sixty-five dollars a month, Finn Burnett. I'll provide bed and board while you're in my employ. Do you have a rifle?"

He was still stunned, choking on the unholy sum as it worked around in his mouth like a chaw of fine Kentucky shag-leaf burley. "Sixty-five dollar a month, Mr. Leighton? Ah . . . no sir. Ain't got a gun but this old pistol papa give me when I come up from home."

"All right, then," Leighton said with a smile. "Here," and he threw the youth the rifle he had slung across his left arm for three days while watching the blacksmith repairing wagon and harness for the long trip west to that faraway land of the Sioux and Cheyenne.

"B-But, sir," Burnett stammered, staring down at the rifle in his hands, twisting it this way and that in the murky red glow of the blacksmith's forge.

"Jesus Christ, Burnett!" the blacksmith himself wailed. "That's a goddamned Ballard he's give you!"

"A . . . a Ballard?" Finn echoed.

"One of the best needle-guns ever!" the blacksmith replied, snatching it from Burnett to admire.

"You just might need a Ballard out there," Leighton had said quietly.

For a moment Finn Burnett studied the eyes of his new employer, and figured Leighton knew whereof he spoke. "Yessir."

"Call me A.C."

"Sure thing . . . A.C. I thankee for the Ballard rifle. I'll take proper care of it, I will. Yes, by God—I'll go with you to Laramie . . . and beyond. Wherever you want me to whip some goddamned mules, I'll go. And I'll see for myself those mighty Injuns of the plains!"

Fortunately for him, Finn Burnett did not see much of the mighty warriors of the far prairie on that trip out. But most of Conner's troops did. That expedition of eighteen and sixty-five proved disastrous for man and beast alike. Except that

General Conner built the fort he named for himself beside the Powder River. Less than a year later the army would want its collective memory cleansed of Conner, and would rename the post Fort Reno.

That fall of 'sixty-five, with the war having ended in a whimper down in Appomattox Wood and soldiers from both sides wandering west as they discovered they had no homes to wander home to, Finn Burnett bid another tearful good-bye to A. C. Leighton and turned his nose south for Taney County.

Funny thing of it, the going home wasn't what Finn had made it out to be over all those lonely nights and long days of remembering. A few of the orange and red leaves still clung to the same high branches, refusing winter's first icy blasts. The wagon ruts along the old road leading to home filled with the same slick of dirty ice as they always had at this time of year. But to Finn Burnett, southern Missouri was no longer home.

Time and again the young man ventured out of the cabin, to stand on the rough-hewn porch and stare off toward the hills that seemed to hem him in now. Making him uncomfortable, like the shirts and britches he outgrew all too quickly as a young'un. Outgrowing the home of his childhood. This place made him feel closed in after seeing all the expanse of prairie and plains where he had come to manhood. These Ozarks could not hold him after laying eyes on those towering peaks where the sun could never melt all the snow.

Finn Burnett finally owned up to what he was and what he was meant to do. And told his mama and the sheriff of Taney County where it was Finn Burnett intended to do it. So it came that on a second cold, frost-licked autumn morning fraught with restlessness and a tingle of fear, Finn Burnett turned in the dusty road to wave one last time to those he left behind. And would never see again.

For the West was bigger than any man. And the remembrance of that country made one young man's heart swell to bursting.

Finding Leighton always in need of a right hand and a young man to trail-boss his freighting outfits, Finn Burnett once again pointed his nose west to the northern Rockies. This time in the summer of 1866. Following Col. Henry B.

Carrington's "Overland Circus" that would reoccupy Conner's Powder River post, then construct two additional forts along the Montana Road to the gold diggings of Alder Gulch first blazed by John Bozeman.

Through that summer and into the fall, Finn Burnett watched Fort Phil Kearny rise from the plateau at the base of the Big Horns, a log at a time. While they buried soldier and civilian alike in the post cemetery, a body at a time.

By the time December snows had closed off all travel north and south along the Montana Road, Finn Burnett had seen his fill of Sioux and Cheyenne. Carrington's forts were effectively under siege as the white men fought for their lives whenever they ventured beyond the stockade walls.

To those walls young Finn Burnett had hurried with the rest to watch as Capt. William Judd Fetterman led eighty men off the crest of Lodge Trail Ridge, following the luring decoys to their deaths.

He would never forget the memory of those frozen, grotesque, mutilated bodies he and the others dared go retrieve on the morning of December 22. Enough Sioux and Cheyenne on these high plains for any one man's lifetime.

Come spring and the first thaw in that country of rarefied air, Finn Burnett was under instruction to take his wagons and teamsters south to Fort Laramie. From there on to North Platte, Nebraska, where he would meet Leighton once more. Into the empty high-walled freighters would go supplies for the starving posts along the Bozeman Road. And if all went well by the time Leighton showed up at Laramie, the horse-drawn mowers he had included in his lading would be put to use up the road ninety miles from Fort Phil Kearny at C.F. Smith.

Back along the Platte River Road, Leighton himself had run on to a pair of wagonmasters out of Ohio who were bringing a load of supplies out to old Fort Kearney in Nebraska. From there both John Morrison and Webb Wood had planned on running empty all the way to Fort Phil Kearny in the Big Horns on a personal errand. Word of all the deaths along the trail had reached Ohio. Morrison was coming to bring family home from that dangerous place where life had proved itself cheap.

Leighton convinced the two wagon bosses to tie in with him and load their fourteen freighters with supplies in North Platte, joining their teams with his to better fight off attacks once past Bridger's Ferry and into the undisputed hunting grounds of Red Cloud's Sioux. At Laramie, A.C. happily learned he had been awarded the contract to cut hay at Fort C.F. Smith. And he learned as well that his wagon train of supplies could travel north under the protection of Capt. David Gordon's troop of 2nd Cavalry accompanying John "Portugee" Phillips north with mail for the three Bozeman Road forts.

"Providence indeed," Leighton repeated now, hoisting his coffee cup laced with the finest whiskey the Fort Laramie sutler could boast. "I not only have the contract at Smith to provide them with hay at fifty dollar the ton, but I have a military escort to accompany me and Morrison north!"

"Seems our timing was on the mark again, A.C.," Burnett agreed, sharing in the whiskey which helped cut the chill that came each sundown to the high plains. No matter that it was early summer and the days could broil a man's brains out. In this country the nights could turn just as mean, and every bit as cold as the days were hot.

"From what I watched loaded at North Platte, we're carrying more than just food north to the posts, A.C."

"That's right, Burnett," John Morrison remarked as he stepped up, clinking his china mug against Finn's. "Bet those new rifles are sorely needed by the army north of here."

"Rifles and bullets both," Finn Burnett agreed, sipping on his whiskey as he sat down on a hard-tack box near the fire, warming his hands after turning up his collar. "By the way, Mr. Morrison . . . been meaning to ask you something, if'n you don't mind."

Morrison found a place to settle beside Burnett at the fire circled with teamsters and contract quartermaster employees who would head north into Red Cloud's land come morning. "Don't mind at all, Mr. Burnett. Ask away."

"Back some weeks ago, when we joined up in North Platte, A.C. told me you and Mr. Wood was heading to Fort Phil Kearny on your own . . . on 'family' business. I ain't mean-'

ing to pry . . . not that at all. Knowing as well as any man what grief there's been come visiting that place."

"Understand you spent the winter at Kearny in the Big Horns."

"That's right, Mr. Morrison. I seen with my own eyes all that passed that place . . . so I ain't one to ask this lightly. Just curious is all. You don't gotta tell me, you don't want to."

Morrison chuckled within his dark beard, winking at both Webb Wood and Burnett's employer. "Out with it, Finn. Will you ask me your question already?"

Burnett cleared his throat. "I don't rightly remember running personal on to any soldier named Morrison. Don't recall anyone of that name up there . . . or at Fort Reno, for that matter. My memory might be going . . . so that's why I ask. You have a brother killed with Fetterman at the fort up yonder?"

Finn watched John Morrison blink, unspeaking for a long moment, his eyes glancing first at Leighton, then Wood, before he stared into the fire. At last he gazed back at Burnett, patiently waiting at his side for an answer.

"I'm sorry, Mr. Leighton . . . I had no busi—"

"Quite all right, Finn," he answered, a hand on Burnett's knee. "You have every right to know." He wagged his head. "No, I didn't have a brother killed with Fetterman."

"I'm glad of that, sir," Burnett sighed, relieved as well for his nosiness had not strayed on to delicate feelings.

"But I did have a relative killed with Colonel Fetterman."

"A relative, sir?"

"Brother-in-law. Fella from Nebraska. My sister's husband."

"You're going to Phil Kearny to claim his body?" Leighton inquired, sitting near Morrison's knee.

The Ohioan shook his head. "No. He'll rest where he's buried. I've come instead to take my sister home."

"Sister?" Burnett asked, his mind wondering on it, tossing the thought from side to side the way a kitten would bat a ball of twine. "Don't remember a woman named Morrison."

He laughed gently. "Finn, she changed her name when she married the settler fixing to homestead in Nebraska."

Burnett nodded. "Nebraska?" His mind suddenly came on it, the way a man would turn a corner onto a familiar street. "Your sister's a widow?"

"That's right, Finn."

"Her husband named James Wheatley?"

"Yes. I'm coming to bring my youngest sister home to Ohio. She needs to be among her own people . . . what with two young boys to care for now. All alone."

Finn Burnett shook his head and whistled, having put it together at last, the way he would fit stones at the edge of fields, building fences.

"Jennie Wheatley," he whispered, remembering the face now, the look of gloom and loneliness and need that freezing day they buried the Fetterman dead. "Poor woman. All alone, and surrounded by wilderness and murdering Injuns."

"Not for long, Mr. Burnett," Webb Wood advised, smiling his crooked smile. "John and I have come to take Jennie home to her people."

"Webb himself has always had eyes on Jennie," Morrison explained, his head bobbing toward his partner.

"Perhaps I can give her and the boys a home and security," Wood began. "Well, we'll have to see how Jennie feels once the mourning is over."

Leighton stood and stretched. "For me, the evening is over. I hear my blankets calling. Tomorrow we turn our noses north, staring the future full in the face, gentlemen."

"Here, here!" Morrison said, rising as well, sloshing the cold dregs of his coffee into the dying fire. "I'm enthused that I'm so close to Jennie. Won't be long now until she is back in the bosom of those who love and care for her in Ohio."

Finn Burnett watched Leighton turn in one direction, Morrison and Wood in the other, headed for their blankets and sleep. And he realized he would be hard-pressed to sleep this night. What with thoughts of the beautiful Jennie Wheatley pushing in the corners of his mind. Thoughts of her and the man who had laid claim to her early on, come that terrible winter at the foot of the Big Horns.

No man with any common sense would seek to trample on those toes, especially the toes of a friend. And if any man besides Jim Bridger, Jack Stead, and Sam Marr could call the Irishman a friend, it was Finn Burnett.

God almighty. Finn thought about it as he settled by the fire once more. *Morrison come to fetch his sister—and Seamus Donegan stuck off up at Fort C.F. Smith . . . on orders of the U.S. goddamned Army itself . . . unable to do a frigging thing about Jennie Wheatley.*

Unable to do a goddamned thing about John Morrison snatching her back to Ohio . . .

Chapter 15

"*I* 'll not allow it!" Capt. Nathaniel C. Kinney bellowed, about ready to stomp his foot down like a schoolboy not getting his way at recess.

"Appears you don't have a thing to say about it," half-breed Mitch Bouyer replied quietly.

But Seamus Donegan read the twinkle in the scout's eyes.

"But . . . but—it's inhuman!"

"What they're fixing to do ain't inhuman at all, Captain," Bouyer explained. "Indians been doing it to each other back in time . . . before the white man even thought of setting a foot in America."

Kinney wagged his head. "If I can't stop the Crow from torturing that Sioux warrior . . . then I'll not be party to any of it." He wheeled on his staff and the guard detail that had accompanied the commanding officer of Fort C.F. Smith to the Crow village near the mouth of the canyon where the Bighorn River issued forth onto the plains in its flow north to the Yellowstone.

"Mount the men, Lieutenant Sternberg. We're returning to the fort."

"Yessir," the young German officer replied.

"You're staying, Donegan?" Kinney asked, gazing down from horseback at the Irishman.

Donegan glanced at Bouyer and Reshaw. Then he glanced at Eyes Talking. "Yeah, Cap'n. I'll stay. Never know when I might get another chance to watch these Crow even the score on the Sioux a bit."

"I see," Kinney huffed, his jaw jutting. "I'd taken you for a civilized man. Not like Bouyer and Reshaw here."

Donegan winked at the half-breeds. "What the army does to its own is what I'd call uncivilized. Not what these Crow squaws are about to do to a prisoner of theirs. We're the visitors here, Cap'n. These Injins are the ones belong out here. It's their rules we'll play by."

Kinney drew in a deep breath of the deepening twilight descending upon the Big Horn country. Already the June sun had dipped behind the peaks as day slid headlong into evening. When he spoke, looking down at Donegan once more, it was with quiet resignation.

"That, perhaps more than any other, is the reason I am retiring from the army, Mr. Donegan. Out here, we are forced to play by Red Cloud's rules. Perhaps the rules of Iron Bull over there. But Indian rules just the same. And Department Command back East refuses to recognize that what we're up against is something they haven't the foggiest idea how to cope with. So soldiers like me and Henry Carrington are sent out here to do only God knows what . . . without enough men and guns and bullets—"

"You miss Carrington, don't you, Cap'n?" Donegan interrupted.

He nodded and sighed. "More than I would like to admit."

"You're both good sojurs, Cap'n Kinney," Donegan said, taking a step backward to salute smartly. "Proud to have known you, sir."

Kinney saluted. "I suppose it'd be all right to salute a civilian, wouldn't it, Mr. Donegan?"

"I won't tell, Cap'n," he replied with a wide grin.

Kinney glanced over at his lieutenant. "Lead off, Mr. Sternberg. I figure the missus has dinner waiting on me. And she's even more anxious than me to get shet of this goddamned privy hole they named Fort C.F. Smith. I'm counting days until I'm relieved, and that poor woman's counting the hours."

"Yessir," Sternberg replied. He twisted in the saddle. "By twos—forward at a walk."

Seamus watched them disappear from the fringes of the Crow village that sat less than a mile and a half from the walls of Fort C.F. Smith on a level plain of land where an abrupt, sheer cliff bordered the lodges on two sides.

"Seamus Donegan?"

He looked back at Bouyer. "I'm ready. Let's go see how these Crow deal with the bastards what stole their hunting ground."

At the far side of the village the women were just then beginning to practice their ancient art of amusement for the menfolk of the camp. Children of all ages and states of undress sat atop the ridge, watching. Other youngsters gathered among the warriors and old ones who stood in a semicircle about the women. And the squaws themselves completely surrounded the lone Sioux prisoner.

Earlier that morning a small war party of Miniconjou had made the mistake of envying the Crow pony herd. They had ridden back to the Bighorn River country to learn something of the goings-on at Fort C.F. Smith. Their mission was to have been entirely secret, and they were to report back to Red Cloud's war council without engaging the soldiers.

Still, it would not matter if they returned to the camps on the Powder with a few Crow ponies, the young warriors had reasoned as they gazed down on the herd from the hills above.

No casualties taken by either side in the running battle that played itself over many miles of the Big Horn valley, ponies laboring beneath their warriors in the chase that took them up Warrior Creek. No casualties, except for one Sioux prisoner taken by the Crow after his pony was shot from under him.

Iron Bull, the Crow mailman Captain Kinney used from time to time, had proudly presented the prisoner to the post commander. And announced through interpreter Bouyer what was planned for their captive that evening. It would be an honor if the commander were present in the Crow village during the torture of the Sioux warrior. Kinney had ridden down to the camp instead to talk the Crow out of their grisly practice. He rode back to Fort C.F. Smith now, his shoulders slumped under the weight of his last days of command, having failed.

The Sioux prisoner, nude but for his tattered breechclout, stood immobile beside a small fire tended by an old woman. Around his neck the squaws had tied a long rawhide rope, the sort used by Crow warriors round their war ponies' necks. At the other end of the lariat stood a giggling assortment of young Crow women. Among them in the deepening twilight, Donegan recognized Eyes Talking.

Every few moments the girls jerked the Sioux off his feet. He struggled to rise again from the dust, his hands bound at his back. Each time, he stared into the night without uttering a word of protest or pain, waiting for the next step in what he knew would be the painstaking process of his own death.

It continued that way for some time, until a few of the older women moved to the center of the circle where they kicked at shins, slammed their knees into the prisoner's groin or stomped down on his bare feet. And the first time their prisoner did not immediately rise from the ground, the old squaw at the fire was ready.

With a movement as quick as a hawk swooping over a nest of field mice, she swept a firebrand from the flames and slapped it against the Sioux's back. The blow sprayed tiny fireflies of sparks into the purple twilight, bringing with it an eruption of cheers from the ring of spectators. Struggling to rise in the midst of an ever-tightening noose of tormentors, the Sioux clambered to his feet, gasping in pain.

Again and again the process repeated itself. The women pummeling the prisoner to the ground. The old woman jabbing the flaming limb at his bare flesh, burning his face, setting his hair to smoldering, jabbing at his genitals with obscene taunts. It wasn't that long before another woman took up a flaming branch and began jabbing it at the prisoner as well. Then a third, and finally a fourth.

Then no longer were the squaws merely touching him with the fiery sticks, they were slapping, then jabbing the hot ends into his flesh, pounding him with all the fierceness they could muster. Repeatedly he tried to rise now, much of his strength and resolve gone the way of smoke from those fiery branches. He remained on his knees, unable to rise. What shred of his breechclout had not burned away was ripped from his waist.

His pubic hair smoldered, as did what had once been the long hair over his shoulders.

Donegan smelled the faint stench of burned flesh and hair. He looked away a moment, sucking deep at the cooling night air.

"Remember those soldiers and friends of yours who died beyond the Lodge Trail, Seamus Donegan," Mitch Bouyer instructed quietly at his side, watching the Irishman quail as the torture turned from sport to pleasure in another man's pain.

Seamus gulped audibly. He did remember. A field littered with severed limbs. Disemboweled bodies frozen in grotesque shapes. Headless bodies stuffed with arrows.

"Does their savagery merit our own?" he asked quietly, not knowing if the half-breeds heard his question.

"It's the only thing a warrior truly understands, Seamus," Reshaw explained. "War is the only thing they respect. This dying as a brave man they respect as well."

"I had no idea it would . . . would turn out like this," Seamus muttered, watching the hunchbacked woman bend over the prisoner.

From her waist she pulled a knife held for a moment aloft in the firelight, joined in a wild shriek of growing passion from the circle of her friends. The knife swept down like a fractured bolt of lightning, then was held aloft again. Bloodied this time. And from her other hand the old one brandished the prisoner's genitals. Penis and scrotum. At her feet the Sioux writhed in agony. No strength to rise. Unable to fight off his torturers. Unable to do anything but to die as quietly as his courage allowed.

Bouyer nodded, his eyes studying Donegan's face. "You find it hard—but you must understand the Sioux dog expects nothing less than this from our women. You must understand this before you can understand the Indian. If the Crow warriors had killed him outright, perhaps using him for target practice . . . the prisoner would believe his captors considered him a coward. A mongrel worth only a coward's quick death."

"Understand this, Seamus Donegan," Reshaw added. "By

turning the prisoner over to their women, the Crow men show their prisoner they regard him as a worthy enemy . . . one worthy of a brave man's death. Any man allowed to suffer such torture before death is a worthy opponent. Cowards die quickly. Only a brave man can die slowly."

"Only a brave man," Seamus repeated, pausing to suck deeply at a breath of air before continuing, "can die slowly."

First fingers and toes. Then one squaw or another hacked off the hands and feet with camp-axes. And in the flurry of blood and firelight, shadow and blurred lust, Donegan wondered if Eyes Talking was impassioned as well . . . in that circle . . . her own knife or axe at work on the prisoner.

Each new appendage severed and thrown into the crowd brought a renewed shriek of fiendish joy from the assembly.

He had heard cries like that before, Seamus realized. *Gettysburg.*

A tiny place on the map of Pennsylvania where men proved their courage, or lack of it. He shuddered with the memory of it. Union cavalry and infantry marching into the valley. Confederate forces marching up as well. And in the center of that growing throb of insanity stood the little village of Gettysburg itself.

Every bleeming bastird cleared out of that town. Every man, no matter what his age. Leaving their women cold, leaving their women behind to suffer the onslaught of two converging armies.

Talk about cowards. The civilized farmers and cow-milkers of Gettysburg . . . running away to save their hides . . . while thousands and thousands more gave their lives to save those farms.

And when it was all over . . . *the spineless bastirds came limping back, creeping back . . . like moles peeking outta some hole in the ground to see if things were safe. Goddamn them! Not one man, young or old . . . not one of them women we fought to protect . . . not a one of those who had no courage to take a musket in hand to protect the homes they considered most dear . . . not a goddamned one would dirty their hands with a shovel to bury our dead in the dirt of their beloved fields . . . fields run red with good men's blood.*

Seamus realized only then that the choked, gurgling,

unintelligible sounds that had been pouring from the prisoner's throat had ceased. The warrior long past the point of pain.

The rain came that sundown. To settle the stinging dust. To soften a bit the stench of gunpowder like a black carpet over the land. And, by twilight, a rain enough to sprinkle itself on the rotting, bloating corpses of Gettysburg. Rain enough to wash the rocks free of blood and gore and splattered brain.

He thought of Captain Kinney suddenly, wondering if the soldier hadn't been right in the first place to refuse witnessing this savage, hypnotizing spectacle. And was quickly struck with a funny thought. Funny, that he think it while watching another man die before his eyes.

Ah, Cap'n . . . hadn't been for what we Union horse did that day, riding under Custer and Gregg—cavalry the finest that ever climbed onto saddles—like as not the army in this Injin country would be wearing the butternut gray of the Confederate army.

Had we not swallowed our fear like a cold stone and shut our eyes and ears to the mayhem around us . . . like as not the Union army would not even be here in this place . . . trying to steal this goddamned land from these bleeming savages.

With the prisoner's head hacked off and brandished aloft at the end of a thick branch, another old woman bent over the prisoner's torso. She tied the rawhide rope beneath the Sioux's arms, looping and knotting the lariat securely before she threw the other end up to a horseman emerging at the edge of the firelight. He was instantly joined by other warriors.

Iron Bull and his friends. Come to drag the headless, armless, legless thing down the valley to Fort C.F. Smith where they would parade around the post compound beneath torchlight to show off their prisoner to the soldiers. Like strutting cocks having driven challengers away from their private harem.

Donegan watched the horsemen disappear into the deepening night. Of a sudden not at all sure where he would stay the night now. Not wanting to return to the fort. To show his face to Kinney and the others after choosing to stay and watch.

And not sure now if he would slip beneath the buffalo robes

in her lodge. Did he have the stomach to lay with Eyes Talking this night?

Did he have as well the . . . courage to last this foreign land and its people?

And then he remembered the half-breed's words.

Only a brave man can die slowly.

Chapter 16

"Captain Dandy, our new munitions are placed in your care," Col. Henry Wessells ordered, a rare look of approval on his face.

"Yessir!" Obadiah Dandy replied, saluting before he turned to Max Littman. "Sergeant, see these wagons are unloaded—rifles and ammunition both stored and secured under lock."

Sergeant Littman, a square-jawed German immigrant, snapped his heels together. "Sir." He turned away, waving for the civilian teamsters to steer their wagon teams across the parade to Dandy's quartermaster stores.

"I believe a drink would be in order, gentlemen," Wessells suggested, swinging his arms out expansively and gesturing toward his office doors. "Mr. Gilmore? Mr. Porter? Please, come in. Captain Dandy, you will join us?"

"Of course, Colonel. About time we received the arms necessary to prosecute this war on the bloody heathens Red Cloud claims are his sovereign nation."

Wessells was at the pine-plank sideboard in his office, pouring the whiskey as red as a blooded bay horse when sutler Kinney clomped through the door left open to admit more of the cooling June breezes here below the Big Horns at Fort Phil Kearny.

"Colonel?" Kinney puffed, then ground to a stop, finding the office filled with the civilian freighters and Wessells's staff.

"Come in, Judge. Come in," the colonel invited, motioning gingerly with his arm as he handed the first two servings of whiskey to contractors Gilmore and Porter. "I believe you've met our guests?"

"We know Judge Kinney of course, Colonel," J. R. Porter said, stepping forward with a hand extended. He took Kinney's pudgy paw into his, shaking it briefly before Gilmore stepped up.

"Judge. Good to see you again."

"Laramie, wasn't it?" Kinney asked.

"Yes," Porter answered. "While you were down there preparing testimony for the commission looking into that Fetterman matter."

"Yes . . . quite," Kinney answered absently. "Thank you, Colonel." He took his cup of whiskey from Wessells. "I will recommend the whiskey to you, gentlemen. As fine as any you'd sample on your tongue back in the states."

"You sell quite a bit of this, do you?" Gilmore inquired, his lips glistening with droplets.

"Not as much as the colonel's men would like," Kinney answered. "Most of the enlisted can't afford it."

"So they satisfy themselves drinking the likes of what we brought along with the goods delivered to your store?"

"Yes," Kinney replied. "A strong . . . potent libation. Though not as . . . fit for sipping gentlemen."

"You were pleased with the condition of your goods, I take it," Gilmore asked.

"Quite, Mr. Gilmore. Everything in order on the bill of lading. What little damage occurred on the trip north from Laramie is duly noted. But that's not what's exciting in the least . . . although it has been one long winter since last I received supplies for my store."

"Oh?" Porter asked over the lip of his cup. "What's more interesting than sugar, coffee, pork and the rest?"

Kinney sputtered, his black beads of eyes dancing from man to man. "Surely, the most interesting item of discussion this day and for days to come will be those new rifles you brought up in your wagons."

"Some of those wagons belong to A. C. Leighton and a pair of freighters out of Ohio," Gilmore admitted.

"I understand Leighton's going on to Smith in a few days," Dandy said, entering the conversation.

"Yes," Porter replied. "He won the hay-cutting contract for the post, and has permission of the new department commander to erect a trading post near the fort stockade, the likes of which Judge Kinney operates here."

Porter eyed Wessells. The colonel knew the others watched him as well with any mention of the new department commander recently assigned and reportedly on his way west to assume the reins at Fort Phil Kearny.

"Leighton will have his hands full with the civilians, I imagine," Wessells said. "Up there at Smith I understand they're quite an undisciplined lot."

Dandy snorted. "As a rule, civilians are undisciplined . . . wherever the army finds them in our employ."

"I beg your pardon," Kinney blurted.

"In no way am I referring to present company in the least, Judge," Dandy apologized. "You're several cuts above the likes of the quartermaster employees I'm forced to hire. By damn, if only the road were more fully open—and I had more a selection of civilians to work with."

"Disappointing, isn't it," Gilmore began, edging over beside Captain Dandy, "the quality of man who ventures west on his own hook."

"The truth be known, Mr. Gilmore—the quality of soldier we're given to fight this war is rarely above the board as well."

"But do the job we must!" Kinney roared, toasting the room.

"And with my new rifles and a hundred thousand rounds of ammunition," Wessells said as he held his cup in the air, "why—we'll finally sting Red Cloud in the backside now."

"Is it true, all this talk we've heard about these rifles sent you?" Porter inquired of the lieutenant colonel.

"What did you hear?"

"That those rifles Captain Dandy's men are off-loading into your stores right now are something more than the normal Springfield muskets your men have been forced to use since Carrington broke ground here last summer."

"You've heard correct, sir," Dandy himself answered proudly before Wessells could speak. "At the conclusion of hostilities in the South, the army had some fifty thousand of a recent modification to the Springfield left over."

"A modification?"

"Something they're calling the Allin conversion."

"Used at the end of the war, you say?"

"Yes," Dandy answered enthusiastically. "A modification tooled on the 1863 models at the U.S. Armory in Springfield, Massachusetts."

"What does this modification do to the weapon?"

"It puts in the hands of our soldiers a Springfield *repeater*," the quartermaster replied, smiling broadly.

"At long last," Wessells added. "You fellas brought us a shipment of the converted rifles that had been reduced from .58 caliber down to .50 caliber."

Dandy edged forward immediately. "Reduced by brazing a smaller barrel tube inside the .58-caliber barrels on the existing rifles."

"We're told that by next year the armory at Springfield will begin replacing the barrels themselves rather than using a barrel insert," Lt. John Jenness added.

Kinney stepped up to Dandy and Wessells. "These are the same, reliable weapons the army has long used?"

"Yes," Wessells was quick to answer the sutler's suspicion. "They maintain the same iron furniture, the same three-leaf rear sight, the same fifty-three-inch length . . . all of it."

Kinney sighed, grinning. "About time the army issued itself an adequate weapon for the job at hand out here."

"Now we can hold our own against any repeater on the market, Judge," Dandy remarked. "While the Winchester and Henry are repeaters, both lack the range and killing power of the Springfield." He curled a fist up before Kinney's face. "We'll have Red Cloud's balls in the palm of our hands before long!"

The judge snorted. "Now all you need is some army commanders with backbone enough to pacify this land for the godfearing white folks who want to husband the prairie, seeing this rich land produce food for our great Republic's food basket."

"More backbone?" Dandy inquired, testy already.

Kinney's cheeks flushed, his thick lips pursed defiantly. "Yes, by God, Captain. Ever since I became acquainted with the army last summer, from that nervous Carrington on down to the present, I've been . . . dismayed at the lack of . . . wherewithal—albeit determination to get the job done."

Dandy took a step forward, halted after that single step behind Wessells's arm. The lieutenant colonel spoke quietly, setting his cup atop the desk, "What job would you, as a civilian and former federal justice, have us do out here, Judge Kinney?"

Kinney's small, feral eyes bounced furtively from the soldiers to the two civilian freighters. "Why, to put outlaws like Red Cloud and his bunch of murderers on a gallows."

"And the rest?"

"The rest?" Kinney echoed Wessells's question.

"Women, children . . . the old ones."

"I'd lock the women and children onto a reservation—the sort that has worked well down in Indian Territory. In fact, that might be where the army should drive *all* the plains Indians as well. Yes!" he nodded, satisfied with himself. "One great, well-patrolled compound . . . where the army can contain the Indian until he learns to civilize himself and till the soil as God Himself meant mankind to do."

"As God Himself intended you to do, Judge?" Wessells couldn't help asking.

He sputtered, then sipped the last of his whiskey before looking back at the lieutenant colonel. "Someone must supply those who till the soil, Colonel. I feel I have been brought to this place at this time to do just that. To be on the cutting edge of this opening of a great land to settlement. A man with my ideas, here to see that those ideas are spread for the glorification of our great Republic!"

Wessells shook his head, briefly glancing at Gilmore and Porter, both of whom wore looks of embarrassment, if not pity, for their fellow civilian.

"I genuinely feel sorry for you, Judge," Wessells said, eventually filling the uncomfortable silence in his office. "It's your kind caused this war my army must wage with Red Cloud."

"M-My kind?"

"That's right. Civilians like you who aren't content to let the Indian be." Wessells saw Kinney swelling up like a cock clawing dirt in a hen yard. "By God, you hear me out, Judge. Your kind makes no bones that it's your God-given right to wrench this land away from the redman. Your right to possess all that walks upon it, or the riches that exist below the surface of the land. And at the first moment you find the redman resisting your theft of what was his—you call for help."

"By damn—" Kinney sputtered, turning to shove his way out.

"You'll listen to me before you go, Judge!" Wessells barked, barring Kinney's exit. "You and all your kind with money and influence and power—you civilians who have the ear of Congress and the Indian Bureau as well—here the army has to come running at your every beck and call."

"I'll not listen to another word of your blasphemous drivel, Wessells!"

"You'll listen—"

"I will not! But you'll hear about this, you can be sure!"

"You'll go nowhere till you hear me out, Judge. There's just one more thing I'll say to you about your kind. It's men like you who always start these miserable little wars. And it's my kind who has to come in and clean up after you."

"How dare you!" Kinney roared. "Mind you, sir—unblock that door!"

"When I'm finished, Judge." Wessells stuck his face down into Kinney's. "Brave men have to come clean up what you stirred up, Kinney. Usually young men as well. Soldiers, Judge. Soldiers asked to do an impossible job by an ungrateful public, like yourself. Men like you—growing fat and rich on the government's welfare."

"Welfare?"

"Your tradership."

"I bid for this position—"

"You and the hundreds of others like you have someone in Washington in your hip pocket, Kinney. Don't try to bamboozle me."

Flushed to the point of apoplexy, Kinney hurled himself against Wessells's arm, forcing his way out the door.

Behind the lieutenant colonel the room remained quiet, the contractors and officers alike stunned into silence. Wessells stood framed in the doorway, watching the squat figure scurry across the parade like a prairie hen furiously after her brood.

Arms fluttering, savagely kicking up gravel, grass and dirt with every step.

"Yes, Judge Jefferson T. Kinney," Wessells repeated. "It's the army who has to come in and clean up after your kind get through stirring things up."

He stared into the brilliant summer sun. Climbing near the middle of the sky, here close to the middle of the *Moon of Fat Horses.*

Dancing.

For more than a day now he had stared at the brilliant sun, then the hours of watching the night-sun track across the starry heavens before seeing a second day dawn in the east. Still dancing. Always dancing round the pole in the center of the huge arbor erected for this annual celebration of life and thanksgiving.

Without food or water for a second day. Hoping for a vision. Some revelation. Some answer to those prayers he sent to the spirits on the shriek of the eagle-wingbone whistle between his parched lips.

Roman Nose shuffled to the left, a foot at a time, following the beat of the drums. So many drums. The loudest throbbing in his skull.

With each step he pulled a little harder, bearing back on the long rawhide tethers lashed to the top of the pole his dance steps slowly circled as the sun crawled overhead. Rawhide tethers reaching down from the sunpole like the fingers of the Everywhere Spirit himself to bind Roman Nose and the others to this dance of self-torture. Willow skewers pushed beneath the pectoral muscles, binding the rawhide-tethered dancers to their vow to dance in prayer.

Prayer for another successful year in the hunt. Prayer that the Cheyenne people would not have to suffer a third hard winter, like that they had just endured. Forced to hear the whimpers of the little ones, the cries of the old ones—no man nor woman left untouched by the great hunger. Game chased off by the coming of the white man. Bellies pinching—as if the spirits were teaching the Cheyenne people to fight back.

Roman Nose remembered now . . . remembered the teachings of his youth: a man with a full belly did not fight long enough, nor hard enough for what he needed. Only a man with an empty belly knew what it meant to fight as a warrior for the lives of his people.

The hot tears stung his eyes again, and his mind cried out. *This! This I give . . . for my people!*

He knew it was his mind. For he could still feel the whistle between his cracked lips. He had not spoken aloud.

Dancing on and on in a circle. Women and children and the hunched, old ones gathered in a ring around the huge arbor. Drummers and the medicine men clustered nearer the dancers. And at the center stood the sunpole itself. Colored red and blue, yellow and green. The sacred colors, one at each of the four winds.

Four buffalo skulls, each painted with stripes and hailstones, sacred sage stuffed in the gaping eye sockets, sat at the base of the sunpole. Gone the time the buffalo were plentiful, like the blades of grass.

Roman Nose brooded darkly, the tears streaming down his cheeks. *But now only the white man is as plentiful as the blades of grass. He kills the buffalo, and so grows stronger. More of him. Spreading the stench of his gathering places farther and farther out onto the land once run only by the buffalo . . . and my fathers.*

His tongue was well past the point of being sticky. It clung to the inside of his cheek like a thin membrane of connective tissue he would slice with his knife in butchering an elk in the cool shadows of the mountains. Where the waters ran sweet and cold.

He pushed the thought of water from his mind, as tangibly as one man would shove aside another who is troubling him.

Trying to swallow again, he gave up. There was nothing left in him to swallow. Roman Nose knew it would come soon. The vision he had thirsted for even more than the cool waters of the streams that flowed through the Piney Woods. Where now the white soldiers defiled the valley with their fort.

The vision would come soon. The one he had begun praying for in the sweatlodge where he sat for more than a day before emerging into the dawn's light yesterday to begin this ordeal beneath the sun. For a second day the bright, unforgiving globe of the life-giver sucking all the juices from his body.

Drying him out, breaking him down—crushing him beneath its hot, stifling paw before it would remake him into a powerful warrior once more.

The powerful warrior his people needed to drive the white man from this land.

A vision begun in the sweatlodge, in fragments like fleeting bits of cottonwood down caught on a spring wind, floating now on the hot air before his eyes blurred by tears and sweat. Stinging . . .

And in his mind the swirling blur began to slow. Edges of his mind began to clear, like the border of a rain puddle on the plains beginning to dry, become more defined. Sharper. And in focus now.

He recognized the fort. Dirt walls.

The one the white man calls Reno!

Dirt walls. *Yes!* He knew it. A vision of what had been the raid on Fort Reno. The four scalps taken . . . but there were so many pony-riding warriors sweeping down on a tent camp of soldiers in his vision.

He tried to swallow, the back of his throat more parched than old rawhide. Scared a little. Unsure as well. For now he realized this was not the Reno fort he saw in his vision.

Roman Nose struggled to remain standing. Stay on his feet until the vision had spoken to him. He sensed his knees softening, like the hoof-meat the women boiled for glue the old ones used on arrow-fletching and hardening shields. Knees softening and giving way until—

Then he suddenly felt the hot, foot-pounded, sun-banked earth beneath his wet cheek. Realizing he was unable to rise. Knowing he was not to rise until the vision had finished with him.

What he saw was not the Reno fort. Another place. Where, he wondered—troubled with each passing drum-throb of his heart as it pounded in his ears.

Then from the walls of the fort marched a caravan of wagons, driven by white men . . . pushing their wagon animals down the river into the wide, grassy valley where the wagons cut the tall grasses, piling the green shafts high, to dry beneath the same sun bearing down now on his brain.

And one of them—a tall one—the only man taller than

Roman Nose himself, stood back from the others, so that now
the Cheyenne war-chief could see his face.

I do not know this one . . . yet.

He said it to himself . . . prayed it to the sun itself, which
had granted him this vision, realizing that one day soon he
would meet this white man who stood alone.

Then, as if caught in the slow flow of a late-summer stream,
the solitary white man seemed to move farther away from the
others . . . until he stood alone on an island in the river by
himself. A single cottonwood tree straining against the sky
behind him. Sand at his feet and his head bleeding . . . the
crimson juice flowing into one eye as he raised his rifle, aiming
it at Roman Nose.

And as the Cheyenne chief forced his tongue to move,
pushing the wingbone whistle from his lips to speak—to yell
out—Roman Nose felt the muscles of a strong pony throbbing
beneath his legs . . . an animal charging down on the white
man who had his rifle raised and pointed at him.

It was to be this way, he knew at the last as blessed, cool
sleep overtook him, the vision blurring around the edges once
more, draining into darkness. Roman Nose understood in the
pit of him that it would come down to something between
him and this single white man now at the dirt fort.

But as his breathing became more regular and he realized
dreamily that some of the old medicine men were pulling his
body away from the sunpole into the shade—where they
bathed his tortured, burning flesh with the cool waters of the
Rosebud—he knew the place had been decided.

He had recognized the soldier fort the white man had
emerged from—it was not the one called Reno.

Instead, Roman Nose knew he would meet the tall,
bearded, black-headed one near the fort built at the mouth of
the canyon where the Big Horn erupted from the mountains.

The place the white soldiers called Smith.

Chapter 17

"*I* 'll never forget that tiny barnyard Sternberg built at the east wall," Amanda Kinney sniffled as she passed the last of the luggage to her husband, Capt. Nathaniel C. Kinney.

He stuffed and squeezed their meager belongings into the back of the ambulance that would carry them south past Fort Phil Kearny, on to Fort Laramie, then east to retirement from the army. His release from service had been accepted on January 7.

Now, the twelfth of June, it struck Amanda once more that for five months she and her husband had been virtual prisoners here at the mouth of the Bighorn, suffocating within the four walls of Fort C.F. Smith, Montana Territory.

"Yes . . . Sternberg," Captain Hartz's wife Lucille found herself sighing. "Bless his German heart."

A favorite of all the women, Amanda thought to herself. Dear, sweet Sigmund.

"Those dear animals he pushed west across that lonely wilderness," Lucille continued, glancing at the mail escort tightening cinches on their mounts.

Why did she say that? Amanda wondered, knowing she had so far to travel. *This tearing apart's hard enough . . . so, who's more fortunate? Those who go . . . or those left behind?*

"After eight hundred miles that milk cow of his still gave the finest cream for our coffee . . . and such splendid pastry!" replied Sarah Burrowes, wife of the officer who would assume command of Fort C.F. Smith until a replacement for Kinney arrived.

She would say that, Amanda reflected, trying to smile. *She's the best cook among us all. Always hoarding those precious eggs of hers. What danger . . . what boredom we shared . . . filling our lonely hours with each other—why, with our coterie of four officers' wives at the post, each had a choice of three homes to visit. Now, we are . . . less.*

"Remember the two piglets who foraged their way north?" Lucille asked. "And Sternberg's chickens!"

"Yes! Oh, yes!" Amanda answered with a brave smile. "Remember dear Sigmund's face when he found half of them had gaped themselves to death in that first snowfall last autumn?"

The women laughed, uneasily. Their laughter rang with a tinny, hollow sound. This was not an easy thing—to let go of friends you had carried in your heart across hundreds of miles of wilderness. Friends whose hands you had held through countless hours of dread. Waiting and worrying till husbands returned through the fort gates once more. Knowing each time soldiers galloped out those gates, fewer men plodded back. Some never returned.

Amanda sniffled, retying her bonnet beneath her chin. "Damn those coyotes!"

"Amanda!" Sarah chided.

The others stood silent, aghast at the sudden curse. Then they all laughed together at their little secret.

"Yes, Amanda," whispered Louise Henry, wife of Smith's assistant surgeon. *"Damn* those old coyotes!"

They laughed together again. More easily now.

"Taking our turkey hen the way they did," Lucille clucked. "Just when she was about to brood some little ones!"

Amanda sensed an unspoken sisterhood among them all. She studied their brave smiles as each one put the best of faces on this painful parting. Through those weeks and months of arduous, unspeakable journey to Fort Phil Kearny, then asked to bear another ninety miles of wilderness to reach this place along the Bighorn River, followed by the rigors of fort construction—their sisterhood had proven a refuge for those women who needed something that could not be found in the company of a husband. Something rare and precious—found only in the warm kinship of their survival together. The homey familiarity of the daily routine—baking, brewing, stewing and sewing. Yet always time for a game of charades or authors, or the challenge of croquet.

"Lucille," Amanda reached out for Mrs. Hartz's hand, "that dear spotted cow of ours tied in Sigmund's barnyard will not be coming east with us."

"Pray tell why not?" Sarah asked.

Amanda smiled as if divulging a secret. "Nathan doesn't think it fitting for a retiring fort commander to be found pulling a cow behind his wagon all the way to Ohio!"

As they laughed, Amanda squeezed Lucille's hand, then patted the swelling belly beneath Lucille's heavy wool coat. "I give the cow to you, Lucy. She . . . with the baby coming . . ."

Amanda choked off the sob at the back of her throat. Then smiled through a fog of tears.

Lucille struggled to clear her own throat. "I won't ever forget Amanda Kinney's Fort C.F. Smith mincemeat pies!" It had such a brave ring to it as she squeezed Amanda's hand.

Amanda snorted back the dribble pendant like a translucent pearl at the end of her nose and laughed sadly. "Just a little beef heart, Lucy. Some dried apples, raisins, and that precious sweetened vinegar from sutler Leighton. You . . . you'll make it for everyone now that I'm gone, won't you, Sarah?"

"Y-Yes . . . oh, God! Yes, I will, Amanda."

Dear God, this good-bye hurts, Amanda thought. *All those days Nathan and the other husbands were too busy to remember their women, we were all we had to each other. Besides our children . . . we were all we had.*

Amanda gazed around as she raked a raw, freckled hand beneath her nose. "I'll never forget this place, you know." The others nodded in silence, staring at the toes of their boots.

Hard to admit what's being torn from us all.

"What grand memories I'll have of this place. Grand! All the buildings complete now—just when Nathan's leaving the service." Amanda sought something happy to talk about. Nothing happy with this moment.

"Thomas says Leighton's men can begin cutting hay for the

winter in a couple weeks," Sarah Burrowes said, attempting to find something to fill the void.

"Yes, more hay," Amanda replied. "Another civilian train. Another soldier escort. More . . . waiting . . . more worry—"

"Amanda?"

She turned at Nathaniel Kinney's voice. "Yes. I'm ready, Nathan."

She held out her arm as the captain helped her climb into the rear of the ambulance. Amanda settled atop the leather luggage and pushed some loose strands of hair out of her eyes. Sighing, she held apart the leather pucker so she could see those she left behind.

Kinney crawled atop the sun-warmed leather of his saddle and signaled the corporal who would lead his mail escort of eight soldiers and the ambulance south, far from this wilderness of blizzards and savage, naked warriors, and . . .

"Sit still, son," Amanda whispered to her six-year-old. "We . . . we have such a long way to go."

"Mama—"

"Hush now, dear."

Amanda swiped again at her nose, no longer caring about her foggy eyes. The boy couldn't see her face. She kept it turned from him. Looking back at her good, good friends. Those left behind. For all they had gone through together, standing steadfast at their husbands' sides while this mud fort was raised and defended . . . there would never be friends like these again.

Not in her whole life. Never again would anyone have friends like these.

Amanda Kinney waved desperately as the ambulance lurched into motion. Her brave smile grown damp.

"Good . . . good-bye."

God almighty!

Sam Marr marveled at the feel of it. Riding along at a full gallop, guns booming in his ears, the whoops and cries of wild, feathered warriors encircling him. Surrounded by Crow horsemen and a handful of civilians. Chasing a band of daring Sioux and Cheyenne raiders who had slipped over Lodge Trail

Ridge to strike the few head remaining in Fort Phil Kearny's beef herd.

Marr and a few of the hardy civilian employees down in their camp near the Little Piney had been closest to the herd itself when the herd guard raised their warning. A few gunshots from the civilians watching the cattle, and a lot of shouting. The sight of painted, naked warriors riding down through the trees at the Big Piney crossing was enough to pucker any man's asshole.

Even an old fighter like Sam Marr.

Captain Marr, veteran of Missouri volunteer cavalry. Cut his teeth twenty years back on Mexicans under Zachary, by God, Taylor it was. And now he found himself chasing after some mounted Sioux warriors, in the midst of some screaming Crow who had been camped near the civilian tents at the sawmill on the Little Piney.

They relish warfare like this, Sam realized. This is their life. *And it may well be the goddamned death of me!*

Time like this, he knew a man needed a good horse under him. And Sam Marr had the best. Seamus Donegan's big gray.

"Son of a buck . . . Seamus never did name this horrid monster," Marr muttered beneath his breath.

Sensing the surge of muscle and fire beneath him. Tears whipping back at the corners of his eyes with the hot June breeze.

He watched a young Crow beside him topple, and looked back to see the body kicked aside by the ponies charging behind.

"Poor bastard," he muttered.

Ahead one of the Sioux tumbled to the side into the sage and stunted grass. Not much of the grass left now. What with the Sioux and Cheyenne sneaking close almost every day now, setting fire to what grass they could. Burning fodder to starve the horses and mules and cattle out. What better way to force the soldiers from this place at the foot of the Big Horn Mountains?

A heartbeat later the long rawhide rope that ran from a loop around the Sioux pony's neck back to the fallen warrior's waist snapped taut. The pony started, prancing to its left.

Then was off again like a bolt of summer lightning. Dragging its unconscious master through the sage and burnt grass. Following the rest toward the Big Piney crossing.

Around Sam Marr the young Crow warriors renewed their yelps of bloodlust, driving their small, ribby ponies ahead of the white men, most of them centering their attention on the unhorsed enemy bouncing through the sage at the end of his tether.

As the old man watched in amazement, two of the young Crow slowly drew closer to the enemy's pony, hampered as it was with its ungainly burden dragged bounding and bleeding across the prairie. First one, then the other sped beside the dragging body. The first struck the unconscious enemy with his quirt. With a victorious wail, the first to count coup on the enemy, he pulled aside an arm's length to allow his friend a chance at the Sioux's flying body.

This time an unstrung bow slapped the back of the enemy's head and shoulders.

The first warrior was beside his companion again, shouting words Marr could not hear. He could only watch the black hole in the Crow warrior's face volving up and down as he shouted his order. The second man obeyed, slowing his pony dutifully, keeping a yard behind the older warrior.

And then as quick as a hungry Missouri toad would catch and swallow a fat bluebottle fly, the first warrior snatched a butcher knife from his belt and brought it down across the rawhide tether.

Suddenly freed, the Sioux pony surged ahead. The second warrior kicked his heels wildly into the side of his mount. This four-legged prize would be his. The older one had his enemy as spoils.

The Crow slowed his pony, reining around in a hairpin near the crossing.

Marr watched the Sioux and Cheyenne reach the far slope leading up the Lodge Trail before any of them looked back to find one of their number gone. Never to cross the Big Piney again.

They waved their arms, held up their breechclouts, obscenely shaking penises and slapping brown rumps at the pursuing Crow and white men. Then as one, they kicked their ponies into motion when they saw the enemy not only had unhorsed one of their own, but had captured a pony as well.

The second Crow recrossed the Big Piney with his prize, a grin as big as any county-fair blue-ribbon-winning farmboy could show.

Sam reined up, throwing an arm into the air to signal the rest of the civilians who had followed him out of camp.

"What they fixing on doing to that red bastard?" R. J. Smyth asked.

He regarded the teamster a minute then smiled. "R.J., you oughtta know better'n that. Those Crow boys fixing to have a little fun with what's left of that red nigger after his pony dragged him through the brush."

Smyth dragged the back of his hand across his dry lips, eyes narrowing. "God, they're all savages, ain't they, Marr?"

"By damned, I believe you're beginning to understand things now, ain't you, R.J.?"

"You gonna stay to watch, Cap'n?"

Marr wagged his head. "Ain't a thing here I need to watch. Saw enough of it already. What I didn't see during the war . . . by God, it filled my craw when I saw what was over that ridge last December."

The smile drained from R. J. Smyth's face. His brown eyes narrowed as he nodded once. "Got my belly full of mutifying that day as well, Sam. Don't need to see no more of it, I suppose."

"What one bunch of red bastards does to another bunch don't concern me now, R.J. I'm thirsty—dry as August ground. What say we go find us a drink of whiskey and a piece of shade afore that quartermaster Dandy wants us to report back for work."

"Sounds fair to me, Sam."

"Didn't think you was one to pass up a drink, R.J."

"Don't ever figure to make it a habit, neither—you god-damned Yankee sonuvabitch."

"Then, I suppose I'll have to drink to your health?"

"Damn well better drink to yours as well, Sam. Sure as hell these red bastards aren't going to!"

"Only reason these heathen Crow got anything to do with

us—we're fighting again' the Sioux and Cheyenne what took their hunting ground from 'em, R.J."

"Maybe you and me best pray while we're having that drink."

"Pray, R.J.? Didn't know you was a praying man."

"I might become such, you blue-belly sonuvabitch! Out here in this godforsaken wilderness . . . having to wonder what red bastard gonna stick his knife twixt my ribs first— Sioux . . . or Crow!"

Chapter 18

"Oh, Sam—I don't know what to do!"

Marr clutched the widow Wheatley in his arms gently, her sobs wracking her small frame. "It's gonna be all right, Jennie. Ain't a soul gonna push you to do something you don't want to."

"Don't know what to do, Sam," she repeated, this time mumbling into his shoulder where she cradled her head. "Don't know what to *feel.*"

"Just let things be, girl," he soothed, sensing even more a responsibility for her now than usual.

Over the top of her head Sam gazed down at Jennie's two young sons. They stared at their mother and the old man, both wearing a look like that of a blue-tick hound caught in a barbed-wire fence. Not sure whether to howl in pain, or bark in anger. Remaining quiet in the meantime, their sagging jowls and sad eyes telling it all.

Sam figured their whole world now had turned upside down. Their mama for the moment no longer the rock to which they could cling in security. Now that papa was gone and never coming back. Marr didn't rightly know how the two young'uns felt not having a pa now who would return from his labors at the end of the day. It had been some six months already that this cabin had been without that man. Another had come forward briefly to fill that shadow.

Marr suddenly felt every bit as sad for Seamus Donegan. Tough job—stepping in to fill another man's boots in the eyes of young'uns the likes of these. A family man himself, with two boys not come home from the war—Sam Marr tried the best he could to take some of the pain from them all.

Jennie stepped back from Marr, swiping the back of her callused hand at a drippy nose. "I'm sorry, Sam."

"No need apologizing, Jennie."

She glanced at the boys, then dragged a sleeve across one reddened eye. "Been doing far too much of this in front of them," she said, trying to laugh as she nodded at her sons.

"Good boys, they are," Marr soothed. "Time they learned their mama's not made of stone, Jennie."

She turned, wringing her hands in the threadbare apron hung in big folds at her waist. "Don't know what I'm made of lately." Jennie stepped to the fireplace, where she swung the trivet supporting the old coffeepot back over the flames. "I'll warm you something to drink, Sam. Nights are still a mite chilly."

Finding himself a stool, Marr settled like an old owl with a tired, rumpled wing. Uncomfortable, but with nowhere better to land.

He glanced at the blankets rolled and bound in straps beside the rumpled, leather cases by the door, then in turning back caught her staring at him. "Your brother . . . he coming back soon?"

She wagged her head, shoving the two-quart cast-iron kettle over the flames in the stone fireplace that glowed with life from well before dawn to well past dusk. Jennie Wheatley, Sam knew, had been a stranger to sleep these past months. He figured he alone at this post might know what the woman was going through, losing a wife himself years gone now. First the hours that would never pass. Then each day crawling from sun to night. But eventually the months marked their miraculous passage on the heart. A pain still there for those left behind, but having made a place for the unbearable loss and hurt, those still living went on with life.

Sam Marr had done what he could to help Jennie Wheatley survive here in the shadow of the Big Horns. Here in the shadow of her loss. Seamus Donegan would have done the same. But it was the army once again that tore man from woman, even when that man did not wear army blue.

In rising, Jennie wiped her coal-smeared hands on the ragged apron and went over to the boys. She pushed the long hair from their eyes and clutched them both against her belly.

"He spends his evenings up at the trader's," she said when she had pushed her sons off to a corner to play.

"In Kinney's place?"

She nodded. "I've given up being afraid John will drink up every bit of profit he made on the trip here."

Marr studied his boot toes a moment, hearing her thick-soled brogans scuff back across the rough plank floor to the fireplace. "And your brother's friend? None of that settled?"

"Webb Wood?"

Sam nodded. "Him."

She sighed. "Nothing settled, Sam. I was so sure I wouldn't marry him when John and Webb first come here. Then I got to thinking that Webb had been like family for most all my life, growing up down the road like he did. Like a brother. Then, come a time he didn't want to be a brother any longer. He wanted to marry me. And I had to tell him . . . no."

Jennie came halfway across the floor, the big ladle out in front of her like a stick an old woman would use to scare a bad dog away with, shaking it slightly. Almost menacingly.

"But, Sam—I got to thinking there . . . with Seamus gone and no word from him. Not even knowing if he really cared for me at all—got to figuring that Webb offered me one hell of a lot more than Seamus Donegan ever could."

He swallowed and cleared his throat, waiting for her to continue. "What . . . what can Webb Wood offer you that Seamus can't, Jennie?"

"He offers me *home,* Sam."

Marr watched something seize her there in the middle of the tiny cabin, seize and shake her almost invisibly. But enough to know she was fighting for control.

"*Home.* That's a mighty powerful thing, Jennie Wheatley. Do you . . . care for the man?"

"I always have, Sam."

"I see—"

"No, you don't," and she shook her head. "Cared for him like one cares for something . . . useful. Like a comfortable pair of mittens in the winter. Or woolen britches so worn and broke in that you don't even think about 'em anymore. Cared for him like that."

"I got an idea what you're saying." And Sam did know. "Man like Webb Wood offers a good woman like you what she deserves—what you got every right to deserve—a home and some security . . . a chance for these two boys here—why, that woman oughta well jump at the chance for that." He said it all in a spurt, like a spray of dancing water at the limestone spring back home in Missouri. Said and shet of it.

"You make it sound like Seamus Donegan hasn't a thing to offer me . . . offer the three of us," she replied after a moment of silent reflection, her arm sweeping at the two boys.

He smiled. "Seamus . . . well now—Seamus Donegan is a different sort, ain't he, Jennie? I suppose you and me know him about as good as any, that's for sure. So, there's no use my mincing words with you. You'd know better'n any what Seamus Donegan can offer you, Jennie."

She bent at the fireplace, busy over the soup kettle for a few minutes. When she finally pushed the rewarmed coffee back from the flames, Jennie turned and straightened wearily.

"Seamus Donegan can give me something I ain't ever had before, Sam. These boys' papa loved me . . . that's for sure. But," and she glanced quickly at them by their small prairie bed, studying her like wrens watched a thicket filled with wooly caterpillars. "I never did love their papa."

"So likely you'd never love Webb Wood."

She nodded eventually, a sob catching in her chest. "I figured—there for just a day or two—I'd found a man to love."

"Seamus?"

"Yes."

"You love him?"

She cocked her head, staring into a corner where a spider's web danced gently and golden-threaded in the lamplight. "I don't know that it is love yet, Sam. I know only that it's something a whole lot different than anything I've felt before. Makes me . . . scared. And at the same time, I'm mad at myself for being scared."

He waited a minute more. "I ain't ever made out to be the kind of man who knows everything, Jennie Wheatley. But one thing for sure, you got the sorriest, hangdog look about you I ever seen . . . that is, since I looked in the mirror when I was courting Abigail Hooper."

"Your wife?"

He nodded and sighed. "That was one woman who knew her mind, so it seemed. A lot like you, Jennie." He rose, turning to the pegs by the door where he took down his coat. As he slipped it over his arms, Sam Marr said, "You're falling in love, girl. And knowing the way Seamus Donegan said he felt for you when he was drove from this place, I think it fitting he should know how you feel about him. That Leighton fella's lighting out with his wagons for Fort Smith in the morning."

"I know," she replied, wagging her head. "Webb's going north for a few days to deliver some of my brother's supplies to the fort up yonder."

"Well, Leighton will be carrying a letter from me, Jennie—if'n I have your permission to tell Seamus what's in your heart right now. I won't do it, girl—less'n you say it's all right."

She took a step forward, then a second, and finally stared up into his tired eyes, her own brimming with moistness. Her full lips quivered.

"Tell him, Sam. Tell Seamus Donegan what I feel."

He stared down at his hands. The Irishman couldn't remember when they had hurt as much as they did right now. He had never fancied himself a soft man, his frame as strong and lean and sinewy as any man's on this frontier. Horses and wagons, harness and single-trees—and he knew of weapons as well. But this . . . this *farming*.

As he swiped the stinging, salty drops from his eyelids, Seamus Donegan had a renewed respect for the man who chose to wrench his living from the soil. Despite the destructive odds of weather and stubborn animals, despite the chance of losing it all to the Sioux.

But be a farmer he must. At least that was what he and the rest of the civilians hired out to A. C. Leighton laughingly called themselves two days ago when they first rode down here from Fort C.F. Smith to begin their hay-cutting. Eight of them joking and full of themselves, ready for an end to the boredom that had been life at the post for too long. Eight men hired by Leighton to supply the fort with hay for stock. And while they would wait for the first cutting to dry, Leighton would have some of his hands at work building his ferry across the Bighorn River.

The man had one idea after another to make money, Seamus figured. But right now, Donegan stared down at his hands. The tall grass nudged insistently against his cavalry britches the way a cat would rub up against his leg. Purring in the breeze as he stared down at the two bleeding palms. Calluses torn and tender. Angrily he grabbed a bandanna from a pocket and ripped it roughly in half. With the ragged pieces he bound his palms, yanking knots in the faded blue cloth with his teeth.

"C'mon, Seamus!"

He looked up, seeing Finn Burnett waving to him from the mule-drawn mower ahead.

"Slow down you bleeming son of a bitch!" Seamus hollered back. "You and Leighton trying to turn a fighting man into a farmer in three days, damn you! Gimme time to heal!"

Burnett rared his head back, laughing. Donegan laughed with him and the others across the field who held their bleeding hands up as well. It was good to laugh in this cool, fragrant meadow. The muscles of your back taut and resisting the new work, the sun creeping beneath the brim of your hat to dry the thick droplets pouring from your flesh. And the taste of cool, sweet water from Warrior Creek, dipper by dipper poured down your throat from the five-gallon keg lashed on the side of Leighton's wagon where it waited for them, wrapped in burlap soaked to keep it every bit as cool as when that sweet water had been pulled from the dancing creek.

Near the beginning of the fourth week in June, Leighton had arrived after tarrying but two days at Fort Phil Kearny to off-load supplies on lading for Judge Jefferson T. Kinney. It did not take long for Donegan to present himself to the sutler who had been awarded the hay-cutting contract, offering his services.

A little traveling money, Seamus had figured. Some money to replace his depleted funds that had seen him through the winter. Army script earned at Fort Phil Kearny and augmented with what he won at the lamplit gambling tables at Fort C.F. Smith. If a man were to travel on to the goldfields of Alder Gulch, he would need him some money.

But once he had read Sam Marr's hen-scratch note, Seamus Donegan realized he would need money before starting out to claim the woman who Sam Marr said had strong feelings for the Irishman.

I can't say come now, Seamus. But you will mind the days, you follow my advice. The woman is pulled by her brother back to home in the weeks ahead, as soon as he finishes his work here with the Judge. Three weeks at the most, Morrison tells me. That's all the time you got to get here and tell her how you feel yourself, Seamus. Three weeks before she's gone for good.

I tried my best to talk her out of going. To wait. But she needs you to tell her. I ain't sure what you said to her before you left Kearny. But it's time you come back— and damn the army! Time you come back and tell her yourself that you want her.

If you don't choose to buck the army this soon again, and you think it best not to come back right now—better you write her. Whatever way it is, Seamus Donegan better tell that gal how he feels. And quick. Her brother's about to take her back home in three weeks. And that Wood fella is planning to make her his wife when they get to Ohio again.

I never gave you advice before. Not on horses. And surely not on women. But you think long and hard on this. And tell this woman so if you want her. If Jennie Wheatley is to stay behind when her brother goes back to the only home this poor woman's ever knowed, you best tell her to wait for you.

Sam Marr

With his sore fingertips, Seamus once more touched that letter nestled inside his damp shirt pocket. He glanced again to the hills surrounding the southern end of this valley. Gone down the Montana Road two days now that Crow mailman called Iron Bull was riding by night now. Hiding by day. Carrying letters and dispatches to Fort Phil Kearny.

Iron Bull also carried an important note in Seamus Donegan's hand. Each letter and word formed carefully. As thoughtfully as each sentence was planned in advance. To tell Jennie his feelings so long held mute.

"You working any more today, Seamus?" Zeke Colvin hollered out, his giant fork spearing more of the tall grass cut by the mule-drawn mower.

Seamus blinked the sweat from his eyes. "I'm working, Zeke. By the saints, I'm working."

So he bent himself over his pitchfork, his mighty shoulders heaving load after load of the grass into monstrous piles. While his heart worked every bit as hard at struggling with the loneliness.

Four nights back he had left Eyes Talking's lodge in the Crow camp not far away. Telling her he would be staying now in the hay-cutters' corral in the meadow far from the fort walls. That had been hard enough, trying not to lie, struggling not to tell her he would not be coming back when Leighton was done with the cutting.

To tear himself from one, a mere girl who had given herself so freely to him while he healed of the hurt of many years. But reluctantly admitting their lives had come down such different paths. Different people, they were. She so gentle. Understanding as he told her of the hay-cutting, her eyes moisting yet refusing to let him see more of her pain in letting the big Irishman go.

And now he was hopeful once more of finding what he needed most with the widow. Before she returned East, back to the place where she and the boys would be safe. Where life would be one hell of a lot easier. Before she went back home where she should be, Seamus Donegan wanted Jennie Wheatley to read his letter.

Chapter 19

"*G*awddamned heathen sonsabitches," he growled, throwing the bone he had been gnawing on at a camp dog, more wild than tame.

Bob North rared back in laughter, hands balled on his hips, watching the animal scamper off, its tail tucked between its legs, the dog glancing wide-eyed over a shoulder as the white renegade barked back at it. North laughed all the louder.

Sonsabitches even think the clap and swamp-cholera and smallpox that the tribes're catching come from the magic the white man's practicing on 'em to steal their lands.

Let 'em be afeared of the white man's magic some more, North thought to himself as he gazed over the ragged Arapaho camp he had called home for many months. *Keeps 'em in line for me, by Gawd!*

Another dog raced up, attempting to nip at his heels. North kicked viciously at it, connecting with the ribs, sending the animal off yelping like a greasy cog.

"Araps no better a'times than their beggar dawgs!"

With the back of a hand he swiped the grease from his lips. Gnawing on bones had become a favorite pastime with him. Convincing himself that by doing so nowadays he grew every bit as rangy and mean as the half-wild wolf dogs that called the Arapaho camp home. Around the Confederate renegade hung the odors of stale meat, old hides, and cheap whiskey. That, and tobacco, when it could be had at the posts.

"Possum up a gum stump,
    Coony in a holler.
Wake, snake, june-bug
    Stole a half-a-dollar."

He sang half under his breath as he sank in the shade of a buffalo-hide lodge. The place where he had mended for many long months from the bullet wound suffered back in the first week of December. By North's reckoning, it must now be July. *Moon of Black Cherries* to the tribes of the northern plains.

Whiskey. His mind burned with the word and the want of it. As much as his tongue hungered for its raw, red-pepper, gut-kicking taste.

Funny, ain't it? Them white soldiers think Red Cloud's Sioux and the rest getting help from half-breed traders come down from Hudson's Bay posts. Shit! That's a cork!

He scratched his back up and down against a lodgepole in the warmth of the morning sun, the way a boar grizzly rubbed himself on a blue spruce.

"Ho, for the maids of Kenanville,
A song for Carolina fair!
We'll sing a stanza of good will
To beaming eyes and flowing hair.
To rosy cheeks and teeth of pearl.
So drink, each one—to our fair girl."

He liked singing. It brought the children round, and with it their mothers and big sisters. He liked that the best. The women. Better yet to smell their rancid bear grease and rotten breath as he rutted with them in the dark robes or tangled with a squaw back in the bushes in the broad of day's light. Wherever he could get his hands on a halfway willing one.

A small group of children was gathering to listen to the strange renegade leader sing his songs in the summer sun beside the lodge he called home.

"And now I'm going southward,
For my heart is full of woe,

I'm going back to Georgia,
And find my Uncle Joe."

North figured it would not be long until he just might command more than this measly bunch of rag-tag Arapaho. What with Man-Afraid staying in the south now, and many of Red Cloud's bands torn apart by arguments over how best to pursue their war on the soldier forts . . . Bob North figured the time might soon come for a man of his talents to wrest control of things from Red Cloud himself.

This summer's war don't go the way that thieving bastard Red Cloud hisself guarantees the Sioux that it will . . . why, ol' Bob North be there to step in and pick up the pieces of this dirty little fight to drive the soldiers out.

He grabbed a swaying, fat-bellied youngster and placed the child on his knee, signaling to the child's older sister with that devilish twinkle of lust in his eye, patting the ground beside him as he raised his voice in song again.

"You may sing about your dearest maid,
And sing of Rosalee.
But the gallant Hood of Texas
Raised hell in Tennessee!"

Ever since that rainy, December day last, North had been sending his Arapaho wards to the farflung posts. More and more often now. Trading for whiskey mostly. A little tobacco a'times. Perhaps some powder and lead. But mostly whiskey. Bob North needed the whiskey.

To control the fire in the wound at his side. To stoke the flames of his hatred for the man who shot him. And with every drink, a swamp-water part of North's soul vowed that he would one day wear the scalp of that man. One day.

He turned, hearing the hoofbeats. A handful of young Arapaho warriors reined their grass-fed ponies to a halt near him. They dropped to the ground, scattering the children as they tethered their ponies to the stakes of the lodge where he sat reclining in the sun, stroking the hair of the adolescent he often caught in the willows by the creek.

North recognized his band of cutthroats, warriors who

thirsted for whiskey almost as much as he himself. Returned from a ride to the trading post at Fort Peck.

The renegade clambered to his feet, unsteadily, an arm clutched at his side against the burn of the healing wound that only recently had allowed him to ride a little more each day, growing accustomed to the throb of horseback once more.

Seeing the crooked smile on the Arapaho leader's face, North nearly lurched toward Sings The Moon, the eldest of the bunch, his eyes wild with anticipation.

"You bring more whiskey?" he growled in Arapaho at the young warrior, his teeth the color of lodgepole pine-wood chips.

Sings The Moon turned his face from the stench of North's breath. When he stared back at the black-whiskered face, he stared silently into the bleak and passionless eyes of this white murderer, eyes every bit as cold as chips from the speckled-blue tin plates he had seen many times in the trader's rooms at the posts from Laramie to Peck. Cold, and more lifeless everyday.

"No whiskey for us, North," he replied, using the renegade's English name at the end of his short string of Arapaho.

"No whiskey!"

He wagged his head.

Behind Sings The Moon, North watched some of the others kick at the ground nervously, their eyes narrowing on their renegade leader.

"We did not go to Peck," Sings The Moon explained. "Got only as far as Red Cloud's camps on the Powder."

"Why'd you stop at that bloody thief's camp?" he roared.

"To eat their meat," he answered. "And learn of the soldiers' forts."

North rared back again, laughing. And as suddenly as a cat could turn on a pouch of catnip, the renegade grabbed the antelope vest Sings The Moon wore. He brought his nose within an inch of the ugly Arapaho's.

"You were gone many, many days . . . and only went as far as Red Cloud's camp of Bad Faces?"

Sings The Moon brought his hands up swiftly, breaking the renegade's grip on him at the same time he took a step backward, a fist wrapping round the knife at his waist.

North saw the gesture. His eyes narrowed. Then his burning, fevered mind began to chew on it the way he chewed on
the shag-leaf burley plugs brought him from Peck and Laramie by the Arapaho. His taut face loosened, and he laughed
again maniacally.

"Stop the fun now," he said with a grin. "Tell me what kept
you so long if you did not go to Peck."

Sings The Moon stepped halfway across the chasm. "We
were told many interesting things in the camp of the Bad Face
Oglallas."

"Like what?"

"We hear talk of the Sioux and Cheyenne planning a big
fight on the forts."

"What forts?" he barked, eyes narrowed and cold once
more.

"The fort by the Piney Woods . . . and the dirt fort in the
north."

"Forget that one," North growled. "Tell me about the fort
at the Piney Woods."

Sings The Moon shook his head, grinning crookedly. "No.
It is the dirt fort you will want to hear of."

North's nostrils flared, impatient. He gazed at the warrior's
hand on the knife at his waist. "It's the Piney Fort I'm interested in, you savage! There's someone there I want to . . . to
see again one day soon."

The Arapaho's crooked grin grew into a gap-toothed gaping smile. Two upper teeth at the side of his grin had been
knocked out back in the *Moon of Deer Shedding Horns,* when
the tribes had surrounded the soldiers and killed them all.
Sings The Moon lost two teeth to the last soldier standing that
cold winter day. The soldier who fought swinging only his tin
horn at his attackers.

"He is there."

North lunged forward again. "Who is, gawddammit!"

Sings The Moon slowly wiped the spittle from his face
where the renegade had sprayed him with his question. "The
one you seek."

"At the gawddamned dirt fort?" North's voice rose two
pitches, his heart pounding as it hadn't through many months
of healing.

The warrior nodded.

North squinted one eye, doubtful. "How you so sure? By taking the word of them Sioux again?"

This time Sings The Moon shook his head. "We were long in returning here with the news." His arm swept over his little band of riders. "We went to see for ourselves. So we could bring you the news you want to hear."

North grabbed the antelope vest again. But this time the Arapaho warrior let the renegade cling to him, as surely as a man would cling to desperate hope.

"You saw him . . . the *big* one? That . . . *tall* one?"

He nodded, his smile widening into a wolf-slash that exposed more of his brown teeth. "Yes. The tall one."

"Where? At the fort?"

"No. It is better. He cuts grass with others. Sleeps in the white-man camp near War-Man Creek."

"How many of 'em?"

"Less than ten hands . . . soldiers and grass-cutters together."

"In a camp away from the fort, you say?" North asked, releasing his grip on the warrior, smoothing the vest, and grinning.

"Yes. Far enough away from the dirt fort that the soldiers there cannot see the grass-cutters' camp."

North smiled, squinting one of those speckled-blue eyes at Sings The Moon. "It is good you did this for me. I want whiskey badly. But I need to know this news even more. It is good you bring me word, my friend. Come now. Bring your friends over here. We sit and talk now. Talk about riding west to this dirt fort the soldiers call their Bighorn post."

Sings The Moon waved the others to follow him and the renegade among the lodges, dogs barking at their heels, jumping in the air as if they sensed some excitement in the beginning of the hunt. Then he looked squarely at the renegade.

"Yes, white man. We go for the one you seek, don't we?"

"He is mine!" North snarled. "The rest—soldiers and all the rest . . . they are yours. That big, black-headed one . . . he belongs to me."

The renegade turned slightly, facing west. "One day real

soon now, I'll catch that slab-sided sonabitch . . . and make hog-paste outta him. He's mine now. He's all mine."

"You're the laziest goddamned drunk I ever knowed!" contractor Pitman Judd growled at teamster Silas Heeley, who ambled slowly toward his lead wagon. "I had my way, I'd see that Captain Dandy let you go—put you afoot and on your own out there with Red Cloud and those red bastards of his!"

"Shit, Judd," Heeley replied, stopping at the front wheel of his wagon and flashing his crew boss a rotten-toothed smile, "you had your way—you'd hand me over to Red Cloud your own self!"

"Damn straight I would! Now get your good-for-nothing Confederate ass in that wagon and haul this timber back to the goddamn fort. Best you earn your pay today, boy—or I'll have your ass to fry tonight."

"Why, boss—I thankee for all your lovin' concern!" Silas cheered. "I'll give quartermaster Dandy your most cordial greetin's."

"Just haul the lumber, Heeley. What you was hired to do." Judd slapped the lead mule on its rump, watching his hired man Heeley slap the reins down across the backs of the whole team. Heeley rumbled off singing.

"Fare thee well! Fare thee well! Fare thee well, my cap-ee-tan!"

Silas Heeley liked his job. All he was called on to do was drive this timber wagon from the fort, past the rolling Sullivant Hills on the wood road, down to the dense woods on Pine Island that lay in the middle of Big Piney Creek. Every day. After his wagon had been loaded with timber chopped by the cutting crews and dragged down to the road by mules in log-harness, Heeley hauled the timber back to the Little Piney Creek just below the fort's water-gate, where Carrington's soldiers had erected their horse-powered sawmill last summer upon arriving here at the foot of the Big Horns. A clumsy, tedious contraption that was—more apt to break down than to work—until army engineer J. B. Gregory had arrived with his steam-powered sawmill and promptly planted it in the middle of the narrow creek, just beyond the stockade gates.

"Fare thee well!" Silas roared off-key, enjoying that early

morning breeze rising out of the valley on its way into the canyons of the Big Horns. Midsummer already, and he wondered if he should have pushed on up the Montana Road when spring broke winter's hold upon the land. Sure, he might be making more money in the Montana diggings. But then again, chances be he might not have much hair left either.

Better to lay out another winter here, Silas Heeley had decided last month. Just like he had decided last summer when he and a few others had straggled up the road from Fort Reno and run onto Carrington's post like an act of divine intervention. Silas Heeley had come to meet Captain Frederick Brown, who proved anxious to hire some civilian drivers for his wood crews. Then Brown galloped over Lodge Trail Ridge with his friend Fetterman and the rest last December.

And got hisself killed for it, Silas brooded. The image of Brown's naked, mutilated body would stay with Heeley until the day he died. Especially the memory of that Sioux lance rammed up through the quartermaster's ass, blood-frozen point protruding from his chest. He shuddered, shaking himself free of that image like a dog shedding water.

"To hell with Pitman Judd! And every slave-driving mother's son like him!" he hollered over his shoulder at the crew boss left standing behind him in the middle of the road. Only four easy miles to go—through the Big Piney Creek bottoms and up along the Sullivant Hills, then down into the bottoms of the Little Piney at last. He knew every rut and rock in the road.

"So do these damn mules," he grumbled, his eyes already heavy.

First run of the day, and here he was dozing off already. "Well, a lil' sleep's quite all right, Silas Heeley. Sun's warm on your face. Rightly put a man to dozing, it will. 'Sides, these mules know their own way back to that sawmill by the fort." He yawned. "Dumbest mule still smarter'n that Pitman Judd . . ."

From one side of the wood road to the other Heeley's wagon rocked in the well-worn ruts a year in the making, swaying him gently from one rut to the other. Like a pineboard cradle, the timber wagon lulled him to sleep. Sleep-caressed by dreams of those Montana mountain streams glittering with nuggets big enough for a pillow. And those Montana whores he had heard tell of who would help Silas Heeley spend all his gold.

Why, yes indeedee! Come next year he'd head for Alder Gulch up by Virginia City. Work every night lapping up traders' whiskey, and wake each morning beside some new toilet-watered chippie. Her huge white breasts suspended over him as she nudged him awake. Shouting at him to get out of bed. Finally, to wake Silas Heeley up, that big-hipped whore would loudly slap the side of the bed with her tin commode.

CRACK!

Awaking with a start, Silas glanced down at his feet, eyes blinking in the bright sunlight.

By God—a arrow! Another whistled past. A third thwacked into the seat beside him.

Great ghost of the saints!

Heeley's eyes shot up the southern slope of the Sullivant Hills. Like boulders tumbling down upon him in a red avalanche, the warriors charged dead on a collision course for his wagon. Scrunching his head into his shoulders like a turtle drawing into its shell, Silas glanced back downtrail to find the other drivers frantically slapping reins against their mules, hurrying not to be the last to the fort. On the wagon's running-gear behind him the logs shifted with a boom like rolling thunder. Up front, the mules strained at the shifting load, their tall ears pricked at the wild warrior shrieks coupled with the clear panic in Silas Heeley's own screech.

With his next ragged breath Silas decided he would never make it to the fort hauling the logs.

No time to dump 'em neither! 'Sides, it ain't the logs they want. They want these goddamned mules!

"Ho! Ho, there! You blessed mean-hearted sonsabitches!"

Silas Heeley pulled back on the reins, standing tall in the footwell against the brake, putting everything he had into getting his wagon stopped. Even before it had rumbled to a complete halt, Silas was on his feet among the mules. His knife sang through the leather harness on the first, followed by a slap on the rump to send the animal lumbering up the slope.

A second and a third he sent on their way. Diversion for the oncoming warriors.

Silas pulled himself atop the last raw-boned animal, grasping frantically to shreds of butchered harness as his heels pummeled the mule into action. Round the hill he bounced, hearing ragged gunfire from the soldiers assigned to escort the wood train. Silas Heeley wanted no part of such doings.

Hard enough for a man to make a living till he gets to the Montana diggings . . . what with getting caught in this gawd-damned Sioux war these Yankee soldiers wanna fight so blamed bad.

He kicked the lean flanks below him more insistently. Praying he could just get his ass on down the road toward the sawmill and the fort, where a simple man could find safety.

Chapter 20

"Relieve the pressure on the wood train and escort it back to the fort!" Tenedore Ten Eyck excitedly sputtered his orders to the young lieutenant who had swung into saddle. Another wood train jumped by the Sioux.

The lieutenant was fearful this attack bode no good, though it brought him a chance to shine before his superiors.

John C. Jenness saluted. "Yessir, Captain!" In that instant he noticed how Ten Eyck's one good eye twitched nervously. "Follow me!" Jenness shouted to the twenty-eight mounted infantry troopers who had been closest to the saddled horses when the sentry's alarm rang across the parade.

Pickets had alerted Ten Eyck that gunfire had been heard down along the Sullivant Hills. The wood train must be under attack, they told him. Still a bit shaky from last night's bout with his private bottle of painkilling consolation, the captain screamed for the first soldier he could lay hands on to lead the rescue.

Lieutenant Jenness felt rightfully proud he had been at Ten Eyck's side when the alarm came in.

After all, this is the way the army is supposed to be, John thought as he galloped down the plateau onto the wood road, racing west toward the southern brow of the hills, where he could plainly hear the rattle of gunfire. Dull echoes booming down in the valley of the Little Piney.

This is the way I was meant to serve all along. Riding at the head of some mounted soldiers . . . throwing our might against the cream of the Sioux nation. By Jove! This is your chance to shine, John Jenness!

Only a youngster when Confederate forces had fired on Fort Sumter, John Jenness had ached to join up when President Lincoln issued his call for ninety-day volunteers. Older boys had marched off to battle and glory. Those three months of service had stretched into three bloody years of war before John could lawfully volunteer his service in the Union cause. After but a few months of savage fighting under Jenness's belt, General Lee and his Army of Northern Virginia had been bottled up in the Appomattox Wood, forced to turn over a dirty hand towel to George Armstrong Custer's Union cavalry in surrender.

With the war finally over, Henry B. Carrington's 18th Infantry was reassigned to old Fort Kearney along the Platte River in Nebraska Territory, where they would relieve volunteers who had attempted to keep a lid on Indian problems on the plains during the war back East. Ideal duty for a young soldier who had yet to see enough fighting to fill his craw. Just about perfect for the newly commissioned Lieutenant Jenness —as he spotted the first of the mounted warriors atop a low ridge ahead.

The Indian whirled round and round, holding a lance over his head from which fluttered feathers and long streamers of multicolored trade cloth and calicoes.

He's signaling the rest of 'em, Jenness's mind burned.

He threw his hand up about the time the loose mules clattered round the bend in the wood road.

"You!" He pointed at a private, "Take two men with you and catch those mules!" He watched the trio rein away, down the hard, crumbling slope into the bottom of the Little Piney.

Jenness was little prepared for what he saw when he turned back around, loud screeches ringing his ears.

A handful of naked warriors swept over the knoll above them, hot in pursuit of the wood train's mules themselves. Surprised to bump into the troopers, they hauled back on their ponies, every bit as startled as the young soldiers who reined up as well, jostling one another, grabbing for their long Springfield rifles.

Jenness tried raising his Long-Tom rifle as he watched the

warriors lift bows when they had their swift, skinny ponies under control. He'd never fired the big rifle from horseback.

Hell, he thought as he clattered to the ground, *these long infantry guns never were meant to be used atop a horse.*

Jenness ripped the hammer back as he slid the barrel over the saddle, the fingers of his left hand inching up the wedding bands. Down the muzzle, one young warrior flung both arms wide, singing out his defiance, while the other five wheeled in retreat toward the crest in dusty confusion. All the time Jenness needed.

Through a puff of oily muzzle-smoke the lieutenant watched the warrior tumble into the dust and sage—then felt the ground yanked out from under him as he got knocked aside himself. His skittish mount hadn't taken at all to standing so close to the roar of that flaming muzzle. A quick-thinking soldier grabbed the bridle and brought the horse to a halt. Jenness picked himself and the rifle out of the dust of the wood road, then clambered back into the saddle.

"There's more of 'em!" Jenness cried out. Some of his detail nodded nervously, their horses prancing, snorting. "Enough for all of us!" He waved and led out, only then realizing he had not reloaded his rifle.

Forgot like some damned green recruit, he cursed himself.

His first action against Indians, and he forgot to reload the big Long Tom. Around the brow of the hill the valley closed in a mite. One fork of the road led off round a low hill toward the southern end of the Pine Island in Big Piney Creek. From the sounds of it, the shooting and shouting came from down along the right fork.

It was there at the western end of the Sullivant Hills that the Sioux held the wood train captive. While they kept the drivers and the military escort pinned down in the dust of the road, the Indians rode back and forth along the slope, in control of the high ground where they could fire their arrows almost at will. When any soldier stood to aim at a warrior, he made himself a dandy target for another warrior somewhere down the slope. With a fierce knot of determination in his gut, Jenness realized that the drivers and soldiers had gotten themselves pinned down with little chance of breaking free.

Up to his right along the slope raced the five warriors who

had bumped into Jenness's relief column back along the road. Spotting the lieutenant's troopers again, the five shouted and waved their weapons, signaling the others for help. Like a covey of quail swooping as one through the dry grass, the Sioux turned from the wood train. Intent on Lt. John C. Jenness and his twenty mounted troopers.

"Skirmish formation!" Jenness shouted, wheeling his horse about sharply. Few of the soldiers knew what he had asked of them. Most did not. There was little time to explain. "By fours—horse-holders to the rear!"

Clumsily, the soldiers dropped to the road, sorting out who would be the fourth man of each group assigned to take all four horses to the rear while the other three troopers dropped to their bellies or knees, spaced some three yards apart. Most got their rifles cocked and aimed just as the warriors rolled down the slope in a wild assault, intent upon counting coup on these soldiers who stood in the open with nothing to hide behind, waiting to die. Like a wave of water, they had rolled from their attack on the wagons toward Jenness's command, freeing the drivers and their escort to train their rifles on Indian backs.

Blossoms of gray smoke bent into the air over Jenness's command, followed by the dull boom of the big Springfields. One warrior clutched his side, reeling atop his sidestepping pony. With a thin, reedy screech he fell to the dusty grass beside the road, unable to stay on his pony any longer.

As the soldiers around him began to fire, Jenness pulled his service revolver free, his finger quickly finding that all six caps were snugly in place. In stunned and envious amazement he watched two young Sioux bravely wheel their ponies through the maze of bullets and scrambling warriors, both hanging off the side of their animals as they swept past their wounded comrade, dragging him from the field, over the knoll in retreat.

With a shrill cry, another warrior waved a long lance decorated with black tendrils of human hair over his head. As abruptly as it had begun, the attack was over. The small ponies swept over the hills like a spring thunderstorm disappearing across the prairie after it had pummeled you with **everything it had.**

Jenness stood, trembling. The last of the escort fired their weapons at the retreating warriors until there were no targets left but clumps of bunch grass and sage along the crest of the hill. In his sweaty hand the revolver grew heavy. Heavier than he had ever believed it could get. He stuffed the weapon into the mule-ear holster, snapping the ear down. It hung at his waist like an anvil.

For the first time in the last twenty minutes, Lieutenant Jenness recognized his own breathing and heartbeat. Snorting like the chugging steam locomotives that whistled past his rural Ohio home. Heart galloping like the hoofbeats of his horse along the sun-baked wood road racing to engage the Sioux horsemen. Then his belly reminded him of what he had just come through.

All about him the other men cheered or slapped each other on their backs self-consciously. Congratulating themselves. And their leader.

"By damned, you dropped one, Lieutenant!" An older, longtime private clamped him on the shoulder. "Gotcha his scalp, son!"

Smiling weakly, Jenness nodded. "One killed," he gulped. "One wounded."

"Not a bad day's work on these naked bastards, is it, sir?"

"It . . ." He tried to explain the feeling to the old veteran before him, to say it with his eyes, but he figured the other man wouldn't understand. "Not like the Confederates. Stand and fight. On our front. Soldier against . . . soldier."

"You're right, Lieutenant," the private answered, suddenly subdued. "The goddamn Rebel graybacks never fighted us this a'way. 'Tween you and me, son—this lil' fracas was downright terrifying. You got every right to be scared."

Jenness sighed, his pulse slowing. "Scared? I'll tell you what's scary, Private—my gut tells me this was only the beginning for me. And it's only gonna get more scary from here on out."

"Them's the guns beat the grand ol' Confederacy."

Sam Marr turned at the sound of the Carolina drawl, watching the wiry rail-thin twig of a man step forward, his thinning hair stuck out in wild, greasy sprigs when he removed his hat to run a dirty hand across his brow.

"S'pose they are," Marr replied. He glanced at the long wooden boxes stacked near the front wall of quartermaster Obadiah Dandy's storehouse. Then he eyed the other man closely. "Hear tell your name's Heeley."

Silas Heeley regarded the gray-headed, long-haired Missourian with a bit of hill-folk caution. "I am. From the sounds of your talk, you hail from the South as well."

Marr chuckled lightly. "Missouri. About as far south as any man got and still fought for the Union."

He watched that bring Heeley up short, the marblelike eyes narrowing. Then the Missourian stuck out his hand to the other.

"Sam Marr, late of the sovereign state of Missouri, our Union reunited. Pleased to make your acquaintance . . . Mister . . . ?"

Heeley stared down at the offered hand for the longest time. "Heeley. Silas Heeley's the name." He finally grasped Marr's in his. "Gawddamned . . . but I'm shaking more Yankees' hands since I come west than I shaked in my whole life!"

Sam chuckled again, nodding at the nearby stacks of wooden crates. "How you know so much 'bout Yankee weapons?"

Heeley smiled, swelling up a bit with himself. "Quartermaster—Lee's Army of Northern Virginia. The Yankees always throwed their best at us. We was always first to get hit with it. Ever' now and then we got us a look at just what they was throwing at us. Like them Springfield rifles of your'n. Repeaters made near the end of the war."

Marr grinned, nodding. "You know your stuff, Heeley." He watched the southerner nod with his own importance. "You working for Porter?"

"Gilmore's right-hand man hired me. Judd's his name."

"Same outfit. They got me running herd duty, on 'count of I know horses."

"Hauling wood up from the woodcutters' camp."

"Was you in that bunch hit the other day, Heeley?"

He smiled, like he had found a sudden claim to some fleeting fame. "Not only in that bunch the Sioux hit the t'other day—I was lead wagon!"

"Don't say?"

He nodded, lips pursed, then spit a long, thin stream of brown juice into the gravel of the Fort Phil Kearny parade. "I do. First time I see'd scalping Injuns up that close. Never wanna get that close again."

Marr laughed easily along with Heeley while the new District Commander, Col. Jonathan Smith, joined Captain Dandy and Captain Ten Eyck in positioning a wobbly table near the stacks of rifle crates, at that moment under the watchful eyes of a covey of guards. Dandy seated himself at the dusty table, a sheaf of papers beneath his pistol paperweight, and without ceremony called forward the first company from formation on the parade. Behind the quartermaster a half-dozen enlisted men who had been cracking off the tops of the rifle crates with iron pry bars pulled the spanking new Springfield repeaters from their nest in the shipping straw.

Marr smelled the familiar gun-oil smeared liberally on the rifles and the soap-oil lathered into the shoulder-straps as each of Dandy's workers hefted two rifles apiece to the table. The quartermaster issued each soldier a new weapon, checking his name off on a muster roll.

Some twenty feet away, a soldier backed out of the plank door of the storehouse, lugging one end of a long box. At the other end hung another trooper. They set the first of the crates assigned to Fort C.F. Smith into the back of a wagon bound for the northern post come morning. When the first wagon had been filled by a steady procession of soldiers struggling under the weight of the wooden boxes, a second freighter was brought up to the doorway. Muted grunts and moans of labor on the periphery of Captain Dandy's issuance of new arms to the garrison at Fort Phil Kearny.

"Hear t'other post's getting a new commander as well as these'r rifles," Heeley whispered loudly at Marr's side as he snapped the blade back into his folding knife. He stuffed the quid of burley he had cut into the side of his cheek.

Marr nodded, smelling the sweetish odor of the shag-leaf tobacco the Carolinian chewed. Black as molasses and as potent as mule dung.

"Bradley. Lieutenant Colonel. Same rank as Wessells. And believe me, I think that fella Wessells is about fit to be tied . . . not getting neither one of these new assignments. The brass back East relieved Carrington and brought Wessells up to watch over things till they could assign Colonel Smith to command."

Marr clucked, as if he could almost sense the disappointment and bitterness of another man. "And then to top it all off, when Kinney retires his command up at Smith, they appoint another goddamned lieutenant colonel to that spot—not Wessells."

"Yankees got a handsome way of screwing each other, so't seems."

Marr studied Heeley from the side a moment. "Shame is, lotta fighting going on for what few commands there are these days. What with the war being over. Most of the Union officers forced to take a drop in rank and cut in pay to boot. Ain't no love lost in this man's army now."

Heeley looked the older man up, then down again. "That why you didn't stay in?"

"That," he answered, "and other things. Plan on going north to Alder Gulch."

"When you going, Marr?" Heeley asked excitedly. "I been heading that way myself. Run outta money back to Laramie, so I hired on to work for Gilmore when he was freighting up here. You take me with you, I'll make it worth your while we get to Virginia City."

Marr studied the thin man. "Don't get your britches warm, Silas Heeley. I ain't going for some time. Got a summer of work yet. Way I got it figured, I can work the summer through for J. R. Porter minding his woodcutting herd. Still have me plenty of time to get on to Alder Gulch before winter settles down hard on this land."

"You going this fall?"

He wagged his head. "Ain't made up my mind yet. Damn thing of it—I'm waiting for two other folks to make up my mind for me."

Sam Marr gazed over the top of Heeley's head, watching a third wagon pull away from the quartermaster's door with a load of rifles. He asked Silas absently, "You hear when

Bradley's heading north with his rifles . . . to take over command at Smith?"

Heeley shook his head. "Don't hear much of any use, 'cept in the sutler's. And I ain't had money to go into the sutler's for couple days now."

"Thought you might know, s'all."

"I'd bet Bradley's going north to the morning, how's'ever."

"Imagine you're right, Silas Heeley. His wagons loading today. He'll leave first light in the morning for Smith." Marr clamped a thick hand on the thin man's shoulder. "I gotta go now. Figure I got someone to see, and a letter to write."

"You write?"

"I do."

"You write me a letter home sometime?"

He smiled, "My pleasure, Silas Heeley. But right now—I got a letter what's needed up to Fort C.F. Smith."

"You got friends up at Smith?"

"Far as I know . . . I still got a friend up there. I ain't heard from him in months. Far as I know, he's still alive. What with a woman waiting on him. But with no word a'tall from him—the man might'a gone under."

"Injuns?"

"Can't be as thick there as they are here, Silas. Likely as not, this fella gone under to a poker player with no sense of humor."

"Your friend fancy at dealing cards?"

"Just . . . lucky, you might say. So, I gotta find out if my friend's luck has run out or not."

Chapter 21

The mosquitoes rose with the falling of the sun in this country of the Piney creeks. Like the cooling winds come to succor the day, the buzzing torment came to trouble man and beast alike.

He slapped at his cheek, feeling the smear of blood above his gray whiskers. "Can't say I blame you, Jennie." Sam Marr said it without conviction.

He sat with her on the rawhide stools before her front door while the two boys played in the twilight, a musty splash of yellow spread on the ground from the coal-oil lamp hung on a peg overhead, beside the doorframe.

"Johnny's going soon." As if it needed repeating.

"I know," and he nodded, watching the boys gallop and cavort with their play horses and stick figures in the dust and grass worn thin and sunburnt yellow in the yard. "Time's coming he's been wanting to take you back to Ohio with him."

"Leaving soon as Webb gets back from up north." She sighed, wringing her hands in the rumpled folds of her patched dress.

He stared at the hands a moment, once soft and the color of the pale cream they skimmed from the butter churns. Hands now grown hard and calloused over years of homesteading on the Nebraska prairie. Birthing two boys, washing clothes in lye soap, plucking chicken and shucking corn. On and on, that lot of the woman who followed her husband onto the

plains. Hands familiar to Sam Marr. His own dear Abigail
followed him to Missouri to bear their children, raise a family
and stand beside him through it all, decades ago.

Might as well been a lifetime ago now, for the way he felt.

"You give thought to marrying that Wood fella, then, Jennie?"

Her eyes came to his, hurt and moist in the yellow light.
They implored him more than her words ever would now,
Sam figured.

*She's steeled herself for what must be. She'll never own up to
what's killing her inside—one husband dead and seven months
gone. Another man she put her trust in what ain't come back
for her when she needs him . . . that goddamned Seamus
Donegan ain't even writ her from that blamed Fort Smith.*

Her eyes eventually fell to her own roughened hands once
more, fingers rumpling the soft folds of the worn prairie dress.
Then she stared at the boys a moment before finding words.

"I ain't decided on marrying Webb Wood, Sam." And there
was something strong in the way she told him.

He felt a small flicker of something live clutch in his chest,
like a small moth, fluttering around inside him.

"Not him . . . nor Seamus Donegan as well. Assuming
he'd ever wanna ask me. Which he ain't . . . and not likely
to."

"Might'n be trouble up to Smith, Jennie." He turned toward her some as he spoke the words. "Some reason we ain't
heard from him."

Her chin eventually jutted forward. Strong along the jaw-
line. And he was reminded once more of a younger Abigail
Hooper.

"Ain't Seamus Donegan's fault in any of this," she went on,
braver with the saying of it. "Jennie Wheatley's got to go on
and do what's right for her and her boys, Sam. Get them
outta here—like my brother says. Take 'em back East where
they can be schooled right. Better'n their papa was. Have 'em
a chance at something."

He nodded, thinking of his own two boys. Buried somewhere in nameless, shallow graves in the South. On some
nameless, overgrown battlefields. Like the thousands and
thousands of others. His own boys . . .

"Them two are what you oughta be thinking of now, Jennie. Much as Seamus is a friend of mine . . . you gotta be thinking of the boys first."

The youngest, Peter, scooted up in the lamplit dust, stopping in a shower of golden flakes a'swirl about his bare ankles to put his head against his mother's shoulder a moment. She clutched his cheek against her breast, running her fingers through his long hair.

"So much like his papa, this one. Looks so much like his papa."

Sam felt the clutch at his throat, this reminder of all that he had behind him in Missouri now. A wife gone the way of her two sons. The little farm he had walked away from when she had died soon after the war, wasting away, not seeing her boys come home. Jennie reminded him of all that was sucked from his life now like fruit left too long on the vine.

"Want you to know, Sam," she said quietly a few minutes later, after her youngest returned to his play in the lamplit yard. "I may have Johnny and Webb drop us off in Nebraska."

"Oh?"

"May not go all the way on back to Ohio with them."

"Change your mind?"

She wagged her head. "No. Just ain't made it up yet."

"Time enough to make it up, Jennie."

She was silent for several minutes more. "Their daddy's people are back there. In Nebraska. They all come from around Osceola. On the Big Blue River." She turned on her stool toward the old man, their knees barely touching, the toes of her dusty brogans rubbing against his boots. "That's east and north some from Grand Island, Sam."

He nodded, and swallowed the lump in his throat. Marr figured that she wanted him to know exactly where, where he could tell Seamus Donegan to begin his search. "I'll remember, Jennie. And he'll know where to fetch you."

Sam watched her shoulders sag, as if finally shed of the worry on it. Loose threads tied up neatly in a knot. Sure in her own unsure way of things that nothing was left to chance now.

"I may be there, Sam. And the boys . . . back there

among their daddy's people. It might be a place for me to start. Johnny and Webb say I should go on east with them to Ohio. Too much chance of Indian trouble still in Nebraska, they claim. The Sioux roaming around here, keeping things stirred up. But I figure it's finally up to me to make up my own mind, Sam. And I think Nebraska's the place for me and the boys to start over."

Then Marr did something totally out of character for him. He gently took one of her rough hands into both of his wrinkled, well-worn ones, patting it paternally.

"By damned, Jennie," he whispered, staring into her eyes, gleaming and brimming with moisture beneath the yellow lamplight, "Nebraska is the place for you and the boys to start over. A fine place for you to wait, girl. Wait for the man you want to come after you."

"Where the hell did those bastards come from?" Capt. Obadiah Dandy demanded as he huffed up.

Lt. John Jenness pointed northeast. "They must've sneaked back of Lodge Trail Ridge, clear 'round to the badlands. Come down the end of the Peno Head on the herd."

"C'mon!"

"Begging pardon—can't, sir. Waiting for my detail to form up. We'll ride down to help the herd pickets."

"Dammit! We won't have a herd, we wait to form up a relief party. Twice now you've taken details out. But right now you and Powell don't have time to wait . . . no time to gallop off down there! I'll tell you what, Lieutenant—you and Powell both can be damned while the red bastards ride off with what's left of our herd!"

"Got my orders, sir!" Jenness threw his hands up in frustration.

"You and Powell can gallop straight to hell for all I care!"

Obadiah wheeled, dashing to the edge of the plateau, leaving Jenness muttering and frustrated, not certain which officer he should obey. Dandy didn't give a damn. It just didn't matter whose toes he stepped on or whose feelings he hurt. He was out to wring that brevet from the promotion board or else.

Job is, scatter those warriors down there before they make it across the creek with my cattle in tow.

Barely minutes ago the alarm had rung out across the parade, disturbing the tranquility of this July Sunday morning. Down in the narrow meadow formed by the junction of the Big and Little Piney creeks, the young soldiers who had been guarding what was left of Fort Phil Kearny's beef herd watched in frustration as Sioux warriors burst from the trees like angry, screeching hornets. Bolting at those first wild shrieks, the spotted cattle lumbered off at a run, scattering before the small ponies carrying naked brown bodies through the herd. Shaken from their lazy, sunrise daydreams, the young troopers seemed confused about what to do. Under orders to hold their fire and conserve ammunition, since each of the pickets was given but ten rounds for his Springfield. Only the warriors' newness in wrangling cattle delayed the Sioux in making their way back across the creek, driving the beef herd before them. Time and again the cattle balked and broke apart, refusing the warriors' primitive efforts.

As Captain Dandy skidded into the northeast corner of the stockade, he peered down into the bottom, watching the herd guard draw their pistols.

"Is that loaded?" Obadiah shouted to the sentry who stared frozen and helpless into the valley as the herd guard finally opened fire. In and out of the maze of cattle the naked warriors weaved, making it less than easy for the pickets to find a target, much less worry about wasting their precious ammunition.

"Sir?" the guard turned to answer, frustrated and frightened. "Yes, sir. It's loaded. I'm under orders not—"

"Back off, then, son." Dandy shoved the soldier from the mountain howitzer, squat and ugly as an iron toad in the sunburnt grass atop the plateau.

"Sir, I can't—"

"I told you, get the hell out of my way!" Obadiah bellowed, instantly shutting the guard up. "This is my stockade. Those are my cattle down there. And if no one else is going to do a goddamn thing about those Sioux stealing army property—Obadiah Dandy sure as hell will, soldier!"

"Y-Yes, sir!" the soldier hollered in reply, stumbling backward, battered by Dandy's verbal assault, saluting for good measure.

As quickly as he said it, Dandy gauged range and distance. *Just like they taught you at the academy. Slow, prepare your charge. Don't rush it . . .*

He cut his Boorman fuse the length he calculated he would need. Just long enough for the flight of the case of eighty .58-caliber balls into the valley below. With a swift movement, he rammed the twelve-pound case down the howitzer's throat, primed the gun, and dragged a sulfur head along the cast-iron breech. He stepped to the side, watching the powder spark the fuse hole. With gray smoke, the gun belched. Sending Dandy's charge on its way over the valley.

"Hurraw!" the young sentry shouted, dancing as he watched the case explode, spewing its eighty deadly balls down upon the warriors and cattle in a spray of noise and confusion and pain.

"Goddamn right, son!" Dandy bellowed, seeing the warriors wheel and turn from their assault on the pickets, retreating through the cattle.

Bastards only want one thing now. To get the hell across that creek before I blow their red asses off their goddamn ponies.

Dandy threw his weight against one wheel, struggling to jostle the howitzer to the left. *That's it, Obadiah. Point it at the creek this time! Good! Hit 'em as they—*

A second twelve-pound case he rammed home after cutting the timing fuse, struck his match. He watched the howitzer belch, sending his renewed greetings into the valley.

"We got 'em on the run now, sir!" the young soldier cheered. "Watch them red niggers go!"

Dandy did indeed watch the Sioux go. Tearing across the creek. One warrior knocked from his pony. Plucked from the ground on the run by another warrior who swung his dazed companion behind him on the back of his prancing pony. The cattle rambled, still frightened from the noise and the lead hail falling from the sky. But they slowed restlessly, and finally returned to grazing as the pickets in the valley surrounded the herd and quieted what few head of beef Fort Phil Kearny had remaining after a year in the shadow in the Big Horns.

"Sonsabitches won't get one damned head of my cattle . . . not if Obadiah Dandy's got anything to say about it!" The captain turned and stomped off, dusting his hands down his sweat-stained blouse.

"And Obadiah Dandy's got a helluva a lot to say about it!"

"You hear that?" civilian teamster R. J. Smyth asked the armed trooper beside him on the wagon seat as they rumbled up the Montana Road, headed back toward Fort Phil Kearny from the hay flats near Lake DeSmet.

"Yeah," Pvt. John Ryan answered, craning his neck. "Sounded like two howitzer shots."

"You don't s'pose the fort's under attack, do you?" Smyth's voice squeaked in fear.

The young soldier waited, then waited some more, staring up the road toward the valley of the Pineys and the fort they could not yet see. After long minutes with no more shots heard, Ryan's shoulders sagged. "Nawww. I suppose not. Be more gunfire if they was under attack."

"Maybeso, you're right," Smyth commented, wishing he had brought along a plug of chew. Wishing he could afford to buy chew more often. "I don't figure them Sioux for real guts —'cause that's what it'd take to make a rush on the fort."

"I'll grant you that," Ryan muttered. "Seems all they do is jump these trains anymore. After what they done to Fetterman and all those—" His voice broke off in remembrance of those mutilated bodies. "Red bastards content now scaring hell out of us when they jump a train."

Smyth turned at the loud clatter of hoofbeats pounding the iron-hardened road. He turned in time to watch a young soldier loping up past the twelve wagons quartermaster Dandy had assigned to bring hay back to the post from the flats near the lake. Down where the Sioux hadn't burned the grass the army's horses and mules depended upon. On each side of the dozen hay wagons rode three mounted infantrymen, rifles ready. R. J. Smyth figured it had to be that last soldier on the west side of the road who allowed his horse to gallop past Smyth's lead wagon.

"Now, what you s'pose that sonuvabitch is up to?" Smyth

grumbled as the horseman trotted past with a big grin cracking his face.

"That's Private Johnson," Ryan answered. "Peter's a loose one, he is. When we were mounting up, he told us he'd be having some fun on the ride back . . . fixing to light out for the post. I declare, but he is a loose one! Said it was too nice a day to spend lallygagging back in the dust with the wagons. Wanted to ride on the point . . . see some of the country."

"See some of the gawddamned country?" R.J. shrieked. "What with them Sioux waiting to loose a man from his hair like they are?"

"Johnson ain't the kind to worry," Ryan answered. "Just look at him up there. Having the time of his life."

Smyth sensed the first twinge of apprehension, brooding that now the caravan had one less gun along for protection.

After all, R.J. figured, *it's the mules them Injuns is always after. They don't have no truck with this gawddamned hay.*

"Hey, soldier . . . don't you think Johnson's getting a bit far ahead now. Better'n three hundred yards. Why'n't you flag him back with us. Make me feel whole lot better."

"Can't now, Smyth. Johnson just dropped off the top of that hill yonder. Down to a ravine. He comes up on the other side, I'll give him a holler and a wave. Don't you go fretting now."

"I'll fret," R.J. spit. "I'll fret, all right. You're not the one liked to lost his hair back to last month on the wood road. Not your hair they was—"

Like shadows flitting across the sun, the warriors swept off the hill to their left and up from the trees on their right. His eyes bugging in hungover redness, R. J. Smyth cursed his luck and glanced at his uniformed passenger.

At the same moment, trooper Ryan bolted upright in the footwell. Searching the road ahead for some sign of Private Johnson. As if to answer Ryan's unspoken question, gunfire crackled from the ravine still a hundred yards away.

"They got him cut off now!" Ryan growled, cocking the hammer on his big Springfield.

"It ain't him I'm worried about, you stupid blue-coated dunderhead!" Smyth screamed as he slapped reins down on the rumps of his team.

"Look!" Ryan hollered, still standing, a'sway with the lurching wagon as Smyth's mules bolted into a gallop. "There he is!"

Up the far side of the ravine raced Peter Johnson, with a half-dozen warriors hot on his trail like wet hornets.

"This way, Johnson!" Ryan yelled, hoarse already. "This way, dammit! You're going the wrong—"

"Ain't no wrong way when you're running from Injuns, soldier!" Smyth growled, bouncing on the seat and glancing back to see where the rest of the hay wagons were.

"But he's headed back to the fort!"

"Just where I'm headed too, gawdammit!"

"Awww, shit! He'd stand a better chance getting 'round 'em and heading back to us."

"He ain't bound to do nothing of the kind now," Smyth moaned, watching up the road in disbelief.

"What you figure made him jump off his horse that way?" Ryan barked. "Man's gone plumb crazy with fear—lookit 'im run! Thrown his pistol away! Can't you make these mules get up and run any faster, Smyth?"

"They running just as fast as they please . . . keeping me away from those Injuns up side of that hill yonder."

"Goddammit!" Ryan groaned as he watched a warrior race right past Johnson, slamming the private on the back of the head with a stone club that dangled from the Indian's wrist. They watched Johnson catapult almost ten feet through the air, crumbling to the dust like a sack of rags.

"C'mon, R.J.!" Ryan yelled suddenly. "Get these mules running now, or I'm fixing to take over the reins on you."

"You'll do no such a thing!"

"Army property this is—"

"But I ain't no gawddamned army property!" Smyth bawled. "Ain't a thing you're gonna do for that stupid boy now. Save our own hides is what we're gonna do."

By the time the warriors broke off their ambush, disappearing into the hills like smoke as quickly as they had appeared, the twelve wagons and escort reached the ravine where the soldiers had watched Johnson attacked. With creaking brakes and snorting, lathered mules, they brought the wagons to a halt. Even before Smyth's lead wagon rumbled to a complete stop, Private Ryan leaped to the ground in search of his fellow trooper.

Johnson's horse had disappeared. That much was easy to understand. The Sioux loved army horseflesh. The pistol Peter Johnson had flung aside in desperation and fear was gone as well. Ryan accepted not finding that either.

Yet most disturbing was that where the young private had fallen after the blow from a Sioux war club, Ryan found only a small patch of dark blood on the grass, quickly soaking into the parched, flaking soil. The ground around the blackened spot of dust appeared torn from many hoofs. None of them wearing the white man's iron shoes.

John Ryan sank to his knees beside the blackening patch of fresh blood. Dipped his fingers in it. And screamed with a cry that echoed off the hills and ridges.

It raised the hairs along the back of R. J. Smyth's neck, that cry climbing into the cool, purple heights of the Big Horns.

Chapter 22

"It is a good sign," Red Cloud said. "High Back-Bone is a grandfather now in the *Moon of Black Cherries.*"

High Back-Bone smiled, accepting the congratulations of his fellow chiefs. "You should not praise me," he said, chuckling lightly and accepting the bowl of stewed antelope as it was passed round the circle in the lodge where the old friends sat in council. "It is my son who had all the fun in fathering this child!"

The lodge rocked with good-natured laughter. Crazy Horse was glad. It had been a long, long time since these men had laughed together. For more than twelve moons these chiefs had not had reason to laugh. Ever since they were told at Laramie of the soldier army coming to shove its fist down the throat of the Indian here in the Big Horn country. This last, best hunting ground of the Lakota and Cheyenne. For more than a year now the bands had drawn close around Red Cloud to press their war against the white men who used the road the way herd bulls would stand off attacks from a pack of wolves. They painted their victories on the winter-count robes—like that Battle of the Hundred in the Hand at the beginning of last robe season of heavy snows, when the soldiers followed the decoys beyond the Lodge Trail to their deaths.

Since then, no civilian wagon trains had ventured north along the Medicine Road that led the white man toward the land of the Crow and beyond, to the places where those white men scratched at the earth for the tiny yellow rocks.

What craziness led those men to risk their lives for yellow rocks, Crazy Horse would never know.

For a long, wet spring of short-grass time, into the summer's beginning spent following the buffalo and antelope herds, the tribes had celebrated and wandered across their hunting ground. And prayed that the harshness of the last two winters would be the last. Knowing the reason the Spirits made hunger visit every lodge was that the mighty Lakota had failed to drive the soldiers from this sacred land.

As long as the white man stayed in this country, living within the safety of his walled forts, the Spirits would bring hunger to the people. This summer the Lakota must drive the soldiers from the land, for all time. No longer merely a war of scalps and manhood for the brave young ones to wage—Red Cloud's war had now become a sacred mission for all. Before the snows of the Winter Man again smothered the land, Crazy Horse knew his people must drive the soldiers from their forts.

"High Back-Bone's grandson is a good sign that means my plans are strong," Red Cloud declared as the lodge quieted. "No more can we merely attack what soldier trains move north along the road. No longer can we content ourselves by stealing a few of the white man's horses and mules near the forts."

"This would take too long," Little Hawk agreed.

"I agree, uncle," Crazy Horse replied, nodding to his blood relative. "We do not have the time. We must join with Red Cloud in planning to attack the forts themselves."

He watched Red Cloud smile at him. They had planned it this way. For the popular war-chief Crazy Horse to announce Red Cloud's scheme for him. Thereby sealing a successful vote of the council in favor of the plan worked out in secret between the two Oglalla leaders.

"Attack . . . attack the forts themselves?" Yellow Eagle asked in the midst of much muttering rumbling through the lodge.

Red Cloud nodded. "We must go into the badger's den . . . or we will never drive him from our land."

"But like the badger," the shrill voice of Red Leaf rose above the clamor, "the white soldier will fight all the harder when we back him into his forts."

"Yes. Make no mistake," Crazy Horse said, holding his hand up for quiet, "the soldiers will fight hard."

"Aiyeee!" roared the Miniconjou chief Black Shield, "it is good they will fight much harder than the hundred-in-the-hand we killed in the *Moon of Deer Shedding Horns."*

"Many of those threw their lives away, yes," replied Yellow Horse.

"But many among them fought hard as well," Crazy Horse retorted. "The soldiers in the forts now will fight as hard against us. But there is no other choice."

"Crazy Horse is right," Red Cloud said. "If the soldiers choose not to stick their heads out of their holes, we will take our war to the forts . . . where we can fight them."

"I have an idea, Red Cloud."

All eyes turned to the aged warrior, the many winters of his life sprinkling his hair with much iron.

"Ice wishes to speak to the council. We are grateful for any ideas you can give us."

"Thank you, Red Cloud," the old man began, his voice quiet and low, like the grating croak of frogs along the wet places on a summer night. "To throw our bodies against the soldier forts is madness."

"But we cannot lure the soldiers—"

"Hear me out, Crazy Horse," Ice continued calmly, his hand silencing the young war-chief. "We must plan to draw some of the soldiers out of the forts. Then we will attack not only the soldiers who come riding out to scare us off, but more warriors still can then throw themselves at the weakened posts."

"This is good!" Crazy Horse said, sensing the surge of excitement like a hot burst of lovemaking through his body. "The forts will never expect an attack. They believe we will only draw the soldiers out as we lured the hundred to their deaths beyond the Lodge Trail."

"It is a fine idea, Ice," Red Cloud agreed with a wide smile, his eyes twinkling, feeling the support of the entire lodge behind him now that Ice had sealed the plan's approval. "We must talk now about a plan to decoy more soldiers from the forts."

"You need no plan!" Ice chuckled. And with his laughter, the sagging skin on his face stretched across his high cheekbones, like an old linen sheet thrown carelessly over the bare bedsprings of a white man's bed.

"Tell me, old one," Crazy Horse began, coming up on one knee and turning full to the old counselor. "Why don't we need a plan to lure the soldiers from their forts?"

Ice laughed, his rheumy old eyes moist and dim. "The soldiers will come. They always do."

"The soldiers always come? I do not understand."

Ice licked his lips. "They always come to help when we attack. And this time, we attack the little camps far from the forts."

"*Yes!*" Red Cloud shouted, seeing the genius in the idea. "The little camps at the Pine Woods where the tree cutters stay!"

Crazy Horse was standing now, beating his bare chest with one fist. "*Ai-yi-yi-yi!* And at the dirt fort on the Bighorn, where the grass cutters stay the nights, sleeping far from the fort walls!"

"We attack them, young ones?" Ice inquired, his old shoulders shaking with sudden laughter.

"Yes, old man!" Crazy Horse roared his approval. "We attack the small camps of the stupid ones who sleep far away from the forts!"

A few high, puffy clouds decked the July blue of the sky overhead this warm, Sunday morning that found Finn Burnett and seven others leading A. C. Leighton's mules and horses from the protection of the post corral to a grassy spot some three quarters of a mile southwest of Fort C.F. Smith. After hobbling all the mules Leighton's crews used to pull the mowers, four of the teamsters returned to the fort, to spend their day of rest at cards or the bottle, whatever diversion a man could afford.

The four who had remained to ride herd on those hobbled

mules, also given the day off from their mower-pulling chores, rode to a low ridge overlooking the green meadow. There they hobbled their horses and sat back in the shade of alder and aspen, chewing on grass stems and watching the lazy clouds drift across the summer sky.

Tony Addinger, Ed Gibson and Charlie White leaped to their feet beside Finn Burnett at the first shouts.

Around the brow of their hill raced two dozen or more warriors. Blankets and pieces of rawhide fluttered noisily in the breeze, intent on stampeding Leighton's mules and horses. The animals struggled, but did not get far in their hobbles. In the meantime, the four teamsters plopped on their bellies, choosing targets among the swaying, prancing Sioux horsemen just down the slope.

First a pony dropped, spilling its rider. As he was quickly scooped up from the meadow, another warrior fell from his animal. Then a second as the white herders' guns boomed rhythmically from the hillside. A gray cloud hung over their grassy position. Burnt powder stung Burnett's nostrils as he reloaded his repeater and went back to work on the attackers.

"They had enough horse stealing, boys!" Sourdough Charlie White growled, watching twenty-odd warriors turn from their futile attempts at stampeding the mules.

"Shit! Looks like they're fixing to run over us, don't it!" big Ed Gibson shouted above the boom of the big rifles.

The four watched as the warriors circled the herd one last time, bunching more closely together as they tore through the hobbled mules and pointed their noses straight for the teamsters' hillside.

From the direction of the post came the sound of gunfire. Then the brassy blast of a bugle.

"By God, will you look at that!" Burnett yelled, rising to one knee and pointing at the fort.

From the front gate poured a hodgepodge of soldiers scurrying pell-mell to the scene, having been alarmed by the sound of shots echoing from the meadow.

"Jesus!" Sourdough growled. "Ain't that Bradley hisself, riding lead?"

"Damn if it ain't!" Addinger shouted. "Now, how 'bout you getting back to watching that gulch down there, Charlie? Covering our backsides and shooting some of these red sonsabitches until Bradley's army gets here . . . provided they get here while we still got our hair!"

"Will do, boy!" Charlie, a master shot, rolled back into the grass and took aim at the approaching mass of naked horsemen. "Another dead buck for Sourdough!" He then crawled off through the tall, dry grass so he could keep an eye peeled on the far side of the hill, where the gulch afforded perfect cover for the Sioux to creep close to the teamsters.

Finn smiled as he set his rifle to work once more, happy with the sight of Lieutenant Colonel Luther P. Bradley at the head of his relief column, clad only in his dressing gown and slippers, his regulation-issue pistol strapped at his hip and a carbine aloft in his hand. Gown tail flapping as he rode, Bradley had issued orders to pursue the enemy without saddles. He bare-bottom hammered the horse's spine like an oak stair banister.

Behind Bradley pounded an unlikely assortment of soldiers, all of whom had leaped atop unsaddled mounts, gripping halters only as they sought to control their wide-eyed animals. Through the gate of Fort C.F. Smith blared the brassy tones of "Boots and Saddles" still, while those troopers left behind scurried to their posts along the walls.

"Lookee there!" Addinger hollered, and pointed with the muzzle of his rifle. "That red nigger's started shooting our mules!"

"Son . . . of . . . a . . . bitch!" Gibson growled. "They can't run 'em off . . . so, the bastards gonna shoot 'em!"

"Not if we got anything to say about it." Burnett ground his left elbow into the dirt and raised the rear sight on his long-range Ballard buffalo gun. Squinting down the barrel for some idea of distance, he dragged a thumb across his tongue and raked the damp thumb over the front sight.

"Here's to luck, boys!" he sighed, nuzzling his cheek against the stock.

He touched off the big-bore rifle, shoved a few inches back in the grass.

"By damn, you done it, Burnett!" Gibson screamed. "Got the bastard!"

Three more of the Sioux who had enjoyed themselves firing arrows into the mules scampered off round the brow of the hill from where they had appeared moments before.

"Goddamn!" Addinger screeched in pain.

An arrow pinned his ankle to the ground.

Another hissed out of the pale sky overhead, its iron head slamming into the ground near Gibson.

"Christ! We're under attack!"

"Don't move! Don't move!" Burnett hollered. "Watch the sky."

"I ain't watching the sky!" Gibson yelled, up on his hands and knees, crabbing away. "Getting the hell out of here!"

Burnett was beside Addinger in a heartbeat. Yanking the arrow out of the ground before he broke off the tip and fletching both, he eased the short piece of bloody shaft from Addinger's leg.

"Where the hell's Sourdough!" Addinger screamed in pain and frustration. "Told him to watch our goddamned backsides."

"I been watching your arse, son!" White hollered as he slid up in the dust and grass. "A fella's gotta see what he's shooting at, boy!"

Finn could tell the old man was as testy as a scalded cat.

"You didn't see the bastards?"

"They can sit down there in them trees and brush, shooting their arrows into the air all day long, and I still can't see 'em."

Burnett realized the whistling missiles had tapered off. A moment later, as Bradley's cavalry raced up the long slope, Finn thought he heard the pounding of hoofbeats and some wild yells disappearing up the valley.

" 'Pears they've gone now," Sourdough advised.

"No thanks to you," Addinger hissed. "You'd got us all killed, watching our backsides, old man."

Sourdough chuckled as he stood, leaning on his rifle, watching Burnett help Addinger to his feet. "Shame, ain't it, Finn."

"How's that, Charlie?" Burnett asked.

"Tony here. Shame that arrow missed its mark."

"Missed its mark?" Addinger shrieked angrily as he hobbled down the slope toward the soldiers.

"Couple more feet, way I figure it," Charlie said with a chuckle and a brown stream spat into the grass. "Couple more feet and them red niggers had your fat ass skewered two ways of Sunday!"

Chapter 23

Roman Nose did not understand some of these white men in civilian clothes. Blue-shirted soldiers he understood. Understood them ever since he had watched a shouting, arrogant soldier kill an old chief near Fort Laramie twelve summers ago. Since that day Roman Nose had grown to manhood learning of the treachery of white soldiers. Now the Cheyenne war-chief found it hard to comprehend this crazy white man trudging along the road on foot below. Heading west. On his way to the white soldiers' fort. Alone.

From the wooded heights above the road leading some two and a half miles back to Fort C.F. Smith, the young Cheyenne warrior watched the white man stop in the shade of some cottonwood at the side of the soldier road. The lone one sat down in the bright morning sun of this *Moon of Black Cherries,* wiping his brow and resting.

Those boxes he carries . . . perhaps they hold something important for the soldier fort.

Puzzled still, he had watched the white man with long hair the color of grass-when-winter-comes leave the white man camp of the grass cutters this morning, taking off up the road to the fort on foot. Leaving the hayfield and the other white men behind.

On foot and alone.

Webb Wood whipped off his floppy hat and swiped a dusty sleeve across his brow. Squinting into the bright sun, he tried to calculate how far he had come since leaving the hayfield corral. Figuring how far he had yet to walk until he reached the fort.

Something like another mile, perhaps. I'll see the fort 'round the next hill.

A warm breeze nudged the hair plastered along his neck. He rubbed a bandanna over the damp skin. Wood gazed down at the two leather cases he had chosen to haul back to the fort on foot.

"Damned heavy," he wheezed.

Whiskey. Webb Wood always had whiskey at hand. A lonely man for most of his life. The whiskey had helped quell some of that loneliness. If whiskey didn't draw other men to him, at least the whiskey had numbed the pain.

Webb recalled Seamus Donegan's words during last night's lamplit game of cards beneath the summer sky.

"Those Injins out there in those hills would delight in clipping your hair, Webb Wood. Closer than any barber back in Ohio."

Wood had laughed easily, stroking his long reddish curls. "Don't you worry none about me, Irishman."

"I'll worry, Wood," Donegan had replied, more serious now. "My eyes have seen what the Sioux do to a man who goes out alone in this country—like that photographer I told you about, the one what traveled up from Fort Laramie with me last summer."

"He was a friend?"

"Didn't know him well," Donegan answered. "But we got as close as any two men pinned down together at that bleeming Crazing Woman Crossing a year ago this month."

Wood chuckled, nervously and without mirth. "But Seamus —with this hair of mine, the Indians will take me for a Mormon. And the Sioux aren't about to tangle with a Mormon, now are they?"

Webb Wood gazed back up the road now, in the direction of the hay cutters' corral. Wondering if he really had done the right thing. It was Sunday. Not a single hay train or supply wagon running between the corral and the fort all day. But he had hungered for some new company. Tiring of the same old talk from the same old mouths. Besides, he was anxious to start back to Fort Phil Kearny where he would rejoin Jennie.

Just this morning over breakfast, Seamus Donegan had again advised Wood against walking back to the fort under any circumstances, much less alone. But Webb Wood had long been a man driven by a strange, misguided sense of courage. During the recent rebellion in the South, he had cowered while other men fought and died.

Now that the hay cutters told him it was a blamed foolish thing for him to strike out alone, Wood considered himself a coward if he didn't take the risk . . . and the road back to Fort C.F. Smith by himself. Besides, Jennie Wheatley waited at the end of the next ninety miles to Fort Phil Kearny.

A risk worth taking for any man. His tongue reminded him of sandpaper on the inside of his cheek.

When the white man removed his big, floppy hat, Roman Nose was reminded of withered, autumn-colored buffalo grass. Not all that many whites with hair that color had the Cheyenne war-chief seen in his short life.

He remembered one—a man who scouted for the army along the Platte River Road. This one with the long, blond hair on his shoulders reminded Roman Nose of blue-shirted soldiers riding into a Cheyenne camp at dawn one cold winter morning. Black Kettle's camp along the Little Dried River two summers back.

Bloodied memories of Sand Creek rumbled like tainted meat in Roman Nose's belly. Reminding him of the anger he felt for all white men who would attack a camp of women and children. For all white men who would defile the dead bodies of Cheyenne women. Or slash open the bodies of Cheyenne babies with their shining sabers.

"Let us see what he carries back to the soldiers' dirt fort," young Two Medicine suggested at his war-chief's side.

"Yes," Roman Nose answered. "I want to meet this one with the red hair. He who is brave enough to venture out alone from the white man's camp along War-Man Creek."

For some reason, Webb Wood sensed them sliding down the hills before he ever saw the shadows of their ponies and the fluttering of their feathers. His heart rose like a cold stone, high in his throat, pumping like a steam piston. Wood's mouth was never so dry.

For a moment he stood fixed where he was, fighting with himself. Wondering what to do. Recognizing at last the same immobilizing fear that had swallowed him during the war. Knowing that this time he could not stand and let the tide wash over him. This time, he would not hide.

The hillsides stood bare of growth where no man could hide himself anyway. And the Bighorn . . . well, the river lay too far away. No cover around him worth a damn for a man to crouch behind and shoot back at the Indians. Even if he did have a gun.

In panic, Webb Wood reached for his belt. Then realized he had packed his pistol in the smaller case with his change of clothing and an extra pair of boots.

Back and forth his eyes darted to the dozen warriors loping easily down the road in his direction. Back and forth while he implored his struggling fingers to free the leather straps from their buckles on the clothing case. And still his heart hoped the warriors meant only to rob him of his clothing and . . . the whiskey.

They're not racing in at me. Not the way Donegan said they charged down on him and Glover at the crossing. These savages don't mean to kill me . . . they don't mean to.

The .44-caliber revolver leaped into his palm as he whirled around at the first shout from the warriors. All feathers and fringe and scalplocks flitting upon the hot July breeze. He watched their mouths round and *o-o-o* as they hollered at him.

Suddenly Webb Wood realized his legs were carrying him away. Sprinting. Abandoning his travel-battered cases in the middle of the road.

Let them have the clothing and boots. My blessed whiskey. I want to live!

With the next thump of his heart, Wood recognized a single set of hoofbeats drawing behind him. He panted, his heart thundering in his ears. Closer and closer he heard that pony drawing. Closer and closer. At an easy lope.

I'm running as fast as I can!

His mouth burning and his chest heaving, Wood glanced over his shoulder. Seeing but one warrior approaching down the trail. Behind him the rest had dropped to the middle of the road and contented themselves in opening his leather cases.

He doesn't want my bags—he wants to kill me! No! My gun —it's my gun he wants!

Webb turned, threw up his hands to show he presented no danger. Staring the young warrior in the face for the first time.

Never so close before.

A Cheyenne war-chief, light shimmering in the black hair hung in a braid on one side of his face. On the other side of the warrior's head hung a stuffed magpie. A warcharm. The Indian slowed, slipping his bow in the quiver at his back.

Wood felt better. *Yes, it's my pistol he wants. Give him the damn pistol and get to the fort. Just give him the damn pistol.*

Without a word, the civilian flung the heavy pistol into the middle of the dusty road. Practically at the warrior's feet. He watched the Indian rein up, stop, glance down at the pistol. Then gaze in his direction again. Wearing the wildest smile.

Wood felt an icy-cold splash down his spine, a cold he had never experienced. Then he whirled, bolting off again, straight down the road.

I wish I could remember that face . . . that smile . . . there'll never be another like it. I'll never see another—

Roman Nose heaved the axe with all the strength in his arm as he galloped up behind the white man with the winter-grass hair.

The blade caught the fleeing runner squarely between the shoulder blades. For two steps, then three, the white man stumbled, one arm flailing at the suffocatingly hot July air, grasping at nothing. The other arm dug frantically backward, scraping, grabbing, clawing for the axe buried deep in the muscle and bone and life of his body.

Now the Cheyenne warrior slowed his pony to a walk, following the stumbling white man, amused at the same time he was intrigued, wondering when the man would fall. The grass-haired man stopped, sighed loudly as his arms fell use-lessly to their sides, then crumpled to his knees. His arms suddenly flailed toward the sky as he cried out. Then he tumbled forward, his face slapping the powdery, dry dust of the white-man road.

"You do not want his clothes?" Two Medicine asked when he and the others rode up on Roman Nose and the white man's body.

"No," the war-chief replied, rising from the body, wiping his bloody knife across on his bare, brown leg. Then he stuffed the long, red-grass scalp beneath the bandoleer of bullets strapped across his naked chest. "You take the clothes, my young friend. You others may take the white man's whiskey as well. I will not drink their evil water." He sighed, smiling that wolf-slash grin of his. "I have all I need, Two Medicine."

Roman Nose patted the blood-smeared scalp at his waist. "All that I want."

Chapter 24

$\mathcal{P}$vt. Henry Ketcham swung his axe again, smiling. Thursday. July 27. Getting closer to Sunday, after all. Reason enough for any young man to celebrate.

Sunlight brightened gay patches of grass beneath the pine boughs where he and two others worked along the slope of Pine Island. Barely a half mile above the pine-slab blockhouse where the timber cutters always retreated in the event of an attack.

Too nice a morning for anything like an attack, Ketcham decided.

A little sun, a good breeze. A touch of summer coolness in the morning air that raised a tingle in his blood.

Ketcham stopped, let his axe slip, and wiped his brow. From his eyes he pushed hair the color of red buffalo grass when the frost comes. He listened to the shrill of the whistle atop the steam sawmill far down the valley at the Little Piney. Closer yet, he heard the ring of axe and the lusty laughter of a dozen more woodcutters about a hundred yards below him on the slope. Ketcham was stuffing the damp bandanna back in his trousers as the first war whoop echoed through the trees.

Shadows flitted through the shafts of sunlight on the slope below him. His other two companions shouted, urging him to hurry. He heard them running, crashing, wildly throwing themselves downhill to escape. Too late Ketcham understood their wild abandon.

More than a hundred warriors had slipped between him

and the rest of the workers down the slope. Ketcham found himself cut off while the others scrambled toward the blockhouse. He darted to the left. Downhill. Shadows loomed out of the trees. He dropped his axe. Stumbled. Wheeled right. He'd take the long way down . . .

They leaped from the dark timber like liquid shadows. Hideous faces, smeared with earth paint and gaping grins. For a moment Private Ketcham froze. The Sioux screamed at him, laughing. And like a frightened doe, he turned to run.

He never really felt the last three arrows. It was the first that burned. Driven deep in his back.

Spilling forward clumsily, Ketcham's face buried itself in the deep musk of a bed of pine needles. The sun grew hot, scorching the back of his neck. So quiet now. Henry listened to the *scritch-scritch* of the ants and beetles crawling through the needles and grass. Searching out the warm blood.

In the deafening quiet of that timbered slope, Private Ketcham dreamed of ants crossing his cheek. Then held his breath, listening to the footsteps on the hillside above him. Below him. Circling in. He ached to open his eyes. Ached to brush the ants from his face.

Thank God! he thought as someone yanked his head out of the pine needles, their fingers threading roughly through his strawberry hair.

Now they'll brush the ants off. Say! Don't hurt me like that . . . He wanted to scream at them. *It's only the ants need brushing off—*

The gray cloud crossing Ketcham's mind flared with sparks of red and yellow. They let go of his head as he heard something foreign, a new sound. A sickening, sucking pop, and a loud grunt.

Henry realized that grunt was his. Just before the red and yellow sparks began to cool and drip across his mind. Melting into blessed blue-black.

Private Gibson wondered what had ever happened to the child. What had ever happened to the child's stunningly beautiful mother. Sam Gibson had loved that woman more than he had ever loved anything. Yet his family did not approve.

Chicago society was like that, Sam brooded.

What could he expect her to do? With all that money Sam's father had given the woman. She had gone. Paid to go away to have their child. Exactly as his family had wanted it. Buy the woman off.

Money can do anything, he remembered. *Anything . . . except buy my bartered soul back for me.*

Disappearing into this frontier army as Pvt. Sam Gibson, there were times he almost forgot who he really was, who he had been and left behind in Chicago. So long ago. So many miles away.

Edgar L. O'Reilly, heir to a fortune of old money. Well, Edgar, you spineless bastard—you're long dead now. One of these days, he knew he would have to reconcile himself to it. One of these days—

"Great Jesus Christ!"

Gibson whirled, startled. Hearing the voice of another picket who sat nearby. Four sentries in all atop Pilot Hill.

Only then did the screech of the sawmill whistle down on the Little Piney reach Gibson's ears. The alarm.

"You see 'em, Gibby?"

Yes, Sam had to admit. He could see them. More than a dozen on their spry ponies, sprinting off the wood road, straight toward the smooth crossing of the Little Piney. Like demons possessed, their bearing on course for Pilot Hill.

"Signal, goddammit!"

Sam heard another soldier growl.

"He is, gol-dang-it! He is!" the third man shouted.

The trooper holding the fluttering flag over his head shouted. "They know! Look at the fort! They can see!"

Gibson wheeled, studying the fort. Streaking across the parade were handfuls of troopers like clusters of dark ants. Bigger splotches of shadow on the parade—the horses. Kept saddled.

Relief was coming. I pray to God they get here soon enough, Sam muttered under his breath.

And watched two of his detail clatter up tugging the four horses. He and the flagman leaped into the saddle. All four scurried down the west slope of Pilot Hill as the relief column splashed across the Little Piney. Up the slope screeched the Sioux warriors, blood still in their eye.

One among them bearing the sticky, still-warm scalp of
Pvt. Henry Ketcham tucked beneath his belt. Next to the
skinning knife he planned to use on at least one of these four
soldiers escaping downhill, fleeing right into their arms.

With a lot of cursing and yanking on reins, Sam stood in
the stirrups, bringing the other three skidding to a stop. "Dismount, boys!"

"You gotta be kid—"

"Every bit as serious as they are!" Gibson snapped, pointing at the feathered horsemen bearing down on them. "We're
gonna make a stand of it."

No more argument was raised beyond grumbling curses as
the three young soldiers dropped from their mounts and
joined Sam in slapping the muscular rumps of their horses.
All four animals clattered away. Downhill, toward the Sioux.

Gibson pointed. "Follow me!"

They dropped into a natural wash scoured each year by
spring erosion. Sam closed the file. Watching the first puffs of
smoke blossom above the relief column.

"Hurraw!" the youngest soldier hollered, standing in the
wash. They watched the warriors halt, mill about in a quick
parley, then bolt away. Escaping down the northern slope of
Pilot Hill, across the Big Piney toward Lodge Trail Ridge.
With twenty mounted troopers hot on their shadows.

"By damned, boys." Gibson stood, leaning on his rifle.
"Looks like I owe you an apology."

"How's that, Gibby?"

" 'Cause of me, we've gotta walk back to the fort. Deeply
sorry about that." He said it all with a big smile.

"You don't owe me no apology, Gibby," the flagman answered. "Gonna be one walk this foot slogger won't mind
taking a'tall!"

Pinpoint pricks of red and yellow light burst across his
eyes. A drum throbbed monotonously in his ears. His head
ached, raw and naked, like a split melon. Then he realized the
drum was his heartbeat.

Private Henry Ketcham's eyes fluttered open, finding his
face partially buried in a pile of pine needles. Ants crawled
across his cheek, clustered at his mouth. Slowly, he brought

one arm up. Fingers brushed his face. Tracks of crusty, moist warmth . . . something all over his face. It hurt like hell to move the arm. His back. Dull pain exploding through his muscles. He'd have to plan the next move before he hurt himself like that again.

His fingers fell from his face. Glistening. *You're bleeding,* he told himself. His head really hurt, throbbing, scratchy pain . . . when he touched it. Henry understood.

I've . . . they scalped me.

He clenched his eyes shut, choking down the sour knot his belly wanted to throw up. *You best start moving, Henry. They'll be back . . . figuring you for dead.*

One leg, then another, he brought under his chest, rising shaky and unsteady on one elbow. Ketcham tumbled to his side, the muscles along his back shrieking in pain.

Won't try that again! his mind cried out.

Choosing to crawl on his belly, Ketcham clawed one hand into the needles and dark soil, pulling himself ahead barely two feet. The other arm he dragged next to his body. Only in that way, he found, would the muscles in his back not cry out so much in torture.

Down the slope he dragged himself, yard by yard, hanging back in the shadows of the tall pines. Across the damp ground left beneath the humpbacked boughs after yesterday's thunder squall. Around him the forest lay deathly quiet. Except for the magpie's protest in the branches overhead. Or the curious cry of a robber jay that flitted about, tree to tree. Studying this strange no-legged creature worming its way across the forest floor below.

Ketcham stopped, laying still, panting. Catching his breath. And wondering where that strange sound had come from. Slowly realizing with his slowed, numb mind that the sound was his own grunt. His own pain.

So he bit his lip each time he inched himself forward. Rhythmic. Swallowing his pain over and over and—

Get to the blockhouse before the bastards find you. They come looking for you soon. Get help soon—

"Aaaiieee!" he squalled like a scalded cat. His back on fire.

Ketcham lay panting, waiting for the hot slivers of light to disappear from behind his eyes. For the pounding in his ears to ebb. Hoping the fog would roll back from his mind so he could sort it all out.

The arrows! That was it. He had snagged the shafts on the low-hanging boughs of the trees.

No two ways about it, Henry, Ketcham argued with himself, swallowing down the last shards of pain. *You either crawl out in the open . . . where the red bastards'll catch you again . . . or you gotta break the goddamned arrows off so the things won't snag on the branches.*

With one hand twisted around and held close to his back, gripping a shaft, Ketcham used the other to fumble and fight until he could snap the first arrow off. He was a good half hour fumbling through it all, snorting, swallowing waves of pain between the ordeal of each shaft. Until all four lay among the bloody pine needles.

This time Private Ketcham crawled, using two hands to pull himself along. Numbing himself to the pain. Making each pull a little goal in itself. Congratulating himself when he had made it. Gathering strength for the next haul. Then stretching his arms out again. Over and over Henry Ketcham won his little battles with himself. Across that half mile of thickly forested slope. Groping his way through the shadows with something like a homing instinct . . . some homing instinct his foggy mind realized few men would ever have to rely upon.

"Holy!"

Ketcham jerked as the first voice crackled above him and not far away. Then the thunder of running feet. Inside his spirit shrank like salted meat. He remembered the painted, shrieking faces pouncing up on him before.

"He's been—"

"Shaddup!" another voice growled.

Ketcham thought he recognized it. Wanting so badly to look into the face. A fellow trooper? Perhaps one of the civilians? But he couldn't. His blinking eyes were filled with pine dust and dirt, ants, and tears.

"Gimme a hand here, dammit! It's Ketcham! Glory—good glory! It's the boy! You're all right now, Henry."

Then Ketcham sensed the hands on him. Many hands.

Tugging at him gently. Lifting him from the dirt. Brushing ants and dirt and hot moisture from his eyes.

"Jesus! Will you look at them broke—"

"I told you shaddup!" the old man's voice barked.

They hurried him into the blockhouse, laid him on his belly on a soft, tick mattress stuffed with pine needles. The gruff voice that had commanded the others into silence now commanded one of their number to dash back to the fort. To bring a wagon and a surgeon.

"He ain't gonna make it. Not stuck and cut like—"

"I'll cut you, I hear another word," the gruff voice thundered. "He'll make it. This boy's 'bout like dog salmon fighting fast water, this one is. He'll make it, won't you, Henry?"

One of the civilians, Ketcham decided as his mind sank into the cool blue-black once more. That old herder . . . the friendly old herder. He was Henry's friend.

"He'll make it," the gruff voice whispered. "He'll make it . . . or my name ain't Sam Marr."

Chapter 25

"You've got nothing better to do than lallygag around all day watching mounted drill?"

From his lips Seamus took the pine splinter he had been using to pick his teeth and gazed up at the mounted officer who had asked the question. "Aye, Cap'n. It's the Sunday sabbath, after all."

"You're Donegan, aren't you?" Capt. Edward S. Hartz inquired.

"No denying."

"You've stirred quite a bit of trouble down to Kearny, so I've heard," Hartz declared, adjusting himself on the sweaty saddle. "Understand that Carrington liked you, though." He smiled for the first time.

"From the sounds of that, I take it you don't think I'm all that bad a fellow?" Seamus stood, letting the chair settle on its four legs. He stepped to the edge of the shade and squinted up into the July sun at the captain. Hartz's blue tunic was sweated with a dark necklace around the collar and beneath both arms.

"I don't come begging, you understand," Hartz admitted after a long sigh. He snagged Donegan's attention. "Just, we've no cavalry here at Smith now. Since he arrived at Kearny, colonel down there never sent us any."

Donegan had to admit he felt intrigued by the direction Hartz was taking. "You're Eighteenth?"

"Right. Infantry. But they renamed us the Twenty-Seventh

last January. Truth of it, none of us foot sloggers fathom much of this horse soldiering."

"Not all that different than foot drill, Cap'n. Just got to get the horse to understand, s'all."

"I'll take any help you'll give. We've got but six officers here to mind the whole post. When there should be at least three for each troop. Damn weather isn't cooperating either. Mercury rising above ninety every day for a fortnight now."

"These men'll do, Cap'n," Seamus reassured. "We'll get busy and show 'em some basics afore the light goes bad and they blow *retreat*. Work on getting your new horse sojurs to mount on call. Dismount on command. Ride column of twos and fours. Most important thing—get it through their thick noggins to fire carbine or pistol *only* when ordered."

"Save ammunition in our new Springfields, eh?"

Donegan nodded. "That, and teach 'em to wait for a proper target."

"By Jove, I think you're just the man Carrington himself said you were." Then he whispered, "Colonel Bradley's got us all toeing the line of late. When can we start, Mr. Donegan? Captain Price's drilling his infantry in loading and firing by file and number."

"Looks to be you've but a handful of horses left you now."

"At stable call this morning we counted twenty-two serviceable mounts."

"Keep 'em saddled from dawn to dusk?"

"We tell the boys to sleep on their rifles . . . in reach of their reins. What with all the trouble the Indians've been. That poor Wood fella from Ohio—found in the middle of the road like he was. We wanna be ready to ride when the alarm goes out."

"That's the whole idea behind cavalry, Cap'n. Strike fast and strike hard."

Hartz nodded. "I figure it's one order Carrington made sense on."

"Cap'n." Donegan ran a dirty hand beneath a whiskey-red nose. "Ever since the army came to this country, a bleeming lot of you been wanting to ride out to try thrashing a thousand Sioux—so you claimed Carrington, or even Lieutenant Colonel Bradley, are cowards, simply because he won't let you run straight into a Injin trap. But to Seamus Donegan, staying put and not charging after any Sioux decoys makes a whale of a lot of sense."

"You aim to help me train these men?"

"That, and I aim to keep my hair locked on this hungover head of mine as well, Cap'n!"

North saddled his warriors in the stillness of predawn light. Awaking some with an insistent toe, sending them off to roust out the rest—his Arapaho, along with some stray Sioux and Cheyenne who wanted to join in the fun had come along. Even some Blood and Piegan from up north beyond the Milk and Judith, come south for a summer full of raiding and horse stealing.

The white renegade smiled as the big camp came to life. The word was spreading, wasn't it now? Bringing 'em in from far and wide to drive the soldiers from this country for good.

Then it can be my little kingdom at last, North cheered himself by the fire. *King of these thieves and cutthroats and poxy sluts I have to bed.*

He grinned, his dirty teeth glimmering in the dawn fire's light. *Them 'rapaho sluts ain't bad when it comes to bedding. Do all a man wants . . . and more.*

He had brought his hundred here the day before. Camping no closer than four miles from the adobe-walled fort, North went with Sings The Moon and his personal bunch to sniff around from the ridges. First the fort. Then the grass cutters' corral.

Bob North didn't spend much time worrying about the fort. If some of the red bastards with him wanted to beat their heads against that stone wall, it was all right with him. But he had squared his jaw and licked his lips when he looked down on the black-ant activity around the corral yesterday afternoon as the civilians and their soldier escort came in from the meadows. Brushing down their mules and horses. Gathering water for the night. Lighting cookfires. Settling in for the summer evening.

One tall, bearded one among them.

Sings The Moon had nodded, pointing eagerly.

North had smiled, slapping the gap-toothed warrior on the

back. "Good work, you gut-stinking bastard!" the renegade had said in English to his brown-skinned right-hand man. "Just mind you," he repeated, slapping his own chest and pointing at the corral, "that'un's mine. Hear?"

The gap-tooth grin widened, and the head nodded.

Some honor among thieves, North figured. Whatever the rest of 'em wanted from the soldiers and civilians, they would damn well leave North's chosen man alone.

He forced them out now without breakfast. Nothing but a little dried meat for the trail and a bellyful of creek water. More time spent on a quick painting of cheeks and chins and chest, after each warrior wet down the bushes surrounding their campsite.

Once atop his nervous, peak-eared Indian pony, North sang quietly.

"And now I'm going southward,
For my heart is full of woe,
I'm going back to Georgia
And find my Uncle Joe.

"You may sing about your dearest maid,
And sing of Rosalee.
But the gallant Hood of Texas
Raised hell in Tennessee!"

The off-key notes drifting into the gray of morning-come, Confederate captain Bob North led his swelling band of bad-hearts across the Bighorn River and down the four-mile trail that would bring him face to face with the tall one.

Chapter 26

"*I*'ll ride with you, Cawpril!" Donegan announced as he swung atop Leighton's own mount.

"Thank you, mister. Make it a habit never refusing an offer of help." Cpl. Ethan Wade turned in the saddle. "Troops, forward at a walk—*ho!*"

"Where the hell you going with my horse, Donegan?" A. C. Leighton burst out of his quarters, pulling up britches and slapping suspenders over his shoulders. "Bring that goddamned horse back, you thieving mick!"

Donegan turned and stuffed a hand high into the dawn air. "Be right back, boss! Gotta ride nursemaid—pull your hay cutters' arses out the fire!"

Sentries flung open Fort C.F. Smith's gates. Wade's relief party cantered past the stockade walls to the martial blare of the tin trumpet ringing brassy into the bright morning air. Down the slope the young corporal led his detachment of twenty-six armed infantrymen and one red-eyed civilian who cradled a Henry repeater in the crook of one arm.

Moments ago the day watch at the fort had sighted a large war party of Indians descending the ridge trail, down the road that would take them to the Bighorn crossing. Right where A. C. Leighton's teamsters and hay cutters had camped on the north bank of Warrior Creek at the foot of a gentle slope. More than a hundred yelling, blanket-waving warriors galloped toward a rendezvous with those outnumbered civilians.

His head hurt again. Few mornings it didn't, what with too

much whiskey or too little sleep. Or just the heat of the coming day scorching these high plains. Seamus cursed the whiskey and the sleep and the new day's sun.

Close to moonrise last night, Donegan had saddled up a mule and bid the hay cutters' camp good-bye, promising to return at first light for the new day's labors. He had better things to do with his night than sleep. There were soldiers at the fort two miles away. Soldiers who liked to play cards and hand their money over to the Irishman. Soldiers who had been paid just the day before.

Seamus Donegan wanted to be one of the first to have a go at all that army script. And if he had to lose a night of sleep to do it, so be that draw of the cards.

As the eastern sky turned gray with the first hint of light, Donegan had excused himself from the smoke-stale, whiskey-soaked room where the gamers had played all night. At the stinking slit-trench near the south wall, Donegan had wet the ground, and was busy stuffing himself back into his cavalry britches when the first alarm rang from the sentries.

Dressed and ready to ride, Seamus loped like a hungry mountain cat toward the hitching post in front of Lieutenant Colonel Bradley's office. He had stopped, quickly measuring the droop-eared mule he had ridden to the fort. Beside the mule stood A. C. Leighton's prize sorrel. Saddled and ready for the contractor's trip to the meadows first thing this morning.

Seamus Donegan never regarded himself as a horse thief, really. Only borrowing the boss's animal . . . to protect the boss's hay-cutting crew and equipment down in the valley. It made one hell of a lot of sense to the Irishman as he clambered atop Leighton's sorrel.

"We'll have our work cut out for us, Cawpril!" Seamus roared as he brought that horse alongside the bay Ethan Wade rode.

"We'll give back everything they give us!"

Donegan liked the grit this young soldier showed. Riding into odds stacked like a whorehouse deck against them. "In spades, sojur. Always give it back in spades . . . for you know not when you'll get another crack at 'em!"

But like many a young soldier, Wade suffered a malady

common among the new, untried army of the west. He let his buffalo bravado overload his better judgment. And pointed his detail up the ridge after exchanging some first shots with the Indians.

On some unseen or unheard signal among their number, the warriors split into two groups. The smallest bunch, numbering no more than thirty by the Irish cavalryman's quick count, wheeled on down the road toward the hay cutters' corral. The rest, he hated to admit, stayed their ground. In the middle of the road they stood, prancing and waiting bold as a general's brass for Ethan Wade's young and untried soldiers to come down for a two-step.

Without warning the sixty-and-more shrieked as one. Pounding their ponies' ribby sides and galloping hell-bent-for-blood at the soldiers. Fixing to scare the troopers into confusion at worst. Surround the relief column at best.

Donegan shook his head and drove his heels into the sorrel's flanks. Realizing the young corporal should have dismounted his command as soon as the warriors swept past on both flanks, intent on surrounding the uncertain soldiers. The Irishman's worst nightmares took shape before his eyes as the formation fell apart, young soldiers jostling against one another wildly. Weapons flailing the air, curses turning the morning sky blue. And few shots aimed at the enemy more by luck than by design.

Tragedy of it was, a moment more and it would be every man for himself as the warriors poured their whistling torment into the confused mass of horseflesh and soldier blue.

Out of the midst of the heavy fire and the milling soldiers, Donegan watched Ethan Wade gallop up, his army revolver in hand.

"Got any ideas getting us out of what I got us into, mister . . . I'll be glad to hear 'em—and quick too!"

"I'll just bet you would, Cawpril," Seamus gritted, studying the prancing warriors very much close at hand. "First off, those red bastards don't look like any Sioux I've ever seen before."

Wade glared at him a moment. "What you figure them to be, Irishman? Mormons?"

Donegan chuckled. "Bless the Pope, and save your sainted soul, boy! I figure them to be Cheyenne."

Ethan Wade nodded. "It's said there's some Cheyenne in this neck of the woods. Arapaho too."

"Their land . . . after they robbed the Crow of it." Donegan wiped the back of a hand across his dry lips. "No matter who those red divils are—we got ourselves pinned down and scattered where they'll start carving away at us. Worse thing for cavalry is get pinned down where they can't move. Look there, Cawpril. We can't ride for the high ground up yonder." He flung an arm up to the east. "No man'd be left in his saddle. Only thing I suggest is that you charge your men straight for the creek. Maybe we can make a stand of it down in the trees. Hold out till—"

Corporal Wade slapped boot heels against his snorting, wide-eyed mount. Gone into the smoke and confusion. Yelling over the shrieks of the warriors and the curses of his frightened men.

Around to the right Donegan tore, shouting for the young soldiers to retreat at a charge, pointing the way with his Henry. His eyes swept the slope. In the space of three more heartbeats, Seamus found himself and Wade acting as file closers. The last men out on the retreat. Nothing new to Seamus Donegan.

"Ride, Cawpril!" he yelled, urging the soldier down the dusty road toward the beckoning cottonwoods at Warrior Creek. "Ride low!"

For your life depends upon it!

A half-dozen warriors drove their ponies down the slope, pursuing the two of them, swinging clubs and axes, not content to use their bows or old rifles at the retreating white men. Two of the six quickly tumbled off their ponies as Wade's soldiers opened fire from the shelter of the leafy cottonwoods along the creek. Another pair pulled up, thinking twice about riding directly into the teeth of those soldier guns.

Despite the narrowing of the odds, Seamus still found himself with a double handful of trouble thundering down the slope after him.

A wildly-painted warrior chose Corporal Wade, drawing an arrow back, firing and missing. Then aiming again. This time the iron point sank deep into the mount's flanks. Stumbling crazily, the animal cantered sideways, pitching its rider into the sage and scrub brush. Without slowing a step, the warrior raced toward the thrown soldier, nocking another arrow in his short, elkhorn bow.

Seamus swung the Henry, aimed instinctively and fired without thought. The warrior catapulted off the side of his straining animal. He had lashed himself to his war pony with a long, buffalo-hide lariat. To the shouts and jeers of the soldiers pinned down in the trees, the pony dragged its master's body back up the dusty slope where the charge had begun.

A burning river of fire suddenly coursed through Donegan's left calf—a pain so intense, he had felt nothing like it since the war.

Seamus stuffed the reins between his teeth, flicking his left hand along the calf the way a man would swat at a troubling wasp. His fingers bounced off the shaft. Sending hot slivers of pain shooting through his leg and hip. His stomach grew queasy. Donegan had been slashed with sabers and shot with minié balls. Never had he worn a warrior's iron-tipped arrow.

A shriek brought him around. He yanked Leighton's sorrel to the left. Protecting that bleeding leg. Up top of the slope he thought he saw a white man among a few warriors. Lighter-skinned than the rest. Waving his arms wildly and directing the charge.

A hand with no fingers? he asked himself.

Then Donegan had more pressing matters to attend to. Another shriek and Seamus whirled to find a young, muscular warrior galloping down upon him, his long lance pointed at the Irishman's chest.

Donegan cocked his Henry. Empty.

Reaching for his pistol, he realized he was out of time.

Just as the warrior swept by, Seamus leaned off his saddle, forced to jam all his 230 pounds onto that left leg. He winced in a flood of pain, swallowing the bile his stomach heaved against his tonsils. A dizzying, mind-numbing pain that sent hot sparks of light exploding through his brain. At the same time he sensed the lance whistling overhead.

Jerking the sorrel around with the reins still in his teeth,

Seamus kicked his right heel against the animal's flanks. The horse bolted off. Heading for the attack its rider planned.

Donegan narrowed the distance on the young warrior. He readied himself as the big Indian haunch-slid his pony around in a cloud of dust, just in time to watch the bearded white man swing the brass-mounted Henry like a double-bladed axe singing into ponderosa pine.

That collision of iron and wood against bone and muscle shook Donegan to his roots. But it knocked the big youth from his pony.

Time to be moving, me boy! The Irishman's mind raced as he drove the lathered sorrel down the slope toward the trees.

His last glimpse at the brow of the hill showed him the white man waving atop the slope. His mouth open like a black hole in his face. Past the white man burst more than a hundred of the warriors screaming down on Donegan's tail, hungry for scalps, charging on a collision course for that gallant little stand Corporal Wade and his soldiers were about to make.

Down the windswept slope the shrieking red tide roared—when the cottonwoods before them suddenly erupted, belching smoke from half a hundred guns. The low boom of the Springfield muzzle loaders coupled with the sharp crack of carbines and repeaters.

By bloody damned! It's them hay cutters, i'tis!

A loud cheer burst from the line of trees along the creekbank as Seamus darted through the skirmish line, his bridle snagged by Ethan Wade.

"You saved my life, mister!" Wade shouted up at the Irishman.

"Aye, Cawpril. Now, you'll be one to return the favor." He swallowed hard. The taste of nausea and last night's stale whiskey choked him. "Me . . . me left leg."

When Ethan Wade dashed to the far side of Leighton's lather-flecked sorrel, his eyes narrowed on the arrow fluttering from the bloody hogleg boot.

"C'mon, Mister . . ."

"Donegan," he gritted in pain.

"C'mon, Mr. Donegan. Step down. I'll help get it pulled—"

" 'Fraid I can't be stepping down, sojur. Here." He handed his Henry down as more heavy fire rattled from the trees.

Glancing up the slope, Seamus saw another handful of warriors tumble, even more of the ribby ponies shying beneath the rain of flying lead. He smiled grimly, watching his fellow teamsters lay down a hot fire into the shrieking Indian horde.

"Can't dismount?"

"Appears I'm a bit stuck . . . now if you'd be kind enough . . ."

The moment Wade wiggled the crimson arrow, Seamus again sensed that peculiar queazy nausea flutter through his belly with heavy wings once more. And Wade himself discovered why the Irishman couldn't pull himself from the saddle. The arrow shaft had Donegan's leg pinned to the stirrup fender.

Swiftly Wade braced one hand back of the bloody leg. With the other he yanked the skewered boot free, watching Donegan wobble a moment as the pain roiled over him.

"Dear Mither of God!" Seamus growled between clenched teeth, regaining his senses and dragging a hand across his damp brow.

Off the far side of his horse he slid, landing on the right leg. Teetering like an aspen in a strong wind.

As Donegan sank among the willow and creepers, up the slope arose shrieks of terror and pain mixed with the wild cries of injured ponies. One of the teamsters roared his approval.

" 'Bout damned time they knock down some of them bleeming Injin ponies!" Donegan laughed. " 'Bout goddamned time, i'tis. We nearly lose our hair! And," Seamus sucked a long draught of air, " 'bout bleeming time you yanked this sonabitch outta me, Cawpril. Nice and gentle, like me tender Jennie-Colleen would do . . ."

He looked away as Ethan Wade grabbed the arrow. Donegan gazed over his shoulder as the confused warriors straggled back up the slope, retreating from the fight and the hay cutters' guns. Enough blood for one day.

Sojur guns are one thing, Seamus brooded as the waves of red pain washed over him.

Inch by horrid inch Corporal Wade pulled the smooth shaft

free from Donegan's calf—raking through the Irishman's muscle just like a glowing poker dipped in a hot rum drink, back in that dear little Boston pub so long a favorite of his.

Injins figured on the sojurs having to reload. Whoever that white bastard was up with them savages on the hill, he didn't count on the repeaters. I'm one happy lad to make our repeaters that white renegade's undoing . . .

Seamus leaned back, wearing a smile, as Leighton's hay cutters and Wade's troopers jostled and cheered and backslapped one another in the cottonwood grove. Donegan closed his eyes, welcoming the cool black pouring over him—dreaming of a cold winter's day and steamy rum drink, back in that dear little Boston pub.

Finn Burnett scratched the bantam tuft of hair he had sprouting just below his lower lip. He wore no mustache. No beard. Just the long, mousy-brown hair he let grow in a stylish tuft down the center of his chin. Scratching at that tuft, he hoped he hadn't caught any lice from one of the other teamsters here in the hay cutters' corral on Warrior Creek.

The sporty tuft made him feel older. At least no longer a youngster. Perhaps more accepted among the older teamsters, some of whom Leighton had brought with him all the way from Omaha and North Platte. And the tall Irishman Leighton had hired on here, despite Captain Kinney's warnings of trouble back in June when the work in these fields began. Finn could laugh at the soldier's assertion of troublemaking Irish. The only trouble the hay cutters had seen came in spades from the naked warriors rushing off the hills more and more often with each new day. Small bands who shouted and waved blankets, frightening stock and the hay cutters alike, forcing the civilians back to their corral until the meadow quieted once more and work could resume.

The Irishman. Finn smiled at the thought of him now as he looked over at Seamus Donegan. *He's the only one. The only one younger than me. And a grand fellow Irishman to boot.*

Twilight glistened summer-radiant overhead. He sighed. Nowhere else in the world was there a sky like this. Nowhere but the high plains, with the Big Horn Mountains hulking behind you like an old friend with his hand warm upon your shoulder. Fires twinkled cheery light as the blue sank into purple beyond the corral and antelope steaks sizzled over the flames, grease popping and spitting while coffeepots steamed their fragrant seduction.

Contractor A. C. Leighton had been going at it in a big way down in the meadows since the last week in June. It made sense to him to establish his teamsters' camp close to his mowing operation. Here along Warrior Creek, with the Big-horn River some three hundred yards away, Leighton's men had completed their first task a month ago—to build a corral for the nightly protection of the mules that pulled the mowers, and a place to which the teamsters could retreat in case of attack. Fort C.F. Smith, some three miles away by a rough road, assigned a rotating compliment of troopers to guard the civilian workers. They too slept near the corral these warm, late-summer nights.

"Coffee ready, Finn?"

Burnett looked up from his work over supper, though he recognized the peaty brogue. No other spoke so thick with the fragrant, green breath of the motherland.

"It is, Seamus. Have a seat and grab yourself a tin. These steaks be a bit longer. Coffee's on."

Seamus held the cup before him as Burnett poured. "You'll not burn my steak now, Finn. A kiss or two of flame, like a Colleen's warm embrace . . . and the inside of my steak as pink as . . . well—an old fella like yourself knows what's most pink and tender."

Burnett and Donegan laughed, joined by a handful of civilians and the three soldiers gathered at their fire. Behind them snorted a few mules tethered at the long picket line run from one end of the corral to the other. Down at the far end stood the army's horses. Nearby rose the fragrant smell of steamy mule droppings. Earthy, mingling with the rising scents of antelope and sourdough biscuits. Charlie White performed his peculiar magic in a Dutch oven again tonight.

Warrior Creek gurgled nearby, just to the south of the corral, dancing over its graveled bed between deep willow thickets as it hurried out of some rough, hilly country that rimmed the wide, grassy meadows Leighton had chosen for his summer's operation.

The teamsters' camp itself was a corral of about a hundred feet on a side. When they first arrived in the meadow, the civilians had chosen this spot a little more than two hundred yards from the plateau rising at their backs. Here midway between the ridges and the Bighorn itself, the civilians had placed logs upright in pairs, spacing them about six feet apart around the hundred-foot square. Then three logs were fastened between each pair of stringers: one laid on the ground, one halfway up the stringer, and the last secured at the top. Between all these stringers, green willow branches from the creek were interwoven. While the leafy boughs would not stop a bullet or arrow, they did provide an effective curtain.

Just outside the corral itself the teamsters had dug three trenches some thirty feet long, all half-moon in shape, each wrapping a corner of the corral. Only the southwest corner lacked a trench. Here Warrior Creek ran closest to the camp, where Burnett and the others squatted now by the cook tent standing just outside the corral wall.

"You cook good antelope, Burnett," Donegan said around a piece of juicy flank, grease dripping into his full beard. "I'll teach you yet the most tender part of the female anatomy—you being such a good student and all, me lad."

The civilians and troopers chuckled wordlessly, each man wolfing chunks of rare antelope and fluffy sourdough biscuits, all washed down with the dark, heady brew that was Donegan's specialty.

There was for the teamsters and soldiers assigned to the corral a sense of isolation here. Although only some three miles by road away from C.F. Smith, intervening bluffs and the plateau kept the corral and the fort hidden from one other. The road leading to the teamsters' camp had to circle north around the base of the tall bluff before it wound south and east past the spur, heading directly for Leighton's meadow.

While the road to the fort ran past the north side, the only entrance to the corral itself was in the center of the south wall. This opening was closed each night by chaining a wagon's running gear across the entrance, locking the wheels to the corral posts. During the day and night, a soldier was picketed on the spur some seven hundred yards down the valley to the east of the camp.

As the purple of twilight slid off the land like rain off a rawhide drum, there arose a shout from the trooper stationed outside the corral near the road to the fort.

"Halt! And name yourselves!"

The teamsters and soldiers at their mess bolted from the firelight, scrambling for their weapons. Near the bright flames was the only place to be if a man had decided on committing suicide.

"Ho, the camp!" rang a voice from the darkness as a half-dozen murky shadows halted on the fort road.

"Saints preserve," Donegan whispered to Burnett, "if that don't sound like Mitch Bouyer himself."

"We're coming in!" the voice shouted.

"Halt, goddammit!" the young sentry ordered, nervousness rising on every syllable.

"That you, Mitch Bouyer?" Donegan flung his voice over the corral wall.

"No other, you goddamned Irishman!" Bouyer hollered back. "You tell this soldier with the itchy trigger finger to let me and my friends ride on in . . . slow and easy like."

"What friends you got out there?" Burnett asked, the hair on the back of his neck relaxing at last.

"Have five Crow with me."

Burnett and Donegan eased their weapons down.

"C'mon in!" Burnett shouted into the murky twilight. " 'Round to the gate."

Finn met the six riders at the corral entrance, the five warriors and Bouyer illuminated in firelight now.

"Damn," Mitch sighed as he kicked a leg off his pony, "you boys sure jumpy."

"We been hit a lot lately," Burnett explained, shaking Bouyer's hand. "I'm Finn Burnett, Leighton's boss here in the field."

"You run things here?" Bouyer inquired.

"Yep."

"So, been hit a lot lately, eh?" the half-breed continued.

"Nothing much. The bastards just swing by, trying to scare

stock . . . or trying to pitch a burning limb in the hay we got stacked to dry out in the meadows."

"Just raising hell," Seamus Donegan remarked as he inched forward, presenting his hand to Bouyer.

Mitch shook it eagerly. "Hey, Irishman—better you keep your eyes open from now on. The Sioux been gaming with you so far."

Burnett looked from Bouyer's face to Donegan's. Both drained of smiles. "Sounds like they're planning something big for us."

The half-breed nodded. He flung a thumb over his shoulder at the Crow riders. "From what this handful tells me, Sioux already quit this part of the country. Heading for Kearny, to work some devil down there."

Donegan chuckled, slapping Burnett on the shoulder. "Then Mitch is right—we are getting a little jumpy . . . what with Red Cloud's bunch ready to turn the burner up on Kearny."

Bouyer stepped closer to Donegan, the smile not returned to his dark features. "Red Cloud's Sioux may be off the Big Horn. But the Crow tell me the Cheyenne and Arapaho are flexing muscle and itching for a big fight."

Burnett glanced at Donegan. "Must be the sonsabitches hit us a few times each day."

"Might be," Bouyer replied. "More likely they're feeling you boys out."

"You got a lot more to say," Donegan growled. "Spit it out, Mitch."

Bouyer scratched his cheek. "Coffee on?"

"Soon as you tell us what you come to say," Donegan remarked.

"The Crow gone to their camps. Heard what Red Cloud's bunch been planning."

"Yeah," Burnett sighed. "They're down to Kearny to jump that post again. Never gave Smith much trouble. Too close to Crow country here."

"Not no longer," Bouyer hissed. "The Cheyenne and Arapahos stayed on hereabouts when Red Cloud went south. These boys tell me they heard the Cheyenne planning to hit the fort tomorrow morning."

"Tomorrow?"

Mitch nodded.

Donegan handed him a steaming tin of coffee which the half-breed slurped noisily. "Tell them others get down . . . have some coffee on us."

"No. We go on to the fort for the night. Attack come, we use our guns from the fort come morning."

"Makes sense, I suppose," Burnett said. "Tomorrow, eh?"

"They'll hit the fort with everything they got, so the Crow tell me," Bouyer said as went back to his black coffee.

"You trust it, Mitch?"

He eyed Donegan over the lip of his tin. "I trust 'em every bit as much as I don't trust the Cheyenne and Arapaho. These boys say the attack will come tomorrow morning . . . you'll see more mad Injuns than you ever wanna see come tomorrow morning."

Burnett accepted the empty coffee tin from the half-breed before Bouyer turned to his pony and leaped atop bareback.

"Thanks for coming to tell us, Bouyer," Finn said, sticking his hand up to the half-breed.

Bouyer shook the offered hand. "No problem, Finn Burnett. Just figured your bunch and that ugly Irishman there needed to know . . . case you hear gunfire from the fort come sunup."

"We'll be listening, Mitch," Donegan said as he waved.

Bouyer signaled his Crow horsemen. They turned, ambling toward the fort road.

"By the way, Bouyer!" Burnett hollered. "You know who's leading this bunch of Cheyenne and Arapaho gonna hit the fort?"

Mitch twisted around on his pony as he disappeared from the corona of firelight.

"A bloodthirsty bastard by the name of Roman Nose."

Chapter 27

*B*ob North had to admit, this was one big Indian. Probably the biggest he had ever seen. Every bit as tall as the white man who had shot the renegade last December, maybe taller. And this ugly Cheyenne war-chief was built like the ox that had pulled North's plow through the rich, steamy soil of his farm back in the South before the war. The chief had a chest it would do the white renegade work to get both his arms around. North shuddered, glad Roman Nose was on his side.

> "Possum up a gum stump,
>   Coony in a holler.
> Wake, snake, june bug,
>   Stole a half a dollar."

North sang to amuse himself during the lull in war talk.

"Arapaho white man sings his medicine song?" the ugly Cheyenne asked with a sneer, his eyes hard as flints in the firelight.

North gulped. "My . . . my medicine song. Yeah! My medicine song," he stammered.

Squatting around the fire were the various headmen of the Cheyenne and Miniconjou bands who would lead the attack on the dirt-walled fort the army called C.F. Smith. With a sprinkling of North's Arapaho thrown in for good measure. Here in their camp of buffalo-hide lodges and blanket-covered willow wickiups, the combined tribes could boast of quite a force of warriors to throw against the soldiers. The Indians had no accurate way of counting. And Bob North was never one to put much stock in ciphering numbers as a boy.

Close as he could count, there were ten-times-a-hundred in this spreading camp. Cheyenne and Arapaho. Even some Oglalla and a few Miniconjou who wanted in on this attack rather than following Red Cloud and Crazy Horse south. Plus a band of Blood and Piegan come all the way from up north near Canada.

Rode down here for a piece of the white man's pie, North brooded now.

The Sioux had ripped themselves apart, trying to decide how to press their war against the forts. Man-Afraid, Little Wound, and Pawnee Killer had gone south in the spring. They would have no more of Red Cloud's war. Instead, they planned to wreak their havoc along the white man's railroads.

Two hundred warriors killed last winter—two hundred, Red Cloud had reminded them in his harangues all through the harsh winter. Killed by the eighty and one they had butchered at the end of Lodge Trail Ridge.

Bob North didn't care who ran this fight. Who called the shots now. He was riding along for one thing and one thing only: a chance to put in his sights the tall, dark-headed one who had shot him last winter. The man who had slipped through his Arapaho attack a few days back.

Roman Nose could have his fort for all the renegade cared. Bob North wanted the tall one to *suffer*.

"Time has come for the Cheyenne to show the Lakota how to kill soldiers," Roman Nose hissed. His voice had a way of slapping a man into silence. His every word a sting upon the ears.

North knew Roman Nose to have a reputation smellier than the Cheyenne's own brechclout. But a bloody, murdering reputation just the same. Roman Nose would kill any white man with half the justification it took for most Cheyenne. The troubling thing was that Roman Nose would kill his own fellow Cheyenne as well—often for less provocation.

His was a respect engendered by nothing more than stark, naked fear. Many a man had Roman Nose killed with his bare hands. Strong, talonlike hands that pointed to the starry sky overhead.

"Most may succumb to the bait of the white man's possessions . . . raiding along the roads and striking the forts to steal what the white man brings with him into our hunting lands," Roman Nose spat. "I make war on the white man like Crazy Horse. For no other reason than to kill the white man. I like the taste of his blood."

North gulped again. For as the Cheyenne war-chief spat out the last few words, he glared haughtily into the eyes of the white renegade.

"Over a long winter of hungry bellies, we have planned with the Sioux our attack on the two forts. They choose the one at Pine Woods. I," and the war-chief slapped his bare barrel of a chest, "I choose the dirt-walled fort." ·

"You can be proud of yourself, Roman Nose," North said quietly, eager to butter-up the ugly warrior. "For better than a year now you've run the war to your liking. Killing your share of soldiers down at the Pine Woods Fort. You have scared off all the civilian wagon trains from this road to the land of the Crows. You have new ammunition and guns. You have prayed at your sundance only a moon ago. Now it is time to forget about Red Cloud and his weakening plans for the war."

For the longest time Roman Nose remained silent, glaring at the white man, who grew increasingly nervous as the logs crackled in the firepit.

"Yes," the war-chief finally said. "Now it is time for Roman Nose to wipe this land clean of soldiers and the filthy white men who follow those soldiers to our hunting grounds. Time has come—for now Roman Nose will show Red Cloud how to kill soldiers."

A man could count the miles on the fingers of one hand. Nothing but a few ridges, some grassy hills and a creek or two separated that war camp of Roman Nose from the hay cutters' corral. Under that same summer moon, while the Cheyenne chief harangued his faithful, the white men cheered themselves that the Crows' predictions had proven false. Congratulating themselves for seeing another day draw to a close without trouble of any kind.

Just the sort of thing to bother Seamus Donegan.

"Something's afoot, boys," the Irishman grumbled to his mess mates.

"You're getting more nervous than a hen about to lay," piped J. C. Hollister, another of contractor Leighton's civilians.

Seamus glanced at the man's eyes gleaming in the firelight. "I am, eh?"

"Just relax, will you," big Bob Wheeling whined. "For God's sake, the Sioux didn't even show a feather today."

"That's what's stuck in me craw," Seamus admitted.

"Shit!" Finn Burnett said, slapping his thigh. "Every man here knows the Injuns are off hunting buffalo and antelope after their sun-dance celebration. Right, fellas?"

Al Stevenson nodded as he leaned forward, pouring himself another cup of coffee. "Finn's right, Seamus. Ain't a Injun in the country. Sit back and enjoy the evening . . . all them stars. Sunrise come soon enough."

"Damned Crows," Wheeling growled, then spit into the fire. "Like a bunch of jumpy old women."

"Their kind sees hoodoos and spooks in every shadow," Pvt. Thomas Navins declared as he came into the circle of civilians clustered at their fire. He squatted. "Jumpy at the wind moving through the grass, fellas."

"See, Seamus?" Finn asked. "The army figures the Crow playing a big joke on us—believing that shit about the Sioux attacking. Joke's on us."

Donegan eyed the old private. Navins had seen action throughout the Civil War. In silence, Seamus brooded that Navins was the sort who would either retire a private or die one. With his boots on.

"Believe the army, eh, Finn?" Seamus asked. "The day I go back to believing what the army tells me . . . that's the day you might as well throw six feet of dirt in my face."

They all laughed with him. Including Private Navins. Him mostly. His thick, colicky brogue barking every bit as loud as Seamus Donegan's.

"Why didn't you stay in the army, Donegan?" Navins asked.

Seamus thought for a minute, then smiled that crooked smile inside his full beard. "Belonging to the cavalry is mostly bad grub and a sore ass . . . and damned little excitement to suit me."

"I figured you for the sort who needed more excitement than most," Navins commented.

"Aye, me friend." He stared up at the stars, with their edges sharp as white sparks set in a ripple of clear water by the sun itself. "Nothing the army can give me to top this, me boon companions. Army makes you work too hard. Man's not meant to work so hard, I say."

Seamus reached for a small canvas satchel nearby, dragging it to his side. From it he pulled a bottle wrapped protectively in his only clean shirt. "Man's meant to enjoy good friends . . . and strong whiskey."

"Here! Here!" Wheeling cheered.

"Pass it 'round, Seamus!"

He worried the cork from the neck with his teeth, then held the mouth against his lips, throat bobbing like apples in a washtub at a harvest festival. Wiping his mustache, Seamus passed the bottle on to Navins.

"Send it 'round the circle, Private."

"After I've damned sure had a drink of my own," Navins growled. "You worked hard enough on it yourself."

Seamus rared back his head, laughing. "Reason I drank like that is I don't figure there'll be a drop one left for me after it goes 'round this circle of rummies!"

Navins sputtered his last swallow, laughing with the rest as he passed the bottle on. "Where be you from, Seamus Donegan?"

"The emerald isle. The warm, fragrant motherland herself."

"I know that, goddammit."

"Born in County Kilkenny. On the southeastern edge of the isle . . . in a little place known as Callan town. Sits nestled on the banks of the river Nore."

"Your parents from Kilkenny, then?" Burnett asked. "Seems I've heard my own folks talk of the place."

Seamus shook his head, watching the bottle slowly make its way round the fire, stars whirling overhead. "My mother's people come from Skibereen, County Westmeath. Ah, the women from Skibereen are oft known to be the most fair in that part of the land . . . but the men—well, the less said about the men, the better."

"You've something against your uncles, have you?" Burnett asked.

"Nothing," Seamus snarled, too quickly. " 'Cept . . . a boy fresh off that goddamned stinking boat couldn't find either one—least not where they wrote me mother they'd be in Boston-town. Left that boy with nary a trace to track 'em."

"But now," Zeke Colvin, ex-Confederate, joined the talk, "now you'll go in search of 'em again?"

Seamus nodded, a faint smile creasing his face. "Hear told one of 'em might be found in Kansas."

"You're still set on leaving day after tomorrow?" Zeke's older brother Al asked.

"Sure as I'm born. Just as soon as Leighton passes out July pay."

Burnett brightened. "By damned, that's right. Day after tomorrow is the first of August, fellas. We got a payday coming!"

"Hurrah!" quiet George Duncan hollered, holding the amber bottle aloft in the firelight.

"C'mon—drink your fill!" Al Stevenson complained, clawing at Duncan's arm. "Best you leave me a drink to toast Donegan's parting in two days."

Dragging a second bottle from the canvas satchel, Seamus said, "No worry any man drinking his fill this night!"

"Won't feel like working tomorrow—we get drunk tonight," Wheeling grumbled.

"Sweat's a waste of good whiskey," Seamus agreed.

"I damned sure don't wanna work beside Hollister's team tomorrow," Burnett remarked as the second bottle headed his way. "Helluva lot easier standing the smell of whiskey . . . than having to listen to it!"

Hollister threw a half-hearted punch at Finn, throwing himself off balance in the process. He fell from the keg he was using as a stool, plopping into the trampled grass outside the corral where the civilians took their mess. Everyone hooted and cheered.

"Tell us about that ship what brought you over, Seamus," Burnett prodded. "I like that story every time," he explained.

"Curse the bastard captain and that scurvy boat," Seamus grumbled. "The hold filled with the teeming, stinking refuse of Ireland's shores. The air so close, and filled with the stench of human excrement and vomit—packed in there like we was."

"You made it, though."

Seamus nodded, his eyes staring somewhere in the middle distance. "Aye. I made it. Not all was lucky as I, Finn Burnett. Not all *walked* down that plank into Boston town."

Finn's bantam tuft sprayed wider as he pursed his lips in sudden silence.

Seamus sensed a darkening to the mood of the gathering. Realizing it was his fault, he suddenly smiled.

"You lads ever hear tell of a song the Irish sing about coming to America?"

"What's it called?" Bill Haynes asked, speaking for the first time that evening.

" 'Amerikay.' Song of a young man talking his love into coming with him to this new land."

"You sing it?"

"Just as beautifully as if me own mother was singing me a lullaby."

"I heard you sing afore," Zeke Colvin growled. "Out in the field, pitching hay. You don't sing like no lullaby."

"More like a bullfrog croaking to find himself a place for his pecker!" Bob Little piped up.

As the laughter died, Seamus swiped a hand across his lips and began to sing.

"My curses attend that savage shore.
  O how came this to be?
That I should leave my parents
  Who reared me tenderly?

"For to follow you through woods and groves
  Where savages wild do play,

That would devour both you and I
  Gone to Amerikay.

"Then he kissed her ruby lips
  And embraced her tenderly,
Will you come with me, my heart's delight
  To the land of liberty?

"When daylight peeps
  No tribute we need not pay;
So forebear to spill those precious tears,
  Come to Amerikay.

"Young man, your moving eloquence,
  You've surely won my heart,
And it's from my old aged parents
  I'm willing now to part.

"He took his bonny lass on board
  By the dawning of the day,
Crowded all sails to reach the shores
  of Rich Amerikay."

Donegan's voice sailed over the log-and-brush walls of the corral, his last notes drifting off into the silence of the summer night. Around him the civilians and soldiers alike sat in stunned and unspeaking silence, each man very much in his own thoughts of loved ones back home. Wherever home might be. Some thinking of loved ones left behind. Others brooding on their own private despair, realizing they had no one left behind.

"C'mon, Navins!" Seamus cheered, sensing the melancholy suffocating their camp like a scratchy horse blanket. "You know 'Union Soldier,' don't you, lad?"

"I do!" the private replied, stamping his foot with a beat of his own making.

He and Seamus sang raggedly together.

"Ye loyal Union volunteers,
  Your country claims your aid.
Says Uncle Abe, a foe appears,
  Are we to be afraid?"

The second time through, a handful of soldiers joined them at the fire. Corporal Wade lent his voice to the song.

Ethan Wade chuckled when the song was finished. "Not much more than two years ago now, it was. And so far away, in many ways. So close . . . so damned close in others."

"The war?" Seamus asked.

Wade nodded, staring at the fire. He finally smiled. "Time has a way of doing that, I suppose. Healing things."

"Not when a man needs him some answers," Seamus replied.

"Your uncles?" Burnett inquired.

He nodded. "Time don't lessen the sting of not knowing what became of 'em. Why they lied to their sister the way they did."

Talk fell off round the fire, like water running down greased rawhide. So quiet they could hear the animals munching fodder nearby. Or limbs crackling in the firepit. Sparks sent like wildly darting fireflies into the night sky.

"Never forget the hard-bread they give us," Navins suddenly blurted.

"Hardtack?" Burnett asked.

Navins nodded. "Damned bread was so full of weevils . . . why—we had to post a guard on it just to keep the bread from marching off on its own!"

Seamus turned his back to the firelight. His pupils widening once more, he stared into the darkness of the hills shouldering in on Warrior Creek and the valley of the Bighorn River itself. Then he began to quietly sing to himself.

"My curses attend this savage shore.
　　O how came this to be?
That I should leave my dear mither
　　Who reared me tenderly?

"For to follow those two through woods and plains
　　Where Cheyenne wild do play,
That would devour both uncles and I
　　Gone to Amerikay."

Chapter 28

"*H*ere come your relief, boys!" Sam Marr hollered over his shoulder at some of the soldiers in the wagon-box corral.

He stuffed a long slice of fried pork into his mouth as several of the troopers in A Company clambered to their feet and joined him in watching Captain Powell's C Company making a golden mist on the powdery road leading down from Fort Phil Kearny.

"By damn, it's time we got shet of this stinking shithole!" an old soldier grumbled.

"Lucky bastard, you are," Marr said, turning, addressing the soldier. "You're going back to the post. Rest of us ain't getting no relief."

"You're being paid handsomely for your work," another soldier joined in. "Gilmore pays lot more than the army does."

"We work for it," R. J. Smyth said as he inched alongside Marr.

"Every penny, eh?" a soldier inquired.

"I suppose these young soldier boys deserve a break, don't you, R.J.?" Sam said, grinning with a wink. "Not every man got the bottom to take it like we have to—day after day—making a target of hisself for the likes of Red Cloud's nasty bastards."

For a little more than a month the teamsters working for contractors Gilmore and Porter had called this wagon-box corral their home while they continued to cut wood on Pine Island and across the slope of the hills bordering Big Piney Creek. Here on a level plain some six miles west of Fort Phil Kearny and in sight of Pine Island, the civilians had removed fourteen wagon boxes from their running gears, stripping both canvas sheeting and iron bows from the boxes. Resting on their bottoms, these wagon boxes formed an oval. A few logs, some extra kegs of rations, sacks of grain for the animals and harnessing were stuffed in the openings between the wagons for even more protection.

At either end of the enclosure stood two wagons with canvas stretched over their bows, boxes still bolted to their running gear. Since both were filled with supplies, the wagons were used to block the two entrances to the corral. They could be rolled into position, sealing both openings when all defenders were inside. The wagon at the east entrance contained woodchopper rations, while that on the west held rations for the military escort. Just beyond the ring itself both teamsters and soldiers alike had pitched their tents, white canvas dotting the green-gold of the summer prairie.

In the event of attack, every man was under orders to make his way to the wagon-box enclosure. There they would defend themselves with everything they had until the post sent out a relief party to drive the attackers off.

"Captain James W. Powell, fellas," the sandy-haired soldier announced as he walked up to the teamsters' fire. He presented his hand around the circle.

"Pleased to make your 'quaintance, Cap'n," Sam replied, shaking Powell's arm. "Sam Marr."

"Captain. Missouri volunteers. Right?"

Powell's surprising remark caught Marr off his guard. "Yes. That's right."

"Let me introduce my second in command, Captain Marr. Lieutenant John C. Jenness."

The young soldier stepped forward, shaking hands all around before he rubbed a hand across his belly.

"Welcome home, fellas," Marr remarked, flinging his arm at the cookfires. "Help yourselves."

"We ate breakfast at the post before assembly," Powell explained, bringing Jenness up short. "I understand some of your men will be ready to make a run to the fort with a load of timber soon?"

Marr nodded. "We load in the afternoon. First thing come next morning, we make the first run of the day. We'll get Heeley off his ass here soon and get hitched up, Cap'n Powell."

"I'm not rushing you," the captain explained. "Just wanted to assure myself of the routine here."

"Not much of a routine here," R. J. Smyth replied. "The far camp cuts wood. We haul it down from the island and the slopes. Injuns show up, the boys up on the hill run to the blockhouse. The rest of us run here to the corral."

"From what we've heard, the Sioux haven't been much of a problem of late," Lieutenant Jenness said.

Marr clucked, grinning. "Son, the Sioux'll come 'round real soon, I reckon. Them bastards never far from this post, they aren't."

"How long have you been in the Big Horns, Captain Marr?" Powell inquired.

"Last summer. Came up with the bunch the Sioux jumped at Crazy Woman Fork."

"Templeton's group?"

"Yep. And that was only the beginning."

"Things safer here in the wagon-box corral, I figure," Jenness commented.

Sam wagged his head with a wry grin. "These damned wagon-boxes was Gilmore's idea. I told him they wouldn't stop the Injuns if they got a mind to rush us."

"The hostiles will actually attack a well-defended fortification like this?" Jenness asked.

"Yes, son. They done it while we was building the fort— Kearny itself. Us civilians made a ring of wagon-boxes like these up on the plateau, busy each day planting the stockade in the ground. Every evening the fellas would play cards by firelight inside that circle of wagon-boxes."

"And?"

"Well, now—one time I went to bed early but was woke up to hear three shots fired near the end of the wagon-box I was sleeping in."

"I'll be damned!" Powell commented.

Sam nodded, gnawing on the last of his skillet-fried pork. "Injuns crawled in real close after dark . . . right through the picket lines . . . shooting up our camp."

"Anyone hurt?" Jenness asked.

"Yep. Three shots. One wounded. Two killed. All near the fire. Red bastards was good shots that night."

"Firelight made a good backdrop, I suppose."

Sam regarded Powell. "I'd say you're right, Captain. Since then, I stay out of the firelight after dark. I didn't get this gray hair of mine by taking chances. And I don't figure on starting now."

"Does make a man walk a little straighter, knowing he has some knocking 'round money in his pocket, A.C.," Seamus declared, smiling at his employer, contractor Leighton.

"Sorry to see you pulling out, Irishman," Leighton replied, turning back to the tailgate of his wagon. "You worked mighty hard—and got hard work out of the others. I'll miss you, Seamus Donegan." He held out his hand.

Seamus took it, shaking the arm solidly. "Likewise, A.C. There's a world of difference between you and that little sutler squatting on his tradership down at Fort Phil Kearny."

Leighton laughed, then sighed, looking over the hay cutter's corral here along the stream they called Warrior Creek. "Never been one to ask more than my share."

Seamus grinned, slapping Leighton on the shoulder. "I never been one to take to employers, A.C. But if a man must have an boss—you're the best a man could have. I wish you luck here at Fort C.F. Smith."

At two o'clock earlier that morning, forty men of D Company had left the post to escort six of Leighton's wagons on their return to Fort Phil Kearny to pick up more supplies destined for the northernmost outpost of Lt. Col. Luther P. Bradley on the Bighorn River. That escort left some 240 men at Fort C.F. Smith, not to mention a full company of forty-odd soldiers assigned to protect the hay cutters' corral.

With the rising of the sun that steamy first day of August, the civilians and soldiers alike had eaten breakfast before some of Captain Powell's soldiers left the corral, escorting a few wagons back to the fort, each straining under a load of hay dried in the previous day's cutting. About the same time, a half-dozen civilians leisurely moved off toward the meadow where they began whipping the mule-drawn mowers into motion, watched over by a dozen young soldiers.

Left behind at the corral were Lt. Sigmund Sternberg and eight of his enlisted men, along with three civilians. It would be up to Finn Burnett and Robert Wheeling to water and feed better than thirty mules tethered at the picket line inside the corral. As he was no longer on Leighton's payroll, Seamus Donegan had found himself some shade by a wagon-box complete with its bowed-canvas top, waiting for Leighton to ride down from the fort. It was, after all, payday. The Irishman had better places to be off to.

And faces to see.

With the stock fed, soldiers and civilians alike pulled blankets from the tents and wagon-boxes, airing the bedding as was their custom each morning. The water barrel inside the corral refilled, Burnett joined Donegan and Wheeling at a hand or two of cards with the lounging soldiers. Some of the troopers pitched horseshoes nearby. Two of the peach-faced recruits busied themselves with letters.

"How many of them redskins you boys figure we can cut down with our new breechloaders?" Robert Wheeling asked those in the circle holding seven of the stained cards from his greasy deck.

Seamus eyed the two pistols Wheeling had stuffed in his belt, figuring the man for a lot of wind and little gumption.

"We can wallop the devil out of all the Indians that can fill the field between here and that hill," the cocky private James Leavey answered first, throwing his arm toward the ridge some three hundred yards away.

"By jinks," said Pvt. Ed Holloran, "I'd like a crack at the red bastards myself. Now we're armed the way we ought'n be."

"Damn right," joined in Pvt. George Frambier. "Way I see it, we could all make them sonsabitches scratch where they don't itch!"

In the midst of the laughing all round, Pvt. Rudolph Raithel declared, "I'd make 'em scratch best of all, I would, bejabbers. For it would be the ground they'd be scratchin' with their noses!"

"I figure we can take 'em all," answered the cocky James Leavey. "Make mince of every last one of them Sioux Red Cloud wants to throw at us—we'll kill 'em all."

"How you see it, Sergeant?" Seamus asked the veteran at his shoulder.

James Horton shook his head, studying the field a moment. "Don't like the idea of having to test them new guns a'tall. Don't like it—with what your contractor done out there in the fields . . . leaving so much grass drying up so dang close to the corral the way he's ordered you boys to do."

"You 'fraid of fire?" Burnett inquired.

"Damn right I am. Fire would play hell with us," Sergeant Horton answered, spitting into the cold firepit. "But don't count on them savages giving us a chance to try out the new guns. They don't fight fair. Nor do they come out when you're ready for 'em. Now that I think of it, fellas—some of you deal out of the game a hand or two—go loosen the screws in the lids on those ammunition boxes. If we end up needing it —we'll need it quick."

Seamus chuckled. "Sergeant, if Red Cloud's warriors come 'round and stay long enough for your boys to thump those five thousand rounds into 'em—there'll be a damned lot of them h'athens needing a surgeon, I'd wager!"

"And by the same token," Wheeling blustered, "there'll be that many more what won't need a surgeon, but good for only the devil when it's said and done."

"Lookee yonder there," Pvt. Charles Bradley announced. "Appears to be your bossman coming now, Burnett."

Finn looked over at Donegan. "Leighton's coming . . . with your pay, Seamus."

The Irishman smiled without real happiness as he laid his cards down on the wagon gate they used as a table. "Looks like I can be going, Finn."

"Gonna miss you, Irishman."

"You as well, Finn Burnett."

When he had settled with Seamus and left the other teamsters' pay in the care of Burnett, Leighton turned to climb into the saddle. "Sorry to rush off, Donegan. Got a couple boys waiting for me upriver. Gonna repair that ferry before lunch."

"I thank you again, A.C. Been a pleasure knowing you."

"Oh—almost forgot." Leighton scratched his cheek before stuffing a hand inside his shirt. He pulled out a thick fold of paper. "Bradley give me this for you. This morning. Said it come in with the Crow mailman some time back."

Donegan took it, seeing his name scrawled across it in an unfamiliar hand. "How long?"

"Said he's had it about a week now."

"A week? Damn."

"I feel the same way 'bout the army, Seamus. Pray it isn't bad news . . . a death in the family."

Alone at last when Leighton departed, Seamus carefully tore at the waxed seal of the paper, finding inside a one-page letter folded over a piece of brittle, yellowed newsprint. He promptly squatted in the shade near the kitchen awning outside the southern wall of the corral to read the letter.

Seamus,

Best to say this off the front and be done with it. Jennie Wheatley's taking her boys back east.

She don't know as things set now how far east she'll get. Leaving with her brother tomorrow. Taking the boys with her. And wanted me to get word to you that she's going. Wanted me to tell you that she cares for you, son.

As it sounds, Jennie might well be waiting in east Nebraska for you. Round Osceola, on the Big Blue River. That's where Wheatley's folks are from. I don't figure she'll get any farther east than that, Seamus. Plant herself there, and wait for you.

Don't wait long. She needs to know how you feel about her. And I need to know if I am to go on to Virginia City with you or without you come fall. Being an old man, I can't wait forever to make myself rich, son.

Newspapers come up the other day from Laramie. Got my hands on this one after it had been the rounds of the barracks. Tore this piece of a story out for you to read. Figured it would help make your mind up if you were going on the Alder Gulch with me. Or back to Nebraska to find Jennie Wheatley.

Or if Seamus Donegan gonna chase after some damnfool ghosts he's gotta get shet of before he can think about settling down.

I'll be working as herder for the woodcutters camp down on the Big Piney, near the island, you come looking for me some day soon.

Figure you better decide before the leaves turn, Seamus. Winter doesn't wait on no man in this country.

Samuel Marr

Donegan swallowed at the hard, dusty knot in his throat, his hands shaky as he unfolded the news story Marr had torn from a page of newsprint. A few feet from where he sat, Warrior Creek ran over its rocky bed with a noise like the westerly breezes nudging a man along in his quest for something unknown. Breezes that whispered his name again and again through the bunchberry and dogwood.

The grass all round him stood full and stiff and stubbornly yellow with summer's age. Beneath the breeze the newsprint rustled like a woman's petticoats, causing Seamus to think on Jennie. And in the next heartbeat Donegan's thoughts of her disappeared as smoke on a strong wind. A brittle, cruel winter wind.

Near the top of the page stood out the bold, black ink:

ROCKY MOUNTAIN NEWS
Denver City, Colorado Territory
May 27, 1867

And directly below it, the banner headline screamed:

HANCOCK ON THE MARCH

Quickly Donegan's eyes scanned the article, wondering why Marr had enclosed the story.

Major General Winfield Scott Hancock, the "Thunderbolt of the Grand Army of the Potomac," will lead a force of infantry and cavalry against the hostile Dog-Soldiers who have been raiding Kansas Pacific Railroad construction crews and carrying on their deadly warfare against settlers along the Republican and Smoky Hill Rivers.

His gray, red-rimmed eyes bounced on down the article, landing here, then there:

. . . grand punitive expedition . . .
. . . special correspondent Henry M. Stanley of James Gordon Bennett's *New York Herald* . . .
. . . artist-reporter T. R. Davis of *Harper's Weekly* . . .
. . . eight companies of cavalry under the command of Lieutenant Colonel George Armstrong Custer . . .

"Why that old son of a bitch." Seamus smiled. "He figured I'd like to know what Custer's up to, I'll bet."

Then his eyes went back to a casual study of the news story, immediately narrowing as he found out that mention of Custer was in all probability the last thing on Sam Marr's mind when he tore the story from the newspage.

As chief scout, Old Eagle-Eye Hancock has chosen none other than the redoubtable James Butler "Wild Bill" Hickock, who has enlisted a dozen of the more noted frontiersmen of these Great Plains to serve Hancock as scouts. Among them are Wheeler Dunn, Bay Creele, Jonah Hexx, Liam O'Roarke . . .

"Liam O'Roarke!" Seamus whispered coarsely. "Damn!"
You bastard, Donegan thought as he clambered to his feet, staring at the name on the old, oft-folded newsprint that rattled in the hot breeze. *I've found you now. All I have to do is run down this grand circus Hancock's calling an expedition against the Cheyenne . . . and I'll have my hands on you, dear Uncle Liam—*

"—God's sake, Seamus!" Finn Burnett's voice cracked through Donegan's reverie. "Look at those red sonsabitches coming up the valley!"

Burnett was beside him like quicksilver, pointing off to the northeast. At the same time a rifle shot boomed from a nearby hillside. Galloping downstream toward the corral tore the uniformed picket Lieutenant Sternberg had stationed on a bench of land overlooking the valley some seven hundred yards away.

More shots echoed down in the valley in the direction of the meadows scheduled for cutting that morning. A moment later those in the corral watched the mowers rattle round the corner of the hills, drivers whipping their teams, the mules snorting and wide-eyed.

Half a hundred screeching warriors were hot on their tails, firing an occasional shot at the fleeing teamsters and soldier escort.

As the mowers made the corral, the warriors reined up, just out of range, taunting, luring the white men to come out and fight.

For almost a quarter hour Seamus and the rest watched the naked warriors throw their curses at the corral's defenders. Standing near the middle of the compound, Lieutenant Sigmund Sternberg was occupied shouting orders to his soldiers, moving manpower this way then that, busting open boxes of ammunition, and all the time assessing the nearness of the warriors.

Donegan looked over at Finn nearby.

"You thinking what I'm thinking, Seamus?"

He nodded. "We both seen what happened to Fetterman's men when they got suckered into a decoy ambush."

"My thought too. Figure they want to draw us out."

"Which means there's one helluva lot more of those red bastards than what we can see, Finn."

"I don't figure where they could be, Irishman."

Seamus wagged his head sadly, pursing his lips within his dark beard. "Look there, lad."

Burnett and the rest stood cautiously as they watched the entire lower valley fill with mounted warriors loping easily into sight of the corral. Hundreds upon hundreds of them whooping and hollering, waving rifles and bows overhead, riding in slowly from the northeast.

"Good God!" Lieutenant Sternberg swore. "That force will surely ride over us!"

Donegan swallowed hard. His throat scratchy from the dust kicked up by the mules growing nervous tethered at their picket line in the center of the compound.

"You don't show them your backs," Seamus hollered, "we can hold our own against undisciplined cavalry!"

Sternberg, a Prussian immigrant to America, almost sneered at the tall civilian. "You're Irish, aren't you?"

"Has nothing—"

"Leave the military strategy to the Prussians, Mr. Donegan."

"Keep my mouth shut, eh?" Seamus asked. "Like good cannon fodder . . . all us Irishmen—"

The lieutenant turned and barked orders as more of his frightened soldiers shouted warnings to him.

The wave of warriors had moved into a hand-gallop, a solid, steady front thundering more quickly toward the corral.

"Man the trenches!" Sternberg ordered. "Everyone to the rifle-pits!"

"Son of a bitch is gonna get his men killed this day," Seamus grumbled as he watched the first of the soldiers reach the opening in the willow branches forming the south wall of their corral.

As suddenly, the bullets whistled overhead and slapped against that wall, causing the soldiers to duck and seek cover inside the corral. Already the warriors had charged so close that the defenders could not reach the three crescent-shaped trenches dug outside the walls without coming under heavy fire. Twenty-one soldiers and nine civilians would have to make do inside the corral now.

The green willow branches lashed between the pine-log uprights had tightened in drying. Although such a wall would not keep arrows nor bullets out, the warriors were unable to see the white men inside. Besides the four canvas-topped wagon-boxes sitting on the ground alongside four wall-tents, all the attackers would be able to see of the corral was that picket line of army mules.

"Spread out, lads!" Donegan shouted, flinging his arm this way and that, watching the civilians crab off along the sides of the corral as the wave of warriors drew dangerously close. "Don't bunch up now—"

"I'll give the orders here!" Sternberg shouted.

"You'll give the orders to your soldiers, Lieutenant!" Seamus replied. "Rest of us covering our own backsides this day!"

Chapter 29

While Lieutenant Sternberg deployed his twenty men around the perimeter of the corral, Finn Burnett watched the other eight grim-jawed civilians disperse into those pockets needing reinforcements along the walls.

Most of the men slid into position by the time the horsemen splashed across Warrior Creek, streaming toward the eastern wall of the corral. From behind the big pine logs that formed the base of the wall, the modified Springfields began to bark, answering the Winchesters and Henrys fired by the shrieking brownskins.

In seconds the warriors had the entire corral surrounded, riding in a wild, thundering, dusty nightmare of screaming torment.

"Stant up, got-tamn you!"

Burnett glanced over his left shoulder. Sternberg stood at the southern, and only, entrance. Fully erect, he chose not to duck behind the hay wagon pulled into place to block the gate.

"I order you to stant up and fight like soldiers!"

Burnett shook his head and then fired again, spilling another warrior. He glanced at Donegan, seeing that the Irishman kept an eye on the brash lieutenant as well.

"He'll stand there like a little tin soldier and get himself killed before the shouting's done," Seamus growled.

"Shame of it," Finn said as he hunkered down to reload, "that'll make one less to hold off the red bast—"

"Watch that sonuvabitch, Zeke!"

Burnett whirled. Behind him across the corral knelt Zeke Colvin, former captain in the Confederate army, straining to peer through the willow branches. Some fifteen feet away huddled Sergeant Horton, his greasy chevrons a splash of color against his dusty uniform. For a moment the two men disappeared from Burnett's view as the mules tied at the picket line jostled one another, kicking up a curtain of fine dust.

"Here he comes!" shouted William Haynes, another civilian on down the wall from the sergeant.

A solitary horseman dashed from the mass of screaming warriors, brandishing aloft a burning torch he had fashioned from dry hay. His wide-eyed, black pony cleared Warrior Creek in one leap, bringing him immediately to the east wall of the corral. Slowing only slightly, he leaned to the side and thrust the firebrand into the dry willow woven among the log railings.

"Shoot the sonuvabitch!" Horton shouted.

Colvin fired as the warrior passed less than an arm's length away. So close that he could not aim at the Indian. The bullet smashed into the pony's chest, spinning the animal around in fear and pain. The horse toppled against the wall, pinning its rider to the ground as it fell, legs thrashing.

For a long moment while Colvin yanked his rifle barrel from one hole in the wall and stuffed it out another, the warrior struggled to wrestle his foot free of the screaming pony. As he leaped up and burst off toward the safety of the willows by the creek, Colvin fired on instinct.

Clawing at his bloody back, the warrior toppled headfirst into the water.

The brave horseman's death drove the rest into a fury. They set up a screeching, whooping howl of dismay, whipping the air with their warclubs and tomahawks.

"This ain't your everyday raid, Burnett!" Seamus shouted over the hubbub.

"Didn't take long for me to figure that out, Irishman!"

"They're painted up good and worked into a lather."

"Feathers tied in the ponies' manes," Burnett agreed.

"Likely they planned to run right over us," Seamus muttered sourly as he rolled onto his back, reloading the Henry in his powder-grimed hands.

Already the stench of powder and the sting of dust clawed at Burnett's nostrils. "How you figure?"

"Ride into the valley. Make quick work of us . . . on to capture the fort."

"The fort?"

"Damned right. But now that they see they're not about to ride right over us, we've gone and made the red h'athens mad."

"Shame, isn't it, Donegan?"

Seamus cracked a smile, then laughed along with Burnett. "A damned shame, i'tis, Finn."

Showers of bullets spat against the logs and willows. Arrows hissed through the dry leaves of the corral wall, sailing inches overhead, to drop in every corner or strike the frightened, crazed mules. Action was hottest now near the southern end of the compound. All along Warrior Creek the hostiles gathered among the willow, allowing the Indians some cover to creep all the closer to the white man's corral. There they kept up a steady, sniping fire at the hidden soldiers and civilians. In turn, the white men made every shot count. Finn knew it didn't take a marksman to make a good Indian every time he pulled the trigger. The warriors pressed thick enough at the walls that every bullet was sure to do damage.

Like swarming red ants the enemy flung themselves at the corral, more deadly, charging faster and more frightening than any Rebel cavalry. And with every wave coming within feet of the walls, the thirty defenders inside repeatedly repulsed the first attacks. Back the warriors fell again and again, dragging their dead and dying with them. Rallying in moments to charge the corral with renewed courage.

"Stant, got-tammit!" Sternberg kept ordering, the Civil War veteran waving his pistol in the air, shaming some of his soldiers into accompanying his bravado.

"No! Get down, Lieutenant!" Burnett hollered, his arm automatically reaching out for the soldier. "Get down, dammit! Don't expose your—"

The impact flung Sternberg's body backward into the dust like a sack of wet oats. Mules snorted and stomped around the soldier, shoving against each other at the smell of blood and the hiss of more arrows.

"Donegan!" Finn shouted as he bolted into a run.

"Damn!" Seamus growled as he slid to a stop beside Sternberg's body.

The young teamster laid his ear against the lieutenant's chest. He slowly raised his head and shook it. "He's dead, Seamus."

"Lieutenant's dead?" a voice sang out nearby through the dusty, yellow prison of their corral.

Burnett laid his hand under Sternberg's cheek lying in the yellow dust. Warm, damp and sticky. He took his fingers away. The back of the lieutenant's skull gone from the bullet that had entered above the right eye.

"Fight, goddammit! Make 'em pay!" Seamus shouted, clambering to his feet, starting back to the wall.

"Listen, goddamn you!" Burnett hollered to the others. "Listen to the Irishman! Sell your lives dearly today! Make these bastards pay!"

"Gimme a hand here, Burnett!" Seamus growled.

Finn turned from Sternberg's body. The Irishman struggled with a mule lashed to the picket line. Severely wounded, the animal stomped and fought the lariat, frightening the others. Burnett threw his weight against the mule. Seamus struggled to free the knotted lariat.

"Gotta get her loose!" Seamus said as his fingers worked the rope. "She'll stampede the others we don't—"

The mule pulled free in the midst of the stinging dust and burnt powder mist hung over the corral. With a lurch, the jenny staggered backward two steps, lumbered in a crazy circle, then toppled her weight onto Sternberg's battered body.

The mule died in a pool of the lieutenant's blood.

"They've gone!" George Duncan hollered.

All around Seamus Donegan some of the soldiers and civilians grumbled their begrudging thanks for this momentary deliverance.

"Keep your eyes peeled, boys," Al Colvin hollered. "They ain't runned off, not by a long chalk."

"Al's right," brother Zeke intoned. "They just gathering for 'nother charge, I 'spect."

Seamus watched the men work silently at their lonely tasks. Reloading. Binding a bloody wound with a piece of torn shirt. Swiping sweat and grit from powder-burnt eyes. And every one among them waiting at the walls for the next rush as the sun rose ever higher, beating mercilessly on their backs. The same sun scorching the rolling hills of sun-cured buffalo grass where the swelling mass of warriors milled restlessly.

"We've gone and made them mad, fellas," Seamus said.

"Damn right, we have," Al Colvin replied. "Figured to run right over us, didn't they, Irishman? Like you blue-belly horse soldiers always figured to run right over Confederate foot."

Donegan glanced over at the former Rebel captain. And found Colvin grinning, his face a smeared painting of powder and yellow dust.

"You Johnnies always had the grit, I'll hand you that," Seamus hollered. "Standing up to odds three, four times your number."

"We'll do the same here today, Irishman," Colvin shouted. "Us . . . together. Blue-belly . . . and Johnnie Reb."

Seamus nodded his head, knowing the rest, soldier and civilian alike watched him and Al Colvin now. Now that Sternberg lay in a pool of his own steamy blood. The back of his head splattered across the trampled ground.

"Where'd you go, Burnett?" he asked as Finn slid back into the southwest corner of the wall.

"Fetch this," he replied, holding forth his ten-gauge double barrel.

"You got loads for that bird shooter?"

"Aye, Seamus." He patted the canvas satchel beside him on the ground.

Donegan glanced round, assessing their defensive island in the middle of a red sea. Zeke Colvin squatted near the southeast corner. Brother Al paced near the northeast corner, watching the milling warriors. Al Stevenson huddled near the entrance on the south wall. Up a ways were the other civilians dotted between the blue shirts of the soldiers, every man among them hunkering down in the shade, alone with his own thoughts. Waiting for the next rush.

At the picket line a handful of the wounded mules whimpered and brayed at times, arrows quivering from their sides and withers like the tough, brittle stems of buffalo grass trembling beneath the onslaught of a prairie blizzard. Others, less severely wounded, stood patiently, flicking ears and swishing tails at the huge summer flies that hung in annoying clouds over man and animal alike. Those mules hungry enough pulled at the dried hay piled along the picket rope. In the quiet of their wait, Seamus listened, the dried and hollow stems bursting apart as the mules ate, making a sound like corn kernels popping in a greased cast-iron skillet.

"You gonna use that Spencer of yours, Zeke?" Burnett asked the younger Colvin brother.

He shook his head. "Not less'n I have to, Finn. Cain't shoot that Spencer the way I can this'un." He stroked the battered Enfield muzzle-loading musket laid like a tree branch across his arms. "I been holding my own so far."

Seamus chuckled. "You have been taking care of your share, Zeke. Where'd you come on that Yankee gun?"

"Took it off a dead soldier. Battle of Wilson Creek."

"Missouri?" Finn asked.

"Yep," Zeke answered. "Figured it was mine to keep. I shot the Yankee bastard." Then his eyes nervously found Donegan's. "No offense, Irishman."

Seamus chuckled dryly. "None taken, Zeke. We was all doing what we believed in, wasn't we?"

"What about now?"

He studied the southern boy's face a moment longer. "I figure we're fighting for our hides right now. You and me can sort out everything else when it's done."

Zeke appeared to accept that. He glanced at his brother across the corral.

Al nodded. "Irishman's right, Zeke. We ain't fighting that bloody war no more. We're fighting these bloody Injuns. Ain't no Yankee . . . and there ain't no secesh out here. We're just fellas trying to hold onto our scalps."

"You fought in the war, Zeke?" Seamus hollered.

"Yep," came the drawl. "General Price."

"Good unit, Zeke. Damned good unit, I hear." Seamus rolled onto his back, reaching into pockets to check his supply of cartridges. For the first time he noticed Al Colvin's weapon.

"You fought for Price too, Al?"

Colvin sank to one knee a few yards away. His eyes darted over the top rail of the corral wall at times. "General Buell, t'was. Captain Colvin. Missouri foot."

"Hey, fellas," Seamus suddenly shouted, snagging every man's attention. "We got a real captain here! I vote for Cap'n Al Colvin to command our unit. Do I hear any disagreement?"

"Hell, no!" Zeke hollered.

"Colvin'll do," Haynes replied.

The soldiers grudgingly agreed. Alone and leaderless, looking for any man to give them direction, if not pull their fat from this fire.

"You're it, Cap'n, sir!" Seamus announced, looking at Colvin's thick, lower lip. From the day Donegan had first met the southerner, that lip had been weepy and sore, perpetually cracked beneath a summer sun on these high plains. Everytime Al spoke or laughed, the lip began to seep and bleed. It was puffy, and bleeding now. "Say, Al—where'd you come on your Henry?"

"Leavenworth."

"Henry better than them Spencers."

"A damned sight better," Al agreed, patting the battered stock of his Henry repeater. He seemed to draw himself up of a sudden and sighed, gazing round their little corral. "So, you fellas want me as your captain, eh? I one time had bars on this shirt, you know."

"He took off the bars," brother Zeke explained. "Kept the shirt."

"Damn right, I kept the shirt, lil' brother! Eight battles and five states I fought with this shirt on my goddamned back. Sonuvabitch grew so used to me, when I tried to shuck it and buy a new one from Leighton, why—the damned shirt marched on over to my bedroll and crawled in with me all by itself!"

They laughed together. For Seamus it felt good. Knowing there was another man, a leader of men, someone else here who knew how to joke in the face of death. To get others to laughing as they stared at the hoary face of death.

"You know, Seamus Donegan," Al Colvin whispered as he knelt beside the Irishman, "chances are none of us never gonna make it outta here."

"You and me been in tougher scrapes than this, Al," Seamus reminded him.

Colvin stood. "Boys, the odds are again' us today. That's by a long chalk. But what say we all take as many of 'em with us as we can while we're here. By God, we'll make these sonsabitches remember this day as long as there's a Sioux alive!"

The corral erupted with wild cheering and huzzahs as Colvin glanced back at Donegan, nodding once. Seamus nodded back. It was all that need be spoken between fighting men come a time when dying was a thing every man did well.

Chapter 30

In a second massed charge, more horsemen raced down on the corral than before.

Screaming wildly, some blowing their eagle-wingbone whistles, gunfire rattling and blackened powder hanging in a noxious cloud over the enclosure . . . a brave hundred leaped from their ponies to reach the corral on foot. Flinging themselves against the wall, scrambling at the willow, climbing frantically, brown hands grasping the top rail, pulling themselves over to peer inside. Intent on bloody close-in work with knife and club and tomahawk. The way they had swarmed over the little groups of winter-soldiers beyond the Lodge Trail.

This time the warriors found themselves blown backward into the brittle grass and dust by lead hail poured into them at point-blank range.

"Brownskins! And thicker'n fiddlers from hell they are!" Seamus shouted, pumping the lever on his Henry until no shells remained.

Burnett saw the Irishman dig into his pocket to reload a half-dozen rounds before knocking some more warriors from their perch atop the walls. One close enough that his hair caught fire from the muzzle blast of Donegan's Henry, before the warrior's own blood and gore put out the smoldering flame.

With wild whoops, another mounted attack unexpectedly swooped in, intent on dragging their wounded and dead from the walls of the corral. From across the creek and along the hillsides their rescue was covered by snipers hidden in the willows and behind trees.

A soldier ten feet from Burnett worked diligently on lessening the odds, though he found himself caught in some cross fire between the creek and the hillside sixty yards away. Waiting for the right moment, he caught one of the warriors exposed. And pulled the trigger on his .50-caliber needle-gun. The Indian flopped from the shady willows along the creekbank, his legs thrashing in the grass as he struggled to rise.

The soldier took aim once more. A bullet splattered the warrior's brains into the thirsty soil.

"By damn, you got 'im!" Burnett shouted. "Good shooting, soldier!"

"Thankee, mister," the old private replied as he sat up straighter to reload.

"Get down—"

Finn watched the soldier's head explode in a crimson spray, flinging the body back against one of the wagon-boxes used for sleeping. For a moment the drone and wheeze of murderous hail faded into the distance as Burnett watched the man's face turn the color of old flour left setting on a millstone. He had seen enough death in his years. But never so violent, never so much of it compressed into so short a time, giving a man no chance to recover from the shock. And never had such violence happened so close. Intimate in its terror.

First Sternberg. Now this nameless, faceless soldier.

"He'p me, gawddammit!"

Burnett wheeled from the soldier's body, finding Zeke Colvin struggling with a burden out of the dust and powder smoke. Zeke practically threw Sergeant Horton into Finn's arms.

"Jesus!" Burnett grumbled as he fought to keep the soldier on his feet.

"Colvin said you knew something 'bout bandaging my wound," Horton whispered hoarsely. "You ain't got any whiskey, do you?"

Burnett stared at the growing blossom of blood encircling the hole in the man's shoulder. "No, I don't, Sergeant. But I know a fella what has some whiskey we all can use 'bout now."

"Seamus!" he hollered as he dragged Horton toward the nearest wall tent.

Together they wrapped the soldier's wound, pouring precious whiskey into the hole, a little more into Horton's gaping mouth.

"Can't handle a rifle now," the sergeant grumbled. "Not against this shoulder. Just gimme your pistol there, Burnett."

Finn glanced at the revolver stuffed in his waistband looking as big as a goat's hoof. Then back to the soldier.

"I got two hands, don't you see, Burnett. I ain't gonna let 'em take me alive."

"You stay in here—"

"Leave me your gun, Burnett," Horton begged.

Finn flicked his eyes at Seamus.

The Irishman nodded. "Leave him your pistol. They come over the walls, Sergeant—we'll need your guns for the close-in work."

"You won't need my guns, Donegan. I'll be there blowing them bloody savages to hell with 'em myself."

"Make way, goddammit!"

Finn turned at the sound of Al Colvin's voice. He and a soldier dragged in J. C. Hollister. The civilian held an arm clamped like a bloody vice over a messy gut wound.

"Belly?" Burnett asked as they dropped Hollister down beside the soldier. He saw the hand Hollister kept pressed like an immobile claw over his stomach. J.C.'s skin had a strange, pale luminescence to it, like old wax. Blood had caked and dried around his fingernails, boldly outlining each fingertip in black.

"Water, Finn? Gotcha any water?" Hollister moaned.

"All you wanna drink," Seamus replied, sweeping up a canteen and pulling the stopper.

Burnett clamped onto Seamus's arm. "Don't go give a man with a belly wound any water."

The Irishman's eyes narrowed and clouded a moment. "Finn," he said quietly, "it's all right. Gonna be . . . fine. It doesn't . . . doesn't matter about Hollister now—let the man have his drink."

"He ain't supposed to have no water," Burnett protested.

Seamus rose, his eyes imploring Burnett to understand. Then he looked over at Al Colvin. And nodded, handing the canteen to the Confederate. Kneeling at Hollister's side, Colvin dribbled some water past the waiting lips.

"THEY'RE COMING BACK!" a frantic voice slashed through the tent wall.

Burnett and Donegan dashed toward their positions. "He gonna die, Seamus?"

The Irishman nodded once as they ran crouched to the wall, the shrieking growing louder than ever now.

"Then water don't matter, does it." Burnett stated it matter-of-factly.

"A friend dies in your arms," Seamus began, huffing into his place, "he gets whatever he wants."

The first shot screamed into the corral, smashing alongside one of the upright wall timbers, sending splinters and dried willow leaves flying, spraying the Irishman with debris.

Looking around, Seamus Donegan noticed most of those nearby already wore a headful of dirt, wood chips and leaves from the bullets wheezing through the flimsy barriers into the corral. Behind him a mule set up a racket, noisy in its dying. Brassy lungs *scree-hawing* as it fought the picket line, kicking up dust and slamming into the animals at its sides before it settled into the urine and blood-dampened soil at its feet.

Out of the misty dust kicked up by the animals, Sergeant Horton appeared like a gauzy specter. The sweat necklace and damp patches under his arms made his dusty shirt look as if it were sewn of two colors. That, and the dark, wet patch spreading from his shoulder. He lurched toward the wall like an ungainly draught horse, blazing away with both pistols.

"He's got no business being here!" Burnett shouted to Donegan.

Seamus shook his head. "Soldier like Horton belongs right where he is . . . his kind don't ever let other men do their fighting for them!"

"Not like that one?" Burnett asked, pointing the muzzle of his double barrel at a nearby stack of harness where it stood wedged up beside some ammunition and hard-tack crates.

Peeking from the shadows of the boxes were two boot soles.

"Who is it?"

"Wheeling," Burnett answered with a snarl.

Seamus had to laugh. "That big bag of air?"

Finn nodded, leaped to his feet as half a hundred warriors swept by, letting fly with first one then the second of his ten-gauge greetings into the red horsemen.

Donegan watched a dozen ponies shy at both blasts, stumbling sideways into others, the riders and their animals alike sprayed at close range with smoky shrapnel from those cruel, gaping muzzles.

"Goddamn, Burnett! That bastard gun of yours makes messy work of the h'athens!"

"You want clean work of it, eh, Irishman?"

"Don't matter to me what they look like after I've killed my share of 'em, Finn!"

Seamus glanced back at the boot soles dragging themselves even farther back beneath the cover of the harness pile. He wagged his head and winked at Burnett as the teamster reloaded both chambers on the ten-gauge. "Happens like this every battle I rode into."

"What did?"

"The ones talk the loudest, strut the most—their kind's the first to cower." Seamus swept his muzzle around the little corral. "Meanwhile, this is the first action most of these boys ever seen. I'd wager a month's earnings on that. But you don't find them hiding like Wheeling."

"No place to run, I reckon," Burnett replied.

Seamus shook his head. "No, even a brave man will sit there, wetting his own pants—and keep shooting . . . because he knows he stands a better chance swallowing down his fear . . . than letting it best him."

Seamus emptied his seventeen-shot Henry twice more before the red tide washed back from the walls.

"Mither of saints!" he roared as he rammed more cartridges into the loading tube beneath the barrel, eyeing the retreating horsemen. "We drove 'em off again, lads!"

"How many of us left now?" Al Colvin hollered as he dashed from the east wall. "Who's down?"

"Horton and Hollister, Al," brother Zeke shouted.

"Any more?"

"Over here!" Stevenson's deep voice rang out.

Al Colvin and Donegan loped to the south wall near the kitchen awning.

"He ain't got his senses," Al Stevenson said, dragging the soldier back from the wall with considerable effort. "Bullet whacked his skull bone pretty good."

"That's Scotty," Colvin said.

"Another sergeant, eh?" Donegan replied, eyeing the arm stripes. Then the blood streaming down the side of the soldier's face, bright and red beneath the midday summer light.

"That bullet break his skull bone?"

Stevenson shook his head. "Grazed him. Lucky bastard."

"Not like that foolish Sternberg. Well, shit—find some shade for him, Stevenson," Captain Colvin ordered. "Wrap his head and get back to the wall yourself—pronto, boy."

Colvin turned, stepping close to Seamus. "That run they just made at us was a short one. You figure they're getting tired, Irishman?"

Seamus wagged his head, pursing his cracked lips inside his dark beard. "They ain't tired at all. Many horsemen as they got out there, the bleeming bastards can keep hammering us all day, they choose to."

"You say they're gonna get cautious now, eh?"

"That's the way I see it," Seamus replied, accepting a drink of warm water from Zeke Colvin's canteen. "They burn us out. Starve us out now. Doesn't look like that peacock Bradley's gonna send us any help, does it? We're penned down here on our own. And the red bastards gonna do their best to wipe us out. But if they can't overrun us—their medicine isn't strong enough to take on the fort."

"Makes sense to me," the Confederate captain replied, staring at the dust between his boots. "I figure they'll try to snipe at us now."

Seamus nodded. "Ain't at all safe out there in the middle of the corral no more. They'll creep in close as they can, force us to keep our heads down so we can't shoot back . . . all while they plink away at anything moving in here."

"Like the mules?" Zeke nodded to what animals still stood along the picket line.

"Yep. Like them mules," brother Al answered just as more shots thundered into the corral from the bluff two hundred yards away to the west.

A mule screamed out in pain and confusion, tearing at the rope line, ripping up stakes as it thrashed wildly. Seamus watched the deadly precision of the Indian marksmen take its toll on the remuda. One by one each animal was singled out for execution. Repeatedly struck by bullets or arrows. At the same time, a few iron-tipped shafts wrapped with burning firebrands of hay slammed into the willow and log walls. The Irishman grew more certain than ever now that the hostiles intended to burn the gallant band of defenders out.

Still more bullets and arrows whined overhead, fired from the willow thickets along Warrior Creek. Chips and splinters flew from the log walls, showering the soldiers and civilians. Dust kicked up by the dying mules added to every man's misery. Holes ripped through that canvas bowed over the four wagon-boxes and the handful of wall-tents. From time to time, a flaming arrow reached its target. And one brave man or another leaped into the dusty maze, making a target of himself to rip the arrow loose and pound the fire out.

Seamus wheeled, the hair at the back of his neck standing on end. He recognized that sound. No horse soldier could forget that screeching cry of pain and fear, especially in his nightmares. It was the horse he had been sold by Leighton for his ride to Phil Kearny.

Onto its hind quarters it crumpled, struggling to rise on its forelegs. The first few feet of gut began to tumble from its belly wound. With four slashing hoofs, the animal continued to tear more and more intestine from its own belly, darkening the ground with blood and stinking offal.

Seamus's mouth went dry. He wanted a drink more than anything at this moment, knowing his whiskey was with the wounded in the tent. As far away as Fort Phil Kearny was now.

The horse was down on its belly now, all legs thrashing as life drained away. Another arrow smacked needlessly into its withers.

"Damn those godless sonsabitches," he mumbled hoarsely. "If a horse don't sound just like a man screaming as he's dying."

Seamus turned away, unable to watch the animal any longer. Seemed things had conspired against him again. Holding him here at the corral this morning when he should have been on the way south to Fort Phil Kearny and Jennie Wheatley.

She's not there no longer, you bleeming idiot, he reminded himself.

Then, by God—you should be on your way to Kansas, Seamus—track down Liam O'Roarke.

A mother's dying wish.

Pray you're not too late for that, you stupid, godless bastard, he cursed himself. *Not too late.*

Not too late to help Al Colvin, he decided next. Seeing the Confederate officer effectively penned down in the corner by some hot cross fire pouring from the hill and the willow thicket both. Seamus yanked the pistol from his belt. All cylinders loaded. He carefully laid the Henry down on some canvas beside one of the wagon-boxes and leaped into action.

First he pulled one end gate from a wagon-box free. Then a second. With them steepled over his head like a hip-pitched church roof, the Irishman lumbered big-footed toward Colvin's position. More lead splintered the end gates. He listened to arrows hiss, smacking into the wood. By the time Donegan slid in beside the Confederate, his eyes were filled with dust and splinters.

"Thought you'd never come, Yankee," Colvin drawled, his head scrunched down in his shoulders as far as possible.

Seamus chuckled, pulling the end gates over them both. "Shame to see a good man get punctured, i'tis."

"Shit, blue-belly." Colvin grabbed an end gate and straightened under its protection. "I'm finding out you Yankees ain't all bad, y'know?"

"Don't go getting sentimental on me, Reb," he growled, and winked. "There ain't a man here who can drink with the likes of Seamus Donegan—'cepting you. So I ain't about to see you go under!"

Seamus tore away to Colvin's laughter, crabbing off with

the single end gate across his shoulders for as much protection as it would give him.

"I'll buy first round, you blue-belly mick!" Al Colvin shouted.

"And I'll buy the last, you miserable Johnnie!" Seamus hollered back once he made his spot at the west wall. "Since I'm usually the only left standing, by the saints—I'll buy the last round!"

Chapter 31

"*Y*ou see that, Irishman?" Finn Burnett asked Donegan as the big man slid alongside him at the southeast corner of the corral. He pointed.

"Darty thieves, ain't they, Burnett?"

Finn nodded. "Appears so, Seamus."

As they watched in amazement, the willows near the kitchen awning rustled and parted slightly again. Atop the plank counter the camp cook used were stacked the tinned dishes and cups cleaned immediately following their breakfast meal. From the willows bordering the creek itself appeared a long, fur-wrapped coup stick, controlled by an unseen hand, inching toward the precious tinned cups stacked on the rough-hewn plank sideboard. Noiselessly, the end of the coup stick worked its way among the cups until a handle had been hooked. With a little elevation the cup slid down the stick, disappearing into the willow thicket.

"I'll be damned, Finn Burnett," Donegan whispered. "Sonsabitches not only out to kill us—they're out to rob us blind as well!"

"I'll bet those tin cups will be quite the prize back in the Sioux camp tonight."

"Not to mention our scalps," Donegan growled.

"What say I show 'em stealing doesn't pay, Irishman?"

Donegan waved a gracious hand. "Your show, Finn. Make the red thieving h'athen pay."

A third and a fourth cup disappeared down the coup stick

before Finn felt confident of his shot. Gauging where the end
of the stick emerged from the willows, he thought he caught a
glimpse of a few patches of brown, glistening hide back in the
safety of the brush. Then a streak of red paint smeared across
the warrior's brown skin.

Burnett's Spencer spoke, spitting fire at the willows.

As the coup stick toppled with a clatter among the dishes
and cups, a voice yelped in pain from the creekbank. The
bushes rattled as the warrior thrashed.

"By God, I believe you got him, lad!" Donegan shouted.
"Good shooting, Burnett!"

For a moment everything grew quiet in the willow thicket
beyond the camp kitchen. From the creekbank sounded a
croaking frog. A signal to the rest.

Suddenly the willow rustled as a dozen warriors burst from
the brush, hightailing it back across the creek to safety.
Burnett's Spencer and Donegan's Henry were barking as
quickly as the targets appeared. Their deadly work brought
two more hostiles down, wounding another three before the
whole bunch disappeared across the far side of Warrior Creek.

Finn was shaking hands with the Irishman when a small,
swarthy soldier crawled up. It was hard to tell with the burnt
powder and dust caked on the man's face, but he appeared in
his early thirties. Old enough to know better.

"It ain't no use, Irishman," he whimpered at Donegan.

"What's no use, sojur?"

Then the man's reddened eyes implored Burnett as he
crawled over Donegan's legs. "We're going to be overrun here
in a few minutes," he whined. "They get over the walls—my
heavens—what those savages'll do to us!"

"Get hold of yourself!" Seamus growled, grabbing the soldier and shaking him.

The private whirled on Donegan like a cat surrounded by
yard dogs. He hissed, white spittle caked at the corners of his
mouth. His eyes muling with fear. "They'll torture us—don't
you see? Carve us into little pieces while we die, Irishman! I
can't take it!"

He was beginning to shriek now, shaking beneath Donegan's grip.

"Shuddup, dammit—"

"I won't take it! Won't! I'll shoot myself first," he whimpered, wagging his head dolefully.

"Sit over there." Burnett shoved the soldier gently. "You lie down over there and help us fight for a while. You'll be all right—"

"No!" he shrieked, yanking away from Donegan's grip. "There's no chance for any of us, I tell you! I'll kill myself! Kill myself before I let those savages at me!"

Seamus wagged his head, glancing at Burnett. Finn asked the question.

"How you figure to kill yourself, soldier?"

"With this ramrod I found," the soldier answered, his eyes lit with fire. "All I gotta do is hold the muzzle up to my head like this . . . just use the ramrod to work the trigger back . . . like this—"

"THEY'RE COMING IN AGAIN!"

Finn and Seamus both turned from the soldier. After the brief wave of horsemen had swept past, showering the corral with arrows and lead hail, dragging off their wounded, the two civilians turned back to find the soldier had crawled across the enclosure to Zeke Colvin. To the ex-Confederate soldier he told his plans.

"Zeke won't put up with a damned coward," Burnett said.

Colvin yanked the Springfield from the soldier's grip. "There now!" he spat. "Get your yellow-bellied ass over there by the wall—you'll find a hole the dogs dug out yesterday, goddammit. I hear 'nother word outta you . . . by God I'll be the one to blow your damned brains out my own self."

"B-b-but . . . you can't take my—"

"GET!" Zeke snarled. "You don't move NOW . . . I take some goddamned pleasure outta splattering your brains on the ground aside you—"

"Goddammit! Goddammit! Goddammit—I'm dying!"

Finn whirled round. Nearby, another soldier lay on his belly, spread-eagled on the ground. A single arrow had passed through the calves of both legs, just beneath the flesh. But from the painful howl he set up, a man would think he was knocking on heaven's door.

As quickly, three of his fellow soldiers were on him. One clamping a hand over the wounded man's mouth. Another

sitting on the man's legs. And the third breaking the arrow off
and pulling it from the wounds. They dragged the screaming
trooper off to the tent where the wounded lay, plopping their
noisy companion between Hollister and Sergeant Horton.

It took but moments for the warriors on the hillside to
begin directing their fire at the tent where the soldier groaned
and screamed. Moments more and the dirty canvas tent top
was hanging in shreds.

Bullets and arrows hissing and whining overhead, Sergeant
Horton rolled onto his side, stuffing his pistol under the
soldier's jaw.

"Listen, boy," Horton snarled. "One more yelp outta your
miserable mouth—and I've have excuse enough to splatter
your brains all over this tent. Now, shut your mouth or I'll
shut it for you!"

Finn didn't hear so much as a whimper from the tent hous-
ing the wounded from that point on.

"Say, Finn," Seamus whispered, nudging Burnett. "I think
we got us another visitor to the kitchen."

Just behind the wooden boxes that held the cook's utensils
and supplies, Burnett made out a moccasin at the end of a
bare calf.

"C'mon over here," Seamus suggested. "You'll see the top
of the bastard's head."

"By damned, I'll pepper that'un's ass," Burnett swore.

Seamus gripped Burnett's arm. "Sit tight, me friend. That
pepper-gun of yours ain't got the range to do the work at
hand. You'll only scare 'im away. Lemme pepper his tail my
way."

"Whatcha gonna do, Seamus?"

"See for yourself. Hand me that old Springfield behind
you."

"This old one. It's just a muzzle loader. One shot—"

"One shot's all I'll need, Finn. Now, dig in your pocket and
gimme a handful of your .32-caliber ammunition."

"For my pistol?"

"Goddamn right. C'mon now—afore the h'athen finishes
licking that pan clean of molasses."

Pistol ammunition in hand, Seamus dumped the lot of it

down the old Springfield's muzzle. Cartridge case, bullets, powder and all.

"Gimme a chance to get outta your way afore you touch that cannon off, Seamus."

"Then get, lad," Donegan replied. "For I'm fixing to show the red bastard the error of his savage ways." Then he winked at Burnett, who had slid ten feet off along the side of a wagon-box. "We'll teach that'un it don't pay to have a sweet tooth!"

While Seamus waited, the dark head bobbed up and down as the warrior licked his tongue slowly, deliciously across the molasses-covered tin plate he had found after creeping up the bank of Warrior Creek into the kitchen area.

When the Irishman eased gently back on the trigger, the gun roared, louder than any of the modified Springfields had, attracting every man's attention. Even more startling was what the handful of pistol shells had done spraying into the kitchen box. Not to mention what a mess it made of the warrior with the sweet tooth.

"Lookee yonder, Seamus," Burnett hollered as Donegan turned from his sniper's work.

"The red bastards're fixing on setting fire to the grass."

At the foot of the hillocks to the west of the corral, some twenty warriors with firebrands of dried hay began setting fire to the brittle, summer-cured grasses.

"Wind's gonna carry it right over us," Burnett complained quietly.

"Their horsemen can't ride over us, they figure the fire'll do the trick for 'em," Seamus muttered angrily. "Those of us don't flush with the fire . . . we'll roast once those flames work themselves up."

While a steady, hot breeze fanned the flames out of the west, some of the soldiers crabbed across the open compound to the east wall. A few more feet of safety from the thick, stifling smoke that boiled over the corral, stinging the defenders' nostrils.

"Those flames reach the wall, Seamus . . ."

Donegan nodded to Burnett. "Don't think about it, Finn. We'll go to the east wall . . . there's nothing for it to feed on in the middle of the compound."

"The smoke—"

"They burn down this wall . . . you just shoot at anything that moves our way out of the cloud."

Yet in the next moment, as the wall of angry, orange flames soared better than forty feet in height over the tall grass, roaring like a thundering steam-powered locomotive beneath an insistent west wind to within a scant twenty feet of the corral itself, the searing blanket of fire undulated twice. As if measuring the resistance of the defenders.

And the moment after, those flames extinguished themselves with a spanking slap, like that of flapping canvas in a hard gale. It was almost more than Seamus could believe.

Like the right hand of Providence Itself. Sweet Mither of Christ!

Still, Providence had not finished with the grass fire that midday. No sooner had the flames been spanked out than the smoldering wall of oily smoke reversed direction, sending the gray cloud swirling back to the west rather than sweeping over the corral itself. Under this cover, several dozen warriors darted in to recover their wounded and dead comrades.

"That did it, boys!" Seamus hollered.

Al Colvin even stood, shoulders bowed, peering over the top of the west wall with the Irishman. "Figure that broke their backs, Donegan?"

"If not their backs . . . then we can pray it broke their will." Seamus found Colvin studying his powder-grimed face.

"I suppose they figure it's bad medicine, eh, Irishman?"

"You're learning, Rebel. You're learning."

"We best not waste this break in the fighting," Colvin suggested, turning toward the corral. "Zeke! You and couple more boys—get that barrel filled, hauling water back from the creek. No telling how long the sonsabitches give us!"

Al directed the majority of his defenders to the south wall to cover his water carriers. With buckets and metal pans in hand, Zeke led Bill Haynes and Bob Little under the wagon at the gate, then the trio made its mad dash to the willows bordering Warrior Creek. With their successful return, Captain Colvin ordered a second trip to the creek.

"I don't get it, Irishman," Al said quietly as his brother and the others scurried to the creekbank a third time. "Can't figure why they're letting us at the water."

"No way to figure it, Al. Best you get some of that water into the tent for the wounded. Your man Hollister's setting up a groan."

"Something awful, ain't it."

"The howl?"

"No," Al answered, wagging his head. "That belly wound of his."

Seamus nodded. "Yes, Cap'n. Man gets it in the belly like that, the old sump keeps pumping blood into his gut till there ain't no more to pump. Man dies drowning in his own juices."

"You seen enough of it too, eh?"

Seamus tried to smile. And couldn't. "Enough to last any man a lifetime, Reb. A lifetime."

"I was to Vicksburg myself. Worst I saw it. Heard tell from other units Vicksburg wasn't nowhere near as bad as Gettysburg."

"Nothing ever be as bad as Gettysburg, Cap'n. Nothing."

"I'll . . . I best get the rest digging in," Colvin said quietly.

"Good idea," Seamus replied, sensing that he had made the Confederate uneasy.

Colvin turned to step off.

"Say, Al."

Colvin looked over his shoulder anxiously. "Yeah?"

"You're doing just fine, Cap'n. You a good officer. In fact— I'm bloody-well glad I never come up against you in that darty war we had down South."

Colvin smiled. "Know what, you blue-belly, mick sonuvabitch? Goddamned glad we didn't either."

"Man hates killing those he's taken a liking to," Seamus cheered, slapping Colvin on the shoulder and shoving him off on his duties.

While the warriors hung back along the hills and out of rifle range down the valley, the grim-faced defenders used the lull to dig rifle-pits behind the bottom logs at the wall. With knives, tin plates, pots, and a skillet or two, the men scratched frantically at the earth. Others dragged a few of the dead mules against the fortifications. Some set to work repairing broken weapons, cleaning the rest. More of the ammunition boxes were broken open and dragged to strategic places on the perimeter of the corral. And when they had a chance, most grabbed a mouthful or two of salt-pork or hardtack sopped in some scummy gravy or molasses that had set out the morning long beneath a forge-hot sun.

Seamus eyed the buttermilk-white orb hung almost directly overhead in a summer-pale sky, pulling the watch from his britches' pocket. A few minutes past noon. Some two and a half hours of fighting already.

And this day's not half-old.

Chapter 32

"Captain?"

Edward S. Hartz turned in his saddle, unconcerned. He was watching his wood detail cutting timber in the clearing near the ridge. Daydreaming mostly. Here in the hills above Fort C.F. Smith, near the mouth of the Bighorn Canyon. Hartz's frost-blue eyes narrowed on the private cantering up, his horse snorting anxiously. He was daydreaming no longer.

"What is it, soldier?"

"Sir—you come take a look at something with me?"

"Is this important?"

His head bobbed nervously, eyes flicking to some of the rest who had stopped their sweat-work among the trees, leaning on axes and saws. "Smoke, Captain Hartz."

"Smoke." He sniffed. Smelling the air. "Those damned Sioux back again? Setting fire to the dry hay in the fields, Private."

Hartz watched the young soldier swallow, as if choking on something hard and thorny. "More'n that, sir. Want you come see for yourself."

When the Civil War veteran came to a halt on the end of the ridge overlooking the valley, what he did see for himself was enough to raise the hackles on any soldier's back. He glanced at the private's face.

"You did well, son." After he took an even better look at

the valley through his field glasses, Captain Hartz kneed his mount around savagely.

By jeeves, the red bastards aren't just striking and running off this time, he brooded as he galloped back to gather his detail, figuring the fight down in the valley would require every man. Besides, with that number of hostiles brazenly out and combing the countryside, flaunting their presence, Hartz knew it would not do to leave his work detail behind, even secreted back in this black timber.

He had his soldiers saddled in the space it takes a man to take three breaths, ordering them to leave their tools behind.

"Time enough to come back and finish our work another day," he declared. "Time now to break the siege at the hay-field corral."

He flung an arm forward as he kicked his mount in the ribs. "Column of twos! On my lead . . . center guide—troops forward at the gallop! *HO!*"

Pulling down the stiff brim of his felt hat, the veteran captain uttered the closest thing to a prayer he had uttered since that bloody day at Antietam.

God help us—that we're in time . . .

So it shocked the captain when he listened to Lieutenant Colonel Bradley's steadfast refusal to send out a relief column to rescue the corral defenders.

"Colonel, I must protest—"

"Protest registered, Captain!"

"S-Sir . . . allow me to take four companies. We have seven posted here. Give me four of—"

"I've said all I'm going to say on this, Captain," Bradley interrupted brusquely, his lips drawing themselves into a thin line of angry determination.

"Three, sir. I request three companies. I'll lead the relief my—"

"You've been here long enough to know, Hartz—the red bastards hit the mowing operations every day."

Captain Hartz shook his head, weary of the argument. "Not like this, sir. I'd estimate more than a thousand of them—"

"You're saying this isn't their routine hit and run?"

"Sir, we're wasting time here. Please allow me three companies to ride—"

"Captain Hartz, do you remember the tale of Captain William Judd Fetterman?"

The captain nodded, swallowing once. Feeling the angry confusion rising in him like bile. "Yes. But I don't know—"

"Then you will pay heed to the lesson learned the hard way by Fetterman's command."

"Sir?"

"Goddammit, Hartz! The same bloody thing will happen to your command, you ride out of this post."

"I'll not allow it to happen to me."

Bradley slammed both palms down on his desk, scattering some papers. "You won't allow it! *I* won't allow it! Permission denied."

Hartz watched his post commander sink back into his straight-backed chair. It scraped across the floor with the irritation of an out-of-tune fiddle. Bradley's adjutant burst into the room.

"Colonel—gates are locked and secured. As you ordered."

"Very good, Corporal. Now see to it the officer-of-the-day doubles the guard immediately . . . and that order will remain in effect until I countermand it."

"Yessir."

The adjutant was gone as quickly as he had come, dashing back onto the dry, dusty parade baking beneath the late summer's heat.

Hartz cleared his throat. "Colonel, you will recall who this fort is named for?"

Bradley glowered at the captain. "I most certainly do. General Charles Ferguson Smith." Bradley cocked his head slightly. "Why the history lesson, Hartz?"

"To make one more appeal to you, sir," the captain said, taking a long step forward that brought him to the front of Bradley's small desk. "This post—*our* post—is named for a fighting man who won distinction during the Mexican War. I think . . . it's only fitting that we carry on in that tradition."

Bradley rose slowly, eyes squinting as he shuffled to the one window across the cramped office. Outside, the parade bustled. Seven companies of soldiers put on the alert. Some 260 men at the ready.

The colonel turned and sighed. "Hartz, I want this understood. Those men knew what chance they were taking when they signed on—"

"Our military escort, Colonel?"

"This is the *army*, Captain. Not some school outing. Every man must understand he might be called upon to die at any moment."

"And the civilians sacrificed as well?"

Bradley glowered once more at Hartz. "That word is a bit harsh, don't you think?" He waved a hand, showing he wanted no reply. "I have been given a fort to command . . . and protect, Captain. It is Fort C.F. Smith I will protect. With the overwhelming numbers of hostiles you say you counted in the valley . . . that skirmish fight in the hayfield will be over very shortly.

Hartz bit his lip to prevent himself from crying out at the injustice, forced to sit on his hands while good men were butchered. He allowed Bradley to finish.

"My only worry now is that I have sufficient forces within this stockade to stem the red tide those half-naked bastards will throw at us once they've wiped out the hayfield corral."

"May I be excused, sir?" Hartz asked, his stomach wrenching with nausea.

"Permission granted, Captain. But—I may need you soon, should the hostiles hit this post once they've mopped up those poor fellows in the hayfield."

Hartz saluted and turned to the door. The hot breeze hit him like a furnace as he stepped onto the parade, feeling the first sting of tears. Frustration. Anger. Utter melancholy.

Those forced to remain behind, doing nothing while good men died bravely.

May God have mercy on our souls, he thought.

"Gimme that Long-Tom there beside you," Seamus demanded.

Burnett slid it over. "You think you can hit that bastard?"

Donegan nodded. Then he grinned and winked. "Worth a try, me friend. Always worth a try."

With the old muzzle-loading infantry weapon packed with an extra charge he knew would knock hell out of his shoulder, Seamus crawled to his feet slowly, inching the barrel over the uppermost log on the corral wall. He snapped up the last of the three leafs on the rear sight, and held his breath a minute as he studied the undulation of the tall grass between the corral and the solitary, brave warrior.

A matter of heartbeats ago, the painted Indian had come to a stop at the bank of Warrior Creek, east of the corral. In plain sight, as if daring the white men to attempt their best shot. He sat there on his sorrel pony, watching the corral, a hand shading his eyes.

"Can you do this, Yankee?"

Seamus recognized the voice of Al Colvin behind him. He smiled at the stock of his Springfield once he felt he had his windage figured out. "It's a far piece, Reb . . . but I'll take a crack. That h'athen's bold as brass. But what say you get that Enfield of your brother's ready—just in case I'm shaky."

Colvin grinned, wagging his head. "A waste of time, mick —fella like you don't miss very often, I'll wager."

Through the muzzle smoke spat moments later from the double-charged Long-Tom, Donegan saw the sorrel rear back, tumbling to the side, pitching its rider into the creek. A cheer erupted from all sides of the corral as they watched the warchief flounder in the water, struggling to rise.

"By jabbers," Finn gushed, "I think that red sonuvabitch is drowning out there, Seamus."

"Damn right he is!" Al Stevenson piped happily. "Hope the bastard takes all day doing it too!"

"Good shot, Irishman!" Captain Colvin exclaimed, slapping Seamus on the back. "We'll do all the damage we can to the frigging bastards . . . while we can."

"You don't figure we'll last, do you, Cap'n?"

Colvin shook his head. "I figure we'll be lucky to make sundown. Between now and then—I want all of you men to take as many of these Sioux with you as you can."

"What about our wounded—come a rush, Al?" Zeke Colvin asked his brother.

"You . . . you take care of them . . . it comes down to it, Zeke."

Seamus watched little brother nod before scurrying back to his spot at the wall.

Al Colvin's eyes found Donegan's locked on him. "You said yourself you seen what them Sioux done to those soldiers of Fetterman's," he explained quietly, simply. "I've already told everyone to keep the last bullet for hisself. Finn here knows what I'm talking about."

Burnett nodded. "But I ain't blowing my brains out until the last minute, Colvin. I won't shoot myself till they're coming over the wall."

"None of us giving up till they're in the corral," Al replied even more morosely. "Won't be a one of us or our wounded alive to torture."

"Cap'n! Here they come!"

Colvin and the rest turned. Two groups formed two lines that poured off the slopes west of the corral. Both groups raced past the west wall, battering the logs and wagon-boxes, willow and tents, with their hissing arrows and whining lead sending splinters and dust and flying shrapnel raining on them all.

A second charge came in to cover those who leaned from their ponies to drag wounded and dead from the open field. With each new body brought to rest on those western bluffs where the hostiles peered down into the corral, renewed howls of grief and despair arose from the women come to watch the victory of their men.

Their high-pitched keening pricked the hair on Seamus's neck. Recalling the high-pitched witches' laughter as the Crow women set to deadly work over the Sioux prisoner.

Hell to pay, you get a Injin woman in a fight, he brooded, glancing at the confusion on the hillside faraway. Then his numbed, weary brain remembered. With Indians, there was no fight that did not include the women. They were part and parcel of it. A way of life. A way of death for them all. Man. Woman. Child.

His Henry reloaded, Seamus slid it back through the willow wall. And for the first time that day noticed a war-chief waving his Winchester rifle, directing another swarming two-wave attack on the corral.

"Duncan!" he hollered. "You see that one with all the feathers down his back?"

George Duncan studied the dusty field of fire down the muzzle of his new rifle. He grinned at Donegan. "Medicine man, you figure?"

"That, or a chief. He's got a lot to do with what this charge is all about. You take him, George."

Duncan grinned big enough to show the gaps in his teeth. "Gladly, Irishman!"

In and out of the dust raised by hundreds of unshod pony hoofs the warriors screeched, racing past the west wall repeatedly. Firing under their ponies' necks. Shrieking out war-songs. Crying out in surprise and pain when they were hit or their animals went down in a tumbling, roiling mass, heels over head each time the corral wall erupted with smoke and deadly hail.

Volley after volley the defenders fired. George Duncan waiting his turn, patient on his shot until he had a clear view of the medicine man with the double-trailer bonnet that dragged the earth with its quaking eagle feathers.

Duncan eased back from the wall, already assured of his success. "Bastard made it too easy, whooping and all!"

"Blowed him right out'n the saddle, George!" Finn Burnett cheered.

More hands pounded Duncan on the back to congratulate the teamster as the screeching rose from the meadow. A handful of warriors swept in on horseback, covering another pair who galloped behind the shield of their bodies to snatch the war-chief from the plain. The lifeless body was carried to the top of the grassy bench, where the rescuers laid it among the other wounded and dead watched and cried over by the women. In the midst of howls and herbs, burning sage-brush incense and boiling roots for bullet wounds, the women keened even louder at the death of this important man.

Roman Nose felt a cold sliver of ice stab at his belly, watching Black Shield's body laid among the dead.

Throughout the morning the Northern Cheyenne had watched the Miniconjou war-chief direct much of the battle from the hillside. Then, in despair, Black Shield rode down to the meadow itself. Drawing close to the deadly fire of the desperate white men huddled behind their wall of willow.

Frustration had already set in, Roman Nose realized. Anger long since gone from his veins. Jealousy before that. Finding that Black Shield would lead this attack. His combined forces of Miniconjou and those Oglalla who had remained behind, plus some renegade Arapaho under the white chief One Thumb—all of those warriors far outnumbering the strength of the Northern Cheyenne under Roman Nose.

Black Shield had taken the power of Roman Nose when he usurped command of this attack on the soldiers' dirt-walled fort as Red Cloud and Crazy Horse rode south to attack the white men at the Pine Woods.

The Cheyenne horsemen were bitter now, bitter that Black Shield's attack had not swept right over the handful of defenders in the grass cutters' camp so they could throw their savage weight against the dirt-walled fort.

And now frustrated that Black Shield himself had been killed. Knocked from the saddle by a white man's gun.

The change of pitch in the wild shrieking snagged the Cheyenne war-chief's attention. He turned in time to see the warriors and women stumble back, away from hovering over the Miniconjou's prostrate body. A cold chill splashed down the spine of Roman Nose as he watched the Miniconjou sit upright with a jerk.

Black Shield blinked, and blinked again. Touching his head, looking around. Slowly coming back to life. Dazed. All around him hands clamped on mouths in astonishment at his trip back from death.

The bullet that had knocked him from his pony had grazed his head, stunning him as it traveled along the skull beneath the scalp before it tore through the skin in its exit. Two bloody wounds.

And Roman Nose realized in that instant that wily old Sioux war-chief would know exactly how to extract the most dramatic effect from his injuries.

Black Shield took his hand from his head slowly, raising both arms to the sky in thanksgiving to his Spirit Helpers. Then he spit into both palms, and rubbed the hands into the dirt. With the ocher mud he had made, the Miniconjou war-chief rubbed both head wounds with this potent medicine.

"See, my children!" he shrieked at the astonished crowd of men and women. "The white man's bullets cannot harm me!"

Roman Nose found the Miniconjou's eyes locked on his, a taunting, haughty light behind them as Black Shield contin-ued to whip his faithful into a fury.

"Follow me now! All who are brave enough to fly into the face of the bullets that do not sting! Follow me—and we will overrun these white fiends together!"

Angrily, Roman Nose glared at the half-groggy Sioux who led his warriors down the slope for another try at the corral.

Come a day soon, The Nose promised himself and his own medicine-helpers. *Come a day soon—I will have the fight of my powerful vision . . . the tall, bearded one with the gray eyes . . . rising up to greet his death in the middle of that little dried river . . . as I ride down on him, my pony's hoofs ripping his body apart.*

Chapter 33

*A*s the sun tilted into the western quadrant of the sky, Seamus Donegan realized much of the fight had slowly hissed out of their attackers.

Fewer and fewer runs were made past the corral walls. Fewer and fewer warriors joined in those sporadic attacks. Had not those brown horsemen worked diligently at removing their wounded and dead from the field of battle, the bloody, naked bodies would have littered the meadow surrounding the corral, covered the willow thickets along Warrior Creek. Dotted the grassy bench above the meadow where more and more of the attackers gathered in sullen knots to vent their angry bile over this unsuccessful attack.

Likewise, they never took their baleful, vengeful eyes from the determined defenders hunkered within the walls of their pitiful corral. Forcing the white men to watch their heads by firing just enough bullets through the walls to keep those defenders at bay.

"Seamus," Burnett whispered. "Need your help."

"What is it?"

"Look at my britches."

Donegan saw what Finn pointed out. "Your pants full of *bullet* holes!" He chuckled.

"Yeah." Burnett ground his teeth. "One of the red bastards out there shooting holes in my britches—"

"Lucky he hasn't shot holes in your arse, me friend!"

"Only reason is these britches was four sizes too big for me."

"Look like two of you could slip in and walk 'round in 'em, for sure!"

"They was brand new down to Fort Phil Kearny a month back. Paid a handsome two dollars for 'em from Judge Kinney."

" 'Tis a shame, Finn. A little big—but a nice pair all the same."

"Big enough I had to tie the extra gather of cloth up at my waist back there."

"I see. That's where you're getting shot, Finn!"

"What I want you to do is watch for muzzle-smoke when I raise up, Seamus."

"Raise up?"

"Every time I move to take aim, I feel a tug at my britches, you see? He shooting at me . . . but I can't see where the shot's coming from."

Seamus grinned. "Go 'head, me friend. I'll spot your bleeming arse-shooter . . . and we'll make a fine kidney pie of the red bastard!"

Finn raised himself ever so carefully, aimed and fired. Almost as quickly, Seamus saw a bullet whistle through the excess cloth bunched over Burnett's ample rear.

"There!" he whispered harshly, pointing out the spot for Burnett.

"The stump?"

"Aye, Finn. Forty yards, and not a foot more. Like falling off a log. He's yours to pepper now!"

"Watch me send this'un to the hunting grounds where all good Injuns go!"

Taking careful aim on the cottonwood stump gnawed by beaver over the years, Burnett fired.

Seamus watched an immediate thrashing behind the creekside stump. Then all was still once more.

"You got 'im, lad."

"Had your doubts, eh, Irishman?"

Seamus grinned. "Me? Not the way you handle your gun, Finn Burnett."

"They're mounting up, Irishman!"

Seamus heeded Al Colvin's warning, turning to see the hundreds of warriors leaping atop their ponies, streaming off the slope.

"Cap'n, my belly tells me they're 'bout to throw us a ringer."

Colvin nodded. "Something tells me you're right." He turned to fling his voice around the corral. "Zeke, you and Haynes stay on the north wall . . . all the rest of you—skeedaddle down here!"

In the space of a moment Colvin had the bulk of his defense gathered at the southern end of the corral. And right on cue, the chief they had knocked off his pony once before led his horsemen off the slope in a wide arc, up Warrior Creek, then swiftly arced left. Heading straight for the south wall of the fort where it might prove weakest at the only entrance to the corral.

"I want that sonuvabitch!" Al Colvin growled. "I'll put him on the ground to stay this time!"

"He's all yours," Seamus replied. "You take that first one 'cross the creek . . . we'll see to the rest, Cap'n."

The headman led his warriors across the creek and up the bank in a headlong rush toward the wall. Coming close enough that Donegan could see the mud smeared on the war-chief's forehead, in his flying, loosened hair.

"Fire with me, men!" Colvin ordered. "By volley! Hold your fire until I drop that bastard!"

Seamus watched them thunder closer and closer, swallowing the dust in his throat, wondering when the Confederate was going to shoot.

And when Colvin finally pulled the trigger, the southern wall exploded with fire and smoke. With a solid phalanx of flame spat at the charging horsemen.

Painted, feathered war ponies reared back and went down. Warriors toppled. Best of all, Captain Colvin watched his hated war-chief straighten back, wobble from side to side, then slide into the dust beneath the feet of a dozen stunned and wounded ponies.

The charge turned back on itself in wild, shrieking confusion. Back across the creek, beyond the willows, into the timber in disarray the warriors poured. Leaderless. Their spirit broken.

Still the guns continued to roar, spitting fire and deadly hailstones into the fleeing riders. Every bit as swiftly, a second charge was formed, riders sweeping in low to cover those who would attempt to recover the body of their war-chief.

"Shoot the sonsabitches!" Colvin screamed, his puffy lower lip leaking blood once more.

They turned the second charge before the warriors could reach the war-chief's body. More warriors lay dead and dying in the meadow between the corral wall and the creekbank. But in the space of a half-dozen shallow breaths taken by those huddled waiting in the enclosure, a third charge appeared out of the dust and smoke of that shrieking, red-skinned hell.

"By God!" Colvin was screaming, possessed, spittle crusting at the corner of his mouth. "Don't let them have that bastard's body! No matter what—I'll hold that chief if I gotta go out there and sit on him my own self!"

And with those forge-hardened riflemen firing point-blank into the face of that third red wave, the spirit of the warriors was broken at last.

"They're running!" Zeke Colvin shrieked, dancing a mad jig through the center of the corral.

"By God, they are running!" piped up Pvt. Ed Holloran. He leaped on fellow soldier Thomas Riley. Both men hugged and swung each other round and round, laughing hysterically with the rest of the defenders.

"Jesus!" rasped Al Colvin, slamming Donegan on the back. "We done it, you goddamned mick! We run the red bastards off!"

Seamus wagged his head, dirt-reddened eyes narrowing down the neck of the valley where the horsemen had headed. "I don't trust 'em, Cap'n. And best thing you don't either."

"Figure they're up to something?"

"Smells bad. They're leaving enough snipers in the hills yonder—take a look."

"I see . . ." Al answered, the air gone out of his enthusiasm like steam from a leaky locomotive fitting.

"They leave a few around us . . . pen us down like this—no telling when they'll come charging back."

"I ain't about to take the air outta the boys' celebrating," Al moaned. "By God, we been at it for over seven hours now, I reckon."

Seamus consulted his pocket watch. "Damn . . . if we haven't been at it that long—"

"Captain Colvin?"

Both Donegan and the Confederate turned, seeing a small, wiry, peach-faced private present himself to Colvin.

"What is it, boy?"

"I asked before," he stammered, clearly nervous. "I'll ask again now that them redskins is skeedaddling. I wanna go to the fort for help."

Colvin glanced at Donegan. With the slightest of nods, Seamus agreed.

"I s'pose time's come. What's your name, son?"

"Bradley, sir. Charles Bradley."

"Get yourself a animal, Private. And we'll see you have a brace of pistols," Seamus said.

Bradley swallowed anxiously. "Only . . . only one horse left what ain't been hit on the picket line."

"One?" Colvin's voice rose two octaves.

"Yessir. And all but three of them mules is wounded or . . . worse."

"Take the horse, sojur," Seamus ordered.

"You get that lucky horse saddled, I'll have a dispatch written to Bradley ready for you, son," the captain said, waving the private off.

With a pair of pistols tucked in the waist of his dirty britches, and his kepi snugged down over his greasy hair, Pvt. Charles Bradley, 27th U.S. Infantry, was ready to ride once Colvin's message had been stuffed down the front of his shirt. Trouble was, the foot soldier had neglected to tell anyone there was a reason he was serving in the infantry.

Only twice before in his young life had Bradley ever climbed atop a horse.

"Take 'er out slow, son," Colvin instructed, pointing. "Slow till you reach the end of that ridge that hides us from the fort. I figure them Injuns try to jump you there. And you

can kick hell out'n this horse then—running like the devil for
the stockade. They'll see you coming. Just get that message to
Bradley. Good luck, boy."

"Godspeed, son," Seamus said, swinging his arm back.

A moment after Seamus slapped the horse's rump to send
the soldier on his way, he realized it would be solely by the
grace of the saints or the Virgin Mary Herself if Private Bradley made it to Fort C.F. Smith with his message.

Unsteady, bouncing on his saddle like a wind-up toy, Private Bradley did make it to the end of the ridge before any of
the hostile snipers made an appearance. And then it was in
force. Better than two dozen of them roared down the slope of
the hill, heading straight for the hapless horseman. So it was
that fear does something to the innocent it will not do for the
courageous.

Bradley rode as he had never ridden before, nor was likely
to ride again. That is until he neared the post itself.

Some seven hundred yards from the stockade the fort road
plunged into a deep gully. It was there the hostiles on their
speedy, grass-fed ponies caught up with the untried cavalryman. So scared was Bradley that he watched the approach of
the warriors over his shoulder and did not see the sudden
drop-off. His horse lurched, pitching the private down the
slope. Bradley rolled into the Bighorn River itself.

Surfacing, sputtering and scared within an inch of his wits,
the soldier realized he had one chance to get his message
to the fort. That was by hugging the willow along the bank for
the next six hundred yards until he could climb out of the
water directly below the fort walls.

After more than seven hours of fighting off wave after wave
of screaming, blood-eyed warriors, it was all Private Bradley
could do to keep from wetting his pants at the closeness of
both the fort and those wild-eyed pursuers.

What with the soaking he took in the river, the young cavalryman finally figured no one would notice if he wet his pants
now anyway.

"Rider coming in, Captain!"

Hartz turned, looking beyond the sentry pointing down the

hayfield road. A crowd quickly gathered along the north wall, watching the horse race down to the river junction.

"He's done for now," one of the sentries moaned a moment later as the horseman tumbled off his mount, careening down the slope into the slow-moving waters of the Bighorn.

"Give him some cover, by Jesus!" Captain Hartz shrieked. "I don't believe you men—that's a soldier, by God! He'll be eaten alive if you don't . . . gimme that rifle—drive those red bastards back, dammit!"

The soldiers answered with their Springfields, shamed by the officer reminding them to shoot at hostiles threatening one of their own. The rifles barking over the top of the north wall along with whining lead kicking up dirt around the legs of their prancing ponies was enough to convince the two-dozen brown-skinned horsemen in the wisdom of retreat.

"You're one lucky soldier," Hartz cheered the dispatch bearer at the fort gate as Bradley stumbled up from the river.

"Colonel Bradley, sir."

"You come from the corral?"

He nodded nervously, eyes bouncing here and there. "Yes-sir—"

"You mean some of you still alive?" Hartz's voice showed his amazement, if not downright disbelief.

Bradley gulped. "The colonel, sir—"

"How many left?"

He shook his head, "I . . . I think we got two, maybe three dead."

"Jesus, son—somebody in heaven watching over you!"

"Got a message for the colonel," and he dragged the wet, folded paper from his dripping shirt.

"C'mon, son," Hartz grabbed the soldier's arm. "I'll take you there myself."

By the time the captain dragged the half-drowned trooper through the post commander's door, Hartz had gleaned a good idea of what was going on down at the corral.

"I have dead and wounded," Colonel Bradley read slowly, repeatedly blotting the paper with a kerchief so as not to smear the carefully penciled letters.

". . . dead and wounded what must have help. The living will have to leave this corral after dark. Most of the Injins has gone down the valley. Have no idea how many is left. Snipers on the hill and some at the creek below us. We cannot stay no longer. If you are a man, Colonel Bradley—you will send relief to our rescue. If you are not a man, then you will surely go to hell where cowards like you belong."

Bradley looked up from the note, his flintlike eyes glaring into the captain's.

"Damn him! Calling me a coward. Why I'll show that—"

"Permission to lead the relief, Colonel."

He watched Bradley snap like a dry twig at the request. Crumpling the soggy paper into a ball he flung against a far wall, the colonel whirled on Hartz.

"Permission denied, Captain," he snarled.

"Denied—"

"Captain Burrowes." Bradley turned to Thomas B. Burrowes, who had served as post commander for a brief stint following Captain Kinney's departure in June. "You will lead the relief."

"By all means, sir!"

He glowered a minute at the angry Hartz. Then spoke his last order to Burrowes softly. "Go pull their civilian asses out of the fire."

"Yessir," Burrowes answered before saluting and lunging out the door, shouting orders.

Without so much as a glance in the direction of Capt. Edward S. Hartz.

Chapter 34

"*D*on't count on those yellow-tailed blue-bellies ever reaching us," Zeke Colvin growled.

Seamus Donegan and the rest watched anxiously as dark-shirted horsemen took shape beneath a dust cloud—Capt. Thomas B. Burrowes's two companies hammering down the hayfield road. At the tail end of his column of twos bounced the mountain howitzer Burrowes had lugged up from Fort Phil Kearney a year ago. Colonel Henry B. Carrington, past commander of this Mountain District, Dakota Territory, had issued Burrowes and Captain Kinney that field piece in August of 'sixty-six when the two had led their companies here to the Big Horn country to build their post, charged with protecting the northern reaches of the Montana Road.

"Those stretchers ready?" Seamus flung his voice back at the tent where the wounded had laid out the duration of the attack.

"Will be, soon enough!" Bill Haynes called back. He and Finn Burnett had lashed together four crude stretchers.

J. C. Hollister was already delirious with pain. His gut wound never bled much from the bullet hole. But the man was slowly drowning in his own juices.

Sgt. James Horton struggled to help the others as much as he could, what with one wing out of commission. Throughout the fight he had repeatedly stumbled from the ragged, bullet-shredded tent when he heard each renewed charge bearing down on the corral. While his wound prevented him from holding a rifle, Horton nonetheless had done his share of damage, keeping his service revolver busy. It had been, after all, a day for close and dirty work.

Pvt. Francis M. Law lay dazed and unconscious. The bullet that had slammed into his eye had exited the temple area, taking some skull bone with it. He would lose his sight, but live to recount this day again and again for his grandchildren.

The last of the wounded, Pvt. Henry C. Vinson, had long since quit whimpering about his leg wounds. The holes made through his calves burned like hell. But watching the stoic bravery of the other three had shut the whining, frightened soldier right up. Time and again Vinson's britches were soaked with urine throughout the daylong fight. But young Henry had grown, as few men would ever have to grow, that hot first day of August in the hayfield.

"I'll be go to hell!" Zeke Colvin shouted.

"Damn them!" Private Holloran yelled.

"They're stopping, goddammit! The yeller sonsabitches are stopping," Al Colvin groaned, turning to Donegan.

As Burrowes's relief column reached that point along the trail where the hayfield road passed beneath the ridge west of the corral, the hidden hostile snipers began to place their whining lead among the horsemen. In horror, the men waiting in the battered enclosure watched the drama on the dusty road strewn with the afternoon gold dust of sunset rays. With the first shots, the column leader threw up an arm, halting his command. There they milled for desperate moments while the snipers played havoc among them.

Then, at the moment the column commander turned his horse and flung his arm back toward the post, a second figure galloped to the head of the march, riding up from the second company in formation. With wild gestures the two men argued, until the second figure reined away, signaled and proceeded with his company. As the other company passed, it appeared the column commander had no choice but to follow on to the corral.

"Gentlemen!" the young officer who had dared pass up his commander shouted as his troopers neared the west wall.

A lusty wild thrashing and hugging swelled over the corral.

Huzzahs and cheers rang in the air while the second company halted and ordered to dismount.

"I want to shake your hand, Lieutenant." Seamus was the first to reach the young officer, Al Colvin and Finn Burnett on his heels.

The lieutenant held his hand out before him, accepting the Irishman's in a crushing embrace. "Didn't quite know what we'd find here . . ." He wagged his head in disbelief. "This . . . this is nothing more than a miracle."

Seamus beamed at Captain Colvin. "You might say that, Lieutenant. Always heard the good Lord helps those who help themselves."

"What's your name?"

"Donegan. This is Al Colvin and Finn Burnett. The wounded are ready to transport."

The young officer wagged his head still, looking over the compound. "It's unbelievable the damage the hostiles did here. Every wagon-box . . . every one of those tents along the west wall—they're riddled, turned to splinters or rags." His eyes swept past the crippled wagon that had been rolled across the corral entrance, not much more now than a bullet-splattered pile of firewood.

"How many animals wounded?" he asked.

"All but two. A horse that went to the fort with the courier . . . and one lucky old mule," Al Colvin announced, grinning.

"Look at the arrows the men are picking up," the young officer said. "And the ground is covered with your cartridge shells . . . like acorns littering a forest floor." He stared at the three civilians a long time before working up the words. "You fellas had a helluva fight here. I haven't seen anything like this since Cold Harbor."

Seamus pursed his lips a moment. "Man does what a man has to do, Lieutenant."

"Name's Houg." He flung a thumb over his shoulder at Burrowes accepting the congratulations of the soldiers who had survived the hayfield fight. "This relief should've belonged to Captain Hartz. He's the one spotted the fighting going on this morning from up there along—"

"This morning?" Colvin squeaked. "You mean the post knowed about our fight this morning?"

Houg nodded, embarrassed. "Colonel Bradley figured—"

"I know just how that pompous popinjay figured," Colvin growled. "Get my hands on him—he'll feel worse than those wounded men do."

"How many dead, sir?"

"Two. Soldiers both. Sternberg and a private. We have 'em in a tent . . . away from the others."

"Lieutenant . . . Sternberg's dead?"

"He fought bravely," Seamus explained. "No one dare not call him a hero after—"

"We're leaving now, Lieutenant," Burrowes ordered, barging up.

Seamus whirled on the captain. "Leaving?"

"For your information, sir—I'm not about to sit around here all evening while you civilians lallygag. My soldiers are prepared to march back to the post at this moment. We'll take your wounded if they are ready—"

"Why, you horse's ass!" Seamus lunged for Burrowes.

Fortunately for both of them, Colvin, Burnett and Houg grabbed the Irishman as Burrowes leaped back.

"I'll have you in irons you lay a hand on me!" Burrowes shrieked like a scalded cat.

"Bet you would at that," Seamus snapped. "A simpering coward like you would talk that other yellow-spined she-dog of a colonel into slapping me in irons."

"I won't take any more of your abuse," Burrowes turned away, slapping dust from his wide-brimmed hat. "Sergeant! Prepare the men to mount."

"You're not going to give us time to get Leighton's property together for the march?" Burnett said, dashing in front of the retreating Burrowes.

The captain jerked to a halt, suddenly surrounded by a few more of the civilians. A grimy, powder-blackened lot they were. His anxious eyes darted over the group.

"You have ten minutes," Burrowes gushed suddenly. "Ten minutes and no more."

While Burnett and Al Stevenson directed the loading of two wagons, Donegan and George Duncan saw to the mules.

They found enough with wounds that would allow them to travel back to the fort, making for two wagon teams. Duncan hitched one team to a wagon Burnett's men were loading with Leighton's goods. The other team Donegan hitched to a hay wagon that would carry the wounded back to the fort.

When the loading was under way, the Colvin brothers led a double handful of Burrowes's soldiers down to the creekbank, where Al Colvin scalped the body of the Miniconjou war-chief he had sworn would not be carried off by rescuers. The bloody trophy held high at the end of his arm, he and brother Zeke watched the troopers hack the warrior's head from his body. They jabbed a spear up through the war-chief's neck and brandished it aloft, promising to display the head in the center of Fort C.F. Smith's dusty parade.

"We'll leave the bastard's body to the wolves," one soldier said to his comrades as the head rose above them.

"Or his friends . . . whichever ones comes back to fetch it first!" another chimed in, followed by the laughter of all.

"Wolves or Injuns, all the—"

"Sergeant! Order: 'Prepare to mount'!" Burrowes hollered as he slipped a foot into the stirrup of his McClellan saddle.

"Prepare to mount!" the sergeant bellowed as soldiers scurried to their horses.

Burnett and the rest hurried to reach the captain's side. "We ain't half done, Captain!" Finn snarled. "We leave without Leighton's gear . . . the Sioux come in here and burn what they don't take! And our wounded—you can't leave us!"

"MOUNT!" Burrowes shouted to his command.

"Mount!" the sergeant echoed.

Al and Zeke Colvin joined the rest at Burrowes's side. Burnett was not the only man trembling with rage. Seamus saw Captain Colvin's eyes search his a moment before Al stepped forward and seized Burrowes's reins.

"Cap'n," the ex-Confederate drawled slowly, but without a hint of meekness. It was the kind of hissing, guarded snarl a yard dog would make giving a man fair warning. "If'n you're so damned skeered to stay here with us long enough for Burnett to get-up his bossman's belongings . . . then I s'pose you better take your yeller-bellied outfit on outta here and get on without us."

"How dare you speak to me—"

Colvin yanked on the reins, shutting the captain up as quickly as a splash of cold water in the face would wake up a hangover.

"These boys . . . we all been fighting the redskins all day long awready. So, I s'pose this handful of brave men can fight our way back to the fort alone, if'n we have to."

The air appeared to hiss out of Burrowes as his eyes searched first the determined look of the civilians, then measured the sinking of the sun behind the hills, and finally glanced at young Houg. The lieutenant sat slightly slumped on his saddle, smiling at the captain's predicament.

"Suggestions, Mr. Houg?"

He straightened, the grin growing like a slash on his face. "Yes, Captain. I say we stay till these men are ready to move their property and the wounded."

"The sun is falling, gentlemen," Burrowes finally gushed, exasperated. "I will appreciate you finishing your labors with all dispatch."

Colvin winked at Seamus. "We'll hurry, Cap'n."

Seamus nodded, looking up at the officer on horseback. "That's right—we'll hurry, Cap'n Burrowes. Far be it from any of us to keep you and your boys from their evening mess —just because of some dirty, little daylong scrap the rest of us had ourselves here."

During the first week of July, civilian J. R. Porter had established his base of operations for woodcutting a short distance east of Pine Island on Big Piney Creek, close to the dense woods where his teamsters, cutters, and herders harvested timber for Fort Phil Kearny's winter needs. On the high plains where summer came late and left about as quickly, the short cutting season meant long days of grueling labor. But men were paid well for the use of their muscles, and for the possibility of losing their scalps to the hostiles who constantly showed themselves on the ridges and hills overlooking the woodcutters' camps.

On the last day of July, Company C, 27th Infantry under Capt. James W. Powell and his lieutenant, John C. Jenness, relieved Company A on guard duty at the wagon corral contractor Porter's men had established along the wood road skirting the Sullivant Hills, where the road progressed eastward toward the fort stockade. With nineteen years experience under his belt, Powell was not an excitable sort. Already he had distinguished himself for cool, thoughtful action on the morning of December 19, 1866, during a running skirmish with Sioux decoys. He had followed Colonel Carrington's orders not to pursue any parties over Lodge Trail Ridge.

Two days later Capt. William Judd Fetterman had ignored that order. And led another eighty men to their deaths.

Enlisting in 1848, Powell had risen to the brevet rank of major during the Civil War, serving with distinction and honor. Already known for his cool bravery, the captain was soon to find himself at the center of Red Cloud's fiercest attack yet on the white soldiers' fort at Pine Woods.

Capt. James W. Powell and thirty-one other men were about to suffer the brunt of Red Cloud's revenge.

When he arrived at the woodcutters' camp, the captain found that contractor Porter had split his men into two groups. The first group was involved in cutting timber on the slope above and on Pine Island itself. In order to remain close to the cutting sites, this small group of civilians camped in the thick woods on the island at the foot of the mountains, across the Big Piney from the main camp. Here Powell stationed a noncommissioned officer and twelve enlisted men to guard the civilian operation.

The second and larger group made its camp on the bare and relatively level plain stretching some thousand yards across about a mile southeast of the woodcutters' camp. This treeless plain, surrounded by low hills, was a good place to graze mules and organize the wagon loads of timber bound for the fort each day. Instead of placing the corral in the middle of the open field, Porter's civilians had set up camp near its northern border so that the level ground stretched away only on the other three compass points. In this ideal location, those in the main camp could keep watch over both the woodcutting operations and the wood road itself.

Here in this main camp the civilian workers had removed

the wooden wagon-boxes from their running gears so that the long logs harvested by the woodcutters could be laid atop those running gears and hauled to Fort Phil Kearny each day. These fourteen wagon-boxes, the ordinary wood wagon beds in use by the Army Quartermaster Corps, stood only four feet tall when laid on the ground in a large oval. They were not lined with iron plate. In addition, the iron bows and canvas tops had been removed before the men augured two-inch holes in the sides of some of the boxes. Loopholes the men would use in firing the rifles issued to the soldiers of Fort Phil Kearny back on the tenth of July.

At either end of the crude oval stood two full wagon-boxes still atop their running gears. At the east entrance stood the wagon containing rations for the woodcutters, while that on the west serviced Powell's troops. These two wagons were eased out of the way during the day, and could be quickly rolled back in place to complete the fortification at night when the stock was driven inside the oval. Or in the event of attack.

Sacks of grain and corn, ox yokes, cordwood, bails of wool blankets, and kegs, along with a few bags of dry beans, filled the spaces between the wagons and were placed inside the outer walls of the boxes for more protection than the thin wood sides could offer the defenders. Blankets lay close at hand, to be thrown over the boxes during attack, so that enemy horsemen charging down upon the corral could not easily spot the defenders.

Outside this oval the men had pitched tents where both soldier and civilian alike slept. In the event of attack, no matter his assigned task or where he might find himself, every man was ordered to hasten to the corral, where extra weapons would be found, along with seven thousand rounds of ammunition for the new Allin-modified Springfields sent up from Fort Laramie. Only in the wagon-box corral, it was supposed, the defenders could hold off an attack by a small force indefinitely, and an attack by a large force for a short period of time while awaiting relief from Fort Phil Kearny.

With the rising of tomorrow's sun, Captain Powell's men and four civilians would find out what it meant to fight for their lives against an overwhelming onslaught of Sioux and Cheyenne warriors intent upon sweeping the white man from their hunting grounds once and for all.

The Milky Way stretched like sugar dusted across the blackening heavens that first night of August as the men in the wagon-box corral finished supper and lit their pipes or cut a fresh quid from their plug tobacco. Out beyond the firelight, Sgt. Patrick McQuiery had stationed his first watch for the evening.

While the fires sank low and the night deepened, McQuiery stepped into the darkening gloom of the summer night. At the sergeant's heels tagged Pvt. Jack McDonough's dog Jess.

"You seen any Injuns, Doyle?" McQuiery sang out in his harsh whisper.

"No, Sarge," Pvt. Tommy C. Doyle answered, scratching the dog's ears when Jess laid her head against his knee. "But, I can smell 'em!"

"Keep your eyes and your nose awake tonight, Tommy-boy. We ain't seen the red niggers for several days now . . . then they up and show this afternoon."

"Run off a few head from the pasture near the fort, I hear."

McQuiery wagged his head. "They're back to devilment. Been too quiet to suit me, it has." He turned to go.

"G'night, Sergeant."

"G'night, Tommy. Looks like Jess will stay out on watch with you. Keep those eyes skinned . . . and you got my orders to shoot anything that don't answer you."

"Yessir."

As McQuiery reached the tent camp, Pvt. Henry Haggerty turned round on his keg stool.

"Ah, Sergeant—we're all in the mood for a rousing ditty, sir. You sing so well, and you're right on time."

He eased himself down on the hard-tack box and accepted a cup of steaming coffee, red coals glowing at his feet. "What'll be fellas? You wanna hear 'bout old One-Eyed Riley?"

"Sure as you're born, Sarge!"

When Patrick began to sing, it did not take long before the others joined in, every man enjoying the ribald tune popular

among the soldiers marching west at the end of the Civil War.
McQuiery bellowed out the first verse:

> "As I was strolling round and round,
> A-huntin' fun in every quarter,
> I stopped meself at the little Dutch inn
> And ordered me up Gin and Warter."

Then the rest joined him in the rollicking chorus:

> "One-Eye Riley, Two-Eye Riley,
> Ho! for the land with one eye, Riley!"

Chapter 35

As drummer boy and company bugler, Private Hines chose his snare to beat reveille on that morning of the second of August down in the wagon-box corral, bringing the men from their bedrolls before the sun had even considered creeping over the low hills to the east.

Sam Gibson, private in Powell's C Company, wiped the gummy sleep from his eyes and scurried to inspection. Lieutenant Jenness finished his roll-call just as cook Hezekiah Brown hollered out.

"Chuck! Get your chuck while it's hot, boys!"

Fifty-three soldiers scampered to lay their rifles away and jostled into line. Everyone but the two pickets who squatted among the tents to eat their pan bread and fried pork, their eyes raking the perimeter of the meadow.

With breakfast out of the way, Powell issued orders for the division of his command for the day. The first train under Lt. Francis McCarthy and Cpl. Paddy Conley leading an escort of twenty men would proceed to Fort Phil Kearny with its load of logs brought down from the Pinery the day before. With McCarthy on his way east, Powell dispatched a second train in the opposite direction, this one to the woodcutting camp in the pine woods under a corporal with a dozen enlisted men. The captain and Jenness themselves stayed behind at the corral with the remaining twenty-six men to guard the contractor's property and livestock.

Lieutenant Jenness's watch showed it was a few minutes prior to seven o'clock.

"Gibson," Jenness called out.

"Yessir?"

"Take Deming and Garrett with you. Get up there and relieve Grady."

"Will do, sir." Gibson swept up his new, unfired Springfield conversion. "C'mon, boys. You heard the man."

"You and me was on guard duty most of the night, Gibby," Pvt. Nelson Deming grumbled.

"It'll be all right. We'll get Garrett to stand first watch while we make us a piece of shade," Gibson explained, slapping his friend on the back.

With a gum-rubber poncho stretched over some willow branches, the two soldiers had their shade from the climbing sun, and Private Garrett standing guard as well. Here on the hillside above the Little Piney, the morning wasn't shaping up badly at all, as Sam Gibson saw things.

R. J. Smyth had come as a teamster to the Big Horn country with Henry Carrington's "Overland Circus," driving an ambulance bound for what eventually was named Fort Phil Kearny. As a proven mule whacker, Smyth had made several trips down to Laramie and up to C.F. Smith, but by and large had kept himself busy and on the payroll driving a mowing outfit in the hayfields surrounding the post and down in the bottoms near Lake DeSmet.

He had joined other volunteers who rode with Tenedore Ten Eyck that bitterly cold December day when the captain had marched off to relieve Fetterman's command. Since that time, R. J. Smyth awoke many a night, cold fear running down his spine like a leaky keg spigot, recalling the sight of those butchered bodies scattered across Lodge Trail Ridge.

Earlier this August morning in the predawn darkness, even before reveille had been bugled across the stockade, Smyth and a hunting partner had slipped from the fort to track some deer in the nearby hills above the woodcutting operations along the Big Piney. Having climbed their horses for better than an hour through the dense woods, R.J. called a breather for the animals. As their mounts blew frosty halos into the warming dawn air, the sun just beginning to creep over the eastern lip of the prairie, both men stretched out upon the damp ground. While Smyth dozed, Billy Lott stared vacantly over the valley below.

"R.J.?"

"Yeah?" he answered, his face hidden beneath his floppy-brimmed hat.

"You seen Injun smoke signals afore?"

" 'Course, I have, Billy."

"You read 'em?"

"God, are you a stupid child! 'Course I can't read Injun."

"Damn."

"Damn, what?" Smyth asked, disgusted at the interruption of his nap.

"Thinking you might tell me what that smoke was saying."

Smyth bolted upright, ripping the hat from his face. "Jesus!" He leaped to his feet. "Why didn't you tell me sooner, Billy?"

Terrified, Lott looked down at both fists gripping the front of his flannel shirt. "They just started a few minutes ago, R.J. Honest. Them there. There. There. And them over there too."

"Jesus . . ." Smyth muttered his oath once more. "Something's afoot, Billy Lott. And we best be getting our sweet asses outta these hills."

"Cain't agree with you more, R.J. Lookee up there."

Smyth followed Lott's arm, pointing uphill from where they stood at that very moment. White smoke, puffing into the breathless morning air of sunrise, signals turned pink with the rising of a bloody sun. As he watched for a few heartbeats, numb and slack-jawed, bright pinpoints of light flashed from the hills bordering the Big Piney.

"You get that animal of your'n downhill and quick, Billy Lott. You're on your own now. I'm gonna try for that wood train heading for the fort—yonder!"

"Don't leave me, R.J.!" Lott hollered out, leaping atop his horse and scampering down through the timber behind Smyth.

The last thing R.J. saw before he headed into what he hoped was the safety of the dark forest was the terrifying sight of hundreds of feathered, mounted warriors just then bristling

atop the hills to the west. And pouring down into the valley—
fast.

He figured if he didn't have time to reach the security of
those twenty-odd soldiers escorting the load of timber bound
for the fort, then surely he and Lott could reach the corral in
time.

Praying that he could reach the wagon-boxes and those
two-dozen soldiers in blue under Powell and Jenness.

Dear God . . . I know I ain't one to get down on my prayer
bones enough and taffy up to you one helluva alot. But . . . I
wan'tcha listen to me close now, God . . .

"Promise me you'll keep to the high places, Seamus," Finn
Burnett implored, sticking his hand up to the Irishman, who
had just climbed atop the horse he was borrowing from contractor Leighton for this ride south to Fort Phil Kearny.

He nodded, smiling. "Bet them Injins is licking their
wounds this morning." He gazed over the stockade wall at the
growing gray light that foretold the coming of a new day.

"Bet they're madder'n wet hornets, you ask me. Licking
wounds or no."

"You just take care of yourself, Finn. Sorry I ain't gonna be
here to bury Hollister today. He was a good man—hung on
long as he could."

"Things could've been worse for the lot of us."

Seamus snorted, passing it off. "You laugh hard enough and
loud enough at death, Finn—that bleeming sonuvabitch'll
turn tail and run. Mark my words."

Burnett stepped back a pace, staring up into the reflected
torchlight at his friend. "You, Seamus Donegan—you keep
laughing all the way to Kearny for me."

He pulled his hat brim down, eyeing the growing gray line
along the east wall of the stockade. "Since I come west to this
Injin country, I ain't never stopped laughing, Finn. Godspeed, me friend."

Seamus yanked on the reins and was off. Through the gate.
Turning immediately southwest across the wood road, aiming
directly for the timbered hillsides. Knowing enough that the
fort was in all probability still watched. He wanted to be into

the forest along the black-timbered ridges before the sun ever peeked over the far rim of the prairie.

No sense in letting any of the h'athens have another go at me scalp, is there? He breathed easier when he reached the dewy coolness of the black timber. *Way things look now, never will have to worry about Injins raising my hair again. Say good-bye at last to this land and all its red divils . . .*

Although he had promised Burnett, Seamus Donegan knew there was little to smile about until he reached the walls of Fort Phil Kearny. Fearing as many others did as to the safety of the post, the Irishman feared even more for the welfare of his old friend, Captain Marr. Sam was down at Fort Phil Kearny.

And Seamus hoped with every bit of his fiber that the widow Wheatley and her boys were out of harm's way as well. Safely on their way south to Fort Laramie. Out of Red Cloud's country and far from the reach of his bloody grasp.

Just keep to the timber and the hills, me boy. Seamus patted the old horse on the neck. *We'll see each other down to Kearny . . . there'll be oats and corn for you, me friend. Whiskey for Seamus and Sam Marr.*

Sweet mither of Jesus—but Seamus Donegan's him got a thirst right now that would make the divil himself blush!

"INDIANS!"

Sam Gibson bolted up, knocking a willow branch over. He fought the gum-rubber poncho aside, searching for his rifle. Tom Garrett hollered again.

"Indians!"

"I heard you, goddammit!" Deming shouted, blinking his sleepy eyes and staring off in the direction Garrett pointed.

"Seven of 'em," Gibson remarked absently, eyes squinting into the new light.

"Single file, in a dead run," Garrett replied, swiping his dry lips with the back of a shaking hand.

"Decoys?" Deming asked.

Gibson swallowed. "Don't have an idea one what they are. But since they're headed our way . . . I figure we're about to find out, boys."

Deming glanced down at his rifle, then at his sweating palms. "I ain't fired this gun yet, Sam."

He grinned loosely, teeth gleaming. "None of us has, Nel. But we're gonna get our chance now. C'mon. Let's knock some off their ponies."

Sam scampered away, the other two on his heels. With a small boulder and a clear field of fire in front of him, Gibson dropped to one knee. He clicked down the first two of the Joslyn leaf sights. Hoping for a long shot of it, he snapped the third leaf into place.

Five hundred . . . no—six hundred yards. He quickly calculated distance and time as the seven horsemen tore down the slope into the meadow at full tilt. Cutting diagonally across Gibson's line of sight.

He touched off the first round.

"You see where that went," he asked without turning to the friends behind him.

"Short!" Deming shouted, excited, hopping anxiously.

"Damn!" Gibson threw open the trap and ran home another of the fat, sausagelike cartridges. He had pockets loaded with them. If the seven warriors turned on the three of them, Sam figured the trio could make a fine show of it with the repeaters. In a way, he itched for a fight of it during that moment he studied the rear sight.

Seven hundred yards, he decided. *And give the bastard some running room.*

That shot struck a small boulder directly in front of the lead warrior as he raced across the prairie. The ricochet of splattering lead caught the pony in the chest.

Stumbling sideways a step, the animal lurched, pitching its rider into the dust before it toppled to the side, wounded and bleeding.

"Hurrah!" Deming shouted, dancing now instead of prancing his anxious jig.

"Good shooting, Gibby!" Garrett hollered, slapping his friend on the back as Gibson rose.

"Uh-oh!"

Sam and Garrett turned to see what had snagged the dancing Deming's attention.

God—there must be thousands of 'em!" Garrett

undreds at least," Gibson whispered, his mouth gone
denly dry. "And we've worn out our welcome here, boys."
Along the foothills to the north there now appeared hundreds upon hundreds of painted, naked horsemen streaming
into the valley from the vicinity of Peno Creek and Lodge
Trail Ridge. Several of the anxious, battle-hungry Sioux could
not be restrained by their war-chiefs and headed directly for
the post herd. There would be time enough to take white
scalps this day. But first, the horses and mules.

Puffs of smoke appeared in the morning air over the herd.
At the edge of the trees where the herders usually kept a fire
going and a coffee kettle hot throughout the day.

"They've jumped the herd, Sam!" Garrett hollered, tugging
on Gibson's sleeve.

Sam glanced at his friend's wide, frightened eyes. Then
looked at Deming. "Go down a ways—see what you can of
the woodcutters' camp. Get an eye on the main corral as well.
See if they've been jumped yet. I need to know what direction
to go."

He watched Deming nod and dash off from the edge of the
timber to a point of land twenty yards away.

"If we're cut off—"

Gibson wheeled on Garrett. "We're not cut off. And we
won't be!" he snapped.

Deming splashed back across the Little Piney, huffing his
way up the slope into the timber. "They run off the herd,
Gibby!"

Sam grabbed his friend's shirt with one hand. "What of the
herders?"

Deming swallowed. "Looks like they're all running for the
mountains . . . straight uphill for the blockhouse . . .
them as ain't penned down—"

"All of 'em?"

" 'Cept one," he answered, turning to point. "I seen him
coming down into the meadow toward our post at a good
lick."

"Headed our way . . . alone?"

He nodded shakily. "Alone. 'Cept he's leading a horse."

"Sonuvabitch ain't riding?"

He wagged his head. "Uh-uh. On foot."

"They got the mules, Sam," moaned Garrett.

Gibson and Deming twisted around, finding some sixty mounted Sioux in among the herd, driving it off toward the north.

"The whole goddamned caboodle!" Gibson swore.

"Looks like the Injuns overrun the camp," Garrett announced, pointing out the woodcutters' camp on the end of the island. A growing cloud of oily smoke told the trio the Sioux were setting fire to the place.

Crazy Horse himself led his screeching Oglallas down on the camp, killing the last four teamsters who had valiantly tried to hold off the war-chief's wild charge. Those soldiers and civilians fortunate enough to escape that sudden death now fought a running battle against the Oglallas as they scampered east, heading straight for Fort Phil Kearny itself and bypassing the questionable safety of the wagon-box corral in the meadow below.

At the same time, those herders who had not headed for the blockhouse were making a beeline for that same retreat. A damned sight closer were they to the soldiers fleeing toward the fort than they were to wagon-boxes. Instead of joining forces at the corral as ordered, Powell's soldiers and the teamsters were scattering to the winds. Every man for himself and remembering that vivid nightmare of butchery across the Lodge Trail that cast its shadow into this valley of the Pineys.

"Damn!" Captain Powell cursed under his breath, his muttonchop whiskers throbbing with every clench of his jaws.

"The hostiles are going to cut off those herders hoping to join up with McDonough's group," Lieutenant Jenness said as he rushed to Powell's side.

Powell as quickly looked around him. "A dozen of you! Follow me!" He gripped his lieutenant's arm as twelve men jogged to the east end of the corral. "John—you're in charge while I'm gone. If . . . if we don't make it back—hold out as long as you can."

"We've plenty of guns . . . and cartridges, sir!"

"That's the spirit, John. The fort will send a relief quick enough."

"Good luck, Captain!"

He smiled at Jenness, turned and led his men from the corral.

Powell hoped to sally out far enough to create a distraction, enough of a diversion to pull the enemy horsemen off the trail of the herders. If he did not, those herders would be swallowed up in a matter of moments and never would reach the retreating wood party and soldiers headed for the fort.

"Fire in volley! At my command and not before!" Powell growled, throwing up his arm. "Form two squads . . . fire six at a time! Ready . . . targets . . . *FIRE!*"

The new Springfields spat flame, six lead pills crashing into the rear of Crazy Horse's Oglallas.

"*FIRE!*" he ordered, waving his arm again, watching the first six soldiers slap cartridges into the smoking breeches of their rifles.

"*FIRE!*" The second half-dozen reloaded.

"*FIRE!*" Powder smoke began to hang at their shoulders.

"*FIRE!*"

"*FIRE!*"

"They're turning, Cap'n!" Pvt. Dale McNally shouted as he pulled a cartridge from his lips and rammed it home.

"*FIRE!*"

"Hurraw!" Pvt. John Grady shouted.

"*FIRE,* goddammit!" Powell shouted even louder, his command answered by another volley. The powder smoke stung his eyes, stank in his nostrils. It clung around his steady soldiers like a whiskey-hungry whore near an army post.

"We got 'em on the run, Cap'n!" Sgt. Frank Hoover shouted into Powell's ear.

"Give 'em hell, boys!" Powell hollered. "Shoot the bastards in the ass, they turn tail like this!"

"Cap'n!"

"Jehosophat! They're coming back at us!"

"Orderly retreat, men!" Powell shouted above the anxious muttering of his dozen. "First squad—keep your chambers loaded . . . fire only on my command. *Second squad*—re-

treat orderly . . . *ORDERLY!* Twenty yards and hold—
ready to fire!"

In that way, Powell kept his dozen from breaking and running in a wild retreat to the corral. Yard by yard, six men
scampering off, turning, and holding the Oglallas at bay while
the other half dozen joined up. Leap-frogging his unit until all
thirteen soldiers sprinted the last fifty yards into the corral.

"You're a pretty sight, mister!" Powell shouted to his lieutenant as he skidded inside the wagon-box oval.

Jenness saluted, smiling. "Thank you, sir! We'll give 'em a
case of lead poisoning this day, Captain!"

"By God!" Powell slapped Jenness on the shoulder. "We
will at that, son. We will at that!"

Chapter 36

Sam Marr hurried the big blue-roan stallion along. He dared not leap on its back until absolutely necessary. Only if the warriors swept down on him. For now, he would use the animal as a shield. Not so easy for the Sioux to spot him if he trotted beside the stallion. Sam pulled and urged and coaxed from beneath the roan's neck, yanking on the halter. And cussing. One hell of a lot of cussing.

"You fellas best come along with me!" Marr cried out as he neared the three young soldiers scampering down that neck of land sloping into the Big Piney meadow.

"We're coming," Sam Gibson hollered back. "If you're headed to the corral, Captain Marr!"

"We don't stand a chance making that bunch!" and Marr flung an arm toward the retreating herders joining with the wood party, the whole lot of them scurrying toward the fort.

"We don't stand much a chance out here as it is!" Nelson Deming groaned.

"They spot us . . . we're soup!" Tom Garrett agreed.

"They spot us—we make a fight of it," Marr explained. "But we'll make it—so buck up, boys."

"Let's go!" Sam Gibson said, shoving his fellow soldiers off behind the civilian.

The four hadn't gone far across the grassy plain, huddled around the nervous stallion, before they spotted some warriors popping up from the creek bottom at their rear. Warriors who caught sight of the four white men retreating to the corral.

"Captain Marr!" Deming whimpered as a bullet whined in the air overhead.

"We got company, boys! They draw close enough to jump us, two of us gonna hold up and stand tight—covering the other pair. Got that?" Sam watched the soldiers nod anxiously, their eyes not on him, but on the warriors streaming from the willows along the creek.

"Leap-frog was always one of my favorite games as a young'un, Cap'n Marr!" Gibson cheered. "I'll stay with you —Deming . . . you and Garrett take off!"

The pair needed no further urging. Fifty yards away they stopped, turned and dropped to one knee to begin placing rounds among the pursuing warriors pouring across the plain on foot. That was Marr's cue.

"C'mon, Sam!"

"I'm hugging your ass, Cap'n Marr!"

When they reached the other two, the Missourian shoved them off. "Git, boys! You're doing a fine job! Fine!"

"Cap'n Marr?"

"Yeah?" Marr replied, firing his pistol once more at the pursuers.

"A few of them redskins look to have Springfields, don't they?" Gibson asked.

"That they do," Marr whispered, his eyes focusing on the distance.

"They got them from Fetterman, didn't they?"

He slammed loads into his second pistol, keeping the loaded one in his belt for the close-in and dirty work. "They didn't buy those goddamned Springfields from Mormons, son!"

"Got one!" Gibson piped as a warrior lumbering out of the creek bottom on horseback tumbled off his pony.

"Good shooting, boy!" Marr cheered. "Our turn! Let's go!"

Gibson took off on a dead run. Marr yanked and struggled. The wide-eyed stallion rared back, nearly pulling the old man off his feet like a limp, rag doll clutching the bridle for his life. The animal backed up. Then backed up some more.

"Gibson!"

The soldier looked over his shoulder, then halted. Darting back.

"Stick your damned bayonet in this bastard's ass, Gibby!" Marr ordered.

"Stick 'im?"

"Now! He ain't going nowhere without a little prodding!"

"Leave 'im here, Cap'n Marr!"

"I ain't leaving this blooded animal for them red niggers get their hands on him."

"He'll be the death of you, old man!"

Marr shoved Gibson off. "Then get up there with the others, Gibby! We ain't got far to go. You boys cover me best you can. Now get! Cover me if you can. Things get too hot for this old warhorse, I'll jump on the roan, go and ride it to the corral right behind you. *GO!*"

Gibson did not wait for more prodding. He was gone. And Sam Marr stood alone, struggling and coaxing the blooded Kentucky thoroughbred stallion. On three sides now the naked warriors sprang up as if from the prairie itself. Rising like a fluttering, shrieking covey of noisy, thieving crows.

"Damned scavengers—all of you!" the old man growled, moving the stallion another twenty yards until a bullet whined overhead. The roan reared again, dragging Marr into the air, legs flopping, his pistol arm clawing at blue sky.

Breechclouts and bonnets. Moccasins and war clubs. Single war-eagle feathers and roached hair. Faces hideously painted: ocher and crimson, charcoal-black and green—faces already close enough that Sam Marr could see the bear-grease colors furred with prairie dust.

The stallion whirled around in a circle, a second arrow slapping into his flanks.

"You sonuvabitch—I'll not find you another mare to stud . . . if you mean the death of me!" Marr swore, steadying the animal with one hand, the other stuffing the second pistol into his belt.

For an old man, the Missourian leaped atop the stallion smoothly, gripping the halter up close to the roan's jaw.

"Now, git—you long-dicked bastard. Run like the devil hisself gonna castrate you!"

* * *

Sam Gibson had witnessed for himself what the Sioux did to soldiers. With his own eyes he had seen the Fetterman dead, frozen into grotesque, tortured positions. Hacked and . . .

The young soldier didn't want to think about it anymore. Refusing to dwell on what would happen should the Sioux cut off the trio of sprinting troopers from the corral. Just run. And keep his two friends with him.

That looks like Littman. His mind burned like his lungs, watching a tall, flaxen-haired soldier scamper out of the corral, around the canvas-bowed wagon and onto the prairie itself.

By God, he's coming out to cover us!

Gibby recognized the stripes on the soldier's arm now, his eyes tearing as his heavy, thick-soled, ill-fitting brogans lumbered over the bunch-grass and sage. He and the others had repeatedly stumbled in their wild dash, nearly falling more times than they would ever recount. But here they were, by nothing more than divine Providence, nearing the wagon-box corral.

Two hundred yards . . .

The whistle of lead and the hiss of arrows overhead.

. . . a hundred fifty yards . . .

Painted, screaming, red-eyed warriors breathing down their necks.

. . . a hundred twenty-five yards . . .

"C'mon, boys!" The tall oak of a sergeant stood, waving his arm, swearing briefly in his native German before he dropped to a knee once more. Firing and reloading.

Sam Gibson watched Max Littman slap each fat sausage cartridge into the breech across those last few yards. Watched the blond-haired, hook-nosed old Prussian calmly blow the stinging, black smoke away from the breech each time he ripped open the trapdoor.

"Sergeant!" Deming flew past Littman, literally diving among the wagon-boxes.

"Thanks, Sarge!" Garrett shouted his greeting as he passed by, not seeing Littman nod coolly.

"You comin' this fine day, Gibby?" Littman hollered, his

cheek nuzzling the rifle stock as the front blade swept across the chest of the warrior bearing down on Sam Marr far in the rear.

"You want help?" Gibson slowed, the Springfield already like a load of bricks at the end of his right arm.

"Get your ass in the boxes, soldier!" Littman growled. "I cover the old man!"

That Prussian's got the heart of a lion, Gibson marveled to himself as he slid round the wagon at the west entrance to the corral. *Look at him, standing there, dirt kicking up 'round him like raindrops on a pond . . . spilling 'em off their ponies like there's no tomorrow.*

Then Private Gibson shuddered with the thought. Looking over the prairie. Watching Sam Marr riding closer and closer. Seeing Max Littman empty another Indian pony of its rider.

There may be no tomorrow for any . . . any of us.

When Sam Marr galloped past the German sergeant, Littman finally retreated, coolly walking backward as the warriors pressed down upon him, firing and loading. Blowing powder smoke from the rifle. His weapon already hot to the touch.

Nearing the wall, Marr hugged the stallion's neck as the blue roan leaped into the air, clearing a wagon-box and skidding into the center of the corral with a dusty cloud. He dropped to the ground, heart pounding.

After their frantic run, the young soldiers still huffed for air as they squatted between the wagons. All of them close to done in from their terrifying retreat to the corral.

Gibson helped Littman and two others push the covered wagon across the west entrance to the enclosure. No more white men would make it to the corral this day. They were alone in that meadow now. Captain Powell and his second-in-command, Lieutenant Jenness. Twenty-six soldiers ringing the wagon-box wall. And now with the addition of Sam Marr as the last man to make it across the prairie, there were four civilians.

Thirty-two grim-eyed white men in all. Each man staring death in the face below a new day's sun inching over the prairie.

Gibson turned from the wagon's single-tree and found Powell nearby.

"Reporting for duty, Captain."

"Gibby! Damn, but that was a pretty run you boys made!"

"Sorry 'bout leaving our post—"

"No apologies needed," Powell replied with the hint of a smile.

"Couldn't hold it against the odds."

"You've done nobly, my boy! No one could've done better," Powell praised, laying a hand on the young private's shoulder. "You four . . . find a place in the boxes. We'll all be fighting for our lives today!"

While Garrett, Deming and Marr all headed to a different wall, Gibson dashed to the north side, where he joined the Irish sergeant Patrick McQuiery and Pvt. John Grady in a box.

"Powell's right," Grady cheered the new arrival. "We all have to fight like *hell* today, kid—if you expect to come out of this scrap alive!"

Gibson made himself a home down among the sacks of oats, moving one sack aside so that he could push the muzzle of his rifle out the two-inch auger hole drilled in the side of the box.

"That old man must be some shot," McQuiery marveled, then spit a stream of tobacco over the top of the sidewall.

Gibson looked over his shoulder. Powell was busy near Sam Marr, motioning three of the younger soldiers to gather behind the old civilian. Bringing their rifles and making them available to Marr when the fight got hot.

"Why's Powell having them give their rifles to Marr?"

McQuiery grinned crookedly, the brown quid almost creeping out of his mouth. "Them's the ones don't shoot worth a hiccup, Gibby. They'll reload them guns for the old sharpshooter. Hear it told that man can knock flies off a postwhore's nose at fifty paces."

"Shit! Hope he shoots as good today!" Gibson laughed, turning back to the prairie.

He saw the blankets stacked in the box behind the three of them. Figuring there were at least five. Good covering to shield the riflemen from the view of the horsemen bearing

down on the corral. Good enough to keep some of the rapidly
rising sun off their backs.

*It's gonna be a long day, Sam Gibson. And then again . . .
maybe it won't. So, the best you can pray for is to hold your
water . . . and ask God for it to be one helluva a long day for
you . . . whatever name you call yourself.*

Already the valley was swarming with more than a thousand mounted Sioux. Adding some two hundred who had
been harassing small groups of white men on foot to the rest
of the Sioux and Cheyenne streaming down the Peno Head
and across the Lodge Trail Ridge, there were more than fifteen hundred of them in full view of the lonely, fourteen-
wagon corral.

Not good odds at all, Sam told himself, praying he would
hold his water and not wet his pants. He never had. But the
old soldiers said it was no shame, said it could always happen
to a man come a battle that would test his mettle. Sam Gibson
figured his time had come.

Dear God, he prayed. *Don't let me die with soiled
pants . . .*

Thirty-two of them huddled in those wagon-boxes now.
Under a rising sun that second day of August of 'sixty-seven.
A Friday morning. And no man among them seriously think-
ing he would ever last to see that sun go down this day.

Out there on that prairie pranced and screeched, cavorted
and screamed, more than two thousand of Red Cloud's finest.
Led by Crazy Horse, Red Leaf, and High Back-Bone. The
pride of the Bad Faces. In their copper breasts beat unre-
quited hatred for white men.

Braver, more daring, more resolute Indians had never been
whelped on these high plains.

All come here under the watchful eye of Red Cloud himself: Brules, Sans Arcs, Oglallas, Miniconjous, Hunkpapas
and a large contingent of Northern Cheyenne who had chosen
to follow Red Cloud rather than attack Fort C.F. Smith with
their war-chief Roman Nose.

The pride of the Lakota nation was about to pit itself
against the pride of C Company, 27th U.S. Infantry.

And four unlucky civilians.

Chapter 37

Sam Marr watched the wiry private Tommy Doyle pile up some ox yokes between two wagon-boxes for his shelter. Nearby, Jim Condon had taken his spot behind a squat barrel of dried white beans.

As he appraised the young soldiers Powell had ordered to stay right behind him, Marr realized the other men in the corral had plenty of weapons as well. Some gripped their seven-shot Spencer carbines proven in service during the war. Others waited patiently at the thin walls of their wagon-boxes, holding their Allin-modified Springfields. That soldier over there beside R. J. Smyth even had a needle-gun. And every one of them had at least a pair of service revolvers at hand. Some of those pistols, even the new Colts he had heard reports of before leaving Kansas with Seamus Donegan, were bound for the goldfields of Alder Gulch, Montana Territory.

Sam wondered now about Seamus. And thought about how crazy men would get for the want of some yellow rocks. Crazy enough to lay their lives on the line. If not crazy enough to leave their blood soaking into the thirsty soil of this prairie.

Damn, if they didn't bring their women and pups along.

Marr gazed cautiously over the sidewall as some of the squaws and children and old ones gathered across the hills to watch their menfolk wipe out this little corral before journeying on to overwhelm the Pine Woods fort itself.

*Bet they wanna see their men rub us out now . . . since
they didn't get the chance to see Fetterman's boys butchered.*

This astonishing force of warriors and spectators had not
reached the valley of the Piney creeks all at the same time.
Instead, more and more warriors and three times their number in women and children appeared along the hills throughout the early morning.

For the most part, the mounted warriors still carried bow,
warclub and lance. The preferred weapons still. While some
did have the newest in repeating Winchesters or Henrys, others brought along the weapons taken from the Fetterman
dead. They would be stingy with the use of those rifles and
pistols. Lead and powder would surely be needed once they
reached the fort itself.

After all, to overrun this corral of wagons the white men
huddled behind would take only a simple charge of horsemen
firing down into the defenders with their sinew-backed bows.
Hardly a fight worthy of precious gunpowder and lead ball.

"Men!" Powell hollered, standing erect and daring at the
center of the corral, a pistol wagging in each hand. "This will
be a long day for most of us. What you see out there on that
field is something that would make any man's innards dry up
and shrivel. Last winter not far from this ground, a little more
than twice our own number were massacred by but a portion
of what faces us now! But we are soldiers, by God—and we
will hold these red bastards off until help arrives!"

Powell waited a moment as a nervous, self-conscious cheer
erupted from his men. The captain drew himself up, swelling
his chest slightly. Already the sweat glistened in tiny pearls
across his forehead and down the sides of his muttonchops.

"And, my friends—you all know what to do should we be
overwhelmed before relief arrives. Let no man be taken alive
by these savages!"

A wilder cheer rose from the oval, crackling into the hot
sky overhead which appeared vacant and ran on forever in its
vastness without a cloud to smudge its blue.

"Captain Powell," Jenness said, nudging his superior.
"Look there on that hill." He pointed to a slope some three
quarters of a mile off to the east. "I believe Red Cloud himself
is on the top of that hill."

"Him and the rest of his bloodthirsty cronies too," Powell agreed.

Marr turned back, for a moment watching some of the older soldiers slipping the laces from their clumsy brogans. One of the young troopers behind Sam asked what the veterans were doing. Dryly, Marr explained why both shoestrings were tied together before a loop at one end was lashed round a foot. A smaller loop then secured in the other end.

His explanation seemed to sober the youngsters some, all but silencing them. If the hostiles ever breached the corral walls, every soldier understood he was to take his own life. The small loop in those shoelaces would be hooked over the trigger of their Springfield. Each man would stand, putting the rifle muzzle under their chins or stuffed in their open mouths before the foot at the other end of the shoestring would twitch.

Leaving no live prisoners for the redmen to torture. Enough stories already had been told and retold around campfires and barracks for even the young troopers to realize that fighting Indians here in this wilderness meant every man looked out for himself in those last moments. Always keeping a last bullet for himself.

"They're coming now, boys," Sam Marr whispered to the three youngsters huddled behind him holding their rifles and supplied with two boxes of cartridges.

None of them spoke. They didn't have to, Marr decided. "Quiet is better at a time like this, soldiers. Quiet is fine."

Across the prairie more than five hundred horsemen had begun an orderly, slow march toward the corral. Sam figured these were special warriors—for some reason allowed the honor of overrunning the corral. Five hundred, while the rest watched.

"Like swatting at a hornet," Sam murmured to himself. Reassuring. "Swat and be done with it."

Max Littman now moved to his chosen location between two wagons and behind a squatty barrel of salt. Most of the soldiers hunkered down even farther into the wagon-boxes, making themselves as small as possible, laying their rifles atop sacks of grain, muzzles poking out the auger holes. Other bags of forage provided protection from Sioux bullets. The inch-thick wagon sidewalls would not.

Five hundred ponies were nudged into an easy lope.

Now Sam began to make out the humming, discordant chant from the horsemen bearing down on the corral. Like an eerie nightmare, the off-key warsong throbbed above the pounding of the pony hoofs.

He watched Powell and Jenness shake hands. Perhaps never to speak to one another again. Never to share that camaraderie only men under fire would ever know. The captain headed toward one end of the oval. Jenness stationed himself by the wagon at the other.

"How many guns we got us, boys?" Marr whispered, trying to smile at the three young faces behind him. Two of them dippled with the fuzz of a Georgia peach. One face already damp with silent tears.

"G-Got us seven guns, sir," answered one of the peach-fuzz faces after he had swallowed a hot stone in his throat.

Marr nodded, glancing once again at the warriors nearing, their hoofbeats and chant growing like a climbing, rumbling crescendo of prairie thunder. He smiled wider, his old teeth yellowed like pinewood chips flying from a woodsman's axe.

"We have eight." He patted his Henry. "I'll take seventeen of the bastards with this gun. Then we'll go to work on them Springfields of yours. Just be sure you keep two guns loaded for me at all times, fellas."

Sam Marr turned back to the prairie. The horsemen had moved into a gallop. More and more of them were stringing out into a wider and wider crescent. Their warsongs and soul-chilling chants were echoed by the hundreds and hundreds on the hillsides, watching. The whole valley rumbled with their promise of death to the white soldiers in the corral. The pounding of those two thousand hooves thundered up through the center of the enclosure like an earthquake threatening to swallow the defenders.

"No man fires his weapon until I give the order!" Powell shouted, running the length of the corral once. He turned around without stopping and ran back to his post repeating his order several times so that every man understood. His muttonchop whiskers drooped with sweat. A dark vee of dampness soaked his shirt between the shoulder blades.

"Sir?"

Sam turned around to the damp-faced one. Marr had seen that look enough times during the war down in Mexico. General Zack leading them to glory over the sun-grinners. Enough times down South, when white man killed white man over black men and for what private reasons they thought important enough to die.

Marr bit his lip, feeling the sting of hot moisture at his own eyes, stroking the brass-mounted Henry. And thinking on Abigail.

"I ever tell you young'uns how me and that drunken Irishman Seamus Donegan held off these same Sioux for a whole day down at the Crazy Woman Fork back to last summer? It was some show, let me tell you. You'll like the story. Well, now . . ."

As Sam Gibson watched the five hundred furiously kick their ponies into a full gallop, Captain Powell darted once more across the enclosure, shouting his orders.

"Men, here the bastards come! Wait for a target. Fire low! Fire low, goddammit! Take your places and . . . shoot to kill!"

And may God have mercy on our souls, Sam prayed, his cheek nuzzling the stock of his Springfield.

He had seen Indians before. A few at a time. Never anything like this. And he wondered if he would ever tell his grandchildren about this day.

You stupid sonofabitch! You aren't even married yet . . .

Then Private Gibson, 27th Infantry, U.S. Army, squeezed the thought out of his mind as he squeezed the trigger of his new rifle, figuring one day every man had to fight for his life. Perhaps even fight for those yet unborn.

"Shoot to kill, men!" Powell hollered again as he recrossed the compound. The warriors were about on top of the corral now. Those final four words would be the last the captain would utter for the duration of this fight in the wagon-box corral.

On both sides of Gibson sporadic rifle fire broke out. He

wasn't sure that his own bullet had hit a thing. But he opened the breech and slammed another cartridge home. Remembering the words of the chaplain who had presided over so many wartime funerals for this battered regiment.

A different chaplain had spoken over the graves of so many of Gibson's friends last winter. Gray-haired, wild-eyed Reverend White.

> "Each soldier joins his brethren in concert. Laying his very life in the hands of his fellows. Trusting completely to the heroism and skill and steadfastness of his friends. Each a soldier—risking without hesitation for the man at his side. Each a soldier—taking the action of his brethren for granted . . . trusting to the heroism of all. Each among them soldiers before God almighty Himself. Expecting no gratitude. For the laying down of one's life for his brothers is thanks enough. Giving a soldier wings through the gates of heaven itself . . ."

It was amazing to even a veteran of the war like Gibson to watch the rest of these thirty men in the corral, coolly waiting as the red horde rode down upon them. Warriors fully expecting the soldiers to withdraw their weapons from the loopholes to reload with the clumsy ramrods. Expecting at this moment to overrun the white men in one concerted rush.

By now the bullets were smashing into the vanguard of the warrior flanks. Dropping a pony here and there. Knocking one naked body after another into the yellow grass and ocher dust. Still the chants hovered over the valley from the thousands watching the charge.

Bullet after bullet smacked into copper bodies. Many of those flattened lead spheres driven with such force through one body that it pierced a nearby rider.

Gibson blinked his eyes, praying it was only sweat clouding his vision. And fired again. With so many riding down on him, his kid sister back home could have killed a warrior with every shot now.

"I can't keep the cap on the—"

He heard Tom Garrett whining in a nearby box. Then the growl of Sergeant Hoover.

"If the cap falls off, Garrett—lick the sonuvabitch first
. . . then jam it down on the nipple! Spit on it first, boy!"

Then their voices were drowned out in an almost concerted
volley as the wave of warriors swooped right, bearing along
the east side of the corral, screaming, screeching, blowing
eagle-wingbone whistles, waving shields and lances, some firing bows and rifles, hanging off the sides of their wide-eyed
ponies, feathers streaming from black hair and manes alike,
feathers and stuffed birds knotted and colored mud smeared
in the tied-up tails of the war ponies. Every one of those two
thousand hooves kicking up clods and a streaming cascade of
dust until there hung a fine, yellow gauze filtering the harsh
white light streaming out of the pale sky overhead.

Because an eroded coulee made a sharp drop-off not far
from the north side of the corral, the warriors circled sharply
about, riding back upon themselves along both the east and
west sides of the enclosure. Upon reaching the southern wall
of wagon-boxes, the warriors again turned back on themselves
and made another sally along the flame-spitting walls of the
white man's corral.

A sudden lull, no longer than three of his hammering heartbeats . . . and Sam realized the first swooping, full-winged
ride-by had left him alive. Sam Gibson knew he would make
it. No wet pants this time out.

The bastards are as close as they'll ever come now.

And prayed he would be right while the south and west
sides of the oval rocked with concerted rifle fire. Slamming
lead into the sides of crying, screeching ponies. Slapping
against copper skin with their stinging .50-caliber messengers
of death repeated over and over and over again. Naked
painted bodies turned crimson as the medicine paint worked
no wonders this hot summer morning, medicine paint and
bear grease unable to turn aside the white man's bullets.

At times a few of the more courageous swept up closer still
to the wagon-boxes, firing their arrows down from horseback
into the corral. A few of the bravest rode in even closer, a long
arm cocked back before hurling an iron-tipped lance among
the wagons. Stone and iron points thwacked into the sidewalls, where they quivered for a moment. Other lances harm-

lessly bled sacks of grain or stood trembling in the ground just beyond the defenders.

Most of those lance bearers paid a terrible price for their bravado, lying sprawled on the dusty grass beneath pony hooves in payment for their foolhardy courage.

Others less cocky and a bit mystified that no lull came in the white man's rifle fire for prolonged reloading, remembering last winter's soldiers across the Lodge Trail Ridge struggling with their ramrods and muzzle-loading, one-shot weapons. Warriors suddenly sensing their own despair as certainty now seeped from their pores while they snapped bows or pulled triggers from beneath pony necks. A *thwunnng!* and an iron-tipped arrow thunked against a wagon-wall. A crack of a new Winchester or captured soldier Springfield and the inch-thick wagon-boards splintered.

Slivers spraying over the defenders huddled at their deadly work, hidden below the wagon-tops. White eyes burned by dust and wood chips and powder smoke. Soldier throats raw and burnt, each man not knowing when he would again taste the sweet, cold water of Piney Creek.

Cool water, Sam Gibson thought, the breech of his rifle scorching his fingers as he threw open the trapdoor again, ejecting the empty cartridge and ramming home another like a machine. He reminded himself of a steam piston on a locomotive that had moved his regiment partway across Georgia before their siege of Atlanta.

In and out . . . in and out . . . each new cartridge . . . in and out.

Then there was a shout. And a cheer. Followed by more huzzahs rocking the little corral. One by one the defenders looked over shoulders, checking on their brothers-in-arms now . . .

Now that the five hundred had withdrawn from their circle ride. Leaving behind the thrashing bodies of ponies and the silent, crawling forms of those fellow warriors not killed instantly. Those left in the grass and the dust, bleeding, crawling off before another white man's bullet would slam into their bodies to finish them off.

Sam grinned, feeling for the first time a hot dampness on his cheeks. Glad there was no warmth between his legs. Not ashamed to be crying openly because so many of the others did the same as they cheered and slapped one another around.

They had turned the first charge. Bronze, bleeding bodies lay among the carnage of animals dead and dying. Ponies screaming out humanlike in pain, legs thrashing, struggling to rise, clawing the hot air as huge snaking guts poured from belly wounds and fresh dung seeped from loosened bowels. A hot steamy hell of a no-man's land ringing that little oval.

By all that's holy, we've turned the first charge!

"We give 'em a little back for what they done to Fetterman, by God!" Sgt. Frank Hoover growled, leading the others in a cheer.

"Damned right!" McQuiery agreed. "Not a man here doesn't remember what these bastards did that day!"

"Ten of these frigging red niggers we'll kill for every one of Fetterman's boys!" Pvt. Henry Haggerty vowed. "Ten of these dogs for every one of Fetterman dead!"

A few sat not uttering a word, not joining the others in their cheers, their Springfields still at work, but more slowly now. Red-rimmed eyes scanning the three-sided battlefield, searching for live ones. Slowly, methodically killing as many wounded as they could before mounted warriors would dart in as expected to drag their injured from the fray.

The corral had turned the first charge, winning the first hand in this very deadly game of draw.

And Sam Gibson sat there wondering how long he and the rest could hold those screeching, wailing, angry, blood-eyed thousands back.

Chapter 38

Sam Marr turned slowly, the pungent burnt gunpowder like grease scum inside his mouth, fouling all taste. His clothes smelled of stale plug tobacco and horse dung and sweat. He smiled at the young soldiers behind him, realizing all three wanted to join in the sudden celebration and anxiously looked to the old man for permission.

He winked, his eyes as gritty from dust and spent powder as his mouth. "G'on, boys! There's a time to cheer . . . and a time to hunker down and get on with the killing. I figure now's about as good as any for busting your lungs. Goddammit—we showed them red niggers what for!"

"Hurraw!" The trio slapped Marr and each other's backs, hopping round and round.

Turning from the soldiers, Sam studied the distance, shimmering with heat haze this mid-morning beneath a buttermilk-pale summer sun. On a hill a half mile to the east, he watched a knot of horsemen glaring down into the wagon-box corral. Other riders came and went. Arms were flung about, pointing here and there. Lances and pennons waved in signal from the hilltop. Mirrors flashed from the surrounding hills.

He glanced in the direction of the fort. *By God . . . if they don't realize we're under attack by now . . .*

Sam wagged his head in disgust. He didn't want any of the youngsters to know his real thoughts. No sense in it. So reminded was he of his own boys. *They were about this age, marching off to fight for Sam Grant and Phil Sheridan—*

Roughly dragging a hand under his nose, Marr forced the painful remembrance away.

No telling how long we can hold out . . . lucky as we was to turn that first charge. Bastards expecting us to reload like Fetterman's boys—and we blow lead into their faces instead.

He blinked some sweat and grit from his reddened eyes, concentrating on the far hill. *That's where the orders coming from, Sam. I'll bet Red Cloud his own self is up there. What I'd give to have me a sniper's gun right now . . .*

"Lookee here, Cap'n Marr." A young soldier loped up, his outstretched arms filled with arrows.

"Where'd you get them, soldier?"

"Off'n the blankets of the wagon-boxes, Cap'n. Filled with 'em!"

"Those red devils came full of sand and tallow this day," he clucked, wagging his head again.

He patted one of the youngsters on the shoulders. "You boys best see to our ammunition. Get every gun reloaded and ready."

"They're coming back, Cap'n Marr?"

He nodded, turning to the frightened youth. "They're not done with us . . . not by a long chalk, son."

"What're they doing out there?" another youngster asked as he slid cartridges into a Spencer's loading tube.

"I 'spect they're changing their plan of attack," Marr sighed. "They figured to run right over us, and we blew 'em back. So they'll try a different way at us here soon. Probably cussing us out something fierce, I imagine—saying we made some powerful bad medicine down here this morning to make our guns fire without reloading."

The last of the trio chuckled, no longer consumed by quiet tears of desperation and fear. He stuffed .44-caliber cartridges in Marr's Henry rifle and said, "Big surprise for them, wasn't it, sir?"

Sam gazed over the sidewall at the hill where the war-chiefs conferenced. "I figure the next surprise is for them to pull, boys. Their turn now."

"Why you say that, Cap'n?"

"You're out here in this country a little more, you'll learn. The Injun comes as the wasp comes—in clouds or alone. Yet he never tries to sting you unless his sting is a sure thing and there's little chance of getting slapped for it. Yessir . . . the Injun won't keep pressing at any attack he doesn't figure he can't win—fair or dirty."

Behind him the rest of the corral went about reloading from the six other cases of ammunition, each wooden chest holding a thousand rounds apiece.

"Know of any wounded . . . or killed?" Sergeant McQuiery whispered as he crabbed up to Marr's wagon-box.

"None here," Sam answered. "Can't say 'bout the rest."

"Looks like we lost Doyle."

"Little Tommy?"

He nodded gravely. "A good soldier. Took a arrow in the throat . . . drowned in his own blood afore anyone could get to him."

"Shame," Marr replied, but taking heart in reading the look of renewed determination on McQuiery's face. "Anyone else?"

"Two boys wounded."

"Soldiers?"

"Yep. One was Haggerty—took a round in the shoulder. Says he can still shoot . . . reload for the rest if need be."

"I was worried 'bout R.J."

McQuiery grinned. "Smyth's about as bad a character as you, Cap'n Marr. Not a arrow made yet got his name on it."

Sam winked and smiled. "Thankee, Sergeant."

"These boys helping out?"

"They're doing me proud," Marr replied. "We'll put our share down."

McQuiery shook his head, chuckling. "This is one hard-assed bunch here this morning, Cap'n. Looks like I'm just about the oldest man in blue. Twelve battles I marched into then out of during the war—and here I am peeing my pants again. Enough to fill a pint coffee tin! Damn—if that wouldn't set my poor mother's teeth on edge!" He nodded and left without a word, chuckling to himself.

A few shots continued to roar at the west side of the corral as some of the defenders finished off the wounded. To the southeast a large body of horsemen formed. From the front of their ranks flashed mirror signals. As quickly, the ridge directly to the east of the corral flashed a reply.

"Fill them hats of yours with cartridges, boys," Marr advised, settling onto his haunches in the wagon-box once more. "The devil himself gonna come knocking on our door any time now."

Indian marksmen turned the rugged terrain at the northern rim of the prairie to their advantage. While the eroded coulee there kept the horsemen from fully circling the corral, this protected area provided the copper-skinned riflemen a place from which they could enjoy some cover while firing down into the wagon-box enclosure, their barrels steadied on crossed sticks. This grassy, willow-covered swale of land arched within seventy-five yards from the corral at its closest point, two hundred yards at its farthest. On the other three sides of their oval, the flat prairie prevented Indian snipers from creeping close enough to do real damage. Only from this north side could the Sioux spray the defenders with rifle fire.

Along that north side of the enclosure, a few of the soldiers and R.J. Smyth set up a valiant return fire, agreeing that if they did not return some of the pressure, the Sioux snipers would soon pin them down. That happen, the horsemen would ride right in to the walls and have their way.

The civilian teamster turned quickly, laying his Spencer in his lap as he reloaded the Blakeslee tube with seven rounds. He glanced at the end of the box, where John Jenness huddled behind a breastwork of ox yokes, barrels and blankets. The lieutenant poked his head up for each individual shot at the snipers, firing more by instinct than taking the time to get a bead on a particular target.

"Want you to remember, Smyth," Jenness advised, "try to make every shot count. Captain Powell figures it's going to be a long day for all of us."

"Doing the best I can, Lieutenant," Smyth replied, finished slipping cartridges in the loading tube.

As R.J. rammed the tube home through the Spencer's stock, he heard that unforgettable sound so familiar to any war veteran. Immediately followed by the grunt of air driven from the lieutenant's lungs as a bullet slammed the soldier backward into the dust.

Smyth shrank his head down into his collar so far his ears scraped his collarbone. He felt his breakfast shove up against his tonsils, watching the young soldier twitch alone in the dirt and burned stubble of the grass. Fingers clawed at the ground. A foot quivered. The ground under the lieutenant's head pooled black with blood, drying quickly beneath the summer sun.

Gulping a few times, R.J. fought down the bile and his breakfast. For some time now the hard-tack and old salt-pork had been waging deadly war in his belly. Threatening to shove themselves right past his tonsils if he wasn't mindful of them.

Perhaps worse for some of them was the growing stench rising from burning piles of dry dung raked to the center of the corral. Minutes ago some bowmen had fired the first arc-ing arrows into the corral, their shafts afire with burning pitch and dry grass. A roiling, noxious cloud hung over the breath-less enclosure, choking each man, burning their eyes more than the hovering clouds of powder smoke.

"Ho!"

Smyth heard a voice call out from the box to his left. It sounded like Private Garrett.

"Yeah?" answered Richard Lang, the soldier huddled be-side the teamster.

"You got any water in there?"

"Not a drop. How 'bout you, Tommy?"

"Uh-uh. Damn them anyway. Red buggers filling our water barrel with holes."

"Don't make difference," Garrett replied. "Barrels're out-side the corral. Can't get to it anyway."

"My tongue's swelled up, with my mouth so dry. Maybeso them coffee kettles got water in 'em."

"Kettles?"

"C'mon," Lang suggested. "Cookie Brown left two kettles by the west wagon. Ready for coffee."

"I don't mind grounds a damned bit!"

R.J. watched, fascinated, as Garrett and Lang bellied along the boxes until they reached the west entrance to the corral, where they slid into the shadows of the wagon-box still perched atop its running gear. Slowly they reached for the two blackened, dented gallon kettles. As they were pulling them gently into the corral, snipers discovered the two thirsty soldiers and opened up on the kettle rescuers. As if the Sioux riflemen had been waiting for the white men to retrieve the precious liquid prize.

Lang sloshed water all over his arm as he yanked his kettle to safety, sinking back against a wagon-box, his heart pounding, breathing in precious gulps. Private Garrett was not so lucky. One of the snipers found his kettle an ideal target, sending a bullet through the fire-crusted tin and out again, nicking the soldier's hand in the process. A cheer around the corral nonetheless. For now they had a little water. Despite the fact that cook Brown had dumped grounds in the kettles in preparation of making coffee, and though the kettles had been setting out in the hot sun all morning—the defenders now had some water.

R.J. jerked around, hearing again that soapy smack of a bullet hitting flesh. A Sioux sniper had found the dead lieutenant's body. Then a second round slapped Jenness's form.

"Sonsabitches," Max Littman growled, crawling on hands and knees over Smyth's legs. "They can't shoot the living . . . they go butcher the dead . . . heathens!"

R.J. swallowed hard.

"You coming help me?" Littman asked, his face inches from the civilian's.

"Help?"

"Get the lieutenant's body, that's it, got-tammit!"

"Yeah, I'll help." His head bobbed up and down as fast as his nervous, turkeylike Adam's apple.

R.J. belly-crawled behind the German, noticing the way Littman's blond hair bristled out from the top of his head like the thorny spines of a chestnut burr. Beside Jenness the sergeant brushed some black ants from the crusted head wounds, bottle-green flies from the open eyes. They buzzed and crawled in and out of the dead man's mouth. R.J. felt his stomach lurch again, threatening. The lieutenant's skin had turned the color of flour paste, stretched over his cheekbones and brow in death like an old, dirty linen sheet thrown carelessly onto bare bedsprings.

After closing the lieutenant's eyes, Littman tried to move the body. He had simply waited too long. Another incoming bullet smacked into the body, inches from the soldier and civilian. Both men scurried back to the safety of a nearby wagon.

"You wanna shoot the sonofabitch?" Littman asked, huffing nervously. "Or you wanna drag the lieutenant's body?"

R.J. gulped. "I'll shoot."

Littman nodded. "Then shoot. Cover me."

As R.J. and another soldier provided some covering fire, Littman attempted pulling Jenness's body to a safer position. After three tries the sergeant gave up. Too risky out in the open, exposed to the sniper. He scurried back and collapsed next to Smyth, catching his breath.

"I suppose," Littman began, his wide, blue eyes flashing an apology, "the lieutenant doesn't mind anyhow."

"No, I suppose he doesn't mind now," R.J. agreed, not feeling so bad about his caution, the way things turned out.

Along the north side of the corral not far away, someone yelled out in warning.

"Look out, boys! They're coming at us again!"

Horsemen, gathered to the south, southeast, and on the east, kicked their ponies into a lope, nosing for the corral with a wild yelp.

"Here they come, Gibby!" Pvt. John Grady shouted, the fear-laced excitement dripping from the old soldier's every word.

"I'm ready," Sam Gibson answered, tasting the bile at the back of his throat once more. War had never set well on the young soldier's stomach.

"The tents!" one of the defenders shouted hoarsely, pointing.

Gibson tore his eyes from the incoming horsemen, looking up into Grady's face. The old soldier hauled his young companion to his feet.

"C'mon, kid! Show me how you young fellas dodge bullets!"

"Whaaa?"

"The tents, goddammit, Gibby! They gotta come down
. . . and now!"

Grady yanked Gibson off his feet, leaving their rifles behind. The work at hand would require no weapons. Only
nerve and a bit of pluck. With a damned good dose of luck
thrown in.

Sam Gibson followed the old soldier blindly. Hoping he
had done nothing in his young adult life that would cause that
fickle bitch Fate to turn her smiling face from him now.

Strange . . . that until this moment, with the coming of
the second massed charge, no one had given a thought to the
handful of tents erected outside the southern rim of their ring
of wagon-boxes. At this moment it seemed every defender was
of like mind, without another word needing voice. The tents
must come down, giving the white riflemen a wider field of
fire, enabling them to sweep from west, to south, back to east,
following the enemy horsemen in their wild ride past the
wagon-box corral.

As soon as Grady and Gibson leaped from their wagon-
box, the Sioux snipers discovered these new and inviting
targets. Moving targets and hence all the more sport. To
young Sam it sounded like that whole hillside to the north
had opened up on them, kicking up dirt in small, angry
spouts. Tearing through the canvas of the tents with an angry
hiss, ricocheting off wood poles.

Without a word between them, the two soldiers bent to
their work while the rest of the corral did its best to cover
their daring. Hands shaking like water about to boil, Gibson
yanked one peg loose after another. First tent down . . .

Arrows arched out of the sun like swooping, hissing birds.

A second tent down . . .

Bullets kicked up dust in front of his hands, spitting dirt
into his face.

Now a third . . .

The tent's ridgepole collapsed above him as a bullet
cracked through, canvas smothering him.

A fourth came floating down in the hot, steamy August
air . . .

One more, Gibson told himself.

Grady looked at him and nodded. This would be the test.

The last tent stood sixty yards off to the south. Farther onto the prairie than the others. Powell's and Jenness's. Apart from the enlisted quarters.

"Get back here!"

Gibson glanced over his shoulder. Sgt. Frank Hoover stood, shouting and waving at the pair.

Grady threw his weight on top of him. Sam found himself on the ground. Bullets whistled overhead.

"You'll get me killed yet, boy!" the old soldier growled, smiling.

"S-Sorry . . ."

"Never mind the captain's tent!" Hoover kept yelling.

"Leave it now!" another voice shouted.

Gibson looked into Grady's face.

"You vote for getting our asses back to the corral?"

Sam nodded. "Y-Yes I do."

He jerked his head, grinning. "What we waiting on, soldier?"

By the time Sam was back in the confines of his wagon-box, his labored breathing echoing Grady's beside him, the horsemen had galloped into rifle range.

"That was a damned stupid thing you fellas did." Captain Powell scooted up on his knees, glaring at the two soldiers. Then a broad smile split his muttonchops. "Stupid . . . but it showed one helluva lot of courage as well. Well done! Well done! Just look!"

He threw his arm in an arc. Gibson saw that his fellow soldiers now had a commanding field of fire on all quarters.

"Well done, soldiers," Powell said, saluting. "Now kill some of these bastards you've stirred up, will you?"

Gibson nodded. Grady crawled off to his loophole without a word as well. Their rifles barked with the rest.

More ponies fell, screaming and thrashing on three sides of the corral. Spilled warriors lay beneath their dying animals. Others tried to crawl off before they attracted the attention of the white riflemen.

Noise and dust. Powder smoke and thirst. Baking sun and the stench of blood. The humanlike cry of the ponies scrambling to rise again until they died. And the moans of the wounded in the corral, calling out for water.

Then the second rush ebbed like the summer thunderstorm that fills the dry coulees of the high plains for but a moment before the ground is left to bake once more.

"By God, I deserve a drink, I do." Private Grady took up his canteen.

Gibson's eyes widened in wonder. "Didn't know you had any water with you."

"Ain't water, boy."

"What is it?"

"Whiskey," he growled. "And that's why I didn't tell you I had any."

Grady put the canteen neck to his lips and threw his head back. As quickly he jerked it from his face and spit the liquid out, sputtering.

"What's wrong with you?" Patrick McQuiery asked down at the end of the box.

"Some . . . someone switched canteens on me, Sergeant!"

"Whadda you mean, Grady?"

"I had whiskey in mine!" he roared, his face and neck red from more than the sun. "This one . . . it has—God . . . it has water! And warm goddamned water to boot!"

"Hand it here, Grady," McQuiery ordered. "I'll drink it."

"Gladly, Sergeant. Warm water isn't fit for a man to drink."

"Unless," McQuiery began, smiling as he wiped off the canteen neck with his dirty hand, "a man uses that warm water to wash down your whiskey, Private Grady!"

Chapter 39

"Captain Powell is a proven commander," Col. Jonathan Smith said, rubbing the sulfur-head lucifer across the flat stone on the desk. He lit his pipe. "Besides, he has a full company of soldiers with him at the corral."

"Not any more, sir," Tenedore Ten Eyck disagreed, pointing out the post commander's window. "The men who just came in are evidence of that. Powell's forces are divided."

"How many made it to the fort, Captain?" he asked, yanking the pipe stem from his fleshy lips.

"All but four," Ten Eyck answered. "They were killed in their retreat."

"How many does Powell have in the corral?"

Tenedore's foggy mind worked at it, the way he would load his own pipe bowl, or stare at the color of the whiskey in his glass, red as a bay horse. Working, tugging, struggling to yank an answer up. Other lives might depend on this.

"He can't have more than thirty men in the corral now."

"Damn you, Captain!" Smith suddenly roared. "You're nothing more than a feeble, whiskey-soaked has-been. No more a soldier than my nigger houseman is! James Powell amassed a credible record during the war. I see no need in rushing a relief to the Pineys for another of these brief forays by troublesome Sioux."

Lt. Col. Henry Walton Wessells cleared his throat nervously, stepping forward. "Colonel, if I may offer a thought . . . it appears from the retreat of the wood-train escort to the fort that this attack on the woodcutting operations is not merely another short-lived foray."

Smith's eyes narrowed on Wessells. The sort of smoky-gray eyes that could broil a man on the spot. Then suddenly the hardened crease between his eyebrows disappeared.

"Am I to understand, gentlemen—that this is a concerted attack on Powell's position?"

The other officers in the room agreed. Most of them had seen enough of hit-and-run attacks since spring. Only Ten Eyck and Powell himself had witnessed what the Sioux could do when they had a small force surrounded and overwhelmed.

Minutes ago, Tenedore had given his sweaty brow one more swipe with the cool cloth, set his hat on a hangover-aching head, and braved the high, midday light of the Fort Phil Kearny parade. Down the graveled walk along officers' row he walked, boot soles crunching, his head aching more this morning than usual. With even more pain at this moment than he had in sitting on the war-torn hemorrhoids that were his legacy of a Confederate prison called Libby.

His midday walk in the high sun had put him near the south gate about the time the sentries along the banquette hollered that two separate parties were hurrying toward the fort walls.

Ten Eyck had been the first officer to reach the gate. The first to receive those initial, garbled, gasping grunts of warning for Captain Powell's command left behind in the wagon-box corral. Tenedore had ordered "Officers' Call" blown by the bugler on duty, a hasty decision that brought Colonel Smith flying from his office door as Ten Eyck loped straight across the parade toward the post commander's office to explain himself and the bugle.

"Is there one among you who would not agree that this fort itself now stands a chance of assault by the hostiles?" Smith asked his officers.

Tenedore glanced from face to face. Some stared at the floor. Others studied a fly speck on the crude walls. It was up to the Dutchman to speak out.

"Colonel, if the Sioux did not attack us those first few days after wiping out Fetterman's command—when the snow drifted high enough for them to breech the walls—I don't think they'll be foolish enough to try us now that this post is at full manpower—"

"And on full alert, Captain Ten Eyck," Smith interrupted. "Colonel Wessells, you will see that preparations are made. Double the guard. All men on alert. Issue arms and ammunition. Captain Dandy, you'll see your men and quarters are put into shape for a siege?"

"Yessir!"

"Colonel?" Ten Eyck asked. "You plan a relief for the men in the corral?"

"I have considered that, Captain."

Wessells had not yet turned from the room. Eagerly he stepped forward. "Request permission to lead the relief, Colonel."

"Permission denied," Smith replied. "I want you to command the forces here at the fort when the full-scale assault comes, Wessells."

"Who . . . who will go to relieve Powell?" Wessells asked.

Ten Eyck saw Wessells's eyes flick at him apprehensively. And Tenedore knew Colonel Smith saw that gesture as plainly as he.

"Major Smith?" the colonel said.

"Sir?" Benjamin F. Smith stomped forward two paces.

"Prepare a hundred men immediately."

"Ambulances, Colonel?"

"Of course, Major. Take a wagon filled with ammunition to the corral as well. If you need it, you will have it. If it is not needed by you, then I'm sure the corral needs restocking."

Wessells inched up, nervously. "Colonel, with all respect— Major Smith has no field experience with these Indians. Would it not be wise—"

"Colonel Wessells, I believe you have your orders. Carry on."

"As you wish." Wessells was a long time in replying. He eventually saluted and disappeared from the door.

"Captain Ten Eyck, you will place yourself at the disposal of Colonel Wessells. You are excused. The major and I have some last-minute plans to formulate."

Tenedore saluted, his head hurting like nothing before.

Wondering if he would have time to go back to quarters for a drink before following Wessells.

In the worst way, he needed that drink. Shivering now as he stepped into the bright light. The heat of a day already climbing over ninety once again. But still, Tenedore Ten Eyck shuddered. Not so much from the pain this time. But from the memory of that twenty-first day of December when he saw the bodies.

From that day the men at this post had claimed the captain was no longer a soldier.

No more than a washed-up, drunken has-been coward.

Ten Eyck decided he would make time to go by his quarters for a drink. The red, red whiskey was what gave him courage to put on his boots and button up his tunic.

Whiskey gave the captain courage to play soldier one day at a time.

Sam Marr watched with pride as Sgt. Frank Robertson crawled on his belly toward Lieutenant Jenness's perforated body. Amid some renewed sniping from the north, Robertson slung a piece of canvas over the corpse.

Hot enough as it is, Marr thought to himself. *No sense that body laying out under the sun like it was. A fine bunch, these. They take care of their own . . .*

After the second mounted charge that swept past the corral walls, the warriors seemed content to make smaller, noisier, and infrequent forays across the open plain. They brandished their tomahawks and warclubs, their Winchesters and captured Springfield muzzle loaders, shouting their warsongs. And time and again Sam thought he saw the same tall giant of a warrior leading the rest across the summer-burnt grass to harass the corral from the east.

Time and again the tall one had escaped their rifle fire while other warriors around him dropped and were dragged from the field when the rest retreated to regroup.

Now the tall one came out once more, waving above him a long spear from which dangled long tendrils of human hair. On the other arm hung a huge buffalo-hide shield.

"Sergeant?" Marr hollered at the man in the next box.

"Yeah, Cap'n?" Frank Robertson asked.

"You any good at long range?"

A slow smile came over Robertson's face. "I suppose I might just be about the best here . . . 'sides you, of course, Cap'n Marr."

Sam nodded. "What say we put some holes in that tall bastard's lights?"

Robertson spit a long stream of brown juice into the dust, causing a small eruption where it landed. "Let's make that sonuvabitch dance!"

Out on the plain the tall war-chief was dancing, alone. Round and round, he inched slowly toward the corral, but never stood motionless. Always daring. Taunting the white men to try once more to hit this huge, moving target. He jumped and cavorted. He spun around and mocked the white men with his spear and shield. All the while his fellow warriors cheered him on, shaming the defenders huddled behind their walls.

"How far you make it, Cap'n?"

"Your eyes better'n mine, Robertson. I say it's close to two hundred."

"I'll lay a bet he's out there two fifty."

"Two fifty it is," Marr replied, adjusting the Merrill sights on one of the big-bore needle-guns Powell had assigned him when the battle began hours before. He slipped the barrel over the top of the wagon-box for a rest and adjusted himself comfortably. "You tell me when you're ready, Sergeant. You fire first . . . I'll fire behind you."

"Sounds good to me, Cap'n. I figure we'll only get one shot at this bastard."

The noise in the corral fell off to an eerie silence as both riflemen nestled guns into their shoulders and cheeks. A minute later as the big warrior flung out his arms, his head thrown back for a heartbeat, Robertson squeezed the trigger, knowing he had held on his target, hoping he had correctly calculated the range.

Another heartbeat and the warrior stopped his wild dance. The iron-tipped, scalp-decorated lance fluttered from his right hand, a hand he brought to his belly. From what Sam Marr could tell over the blade of his front sight, Robertson had dropped a huge round through the Indian's gut. The old civilian blinked, clearing his eyes for the last time. He took in a long breath, let half of it out . . .

The big-bore gun exploded.

Its high-powered lead sphere tore into the top of the warrior's chest as he stood in his tracks, staring down at his belly wound. Marr's shot knocked the Indian backward five feet, landing spread-eagled. Dead before he kicked up a small cloud of dust in falling.

When the cheering and joy in the corral died, the defenders heard the chilling wails from the other warriors and the women who had seen their hero killed so easily. Then from that hilltop a half mile to the east arose one voice. It was but a moment before that single voice silenced all others. Haranguing them. Challenging them. Cursing the white men. Vowing death to the soldiers.

Sam Marr grinned as he looked at the three young troopers assigned his wagon-box. "Bet that's ol' Red Cloud hisself. Angrier'n a bear come outta his hole a month early!"

A large force of mounted warriors swooped down the Big Piney valley out of sight. Another group of horsemen, still numbering several hundred, gathered on the plain to the northeast.

"They'll come in again, boys. Them guns ready?" Sam asked.

"Yessir, Cap'n Marr. They're ready, by God!"

"Good work, son. Good work."

"They ain't riding down on us," Robertson shouted from the next box. "They're . . . they're just sitting there."

It was eerie, uncanny, waiting there beneath that glaring sun and watching those hundreds of mounted horsemen waiting in a long phalanx on the plain. Not a chant being sung. Not a war cry uttered.

Then something happened that raised the hair along the back of Sam Marr's neck for the first time that day. Over the shimmering, gold-coated silence of that dusty prairie, there arose a low hum.

"That them squaws crying over their dead up there on the hills?" one of the soldiers across the corral called out.

"The sound don't rightly come from those hills up there," answered another.

Instead, the hum seemed to shift more to the northwest now. Marr wasn't sure if it really was a humming any longer. More of a spooky chant. And growing louder with every throb of his heart.

Then on some cue, the warriors on the plain dashed forward with a single, deafening cry. Those with guns fired them at the corral. Once more the defenders made themselves small in the wagon-boxes and turned their destruction on the horsemen sweeping down upon them. And still, beneath all the rattle of rifles and screams of horses, the cries of men hit and dying, that eerie humming grew louder and louder and louder . . .

Until the attacking force turned away as suddenly as it had swept down on the corral, retreating from the plain. Withdrawing. Turning. And waiting. As if something momentous were about to happen beneath the growing, ghostly chant.

"My God!"

"HERE THE BASTARDS COME!"

"Look at that, will ya?"

Sam looked with the others, finding a sight that would chill the blood of a lesser man.

Up from the ravine to the north of the corral, little more than ninety yards away, poured hundreds and hundreds of warriors on foot. Clad only in moccasins and breechclout. Every one of them carrying two weapons. Pistols, knives. Tomahawks and clubs. All chanting the same, eerie blood oath.

Marr realized time had come that Red Cloud wanted the corral wiped off the prairie. Time had come, Red Cloud threatened, for the close and dirty work of seeing your enemy's face an arm's length away.

The seven hundred burst from the ravine in a wedge, the point of which was a large, barrel-chested warrior wearing a long, trailing bonnet of feathers fluttering in the hot breeze.

That determined leader of the Bad Face Oglallas had grown weary, angrier still at the progress his warriors made in rubbing out the white men in the corral. He wanted to move on to the fort itself. Red Cloud had designated his own nephew to lead the seven hundred down the ravine. To spearhead this attack that would swamp the corral defenders.

At the first volley from the soldiers, more than one bullet caught the attack leader in mid-stride. His feathered head snapped violently backward. The long-trailed bonnet tumbled to the side in a spray of brains and blood and gore. Crushed beneath the bullet-riddled body. Ermine and war-eagle feathers muddied among the dust and crimson and the trampled sage.

"Fire, goddammit!" Powell hollered behind them all, dashing up and down the corral. "This is it, men! Them or us—drop them! Kill them *now!*"

Volley after volley spat fire at the charge of enraged, yelling, wide-eyed warriors surging closer to the corral than ever before. The ponies had provided big targets, easier shots. But this charge on foot was something altogether different. The wagon-box defenders killing row upon row of naked warriors. With more coming, pushing behind them.

Again and again Sam Marr held out a left hand. A young soldier slapped a reloaded weapon into it, another of the trio taking the empty rifle from the civilian's right. Rifles with little chance to cool. Under his breath, Sam prayed that none of the corral's weapons would jam with the heat and the burnt powder in the breeches.

He suddenly smelled the stench of burning blood. A new fragrance to the old man.

It dripped from his head as he leaned over the trapdoor, working the breech block, slamming home the cartridges he hung between the fingers of his left hand like a row of glittering brass sausages. His head swam. The field before him shimmered and danced. Out of focus, the hostiles came on like flitting, cavorting blackbirds before his tired eyes. Sam swiped a hand across them quickly, smearing the blood. More blood than he could stop now. Two wounds, dripping blood into the heated breech of the Springfield. Blood sizzling. Bubbling in the breech. Cooked like blood-sausage back home in Missouri.

He liked the sound of that in his head. The cool, shady places of home. *Missouri.*

"C'mon in here, you blathering sonsabitches!" Marr shrieked, working the breech block, struggling with the cartridge stuck to his hand in congealing blood. The rifle hot to the touch. The sticky, crimson damp down his front now, matted in whiskers, spilling on his legs.

He blinked, his eyes clearing for a moment, able to see more of the human waves rushing down upon them. His old eyes sharp and intent. Like the redbone hound's back home who always loped at his heels as he would seek out those cool places where the squirrels hid up in the forks of the blackjack oaks. Eyes like those hunting dogs watching him skin those squirrels, waiting . . . waiting . . .

"C'mon, you red bastards!" he hollered again. "We'll lick the whole bunch of you!"

"We ain't got a chance!" whined a soldier.

"Shuddup and load!" growled another of the scared recruits behind him.

"We can't sit here—"

"You move and I'll shoot you myself," the second one warned, finding some courage perhaps never before tested.

Sam Marr's gummy fingers fought the fat cartridges into and out of the breech, sticky with blood. His nose running now where a flying splinter of wood had ricocheted off the sidewall he knelt behind. Still the blood dripped slowly into a pool between his legs.

"Where's my Henry?" he snarled, turning slightly toward the youngster behind his left shoulder. Sam wanted that seventeen-shot repeater in a bad way. The work was close at last. What he had been waiting for all morning.

He snatched the Henry up, rising, locking the butt into his right hip, pumping the lever. Again and again he pumped as he rose, until he stood full height. Screaming out in pain and frustration and fear of dying here. Pumping the lever again and again and . . .

Until the hot, hot blow spun him around. Throwing him backward with the shocking brute force of that old bull he kept in the pasture back home.

He sensed many hands on him, pulling him down. *Strange, Missouri isn't home anymore. The boys ain't there. Sweet, sweet Abby—where are you? Dear God, where . . . just where the hell does a man go when he dies . . . and he doesn't have a home where he can be buried?*

Sioux and Cheyenne came on.

Glistening, sweating, bleeding copper bodies stumbling over the fallen, bloodied bodies of those gone before them. Never slowing. Coming on. Coming on resolutely through the golden haze of yellow dust hung like gauze in the slanting sunlight.

Coming on still through the clouds of stinging powder smoke.

Chapter 40

$\mathcal{T}$he screaming warriors got so close to the wagon boxes that Sam Gibson could see the whites of their eyes.

It was something he would never forget. Watching that attack come at them with no end. Wave after wave of glistening, sweating, paint-smeared, dust-covered, copper-skinned bodies hurling themselves forward without thought of death.

Mindlessly hurling themselves against the smoking muzzles at the corral walls.

By now most of the defenders had risen above their wagon-boxes, up on one knee to meet this nonstop onslaught. A lot of yelling. Swearing. Loud voices matching those shrill war cries thundering off the hills around them, echoing across the grassy plain littered with horse carcasses and bleeding, whimpering wounded.

In the box beside him, Gibson watched Sergeant McQuiery sweep up one of the big augers they had used to bore the holes in the sides of the wagons. McQuiery hurled it at the advancing horde, not taking the time to reload. Other men as well, each grabbing this tool or that sack of beans, flung them into the faceless, brown-skinned mass.

And for the first time Sam Gibson thought on dying. Wondering where the lanyard was that he had made from his shoelaces earlier that morning. Glancing quickly to the right as he saw the old civilian frontiersman knocked backward into the trio of reloaders Powell had assigned him. Closer and closer the charge surged from the dust and powder smoke. A haze so thick now that the warriors drew desperately close to the walls before they were discovered looming out of the sticky haze. Closer and closer still before the defenders shot each glistening body in desperation.

Gibson's thoughts hung on dying. Wanting it to come struggling hand in hand with one of these sticky, sweating crimson bodies lurching out of the powder smoke toward the corral wall. He wanted to die fighting. Not with the muzzle of his rifle jammed under his chin at the last moment . . .

Three fluttering heartbeats later Sam Gibson found himself shooting the fleeing warriors in the back as the wave retreated. None of them took the time to drag any of the dead from the field. Just yards shy of the west wall the attack faltered in the face of determined men who had stood their ground, swearing to sell their lives dearly. Casualties too high. The field littered with the dead and dying. The rest just running.

"They're turning tail, men!" Powell shouted, seeming to appear everywhere in the corral at once. His head bandaged. A brown smudge over one eye where his blood had dried.

"By jabbers! They running like jackrabbits!" Sergeant Hoover hollered, standing tall, shaking a triumphant arm in the air.

As the pell-mell rush swept from the prairie in a disorderly retreat, most of the soldiers quieted. Remembering their rifles. Intent now upon reloading the weapons still capable of firing. Those rifles not jammed, or caked with burnt powder, or seized with an oversized cartridge, or just plain overheated and gummed with blood.

"Shoot every one of the bastards that moves!" Sergeant Robertson ordered as he skidded on one knee along in the trampled dust behind each wagon-box, checking on the ammunition supply in the upturned hats beside each rifleman.

Guardedly, the defenders inched their weapons over the sidewalls of their boxes once more. Eyes scanning the prairie carefully. Watching for movement among the bodies. Looking for puffs of powder smoke among the sage or thrashing pony carcasses or naked brown skin. Their sights methodically lined up on the warriors attempting a crawl to safety. Red-rimmed eyes sorting the dead Sioux and Cheyenne from those wounded who fired from the blood-soaked dust of their dying place, determined to take more of the white men with them to the other side on this good day of dying.

From time to time some of the old soldiers poured a bit of warm, precious water on the breeches of their rifles. Cooling them. Weapons allowed little rest from their killing work.

Red Cloud ordered his skirmishers forward again. Yet this time the soldiers saw something different. The medicine had gone out of their charge. Instead, most warriors galloped across the plain only to lean from their ponies and snatch up a raised hand from the field. Others cautiously inched forward on their bellies, covering those who worked among the dead and dying behind large buffalo-hide shields, dragging limp bodies back to safety. On three sides of the corral the soldiers watched as rescuers slipped rawhide pony lariats around ankles or wrists, dragging friends or brothers or uncles back into the sage and willow, out of range from the white man's big guns that barked again and again and again . . .

Already the Sioux and Northern Cheyenne were speaking among themselves of this day when the soldier guns talked without stopping. Already Red Cloud's bewildered legions were calling this the *Battle of the Bad Medicine Rifles.*

Yet what this fight was to be called when painted on the winter-count robes did not matter to the women and children and old ones gathered on the hilltops, watching the pride of their bands thrown against the tiny corral of white man's wagons, watching that pitiful handful of defenders repeatedly repulse the screaming charges. From those hilltops their voices now rose in eerie cries and wailing laments, a melancholy keening as many of them hacked off locks of their own hair or dragged knife blades across arms and calves to bleed themselves or chopped off fingertips in mourning. A great, red wake on the hills overlooking the Big Piney meadow.

"Captain Powell says he wants you on the east wall, Gibby."

Sam scurried across the compound to where Powell knelt among seven other soldiers.

"I don't know what this gathering of their dead means, fellas," the captain began in a hoarse whisper, "but I'll have the rest of the men keep the red bastards honest. In the meantime, I wanted my best marksmen—each of you—to take ten rounds, and ten shots only, at that hilltop."

Gibson's eyes joined the rest, studying the slope to the east. From that moment of the first attack on the corral, that slope had appeared to be the hostiles' command center. Couriers rode back and forth to the site. Blankets flagged messages and mirrors flashed replies across the valley from its slopes.

"Red Cloud, Captain?" Hoover asked.

"As sure as I'm born, Sergeant."

"Take your time, boys," Powell concluded. "If they throw more weight against us, hurry back to your assigned boxes. Until then . . . see what you can do to bag yourself a Sioux chief. Good luck."

One by one the soldiers dispersed along the east wall of the corral, making their rests, counting out their ten rounds to conserve dwindling ammunition. Adjusting leaf sights up for the farthest range, murmuring amongst themselves on just how far away the hill really was from their compound.

Sam waited, watching a few of the others firing, walking their rounds up the slope of that hill. To figure range. Once those three had used up their allotment, the rest hunkered down to do their best in flushing the Sioux commanders from their nest.

"Damn if I wouldn't give a month's wages to make that Red Cloud a *good* Injun," Max Littman whispered to Gibson.

As the lead hail rained down around their ponies, the enemy horsemen once again waved blankets, flashed mirrors, shouted orders over the valley. Some of their animals reared uncontrollably, spilling riders, frightened by the incoming rounds.

Then over his front sight Sam Gibson worked his last four bullets down the slope into the faraway meadow. Following the attack leaders as they retreated. Some of the marksmen growled their complaints of having to hit long-range moving targets. Others silently calculated windage and distance. Attempting to walk their bullets into the mass of warriors the way an artilleryman would walk his case shot over an entrenched infantry position.

"*HURRAW!*" a sudden cry erupted along that east wall.

Gibson jerked up. A second soldier leaped to his feet, arms in the air to join the first in a wild jig.

"What was that?" Hoover asked, turning to watch the commotion behind him in the corral.

"Did you hear that?"

"By God, I did! Was that—"

"They're coming! Sweet, sweet Jesus—they're coming!"

"Who's coming?"

Then Sam Gibson saw the next puff of faraway smoke rising on the hot valley air. A few seconds of air flight later, another eruption of smoke was visible, even more smoke this time, filling the neck of the Little Piney valley to the east.

"It's canister!"

"—dropping howitzer pills around their damned heads!"

"We're saved!"

"They're firing cased shot at the bastards!"

"—'bout damned time!"

"—saved now!'

"—running 'em off!"

Then, through the leafy green branches of the trees lining the wood road along the Sullivant Hills, young Sam thought he spotted movement. This time a swelling, blue movement. And only when that column of troopers had cleared the trees where hours before another frantic group of soldiers had retreated from the wood train did Private Gibson sense the sting of hot, salty tears at his eyes. He wheeled on Sergeant Hoover, his mouth moving, no sound coming forth.

Hoover nodded, landing his big, swollen and bloody hand on Gibson's shoulder. Smiling that crooked-tooth smile he rarely gave any man. "Likely we'll get back to the fort in time for dinner, Gibby."

Gibson fell against the old soldier, shaking, trying to control his tears, his shoulders quaking. Afraid he might never stop sobbing. And the old sergeant held him there with that one good arm he had left now. Clinging onto the young soldier, for if he didn't, Hoover might fall himself, his legs gone weak and watery.

All round the corral the men danced and hugged and slapped and cheered, throwing their hats into the air. The strain taken from their shoulders at last. Every one of them watching that long column of a hundred men and the big, brass-mounted, mule-drawn howitzer bouncing hurriedly into the valley. And behind them all rumbled the six wagons and four ambulances rocking in the sun-baked ruts of that dusty wood road, spinning iron tires kicking up tall cascades of golden haze. Hurrying to the rescue.

In the middle of the smoky compound stood their commander.

Powell's eyes did not tarry on the relief column long at all. He alone among those in that corral knew how the Sioux and Cheyenne could circle back on a unit. Two days before these very warriors had wiped out Fetterman's men, the captain led his own command to the crest of that same Lodge Trail Ridge, on the heels of those same enticing decoys. But Powell had followed Colonel Carrington's orders not to pursue that seductive lure into the valley of the Peno.

To the disappointed groans of his men that cold December day, Powell turned his troops about and retreated to the fort. Leaving the angry two thousand warriors waiting in ambush to wait another two suns.

Two suns had come and gone when many of those same soldiers trotted off behind Fetterman over the crest of the Lodge Trail, onto the spur ridge where this time they would give their lives in the successful closing of the redman's bloody trap.

These men here in the corral groaned and complained every bit as loudly when Powell ordered them to break off their celebration.

"Back to your wagon-boxes . . . *now!*" Powell wheeled on the rest. "That goes for all of you!"

"Ahhh, Captain . . . can't you see—"

"I'll drag you back there myself, McQuiery!" Powell barked, starting for the sergeant's box.

"I'm going, Captain! I'm going, goddammit!"

"We'll wait for the column to draw closer, men." He said it quietly this time, as the air hissed out of their premature celebration.

"The bastards are running, Cap'n!"

"The day you trust an Indian, Robertson—day you'll be a dead man."

"They've turned tail!" McQuiery argued.

"As many as we've killed," Powell hollered above the protests of his men, his hands trembling to control his rage and remembrance, "Red Cloud's still got more than enough with him to descend on that relief party . . . and wipe those men out."

"They didn't overrun us!"

Powell whirled on a young soldier, one of those who cradled Sam Marr across his lap. "By damned—we weren't caught in the open like they are, soldier! You pray to your God this moment—and thank the almighty for these wagon-boxes and ammunition."

Sam Gibson watched the contrite soldier nod, pursing his lips as if ashamed of his blasphemy.

As the relief party descended from the Sullivant Hills into the meadow, the men in the corral could contain themselves no longer. First one, then two more, and finally more than half of them leaped from their boxes, racing the last two hundred yards across the prairie grass littered with the carcasses of dead and dying ponies. Strewn among the painted, feathered, copper-skinned bodies fallen too close to the corral for rescue.

Major Smith's rescuers broke formation as well, rushing forward at double-time now. Many amazed to find so many from the corral still alive. Truly awed to look upon those hardy, sunburnt defenders, their faces smudged with blood and blackened with powder soot, eyes reddened by flying dust and smoking dung piles and tears of joy.

"Cap—Captain Powell, C Company, reporting, Major."

Smith returned the salute, wagging his head in pure wonderment before he found words. He swallowed hard. "Your casualties, Captain?".

"Near as I can tell, Major—we have three killed. Two wounded. One civilian wounded."

"Civilian?"

"Our marksman, sir. He as well as any man accounted for making Red Cloud one unhappy chief during the battle. I say that without reservation."

The major's eyes continued to scan the corral. "Will he live, Captain?"

Powell sniffed, running a hand under his nose. "We get him back to the post in time, he might. It's . . . he's no longer in our hands, sir."

"Surgeon Horton accompanied us. He can see to your wounded while the men load your dead into the ambulances as quickly as possible. I do not relish the idea of seeing the sun go down on us here, Captain."

Powell straightened his back, saluting. Sensing the strain suddenly in every muscle now that the fight was over. Like cat-gut fiddle strings loosened after a vigorous playing. "As you say, Major."

At the west end of the corral Dr. Horton leaped from his ambulance with a large canteen under his arm. He hurried up to Powell.

"Captain! By God, it's good to see so many made it through your . . . your emergency!"

Powell nodded. "Thank you—"

"May I have your permission to give your wounded a dram of the whiskey I've brought along?"

The captain smiled at Horton, his muttonchops quivering a moment. "By . . . by all means, Surgeon. And, if perchance there's any left when you've given all the men their due, I would like to share a drink with you, friend."

Horton stepped up, holding his hand out between them. "James, I'll buy you an entire bottle myself this evening! That's a promise!"

Powell squeezed the surgeon's hand in his own blackened one. "And I'll see you keep that promise, Sam!"

Some of the relief party methodically worked over the Sioux and Cheyenne dead abandoned on the field, scalping every body and even chopping off one head to present to the post surgeon for his examination. In the midst of that raucous, bloody work, most of the corral defenders slumped against the sides of the wagon-boxes, silently determined to replace their army-issue brogans now that the fight was won.

When they had Jenness and Doyle and Haggerty gently laid among the folded tents and bedding and rations in the wagons, and had the wounded helped into an ambulance, Major Smith gave his order for the columns to move out.

Powell turned to Smith at the head of the march and sighed. "Do you . . . would you have the time, Major?"

Smith pulled the silver chain at the end of which hung the cased watch. He pried it open. "It's a little past two, Captain."

Powell stared over his shoulder, off to the northwest, pointing at the long columns of Indian ponies laden with travois of wounded and dead. "They charged down on us at seven-thirty, Major. We . . . by damned—we held them off for more than six hours."

Smith's eyes turned from the retreating Indian columns, finding Powell's eyes misting. "A fight you can take pride in, James."

"I tell you, it feels like we held them off for six days."

"Before I left the post, Colonel Smith talked of recommending every one of your men for the medal of honor."

Powell grinned crookedly inside his dirty, smoke-smudged muttonchops. "Right now, the best thing I could hope for is some of Surgeon Horton's whiskey."

Chapter 41

"Sam . . . can you hear me?"

Seamus Donegan watched the old man's eyes flutter, then crack open into narrow slits. He leaned back some, his big hand beneath Marr's head, cradling it gently as a thumb stroked the old man's leathery cheek.

"It's Seamus, Sam. Seamus Donegan."

Marr nodded weakly, his dry lips moving like the trembling breast of a hummingbird working among lilac blossoms. "Waaaa . . ."

"Water?" Seamus asked, then held the cup to Marr's lips without waiting for an answer.

He drank a little, sputtering on it, then let his head droop back against the straw-filled pillow again. Donegan dipped his fingers in the water, slowly running them back and forth along the old man's lips. Watching the tip of Marr's tongue occasionally dart out to lick at the droplets.

As the sun inched over the horizon that morning, Seamus had shown up at the north gate of Fort Phil Kearny, minutes after he had found some of the civilians lighting their morning fires under coffee kettles and breakfast skillets in their camp near the sawmill on the banks of Little Piney Creek. Emerging from the shadows and timbered hillsides after a three-day ride south from Fort C.F. Smith, the Irishman was relieved to find the post still standing and, from all appearances, practicing the same routine it had for the past year of its existence here in the lee of the Big Horns.

Yet before that first kettle of coffee had begun to boil, the rest of the story spilled from the lips of R. J. Smyth. Without waiting to drop breakfast into his pinched belly, Seamus leaped atop the tired army mount that had carried him south. He had to see to his old friend, whom R.J. said was under Horton's watchful care.

He had banged on the gate and been allowed into the stockade to dart across the parade on foot until he hammered for admittance to the infirmary. Waking one of Surgeon Horton's two stewards, who tried to calm the tall Irishman, Donegan was told they had kept a twenty-four-hour vigil over the crusty, old civilian across the last three days.

With a head wound, things were never certain, the young soldier in the white gown had explained helplessly.

Flinging his hat at the foot of Marr's bed, Seamus had dragged up the ladder-backed chair that groaned beneath his weight when he settled beside Horton's sleeping patient.

Seamus took his fingers from Sam's lips now, setting the enameled cup aside. For a long moment he studied the bandage wrapped round Marr's head. Two dried, crusty brown patches contrasted against the dressing, stark and white in the sunbeams streaming like warm buttermilk into the room. The shafts sparkled like gold dust whenever a person moved down the long aisle between two rows of neat, blanketed beds. Marr's cot had been partitioned off from the rest of the ward. Sick soldiers only. The other wounded from the wagon-box fight had reported back to their units yesterday.

"R.J. told me the blue roan was killed."

Marr nodded weakly, turning his head away from Seamus slightly.

"Sorry to hear that, Sam," Seamus said, trying to make up for mentioning Marr's prize stallion. "Know what he meant to you." He laid his big hand on his friend's forearm and squeezed. Seamus did not take his hand away.

Sam eventually turned back to him, tears misting in his eyes. "He was a good horse, Seamus. A might touchy 'bout his feed . . . but a good horse."

The Irishman nodded, not knowing what to say more than, "You've had good horses before as well, Sam. And you'll find a good horse again."

"Not in this hellhole, I won't," he growled in no more than a raspy whisper, his throat unaccustomed to talk these past three days.

Seamus smiled, squeezing the arm again. "No, I suppose you won't, you old horse thief—unless you heal up and crawl out of this bed to find you one among Cap'n Dandy's stock."

"A army horse?" he croaked.

"Don't you remember you were buying horses for the army when I met you in Kansas, old man?"

Marr nodded once, a hint of a smile crossing his cracked lips. "Tried to buy that big stallion of yours."

"You didn't try to buy him, Sam Marr. You tried to steal him from me!"

Sam looked squarely at Donegan. "That big gray of yours, Seamus. How come . . . you never named him in all this time?"

"I . . . never thought about it—until I was riding down here from Smith. Saw him this morning, down in camp. Looks like he's fared well in your care."

Marr studied his friend. "Too damned long since he's seen you, son. Half a year now. I rode him when I could. But, he knowed the difference atween you and mean, Seamus."

"I can't repay you for minding him."

"Maybeso you can tell me what name you give the big sonuvabitch though?"

"General."

"General?"

He nodded. "General Lee."

Marr nodded as well. "General Lee. My God, that does sound good, don't it, Seamus? Sonuvabitch big enough to carry Lee proud."

"Southern bred as well . . . just like your best studs, Sam."

"True. True. General Lee. Fine name, Seamus." His eyes blinked at some moisture. "If only I could find a animal with half the sense that blue roan had."

"Dandy's got some fine stock to look over—"

"What that quartermaster has left in army stock? Shit!"

Donegan nodded. "So you figure to raid Red Cloud's camp for one of them mangy, ribby Cayuse ponies they ride?"

Sam Marr sputtered a moment, his eyes flashing fire at his young friend. "I s'pose I ain't got much choice, do I?"

"About the horse? Or, about getting your good-for-nothing lazy ass out of this bed and back to work?"

Marr sputtered again, then broke out laughing weakly. He laughed with Donegan until it hurt the chest wound and he broke off in a hacking cough.

"Careful, Sam," Seamus soothed, patting the old man's chest gently. "R.J. says Gilmore and Porter need you bad."

"Oh?" he replied, then rolled his head to the side slightly, his eyes gazing off.

For a long time Sam remained silent. Seamus allowed him his pout, watching the Missourian's lips curl up childishly. Donegan figured it was good therapy for the old man's healing. Eventually Marr turned back, glaring at his young friend with a flinty stare.

"You talking 'bout R.J. and Gilmore and the work—I s'pose that means you've decided to head back east to find the widow?"

Seamus pursed his lips a minute, and squeezed the arm before answering. "No, Sam. Not going after Jennie . . ."

Marr seemed to rouse at that declaration. He tried to push himself off the pillow, pressed back down against the prairie-tick mattress by Seamus. "That means we can get outta this hellhole army slip-trench latrine of a post and get on to Alder Gulch where a man can make his fortune. Way I got it figured, Seamus—Red Cloud's off licking his wounds, and the road north of here gonna be safe just as long as we—"

"Sam . . . Sam—quiet down," he soothed, holding his friend on the bed. "You aren't in any shape to be talking of going on to Virginia City for some time now—"

"I'm healing, boy! You go ask that sawbones Horton yourself!"

"Sam," he cooed again, wondering if there were any other way to say it than straight out. Any other way but straight out that might make it easy on the old man. "We aren't going to Alder Gulch."

"We . . . we aren't?"

Seamus sensed something go out of the old man's body as it sagged with those words, sinking back into the mattress beneath the sheet like a small and helpless thing. "Maybe I should say . . . *I'm* not going to the goldfields. Not . . . not just yet."

The old, watery eyes searched his until Seamus had to look away. "We . . . we're not gonna dig for gold like we planned for so long, Seamus? What . . . what you expect me to do?"

"I figured you'd stay here. But when I come back and don't find you here, I'll wander on up to the Montana goldfields looking for you."

"When you *come back?*" he squeaked. "You ain't going after Jennie . . . then where the hell you going?"

"You old fake," Seamus said with a chuckle. "You know bloody well where I'm headed. Put me on the scent yourself, Sam."

"I did what?"

"Sent me the clipping from the newspaper."

"I did?"

He nodded.

Marr ground his teeth a moment. "S'pose I did. No telling what stupid stunt a old man like me will try, is there?"

"Nothing stupid about helping a friend, Sam Marr."

"Am I your friend, Seamus?"

"You're the best I got in this world," Donegan answered, the knot of sentiment grown hot at the back of his throat. "That's . . . that's what's hardest about this, Sam. Leaving you behind, especially like this—"

"You don't have to leave me behind! I'll go with you, boy . . . gimme a day or so . . . I'm on the mend—"

"No, I can't take you with me, Sam," he whispered, holding the man down on the bed beneath his big hands. "Not where I'm going. You're in no shape to travel for some time—especially riding south to Laramie, through the gut of Red Cloud's hunting ground. You remember our long day at the Crazy Woman?"

"Shit! Remember that bloody ground? 'Course I do, Seamus—"

"Then you know why I can't take you down to Laramie with me," he explained. "And from there the maps I looked over up to Fort C.F. showed I've got to ride south and east across Colorado Territory. Into Kansas."

Marr finally nodded, his eyes softening. "I'd hold you back, wouldn't I? Maybe . . . maybe even get you killed."

"What I have to do is a one-man job as it is, Sam."

"That uncle of yours?"

"Liam O'Roarke. Said to be scouting for Hancock this summer."

"By the time you get down to Kansas, Hancock's summer circus gonna be only a piece of history, Seamus."

"So?" he asked, cocking his dark head and scratching his full beard.

"You stupid mick Irishman!" Marr chuckled weakly, trying to fling a fist at Donegan. "So Hancock's campaign against the Sioux is over and done with—the army goes into quarters for the winter, and they muster out their scouts . . . that's what!"

"Muster out the scouts?"

"If a army ain't marching against the Indians, they won't keep a bunch of scouts on the payroll, now will they, Seamus?"

He shook his head, feeling the sense of dread rising in him like a grease scum rising to the top of a kettle of blood soup. Sensing the fleeing of that hope he had nurtured over the last few days since reading the news story that told of Hancock's scouts. Hope brought by that and a long day's fight on Warrior Creek.

"I suppose I can hope, Sam," was all he thought of to say.

"I know you gotta go, Seamus," Marr finally admitted quietly. "Even if you don't find him down there. You'll likely find his trail, won't you? Now that you got his scent."

Donegan nodded. "Even if I don't find him, I feel like I'm close. Damned close."

"You come find me, Seamus," he said as he slipped a hand from under the dusty sheet. Marr squeezed the Irishman's big paw. "Come find me when you're done doing this for your mother."

"How you know about her?"

"I read the letter she wrote you . . . wanting you to find her brothers. Both of 'em. Bring 'em home."

"Before . . . before she . . ."

"Before she passes on, Seamus. Ain't a man can find fault

with you doing what your mother wants of you. Even if it turns to some bloody work atween here and there."

For the longest time Seamus stared down at that ruddy, fevered face below him, looking all the more frail against the gray sheeting. The skin sagging over the brow and cheekbones, cadaverous.

"Tell me, Sam. Why'd Jennie go? After I sent me my letter, asking her to stay put here . . . telling her I'd be coming for her soon. Why'd she go east on me?"

"Letter?" Marr squeaked. "She didn't get no letter from you that I know of. We never heard a word out of you, neither of us, Seamus."

"I wrote," he stammered, confused. "Sent it down with the army mail. Told 'em to deliver it to you personal."

"Mail goes across the colonel's desk."

He nodded, recognition slowly clearing light at the corner of his mind. His jaw squared. "Never have been too popular with the brass, have I, Sam?"

"I expect your letter disappeared, son. Sonuvabitch probably started one of his fires with it, I'd imagine."

"Letter isn't all that important now, I suppose." He studied the old man's watery eyes again. "You'll make it . . . won't you, Sam?"

Marr smiled weakly, gripping the big hand in his. "I'll be where you can find me . . . you get things settled with your uncles."

Seamus sighed, holding the wrinkled hand still crusted with burnt powder, the blood caked around the fingernails like dark crescents. He stood slowly, nudging the ladder-back chair out of the way, still clutching the hand.

"How many of those Sioux do you figure you put down?"

Marr smiled crookedly. "Damned near all of 'em, Seamus. You oughta know better than ask me a question like that. As I'm laying here at night, it gets damned quiet. Seems I hear the wailing in Red Cloud's camp from here, boy! All the way from here. If I turn my head just right, I can make out the old nigger himself cussing me out for the damage I done his warriors."

"You're too ornery to die." Donegan swallowed, fighting

the feelings the words welled up inside him. "I . . . I best be going, Sam."

"Going south alone?" he asked, refusing to release the big hand.

Shaking his head, he answered. "Nawww. Jim Bridger says he'll ride down with me far as Laramie. The colonel here doesn't have him on the payroll no more. So Jim says he'll wander south. What with winter coming."

"Comes early . . . this part of the country."

"Stays a while as well, don't it, Sam?"

"It does, that, Seamus Donegan." He choked a moment before he got the words out. "I . . . I wish you Godspeed," Marr whispered.

"My prayers stay with you as well, old friend." His eyes were misting now, and the old man swam out of focus. "I'll think long and hard on you while I'm gone from your side."

"Just get this stalk of yours over and done with, Seamus."

"Stalk? You make it sound like I'm hunting down trouble."

"Isn't that what you're doing, Seamus Donegan? Stalking trouble . . . like enough of it doesn't find you on its own?"

"Never looked for trouble in my life, Sam. But, you're right —enough trouble just naturally haunts most of my days as it is."

"Watch your backside, Seamus Donegan," he reminded, shaking the big hand, then letting his drop to the sheeting.

"I got this scar on my back, left there by Confederate steel and fumaric acid," he answered. "It burns when there's danger ahind me."

Then Seamus did something that he figured they might talk about for days to come at Fort Phil Kearny after the big Irishman had gathered up the big gray horse and General Lee's hoofs hammered south toward Fort Laramie. And the plains of Kansas.

He bent over and planted a kiss gently on the old man's cheek. As he pulled away from Marr's face, Seamus saw the tracks of water glistening down the leathery skin.

"Damn, if you can't turn a he-boar into a whimpering sissy," Marr sputtered angrily.

"Sorry, Sam," he apologized. "Just . . . just that you're the closest thing I've known to a father . . . hardly knew mine. Suppose . . . that's why my mother always put so much faith in her own brothers. Hoping as she did one of them might take the place of me own father after he was killed. Until, they both run off to America."

"You're the first man what's kissed me, Seamus," he sobbed quietly. "Wished . . . I'd kissed my boys afore they enlisted and were gone off to the war. Wish I had."

"You watch your hair. 'Cause I'll be back, Sam Marr," he reassured, straightening after grabbing up his slouch hat. "That's a promise."

Seamus turned on his heel, listening to the sound of his boot soles on the rough-hewn plank floor as he made his way down the row of beds, stomping noisily through the brilliant shafts of gold streaming in through the windows.

You're burning daylight, Seamus Donegan. Best get south while you can.

And he worked at scuffing up more noise with his boots as he hurried toward the door at the end of the infirmary.

"Godspeed, Seamus Donegan!" Sam Marr hollered out from his bed, the voice stronger than before as he struggled up on one elbow to hurl his words down the aisle. "Man goes on a death stalk like you—I'll keep you in my prayers!"

Seamus worked at making still more noise with his boots now as he neared the infirmary door, passing by Horton and his stewards. More noise, so no man would hear the sob catch in the big Irishman's chest.

"I'll pray for you, Seamus Donegan!"

Epilogue

$\mathcal{U}$p north at the hay cutters' corral near Fort C.F. Smith, the Indians returned the morning after their daylong fight with the white men. Licking their wounds and eager to wreak vengeance on anything the defenders had left behind.

The bitter warriors hacked to death all the wounded mules abandoned by Captain Burrowes in his haste to return to the fort. They set fires here and there in the fields, flames having the last, purifying word on the flimsy corral wall.

Days following that second of August, a band of friendly Crow rode into the post with intriguing news of seeing first-hand Red Cloud's villages on the Rosebud, filled with wounded. Each morning following their visit to the Sioux camps, the Crow informed the soldiers that more of those who had died through the night were taken from the villages into the surrounding hills. Sioux and Cheyenne and Arapaho squaws wailed their ancient, keening cry of lamentation.

The soldiers figured the Crow were doctoring the truth, if not outright lying.

So to prove what a horrendous toll the corral defenders had exacted from their attackers, those visiting Crows guided some soldiers to a sandstone ledge not far to the east of where the hay cutters' corral had stood that hot first day of August. In caves dug out of the ledge, and in the trees dotting the valley itself, the Crow explained they had counted more than fifty bodies buried by the retreating hostiles. Because Red Cloud's warriors were still about the nearby country, the soldiers declined to go in search of more graves at a site farther down the Bighorn River where the Crow claimed the white men would find even more bodies.

On the morning of August third a detail from Fort Phil Kearny rode down to the wagon-box corral. When Major Smith had brought his noisy relief party and the mountain howitzer to the rescue the day before, Red Cloud's hostiles had been forced to abandon many of their dead, especially those fallen close to the corral. Upon reaching the meadow that next morning, the soldiers found not one Indian body remaining on that field all but ringed with the silent foothills of the Big Horn Mountains.

Those fierce and jealous guardians of this hunting ground had done exactly as Col. Henry B. Carrington himself had done the day after Fetterman's command suffered annihilation. They returned to the scene of their defeat to retrieve their honored dead.

A September sun streaked the eastern sky with the pink of dawn as Seamus Donegan finished lashing his bedroll to the back of General Lee's saddle. He sighed and turned back to the fire, accepting the cup of coffee Jim Bridger offered him.

After a mutual silence for long minutes, the Irishman finally spoke. "I'll miss your coffee, Jim."

The old man grinned crookedly, then tossed a twig into the flames that danced around the skillet in which he was grilling slices of venison. "I see you're serious about leaving this morning, son."

Seamus blew steam from his cup into the chill, predawn air of the high plains. Then nodded. "I stay here any longer, I'll not make Kansas before the snow flies."

Bridger never looked up. Continuing to poke and prod the venison steaks with a peeled willow twig. "I ain't good enough winter company, eh?"

Donegan chuckled. "Some of the best company a man could hope for, Jim Bridger."

As the old trapper pulled a steak from the skillet and slapped it on the tin plate he nudged across the ground toward Seamus, Donegan continued to stare at the flames.

"You never talked about the woman . . . all the way

down from Kearny, son. So tell me, you fixing on going after her now?"

The Irishman drew his knife blade across the tender meat taken from the doe found less than a couple miles from Fort Laramie yesterday afternoon on their hunt for Donegan's trail food. The steak fell apart under the steel, red juices seeping from the tenderloin.

"Got some family business to attend to first, Jim," he answered, not irritated with the old man's natural inquisitiveness.

Bridger spoke around a chunk of steak he shoved into his wrinkled mouth. "Just as well, son. Women get a man so bedizened . . . he'll tromp through hell to find the one he loves."

Donegan stopped chewing. "Sounds like you speak from experience, Jim."

His grin cracked the well-lined face that was like a war map of his forty-plus years in these mountains. "Lots of experience, you young lop-eared pup!"

"You figure Injin women make the best wives, eh?"

"Don't you? Man like you's laid with all kinds, way I see your stick float. So, you tell me about women, Irishman."

Seamus wagged his head. "For better and for worse, old man . . . usually means *for good.*"

"And that scares you, don't it?"

"Damned sure does, Jim!" he sighed, thinking on it. "But, then another feeling comes roaring in that tells me what I felt with Jennie was good. God help me, I can't begin to tell you how it was . . . without even laying with her. Feeling something so strong I could taste it." His eyes sought Bridger's, imploring them, wanting the old trapper to understand. "I want to go on tasting it till my candle's snuffed out."

"Why'n't you following the Platte to Nebraska, son?"

"It's just . . . just that I have this to do."

The old trapper clucked like a sage hen, stuffing another chunk of venison between his lips. "Take the word of a old man what's seen a bunch of country, son: the farther you run . . . the longer the way back."

The memory of her clutching him, clinging to him like ivy to an oak, was the most bitter potion Donegan had ever tasted. And with this moment Seamus fully realized he must drink a little from that cup every day. Drinking every day until he finished this stalking of men and could go in search of Jennie.

After brooding on his own thoughts a few minutes, Donegan sat his tin cup aside and began whittling a fine stick he would use to pick his teeth. "You'll stay here for the winter, Jim?"

Bridger nodded, rubbing his belly. "Damned good venison you shot, boy. Yeah—I'll stay here. The folks good to me. Not like they are up the Montana Road some. Just as well stay here, since they don't need me up there no more."

He paused, sensing that Donegan was not really listening at all. "And you, son. What about you? Nothing gonna turn you from hunting down this uncle of yours?"

Seamus wagged his head, never looking up from the fire. "You might say I promised someone I'd see this through, Jim."

"Lot of space out on them Kansas plains."

"You wanna come show me?" Donegan's voice rose with a twinge of excitement at the prospect.

"Shit! I don't belong there no more'n farmers belong out here among God's greatest creations. Farmers—hear they're pushing 'crost Kansas now."

"That's why the army's there."

"Damn right, son. And that's why the buffler ain't."

"Maybe I'll see me some buffalo in Kansas, Jim."

"Could be," he replied absently, still mad at the unseen settlers farther east. "What's a fella like you to do this winter in Kansas? You find yourself a place to stay warm and your belly full?"

Donegan laughed. "Worse comes to worse, Jim—I'll wait out the winter hanging 'round one of those army posts. Find me something to do. A good horse there—General Lee is. And I reckon the army will fill me belly least once a day. Besides, their beds are warm and dry."

"Sounds like you see yourse'f wearing army blue again, boy."

Seamus wagged his head and chuckled. "Not just yet, Jim.

But the army does give a man a good horse, full belly, and warm bed. All that some men truly need."

"My way of callating—you need something more."

Seamus rose, rotating an aching shoulder, flexing the muscles of his left calf which complained more and more with autumn coming ever since a Cheyenne arrow had pinned him to Leighton's horse.

"I do need something more'n the army can give me right now, Jim."

"Scouting's a fair game. Lookit me."

Seamus nodded, smiling warmly. "Perhaps I'll give it a try someday. Had a good teacher in you."

Bridger tossed back the last of the coffee in his cup. "Lot more to learn than what I teached you riding to Laramie, Irishman."

Donegan took hold of the reins of the big gray, then finally turned to look over his shoulder at the old trapper. "Way I see it, Jim—you've forgotten more about scouting than any the rest of us will ever know."

Bridger hobbled over quickly as he could, hunched a little more with the morning chill, his rheumatism refusing the hips much motion.

"You always knowed what to say to this old man to make him feel pert, Irishman." He stopped in front of Donegan, pulling a long, well-oiled thong from round his neck. "Want you have something afore you tear off for the prerra on your own hook."

Bridger pulled the small medicine pouch over his head, spreading the thong with his hands. Seamus yanked his felt hat from his head then bent his great height forward as the old trapper slipped the pouch around his young friend's neck.

Jim sighed, squinting an eye up into the new sun peeking over the great plains of the Platte River stretching endlessly east from their camp.

"Here's something to have, case we don't run onto one 'nother again."

Donegan examined the small, elkskin pouch trimmed with red wool and porcupine quillwork. "What . . . what is this?"

"Medicine bag. Carried it for many a year now. Near as I can callate, I had that 'round my neck 'bout as long as you been alive, young'un."

"A good-luck charm?"

Bridger snorted, throwing a punch at the big man. "More'n good luck, Irishman. Injuns got medicine helpers . . . the spirits that live in rocks and trees and such. It's all in there. Feathers and ashes . . . all that."

Seamus squeezed it, sensing something warm and uncanny in his palm. "It will be my medicine helper as well then, Jim Bridger. But I have nothing to repay you—"

"Wagh!" Bridger snorted the grizzly's battle cry, chuckling. "I don't need nothing in return. I'm an old man, Irishman. Lived me a damned full life out here in these spaces. All I need is up here." He tapped a gnarled finger against a temple. "And what no man can ever take from me in here." Bridger brought the finger to his heart.

Donegan reached out slowly so as not to scare the smallish man before him, having never touched Bridger before in the year they had stood the test of Red Cloud. Yet now, to the Irishman, it seemed only fitting that in this parting he should do exactly what he felt.

Seamus pulled the hunched, brittle old man into his embrace, feeling like a mighty oak sheltering the aspen seedling.

When Bridger finally pulled back, he sniffed once, dragging a hand under his nose through the white, week-old mustache. He hobbled back to the fire muttering as Seamus slipped a foot in a stirrup and rose to his saddle.

"Time was, Irishman," Bridger spoke up, his back to Donegan while he knelt over the blackened kettle and poured more steaming coffee into his battered tin, "this ol' man come to the mountains but a child o' seventeen. Young'un makes mistakes a'times, you know? I did."

Jim rose painfully from the fire, the coffee tin smoking like a cup on fire itself. "That first trip to the mountains . . . I offered Gen'l Ashley to stay with a man I figured would be a day or two in dying. Got mutilized by a sow grizz. Me and another said we'd stay till he died . . . out east it was a ways . . . near the Grand River as I recollect. That fella—ol' man named Hugh Glass—he never died. Day after day . . . but the other'n—he talked me into leaving ol' Hugh there . . . aside the grave we scooped out'n the sand for him along that creek where the sow grizz jumped and mutilized Glass."

Seamus nudged General Lee toward the firepit.

"Me and Fitzgerald spooked and got high tails behind us . . . pulled out on Hugh. Left him to die by wolves or red niggers—whatever hap't on him first."

"You've always been sorry you left him to die."

Bridger wagged his head, rolling his lower lip between a thumb and forefinger thoughtfully. "Naw. Hugh Glass didn't die. He come looking for me and Fitzgerald. Ol' man found me that winter up to Henry's fort. I was a pup then—seventeen years old and my first winter in the mountains."

"So, this Glass figured you owed him, right?"

"Plain and simple, I was his meat. He had every right to kill me for leaving him for dead. But, after holding his pistol again' my brow for a few minutes, he took 'er away. Saying I was just a pup and didn't know no better."

Seamus nodded. "Those fortunate among us learn in the journey across our years, Jim."

Bridger chuckled, taking a sip of the scalding coffee. "Taught me, that ol' man did. Across all my winters in these mountains, Jim Bridger's never left a wounded man behind again."

"I recall you arguing with those cowards who were not in favor of Carrington's plan to retrieve Fetterman's dead."

Jim snorted into his coffee, his eyes narrowing on the tiny flames. "I learned some powerful medicine once I gave up thinking I knowed everything, Irishman." He looked at Seamus.

Donegan sensed more than Bridger's eyes boring into him. It was as if something wise and far smarter in that old man's soul were peering right into the pit of him.

He smiled. Holding down a hand to the old trapper. "You've taught me well, old friend."

Bridger took the big hand and shook it, his rheumy blue eyes twinkling. "I trust you will fare well in your search, Irishman."

"I got your medicine watching over me now, old man. Got your spirit helpers riding with me."

Seamus Donegan gently nudged the big gray off, easing the animal through the shafts of sunlight slanting into the cotton-wood grove here beside the Platte River like fractured yellow streamers. Shadow. Then sunlight. Shadow. Then . . .

HERE IS AN EXCERPT FROM *THE STALKERS*—THE NEXT VOLUME IN TERRY C. JOHNSTON'S BOLD NEW WESTERN SERIES—*THE PLAINSMEN*:

Prologue

"*I* don't figure this got nothing to do with you," the sergeant growled, his red-rimmed eyes glaring harshly at the civilian striding up to the hitching post. He reminded the newcomer of a skinny wolf.

"None o' your business, stranger," echoed a second soldier.

A third dressed in dirty army blue lunged up, shoulder to shoulder with the first. "You heard the Sarge here," he spat. "Best you g'won your way now, sonny. Afore you get hurt."

"Not so sure it's me what gets hurt here," the tall Irishman replied, the hint of a smile spreading his dark beard. Almost a head taller than any of those five soldiers now crowding him at the hitching post, he gazed down at the shiny, blood-smeared face of the Negro soldier sprawled in the dust of what Fort Wallace, Kansas Territory called a parade.

"A mick he is, boys!" the sergeant roared in hearing the stranger speak, his reedy laughter goading the other four shouldered close round him like a pack of wolves with downed buffalo calf in sight. "As if there ain't enough of 'em in this goddamned man's army . . . we got loud-mouthed ones wearing civilians' clothes too!"

"Sarge—this'un makes out like he owns them army britches!"

The older sergeant's eyes narrowed, studying closely the patched and worn union britches the tall civilian sported. Complete with yellow stripe down the outside of each leg.

"Cavalry was it, Irishman?"

"Aye," he answered, taking one step back as two of the leering soldiers slowly flanked him.

"That's horseshit, if I ever heard it!" the sergeant spouted. "Ain't an Irishman been borned what can straddle a horse long enough to be a cavalryman!"

The five roared with crazy laughter.

The Irishman swallowed the knot of pride hot in his throat and lunged, snagging the soldier inching up on his right. Flinging him back against three others, the stranger spoke as calmly as he could. "Like I said when I walked up on your little party here . . . your fun's over, sojurs. I asked you polite to quit jobbing on the darkie here."

"Oh, he asked us polite to quit jobbing on the darkie, was it now?"

"I suppose you sojurs wanna dance?"

"And what army imposter would be asking me now?" the sergeant snarled.

"Seamus Donegan . . . formerly of the Army of the Shenandoah," he answered. "And by the looks of your dirty uniforms . . . you all must belong to the Seventh Cavalry I hear so much about . . . from Julesburg on south!"

"Heard about us, he has?" roared one of the corporals as he scuffed backwards and grabbed a handful of the dirty blue blouse worn by the Negro soldier, yanking the bloodied man off the ground to his feet. "Have you heard we don't take to these here darkies the army sends out here to fight Injuns as well?"

"Heard your regiment's led by a man named Custer," Donegan replied. "Word has it up to Laramie that Custer got himself in trouble having some of you nice fellas shoot deserters this past summer."

"Any man deserts General Custer deserves what he gets!"

Seamus smiled. "I was there when that curly-headed sonuvabitch strung up some Johnnies at Front Royal in the Shenandoah—"

"You called Custer a . . . a sonuvabitch?" the sergeant roared, spittle flecking his cracked lips.

"Figured I had to get you fellas riled up some way. Let's *dance!*"

With the last word off his tongue, Donegan swung his big

right hand in a mighty arch, scooping the sergeant off the ground. Before the soldier landed in the dust, Seamus's left fist jabbed the man rushing his flank. As quickly, he flung his boot at another before dancing backward, both fists up before his face, shoulders hunched and bobbing as the five soldiers assessed their three casualties in those first few seconds.

Stunned, the sergeant brought his fingers to his mouth as he sat sprawled in the dust. The fingers came away stained and damp. With a tongue he rocked some loosened teeth. "You stupid bastards—tear his eyes out!"

The three soldiers who were still on their feet charged him at once, swinging wildly with all they had. Backwards Seamus pedaled, jabbing and swinging when an opening came. Bobbing right then left as fists shot his way in a blur of dirty fingernails clawing for his face.

From the corner of his eye he saw two more soldiers in dirty blue tunics bolt from the shade of the nearby porch, on their way to help their kinsmen. The sergeant clambered clumsily to his feet, charging back into the fray.

"Now you'll pay for sticking your mick nose in where it don't belong!" the sergeant roared.

Five of them descended on him at once. Pinning down his arms so that Donegan couldn't swing. He sensed the blow coming more than saw it, the great, white scar along his back gone cold, prickling with warning. Then recognized the metallic clunk of the pistol-barrel against his skull. A glancing blow, but enough to jar him to his boots. Enough to bring him to his knees.

"Now we'll show this big-mouthed bastard what the Seventh Cavalry does to them that talks bad about the general!"

Seamus gazed up through the meteors in time to see the play of October sunlight glint off the knife-steel twisting in the sergeant's hand.

"What say we cut out his tongue, Sarge?"

"Good idea. Teach this mick not to talk bad 'bout Custer, won't it?"

The sergeant no more than got it said while hauling down on Donegan's chin whiskers, intent on opening the Irishman's mouth, when a black hand swept round the soldier's neck, yanking the sergeant off his feet. Seamus figured that was his cue.

Two of the soldiers imprisoning Donegan made the mistake of lunging to help their sergeant.

Wrenching his left arm free as the pair pulled away, Donegan put that powerful oak-rail arm and mallet-sized fist to work. Swinging it across his body with sudden effectiveness, the first soldier stumbled backward. Stunned, holding a hand to a nose spurting bright gouts of blood.

That left hand pistoned back and jabbed the second soldier who waited too long to make his move. Petrified too long as he watched his friend back off bleeding, he himself crumpled backward into the dust as the Irishman's quick left jab cracked against the side of the soldier's head.

Whirling, Donegan was pleased to find the mouthy sergeant had his own problems. In one hand the sergeant still gripped his knife. While the other clawed at the black arm clamping his throat in a vise, barely dangling the soldier above the ground. Above the clamor, the sergeant struggled to growl orders for the four soldiers to come to his aid. His voice no more than the squeak of a field mouse caught in the jaws of a trap.

The sergeant's four gallant rescuers pummeled the black soldier from all sides. Swinging, yanking, wrestling to free his death-grip on the sergeant and his knife. Tiring of the struggle, one of the four freed the mule-ear army-issue holster at his right hip and cleared his pistol, swinging it overhead toward the shiny black face.

Hurtling forward, Donegan caught the hand before the pistol cracked into the unsuspecting skull. He wrenched the soldier round, stared a moment into the surprised eyes, then jabbed his fist into the face, blood spurting from his nose.

Stumbling over the body as it sank to the trampled dust, Seamus dug his fingers into the hair of two more attackers, trying to yank them off the black soldier. They only yowled in pain. One lashed out with a dusty boot. Both hands still in their hair, the Irishman cracked the heads together like a hickory axe-handle whacking the staves of an oak water-keg. They crumpled without protest.

He turned in time to see the last of the rescuers dig his

fingers into the black soldier's eyes, pulling the darkie off the sergeant. Gasping for air, one hand clawing at the neck of his sweaty tunic, the sergeant fought to breathe, his eyes bulging. Then turned in one swift motion, bringing the knife into the air once more as he lunged up the Negro soldier's back.

Donegan caught the arm from behind, clutching the white wrist in both of his hands. Wheeling beneath his own arm, the sergeant brought a knee violently into the Irishman's groin. Seamus stumbled back a step, then a second as another blow came his way. Yet he refused to release the knife hand. The sergeant connected with a third boot.

A rush of gall and puke flung itself against his tonsils as Seamus sank to his knees. Almost more pain than he could bear. Watching the sergeant through the sweat dripping in his eyes. A swirl of dust around them all. Faintly heard, the murmur of voices ringing from all directions. That knifeblade glimmering in the bright autumn sun here on the far western plains of Kansas.

The knife falling toward him in a streak . . . a streaming sliver of sunlight off the blade, like that dusty trail smeared behind a falling star against a prairie-night sky . . .

A gunshot cracked through his pain.

The crack of a pistol.

"HOLD IT!"

That stopped the knife hand in its fall.

Seamus glanced up at the sergeant, recognizing in those red-rimmed eyes the look of an animal suddenly caged. Something dark and dangerous shut off behind those whiskey-soaked eyes. Again the pale saber scar along his back warned the Irishman. He whirled around, staring into the muzzle of another pistol held by a soldier with a smashed and bloody nose. The lower half of his face glistening pink in the midday, October sunlight.

"BELT YOUR WEAPONS!"

He watched the pistol tremble for a breathless moment before the soldier dropped his arm, and reluctantly stuffed the weapon into the holster on his right hip.

"I don't have enough to worry about here," said the same deep voice, drawing closer. "Cheyenne and Sioux tearing up the tracks . . . Kidder's men got theirselves butchered . . .

I can't keep the mail-lines open to Denver—and now you boys get yourselves all oiled up and jump this civilian and one of Carpenter's brunettes!"

Seamus clambered to his feet, studying the big-framed soldier striding up at a ground-eating gallop. A thick shock of hair atop his head, wild and unruly, and now slightly flecked with gray. Shiny teeth in a neat row beneath the iron-colored mustache, waxed and curled at the ends.

"Sergeant-of-the-guard?"

"Yessir."

"Bring those others over here until we make sense of this."

"Yes, Captain."

"Give me your knife, Larson."

"Captain . . . weren't our fault—"

"That was an order. Gimme your knife!"

"Yessir."

The officer turned on Donegan. "Who are you and what business have you here at Wallace?"

Seamus took a moment in answering, dusting the front of his sweat-stained shirt. "Donegan." He looked square in the officer's eyes. "Seamus Donegan. Come here looking for word of me uncle. Heard at Fort Hays he might be here."

"A soldier?"

"No, Cap'n. Civilian. Scout, so I'm told. Working for you."

"This uncle of yours has a name, I take it."

"O'Roarke. Liam O'Roarke."

"Indeed he is a scout for us. Or," the officer paused, "I should correct myself. He was a scout during Hancock's summer campaign."

"He's not here?" Donegan asked, craning forward anxiously.

"Not any longer, stranger," the officer replied. "Hancock's campaign over . . . Colonel Custer brought up on several serious counts of courts-martial . . . the army let its scouts go for the coming winter."

"Let him go?" He bit his lip. "Where? You hear where he was heading?"

"Hold on, stranger. O'Roarke said he was heading over the Rockies to spend the winter in the City of the Saints."

"City of the—"

"Salt Lake. Brigham Young. Mormons," the officer instructed impatiently. "You heard of Mormons, haven't you, stranger?"

He shook his head. "No."

The officer sighed. "You will out here. If it ain't Cheyenne stirring up trouble . . . it's Mormons migrating to their beloved City of the Saints. Or on the road east to sell their goods. And if ain't Mormons . . . it's soldiers like these with too much time on their hands, jumping Carpenter's brunettes. I wish Bankhead would get Carpenter and his darkies transferred outta here," he muttered.

"What would he be doing in the City of the Saints?"

"Not that I have anything against Negras, you understand," the stocky officer explained, still deep in his own thoughts. "I was born in Virginia and raised out Missouri way —fought for the Union, mind you. A Union man tried and true—"

"Captain—what would Liam O'Roarke be doing in the City of the Saints?"

"O'Roarke? Why, probably looking for work."

"Work?"

"Brigham Young always has something for a man to do on the other side of them mountains," he said wistfully, pointing off to the west beyond Fort Wallace's pink limestone walls. "Any man that's good with a gun and can stay atop a horse at a full gallop. I hear he calls that bunch of renegades his 'Avenging Angels' . . . Danites. Damn—but there's times I wish I had a few like them myself. If I only had some that were good with a gun and could stay nailed in the saddle at a full gallop—"

"How do I get there . . . to this City of the Saints?"

The Captain laughed. "You aren't going there now, stranger. Unless you're planning on taking the long way around. Them mountains out there would chew you up this time of year . . . spit your bones out come spring. What's left of you, anyway. Wouldn't be a scrap of meat left after all those winter-gaunt critters get through with you."

Then suddenly, the officer clamped a hand on the Irishman's shoulder. "Best you stay on this side of them mountains for now. Come back here in the spring . . . early summer. Liam O'Roarke will return here then as well."

"Back here?"

"He knows I've got honest work for him next year," the captain replied. "Another summer. Another campaign against these infernal Cheyenne. Keeping the wires up and the telegraph open. Pushing the railroad to Denver. Honest work for a scout . . . not like working for Brigham Young."

Seamus watched the captain direct the guards off to the stockade with the grumbling, cursing soldiers. "I'll be back . . . come spring."

"Suit yourself," the officer muttered, reluctantly tearing his eyes off the far western mountains. "Now you," he flung his voice at the black soldier. "Get your ass back to Carpenter's camp and stay there! For your own good!"

"Yessir! Cap'n, sir!"

"Hold on, sojur," Donegan ordered. "I'll walk 'long with you." Then he turned back to the officer just starting back to the shade of his post commander's office.

"Say, Cap'n. I want to thank you for your help . . . the information on my uncle."

The officer stopped in stride, turned. "Quite all right. I'd appreciate a return of the favor by you taking yourself and the darkie out of here. I don't need any more excitement this week."

"Did not catch your name, Cap'n."

He smiled beneath that bushy mustache, pushing a shock of dark hair from his eyes. "Benteen. Fred Benteen. Don't believe I caught yours."

"Seamus Donegan."

"Been nice talking with you, Donegan. Best now that you make yourself scarce before any more of these drunk, sullen soldiers take a carving knife to you."

"See you come next year, Cap'n Benteen."

Seamus turned back, finding the Negro soldier awaiting him.

He ground his dirty kepi hat between his two huge, black hands, both scarred with light-skinned tracks. "Wanna thankee, sir."

"No thanks needed. You're a freedman, aren't you?"

His shiny face bobbed up and down. Flinging drops of sweat. "I am."

"Hot enough to boil the fat off a flea, sojur." Donegan started off. He watched the sullen, glaring faces of those soldiers lounging in knots round the parade, faces filled with distrust and downright hatred for the black soldier at the Irishman's side.

"I'll go back to my unit now."

"Think I'll walk you there," Seamus replied, nudging the soldier off. "Not much of a happy place, this Fort Wallace."

"Thank you again . . . for coming to help me with them boys hacking on me. I owe you one, Mr. Donegan."

Donegan smiled, slapping the soldier on the back as they trudged toward the far side of the parade. "Call me Seamus, sojur. What's your name?"

"Waller, sir. Given the slave name of Reuben. Took my old field-boss's name after my master was killed in the war . . . when I run North to fight in the war on the Union side."

"Reuben Waller, is it?" Seamus said with a grin, gingerly feeling the growing knot at the back of his skull. "Glad to meet you, Reuben Waller!"

DON'T MISS *THE STALKERS*—VOLUME 3 IN THE *PLAINSMEN* SERIES BY TERRY C. JOHNSTON—COMING IN DECEMBER 1990!